PASSING AND PEDAGOGY

Philip Evergood, *Passing Show*, 1951, oil on canvas. (© Daniel J. Terra Collection. Reproduced courtesy of the Terra Museum of American Art, Chicago, Illinois.)

PASSING AND PEDAGOGY

The Dynamics of Responsibility

Pamela L. Caughie

UNIVERSITY OF ILLINOIS PRESS

URBANA AND CHICAGO

©1999 by the Board of Trustees of the University of Illinois
Manufactured in the United States of America
1 2 3 4 5 C P 5 4 3 2 1

∞ This book is printed on acid-free paper.

Library of Congress Cataloging-in-Publication Data
Caughie, Pamela L.
Passing and pedagogy : the dynamics of responsibility / Pamela L. Caughie.
p. cm.
Includes bibliographical references and index.
ISBN 0-252-02466-4 (cloth : alk. paper)
ISBN 0-252-06770-3 (pbk. : alk. paper)
1. Literature—Study and teaching (Higher)—United States.
2. American literature—History and criticism—Theory, etc.
3. English literature—History and criticism—Theory, etc.
4. Arts—Study and teaching (Higher)—United States.
5. Passing (Identity) in literature.
6. Passing (Identity)
I. Title.
PN61.C38 1999
807'.1'173—ddc21 98-58007
CIP

To C/Zinc
WITH THANKS

pass \'pas\ *vb:* to move; to go past someone moving in the same direction; to surpass or exceed; to cross over; to go from one quality, state, or form to another; to go from the control, ownership, or possession of one person or group to another; to be exchanged as or in a social interaction (words passed); to give approval to; to complete successfully a course of study; to withdraw from the current poker pot; to be accepted or regarded as; to identify oneself or accept identification as a white person though having some Negro ancestry; to go uncensored, unchallenged, or seemingly unnoticed

—Adapted from *Webster's Ninth New Collegiate Dictionary*

CONTENTS

ACKNOWLEDGMENTS

I first saw Philip Evergood's painting at the Terra Museum of American Art in 1990 when I was writing an essay on Nella Larsen's *Passing,* an essay that eventually turned out to be the genesis of this book. The tension between fantasy and reality, between caricature and realism, visually captured the kind of analysis of social issues and identities that I hoped to promote in my writings on passing. The double entendre of the title, *Passing Show,* conveys the notion of performativity that informs my use of passing while the visual image insists on the materiality of the desires that motivate our performances. In choosing this painting for the cover, I also want to feature the Terra Museum, a Chicago institution whose exhibitions of American artists, from Henry Ossawa Tanner to Gertrude Stein to Duke Ellington, has taught me much about the centrality of racial representations to American cultural productions. I gratefully acknowledge the Terra Museum for permission to reproduce the image.

It was Anne Callahan who first pointed out to me the relevance of *Passing Show* to my writing when we happened upon the painting during a visit to the Gertrude Stein exhibit at the Terra Museum. In acknowledging those who have helped me most with this project, I must begin with Anne, my friend, colleague, interlocutor, and sometimes collaborator. Along with Susan Cavallo, Janice Mouton, and Eleanor Honig Skoller, with whom we constitute an informal writing group, Anne has been indispensable in my conceptualization and realization of this book. All four friends have been more than generous with their time, their comments, and their criticisms. Writing with them over the past few years has been, and continues to be, immensely pleasurable.

Others who have read and commented on the manuscript, or portions thereof, include the editors and readers for previously published pieces and colleagues and students from my department. I thank them all for the suggestions I have incorporated and for the criticisms that keep me pushing against the limits of what I can do. I would like to thank in particular Christopher Castiglia, Ann Dolinko, Judy Massey Dozier, Marian Staats, Susan Jarratt and Lynn Worsham, Isaiah Smithson and Nancy Ruff, Domna Stanton, and especially Ann Lowry, my editor at the University of Illinois Press. I am grateful as well to numerous research assistants over the years who have worked with me on this project, including Sarah Ruhl from Brown University and Danielle Glassmeyer, Steve Venturino, Michele Troy, Dagmara Sarudi and Kristen Kapica from Loyola University Chicago, and to the numerous students in my classes at all levels whose writing and participation have inspired, and in some cases contributed to, these chapters. It is indeed a pleasure, and a challenge, to teach and write among such stimulating and talented students. A fellowship at Loyola University's Center for Ethics in fall 1992 and a leave of absence in fall 1995 were instrumental in helping me to complete this project.

Finally, I want to convey my love and gratitude to Doug and Evan, who have helped me (sometimes forced me) to keep my writing in perspective and who remind me daily that I have a life.

I gratefully acknowledge permission to republish the following material in this book:

Portions of the introduction and chapters 2–3 appeared in "Passing as Pedagogy: Feminism in(to) Cultural Studies," in *English Studies/Culture Studies,* ed. Isaiah Smithson and Nancy Ruff (Urbana: University of Illinois Press, 1994), 76–93.

Chapter 3 appeared as "'not entirely strange . . . not entirely friendly': *Passing* and Pedagogy," *College English* 54 (November 1992): 775–93.

Chapter 5 appeared as "Let It Pass: Changing the Subject, Once Again," *PMLA* (January 1997): 26–39; reprinted in *In Other Words: Feminism and Composition Studies,* ed. Susan C. Jarratt and Lynn Worsham (Modern Language Association, 1998), 111–31.

PASSING AND PEDAGOGY

IN PASSING:
PREFACING REMARKS

> I would love society as others do if I were not sure of show-
> ing myself not just at a disadvantage but as completely dif-
> ferent from what I am.
> —Rousseau, *Confessions*

Remarks made in passing can get us into trouble in any social situation. Whether uttered in full awareness or embarrassed ignorance of the personal histories and self-identifications of those present, a passing comment can also abruptly open up the possibility for what I am almost perversely calling pedagogy. Passing remarks may be taken to be all too revealing of a speaker's own identifications and political agendas, evoking charges of racism, sexism, homophobia, anti-Semitism, reverse racism, backlash, male-bashing, or, even worse, political correctness, and prompting equally passionate denials of the accusations. Certainly passing comments can be misunderstood or blown out of proportion, but such remarks are anything but incidental.

What we need in the face of passing remarks is a structure that provides a means of owning up to the implications of passing rather than trying to explain or deny the violating remarks—that is, we need a structure of response (Piper, "Passing" 28).[1] A passing comment is too often seen *only* as a slip of the mask, revealing the true character behind the persona. We need a way of responding that moves us out of the initially defining situation, which so often locks us into the structure of accusation and defense. To name and conceptualize such a structure of response, one that confronts instances of passing as central to the structural dynamics and ethical imperatives of the pedagogical relation, is the principle aim of this book.

1

We are at a critical moment in literary studies, both in the way we represent each other and in the way the debates in academe are currently represented in media accounts aimed at informing the general public of the antics of our profession. This book responds to the need for a strategic and
pragmatic intervention in several distinct but related debates that continue
to preoccupy us: the place of cultural diversity and identity politics in academic discourse; the institutionalization of a multicultural curriculum and
a cultural studies paradigm; the politics of postmodern theories and the
hegemony of Theory itself; and the aims of what some call critical pedagogy
and others call advocacy teaching.[2] Instead of fighting with the media and
scapegoating one another, we need to find ways to make the political and
social relevance of these extremely complex inquiries clear, urgent, and non-
threatening—even if risky. My contention is that it can be pedagogy in its
most widely applied sense—and what we *do*—that will move us out of the
impasse of these debates and into the ethical practice they call for. The material in this book is made up of various examples of how this move might
work. By revealing their common structure, which is related to the deconstructive double gesture, I propose pedagogy to be a social and ethical practice that is not limited to the classroom.

In each of the following chapters, I take my readers, as I take my students,
through creative sites of conflict (in literature, film, performance arts), where
one is moved into new and even alien subject positions with relatively little
risk, and into cultural sites of conflict (legal hearings, art exhibits, classroom
scenes), where the risks are greater, to reenact how and why it is so easy to
forget in practice what we so often advocate in theory: namely, that all subjectivity is passing, even the subject position of the teacher-scholar who is
engaged in the deconstruction of identity.[3] I want to probe my readers' mem-
ories for those moments when passing—the performance of identity as redefined in this book—happens. It happens in reading, in writing, and in
teaching. My goal is to disclose the structure, in example after example, so
as to make it as easily recognizable as the construction of race and gender
has come to be for us, so that we can exploit it for the ethical possibilities it
offers. Beyond the mere fact of advocating a certain political or theoretical
position or a certain concept of identity, the ethical practice described in these
chapters means taking responsibility for the positions we assume and put into
play in our teaching and in our writing. *Passing and Pedagogy* provides
specific examples of the forms this ethical practice might take.

Passing remarks can be both efficient and enlightening when they function like the supplement that Jacques Derrida, after Rousseau, has characterized as "dangerous." We fear that a passing comment shows the speaker

to a disadvantage, revealing more of the self, and a different self, than the speaker would consciously present and thereby revealing the speaker's non-identity with that self. Having recognized the power of speech to "[dislocate] the subject it constructs," Derrida writes, "[Rousseau] is nevertheless more pressed to exorcise it than to assume its necessity" (*Of Grammatology* 141). The dangerous supplement becomes writing, thought necessary to protect the subject from misinterpretation. Yet as Rousseau's writing itself proves, writing never delivers the control it promises, for we still expose ourselves in ways we had not intended or realized. The double logic of writing—at once a way to avoid exposing the referential Self, whether *through* slips of the tongue or *to* the exigencies of the immediate speech situation, and a way of exposing more of the self than one could ever divulge in the expressive communication of the face-to-face encounter—is the logic of passing.[4]

The double logic is the logic of supplementation that undermines the identity in (self-)identifications, making any identity nonidentical with itself—Rousseau's famous *je suis autre* (I am other). What passing comments expose, then, is less the true character of the speaker than the binary logic of identification that would equate the speaker (embodied person) with the "I" (grammatical subject), the very logic that locks us into the structure of accusation and defense. "Any rhetorical posture," writes Susan David Bernstein, "whether in an article or in the classroom, is already mediated, compromised by desires, by forces of language and culture, that cannot be grasped together by any one 'I'" (127). The recognition of this deconstructive insight into the functioning of language has provided a powerful stimulus to the revolutionary critiques of identity and identity politics that have politicized the academy for the good. At the same time, this very same recognition has produced an equally powerful and passionate reaction against the critique of identity it allows, even by those who have promoted such a critique. Those "more pressed to exorcise [this logic] than to assume its necessity" would dismiss deconstruction as politics (whether for its lack of politics or for the wrong politics) rather than assume responsibility for working through the possibilities and implications of the double logic of supplementation.[5] The classroom is one site where such responsibility must be assumed.

In the chapters that follow, I will reconceive the term "passing" (a concept that implies a misrepresentation of oneself) in terms of this double logic rather than in terms of the binary logic that governs its common uses. The double logic is a "nonintuitive logic," Barbara Johnson writes, in that it cannot be held in the head but must be worked through in writing ("Writing" 45). I exploit the full potential of "passing" in the way Derrida's reading of Rousseau exploits the full range of possibility of the logic of supplementation. These chapters are best understood as a series of related explorations; they do not attempt to provide a model for pedagogy. Indeed, my approach works against the belief that certain pedagogical difficulties can be resolved by a model.[6] Instead, pedagogy becomes, in these chapters, both the site of and a figure for the failure of control that writing promises. The dynamics of the pedagogical exchange can render ineffectual, even suspect, the positions (subject positions, but also theoretical and political positions) we so carefully assume in our writing, forcing us to be more accountable than we can possibly be in the relatively isolated and structurally bounded act of composing. The anxiety we may experience in the classroom not only comes from our exposure before and to others but is the very effect of our writing as well. We need to move the pedagogical relation, with its risks of exposure, to our writing and to move "passing" out of the classroom into cultural sites, including the cultural site of our own writing.

"Passing" as I deploy the term is closely related to performativity, a theory of subjectivity that conceives identity as something we *do*, not something we *are*. The concept derives from J. L. Austin's category of performatives, those utterances that bring something into being rather than referring to something that already exists. In *How to Do Things with Words*, Austin introduces this category to challenge the Descriptive Fallacy, the assumption that the primary function of statements is to describe some state of affairs (1), and the True/False Fetish, the notion that statements can be evaluated in terms of how accurately or inaccurately they present some state of affairs. Insofar as performatives do something rather than describe something—"the issuing of the utterance is the performing of an action" (6)—they cannot be evaluated as true or false but only as felicitous or infelicitous. They either succeed or misfire. Austin's performative has ethical implications. The "solid moralist," Austin says, believes that "accuracy and morality alike are on the side of the plain saying that *our word is our bond*" (10). Austin decouples the copula, driving a wedge between word and bond, by introducing the possibility of misfiring into all speech acts, even supposedly descriptive ones: "Infelicity is an ill to which . . . all *conventional* acts" are subject (19). The covenant between word and bond is broken.

Austin's performatives interrogate the limits of language, meaning, and responsibility. Insofar as we understand such interrogations as leading to new guarantees, both the deployment of performativity by theorists such as Derrida and Judith Butler and my deployment of passing will misfire.[7] In contrast to common usage, "passing" in my use does not assume that there is a prior or extradiscursive subject position that one acts and speaks from and is responsible to. Passing becomes visible, and inevitable, in the wake of the decoupling of the copula. The break in the covenant opens a space between the "I" who writes or speaks and the "I" who is the subject of that discourse.

If I prefer the term "passing" to "performativity," it is first of all because passing is a social practice, not a philosophical or linguistic concept. As a gerund, "passing" connotes movement, process, a dynamics: passing on, passing through, passing by, passing over. "Passing" is colloquial, "performativity" is jargon, alienating rather than familiar. Passing must be understood in relation to specific practices and circumstances and not just in relation to a theory of the subject. Indeed, I offer no new theory of the subject here, nor do I want to defend a specific theory in the abstract. I am not simply arguing that identity in postmodernity is a form of passing (although that is one argument I make) but that passing is also one of the practices through which we try to refuse the identities that have been historically offered to us and that continue to structure our responses even or especially when we seek to move out of them. Even more than the term "performativity," passing signifies the *risk* of identity in that the practice has social, economic, and even physical consequences. Passing can be literally a matter of life and death. Thus, passing marks the site of an ethical choice (Butler, "Imitation" 14–16).

I am aware of the dangers of employing the figure, for my use of "passing" can all too readily be translated into familiar terms and thereby fail in its objective to reconceptualize the familiar. This is a danger that has always attended deconstructive critiques. John Searle too quickly translates Derrida's argument in "Signature Event Context" (a key essay for a theory of performativity) into familiar terms and thereby misses the ethico-political import of Derrida's project.[8] Such ready translations are at once the obstacle to teaching theory (for its difference is explained in terms of what we already know) and the very possibility of its being understood (for its difference can be understood only in relation to the familiar). For example, one cannot understand Ferdinand de Saussure's concept of the sign if one translates "signifier" and "signified" into "word" and "meaning," as beginning theory students inevitably do. And yet the inevitability of that mistake can itself help students to understand why Saussure needs the concept of the sign to challenge precisely the concept of language bound up with word-meaning and thereby to grasp the importance and the long-term effects of the structuralist revolution. The initial slip in translating the theoretical concept into familiar terms is a necessary one in order to conceptualize the difference a theory of the sign makes to thinking about language. The gravest error I make as a teacher, and also the greatest temptation I face, is to keep my students from making such slips. If readers initially read my "passing" as "passing as a"—that is, as an intentional act rather than a performative effect—that slip can itself be revealing. Sometimes you just can't tell the difference, even when that difference makes all the difference.

Deconstructive reading requires, in Johnson's words, "read[ing] what is written rather than simply attempt[ing] to intuit what might have been meant" ("Writing" 46). Analogously, passing requires that we read the performance rather than reading through it to expose the "real" identity behind it.[9] The danger that the figure will become only a metaphor for subjectivity, that it will (re)locate the risk of identity only in the experience of writing and not, for example, in institutions and relationships, in part motivated my choice of a term signifying a social practice rather than a linguistic one. Passing, as a concept, provides "a critique of the vanguardism of the theoretician," as Gayatri Chakravorty Spivak characterizes Derrida's project in "SEC," that is, the belief that we theorists understand the performativity of subjectivity while those in the popular domain do not.[10]

The first chapter, "Passing," defines my use of "passing" to name and conceptualize not just the condition of subjectivity in postmodernity but the ways in which subjectivity is performed, in the arts, in academic scholarship, and in lived reality. I use the term to link critical practices to popular culture. There is no necessary relation between these, or between our theories and our practices, but there is, I argue, an imperative to make connections between them. It is that imperative that defines the ethical relation. I am concerned with the ethics of passing but not in the sense of determining whether it is right or wrong, legitimate or illegitimate, liberating or appropriative; while I argue that passing happens because of the choices we make, it is not itself a choice. Instead, I am concerned with how we negotiate passing as a practice that is implicated in a political, social, and ethical dynamics and with whether and how we become answerable for the choices we make. If traditionally, as John Rajchman writes, "the question of who we are—historically, libidinally, or 'aesthetically'—is a secondary one" in moral theory (143), today, I would argue, that question is a primary one in literary pedagogy.

"Pedagogy at Risk," the second chapter, looks not just at the risks we run as professors in teaching certain subjects and promoting certain practices considered to be political, and not just at the risks we ask our students to face, but, more important, at the ways in which passing puts pedagogy itself, and thus the profession of literary studies, at risk. For me, "at risk" signals not an imminent collapse that requires a return to standards but the inevitable, and positive, outcome of the changes brought about by the institutionalization of theory and the diversification of our classrooms and curricula. Together the first two chapters set up the theoretical arguments for the chapters that follow.

"Museums Do Have Walls," a performative interlude, takes pedagogy out of the classroom into other cultural sites, specifically, that of the museum exhibit. The next four chapters, which were written for different occasions and in response to specific pedagogical situations, provide example after example of the different ways passing occurs in the writing, reading, and teaching of literature. The conclusion, playfully titled "Coming Out," has less to do with the practice of disclosing one's "true" identity, the apparent contrary movement to "passing," than with the process of coming to terms with subjectivity as passing through writing about one's life.

There is a certain amount of repetition from chapter to chapter that is inevitable in a project such as this. "Teaching," Barbara Johnson writes in her preface to *The Pedagogical Imperative*, "is a compulsion . . . to repeat what one has not yet understood" (vii). Pedagogy is the art of repetition. One repeats in order to bring home a point, and in doing so, one finds out what can and cannot be repeated. The fact that we may discover, over and over again, that what happens by accident in the classroom—the random and contingent event—is the best pedagogical device does not lessen our desire to repeat the event, to reproduce its effects in subsequent classes. More than once I have caught myself wishing I had videotaped a class or conference during which the students and I worked through a particularly knotty issue so that I could capture the exchange and replay it for my classes. *Then*, I think, they would get it, if only I could get the arguments and the presentation right. But the repetition never quite comes off, for the very thing I would have them get cannot be learned without the lived experience of that exchange. Pedagogy entails the site of our actual engagement with others, and yet so much writing about pedagogy elides the messiness of actual engagements for the safety of the clear position or the security of the moral high ground, admittedly a difficult position to avoid in writing about pedagogy. The repetitions here are not only a conscious effort to get us unstuck from certain habitual ways of thinking and acting but are also symptomatic of my inability (and, I would argue, anyone's inability) to get it right—that is, to lay bare the structure of passing as if we could then break free of it. The point of the repetition is not to get us out of the structure of passing but to make it noticeable and thus to make us responsive to it.

The repetition may well be annoying to readers habituated by new technologies to "point and click," a phrase that for me has become a shorthand expression for the restless reading habits of a society for which information

is so readily accessible that learning seems to be a matter of locating and re-
trieving material. The phrase signifies a certain resistance to reading that Paul
de Man associated with theory. In the age of hypertext, and hyperreaders, I
no longer write with the expectation that I will be read through or that my
insights will not be lost in the distractions of browsing. Repetition is a strategy that seeks to compensate for, as well as respond to, a new technology of
reading. To those readers who may find the attitude that guides the writing
of this book somewhat foreign, I offer the following observation from Michel
Foucault: "As to those for whom . . . to begin and begin again, to attempt and
be mistaken, to go back and rework everything from top to bottom, and still
find reason to hesitate from one step to the next—as to those, in short, from
whom to work in the midst of uncertainty and apprehension is tantamount
to failure, all I can say is that clearly we are not from the same planet" (*History of Sexuality*, 2:7–8).

　There is as well a certain sliding of terms throughout. Poststructuralism
and postmodernism, postmodern theories and Theory, multiculturalism and
diversity, political correctness and identity politics, cultural studies and cultural criticism, passing in its conventional sense and passing as I reconfigure
it—all these concepts slide into one another. Such sliding of terms is also
inevitable in a project that is all about recognition and misrecognition. The
slipperiness of these terms is what makes these concepts relevant, for there
would be no need to work through the dynamics of passing if the boundaries around such concepts were clear, secure, and undisputed.

　Writing this book over the past six years, I have been continually aware
of the risks of employing the figure of passing. I have found many reasons
to hesitate, and more than once I nearly abandoned the project because I
kept coming up against myself, continually confronting the conflict between what I wanted to do and how I was afraid of being perceived. I wanted
to show the ethical and political potential of practices that are by no means
pure, and at times downright suspect, without being perceived as *endorsing* suspect motives. I wanted to write about ethics without sounding morally superior. My worry was that I could not always tell the difference between the practices I was engaged in and those that I critiqued. In the face
of criticisms and indictments coming as much from myself as from imagined readers, I kept forgetting one of the main insights conveyed by my use
of "passing": that that difference cannot be known in advance, can never
be guaranteed. I had to reaffirm, again and again, the very commitments
that led me to undertake the project. To risk oneself, to risk exposure, can
itself be a responsible act and can have transformative effects, however lim-

ited or partial, while to write always in relation to an imaginary hostile reader and to seek a safe position from which to speak will likely produce no such transformative effects or, at least, very little real change in the structures in which we hope to intervene. Writing against recent policy and funding decisions at the National Endowment for the Arts, performance artist Karen Finley remarks: "We have lost our inventiveness for the sake of appearances" (A17). The concern that motivates this book is that as cultural critics and literature teachers, we have reneged on the promise of our theories for the sake of appearances, and thereby have foreclosed on the ethics of passing.

In the years that I have been writing this book, many books and articles on the topic of passing have appeared, and just about everything published on pedagogy and higher education has seemed relevant. I cite many of these publications here, some I even use. Given the particular emphasis of my project, however, in regard to these works, I will, as the French say, *saluer en passant*—mention in passing and pass over.

NOTES

1. In reference to the racism that will inevitably emerge "despite our best efforts at concealment," artist Adrian Piper writes: "The question should not be whether any individual is racist; that we all are to some extent should be a given. The question should be, rather, how we handle [racism] once it appears" ("Passing" 28).

2. Geoffrey H. Hartman criticizes advocacy teaching as a loss of the ethos of inquiry. However, in response to recent debates over advocacy in the classroom, the point, I would argue, is neither to defend advocacy teaching nor to resist any kind of imposition as a power ploy, for the difference between advocacy and inquiry will be realized only in practice and experienced differently on different occasions. My focus on the dynamics of responsibility, for which the classroom serves as a paradigmatic example, is meant to counter such efforts as Hartman's to define "inquiry" and "advocacy" in the abstract, outside of particular practices and situations, and to offer an ethics that neither posits nor desires normative criteria.

3. Carole-Anne Tyler writes, "No matter how self-consciously we deconstruct identities, no matter how self-reflexively we perform our selves, we are still 'doing' them" ("Passing" 222).

4. Derrida elaborates the double logic of writing in his reading of Rousseau. See *Of Grammatology*, pt. 2, chap. 2.

5. Resistance, writes Elizabeth Grosz in a 1995 essay on Derrida's politics, does not lie outside dominant regimes of power but "is conditioned and made possible by them." What the logic of the supplement confronts is the "constitutive binding" of any oppositional practice to the law it would subvert (117).

6. On this resistance to models, see Jean-François Lyotard, *The Differend,* and

Lester Faigley's discussion of Lyotard in *Fragments of Rationality,* as well as Derrida's *Acts of Literature.*

7. Timothy Gould writes that Austin's performative resists "philosophy's desire for a guarantee of sense and relevance" (33). Gould's essay provides an excellent critique of common (mis)representations of the performative that neglect the more radical and disturbing political and moral implications of Austin's category. I reiterate Austin's theory of performativity in chapter 2.

8. See Gayatri Chakravorty Spivak's "Revolutions That as Yet Have No Model" for an explanation of Derrida's ethico-political project. John Searle's essay "Reiterating the Differences" is summarized in Derrida's *Limited Inc.,* which reprints "Signature Event Context" (hereafter abbreviated "SEC").

9. For an excellent analysis of passing as a reading strategy, see Robinson ("It Takes One").

10. Quoting a key passage in "SEC" in which Derrida asks, "But am I serious here?" Spivak comments: "Within the disciplines of philosophy and literary criticism, that is the question that many readers of Derrida have not been able to answer. Yes, Derrida is 'making fun of' Searle: and 'one does not write philosophy like that.' But also, to repeat, the charge is precisely against that seemingly impenetrable but ultimately perhaps even stupid seriousness of the academic intellectual; that is the 'condition or effect—take your pick' of ethico-political repression. And one should give Derrida the benefit of the doubt that, when he asks such a question it does not only mean 'you can't tell, can you?' but that, 'given the implications of my critique, I can't tell either; yet I will take my stand and make the critique nonetheless.' . . . I should insist that, to undermine the plausibility of one's arguments, to give the reader the ingredients for 'situating' one's own 'intention,' remains a considerable risk. . . . It is a sign of the dynamism and power of ideology that Derrida questions that this undermining can be recuperated into varieties of esoteric game-playing" ("Revolutions" 44–45).

ONE

Passing

Many things in the world have not been named; and many
things, even if they have been named, have never been described.
  —Susan Sontag, "Notes on 'Camp'"

On her 1992 album *Arkansas Traveler,* featuring such songs as "Jump Jim
Crow" and "Prodigal Daughter (Cotton Eyed Joe)," pop rock singer Michelle
Shocked claims her original idea for the cover design was a picture of herself in blackface. "Aside from providing controversy for hatemongers or offending the delicate sensibilities of the politically correct," Shocked writes,
"my sincere intention was that it would provide a genuine focus on the real
'roots' of many of the tunes included; blackface minstrelsy. It's my contention that a blackface tradition is alive and well hidden behind a modern mask.
I believe that 'blacking up' should be done correctly; as an exploration for
the source of that hollow ring we mistakenly believe was immaculately conceived in Las Vegas, and in a context of true respect for the cultures we ape."
  The audacity of a white performer considering wearing blackface as a sign
of "true respect" and professing through that mask to tell us how "blacking
up" can be done correctly is not what motivates my impulse to begin with
Michelle Shocked's words. Shocked's professed intention, and the complex
identifications and desires that motivated it, emblematize, for me, a pervasive
phenomenon in popular culture and in academic writing that evolves around
identities and the ways in which they are performed, not just in the arts but
in lived experience. It is a phenomenon I have come to name "passing."
  Examples abound. Sandra Bernhard impersonates black female performers in her 1990 film *Without You I'm Nothing.* A group of Irish working-class

musicians identify themselves as the blacks of Dublin, performing American soul music as an emblem of their disfranchised status in Alan Parker's 1991 film *The Commitments.* In 1991 ICA/Off White Productions, Inc., presented Jennie Livingston's *Paris Is Burning,* a film about the Harlem drag-ball scene, where black and Latino gay men impersonate recognizable and normative gender roles. In 1993 Noel Ignatiev and John Garvey founded *Race Traitor,* a journal premised on the belief that "race" is a fiction and devoted to abolishing the white race in part through whites identifying with, and identifying themselves as, nonwhites. In a chapter entitled "Reinventing Ourselves as Other" in *Whose Science? Whose Knowledge?* (1991) Sandra Harding urges us to take on "traitorous" identities. Eve Kosofsky Sedgwick writes from the position of a gay man in *Epistemology of the Closet* (1990) and speaks not just of her identification with but of her identity as a gay man in her essay "White Glasses." Henry Louis Gates Jr., in the *New York Times Book Review,* ties his scholarly writings to his effort to learn how to speak in the voice of his mother ("Whose Canon"). Jacques Derrida, in an essay on Emmanuel Levinas, "At This Very Moment in This Work Here I Am," writes in the voice of the feminine interlocutor (*Reader* 405–39). Richard Rorty uses the feminine pronoun for the position he occupies, the liberal ironist, in *Contingency, Irony, Solidarity* (1989), signifying by his move into the "she" his openness to redescription.[1] Gilles Deleuze and Félix Guattari write of "becoming-woman," by which they mean neither impersonation nor transvestism but the process of deterritorializing one's "major" identity (25, 29). Jaye Davidson becomes a woman in Neil Jordan's film *The Crying Game* (1992), "a love story . . . beyond sex" (qtd. in Corliss 57). Harlan Lane, a hearing person, writes on behalf of the deaf in *The Mask of Benevolence: Disabling the Deaf Community* (1992). Arnold Krupat writes, without any "experiential authority" (30), from the perspective of Native American culture in *Ethnocriticism* (1992). Sociologist Judith Rollins passes as a domestic to obtain firsthand experience of domestic service for her book, *Between Women* (1985). Nancy K. Miller in *Getting Personal* (1990) confesses that she moved from the French to the English department because she feared that a gender mistake or a misfired joke would expose her as an impersonator, the misperformance of the improvisation revealing that she was passing as "a near native speaker" (48).

I do not mean to suggest that all these examples have any one thing in common—*except that each engages passing as an ethical practice.* If, as it has been suggested, self-privileging through the pathologizing of the other is the key move of a metaphysical or modern theory of value,[2] then, I would suggest, self-divestment through passing as another may be the key move in a postmetaphysical or postmodern theory of value. "Maybe the target nowadays," writes Foucault in "The Subject and Power," "is not to discover what we are, but to refuse what we are" by resisting those "techniques of power" that attach the individual subject to her or his own identity (212–16). "'Crossing the line' to a new and improbable identity" (216) is, for Foucault, the ethical imperative of our day (Rajchman 13). Putting one's self-identifications at risk is just the first step in an ethics of passing. The dynamics of following through, and the ways in which we tend to slip, are the subject of my book.

Passing, with its corollary, coming out, has become an obsessional interest in popular entertainment and a major topos of our critical and professional activity.[3] My interest is not only in the act itself but in how the performance of the rhetorical figure of passing helps us to conceptualize certain difficulties we face as cultural critics and literature professors when we attempt to put our theories of the subject, our politics of identity, and our ethics of diversity into practice in writing and in teaching. The metaphor of passing describes the position of scholars, teachers, and students in a classroom and an institution profoundly changed over the past few decades. These changes are due in part to the academy's efforts to acknowledge diversity in response to the changing demographics of the university by institutionalizing studies programs (e.g., women's studies, African American studies, composition studies, gay/lesbian studies) and by promoting a multicultural curriculum; and also in part to theory's efforts to rethink the notion of difference and to critique the concept of identity on which those studies programs are founded. When various postmodern theories that deconstruct the "self" converge with various studies programs that revive it, anxiety arises over the positions we find ourselves in as professors and learners in the newly configured university. Passing is an appropriate figure for the anxiety of having no secure position. As Amy Robinson puts it, "in an academic milieu in which identity and identity politics remain at the forefront of a battle over legitimate critical and/or political acts, the social practice of passing offers a productive framework through which to reimagine the contours of this debate" ("It Takes One" 716).

Passing in my book, however, is more than a metaphor for a new subject position, and it is not limited to the social practice of Robinson's statement. I use it to name and conceptualize a pervasive phenomenon that has gone by so many names that it, like Sontag's "camp," has never been adequately or usefully described. "Catachresis" may be a more apt figure for my deployment of passing than "metaphor," insofar as "passing" names something that does not exist or for which a literal term cannot be substituted.[4] In other words, "passing" is a dynamics, not something that stands for or represents another thing. "Passing" as I use it is closely related to "performativity," the notion that any "I" comes to be a subject only through a matrix of differential relations that make certain kinds of being possible.[5] I prefer "passing" because the phenomenon I am describing is not just a philosophical or linguistic concept but a social practice with a history. I use "passing" in each example I cite above not to suggest that there is a unifying element in all its applications but to say, paraphrasing Ludwig Wittgenstein, that these practices are related to one another in many different ways (#65). The examples I give above and those to follow, all of which are performances of one kind or another, register various (and variously effective) responses to a psychopolitical dynamics that involves the same kinds of imperatives, constraints, and impasses. More precisely, each of these instances of passing is ethically and politically motivated by a desire to respond to the claims made on the kind of cultural work intellectuals and artists do by the changes—theoretical, social, technological, economic, attitudinal—designated by the term "postmodernity."

Postmodernity is at once a function of the increasing inclusion of so-called minority populations and marginalized experiences in the dominant culture and a function of broader "macrolevel" changes, in information technologies, multinational corporations, genetic engineering, reproductive technologies, the global village, and life online. Crucial to my use of "passing" is the notion that these changes are felt most immediately as a threat or challenge to the individual subject, putting at risk one's most profound understanding of what it is to be a person or agent. Insofar as subjectivity is constituted through public practices and public property (namely, language), changing notions of what it means to *be* a subject or to *have* an identity are as much an effect of postmodern culture as of postmodern theories.[6] Passing entails both an effort to divest oneself of privileged subject positions that have been made increasingly untenable by the emergence of certain political and social groups into the general culture, and an effort to resist certain identifications that have long proven to be oppressive by tying our subjectivities to a particular identity seen to be "given." For example, identifications as a woman, as a woman of color, and as a mother are now as problematic as those of white, male, western intellectual. Indeed, identification itself has come to be a political, ethical, and pedagogical imperative.[7]

That so many professionals today are, in Sedgwick's words, crossing "politically charged boundaries [of] group identification" (*Epistemology* 59–60) has led just about everyone, it seems, to question who has the right to engage in certain practices, who can cross over and for what purposes, or who can speak as, for, and from what positions. Whether such critiques are directed at one's own practice, or at others with whom one may be seen to share a practice, exploring and exposing the phantasmatic bases and the cultural politics of "what we think we are doing anyway" has become the order of the day.[8] How has this situation come to pass? What does it mean to call it "passing"? What does this description enable us to do?

In this chapter, I can only begin to answer such questions, which I will pursue in the following chapters in terms of specific texts, certain theoretical problems, and particular social, political, and pedagogical contexts. Here I want to lay the groundwork for the performative readings that follow (readings that seek to engage the dynamics of passing rather than to formulate an appropriate response to it) by briefly defining "passing" as it has been traditionally used and as it is currently being redefined by literary and cultural critics, and by discussing some specific instances of the phenomenon I am calling "passing," identifying in each a common structure of response to a shared set of theoretical and political concerns. But first I want to return to my opening example. The pop rock singer's justification of her shocking, if only imaginary, cover design can tell us much about the function of racial impersonation in the white Imaginary, certainly; but the performance artist (who, after all, calls herself *Shocked*) can also teach us something about the performativity of critical discourse and about the anxiety that attends our own crossover performances.

Shocking Performances

> If I knew your secret I would make it mine.
> —Michelle Shocked, "Jump Jim Crow" on *Arkansas Traveler*

> The most important lesson music still has to teach us is that its inner secrets and its ethnic rules can be taught and learned.
> —Paul Gilroy, *The Black Atlantic*

Michelle Shocked's statement which opens this chapter not only epitomizes our contemporary fascination with the theme of passing and the practice of impersonation, it also challenges popular conceptions of these practices. If the deliberate assumption of the blackface mask makes Shocked's disclosure so flagrant, the malfunctioning of the very concept of the mask, what we might call its slippage, gives the statement its force, especially when used to read the various forms this slippage takes in the examples of passing discussed later in this chapter.

On the one hand, Shocked would flaunt the mask to taunt racist "hate-mongers" and "politically correct" liberals, presumably those who would find such parody offensive in its racist stereotyping and its apparent indifference to the history of racial oppression that blackface has come to signify. On the other hand, Shocked would wear her blackface straight-faced, as a "*genuine* focus" on this music's "*real* 'roots'" and to show "*true* respect" for the culture musicians like herself "ape." The juxtaposition of "sincere," "genuine," "real," and "true" with the blackface mask is jarring. Yet that disconcerting effect brings into strong relief the fact that "aping," the very form of mimicry racist whites attributed to blacks through such parodic figures as Zip Coon, a stock character of blackface minstrelsy, is here attributed ostensibly to white musicians who want to sound black *without* wearing the mask. What is being mocked in the guise of blackface is not black people but white performers who would hide or disavow the miscegenated history of the contemporary pop rock, blues, and bluegrass sound they produce, in effect denying that they are in blackface whenever they perform this music.[9] The real mask is the straight white face.

Michelle Shocked would don the minstrel mask neither to participate in blackface as racist mimicry nor to celebrate, through these songs, an authentic black or folk culture, which would be, in effect, to mistake blackface as a signifier of or on a real black face. Instead, and more important, both her performance of this music and her defense of it raise the issue of the social relations of its production. In paying tribute to blackface minstrelsy, not actual black people or culture, as the source of the songs she performs, Shocked acknowledges that a southern folk tradition as it has been passed down to us in popular entertainment, especially musical performances, was not "immaculately conceived," either by whites or blacks, but finds its "real 'roots'" in the already imitated, appropriated, racially mixed and commodified sound that passes as the real thing. Blackface is neither disguise nor simply impersonation but a performance that signifies the racially mixed origins of this music. The whiteness on display in these performances is every bit as much a mask, a cultural construction, as the blackness it would seem to appropriate, not the origin(al), and certainly no immaculate conception. In performing this music, there is no way to remove the mask, Shocked would seem to suggest, no matter how politically correct that gesture may seem, for the impersonation is, if not the "real thing," then at least what performers, white and black, in this tradition must always negotiate in any effort to represent the real thing. The miscegenated history that Shocked's blackface

would signify positions writers and performers alike complexly, even uncom-
fortably, in relation to those we identify as or with in our cultural productions. That history calls into question the belief that we can get beyond or
beneath the commodified image to the real thing—a belief that always entails a disavowal of the mask, the performance itself.

If the performance artist insists, as do so many cultural critics, that "minstrelsy has never really died out,"[10] her point is not simply that whites continue to mimick, and to stereotype, blacks in their cultural appropriations
of black art forms; rather, it suggests that a minstrel tradition means that pop
blues musicians, whether black or white, cannot help but wear the mask when
they attempt to represent a genuine black sound or look—something Bert
Williams and Josephine Baker knew only too well, and something Jimi Hendrix and Michael Jackson have profited from. Michelle Shocked would have
us neither forget nor disavow the impersonation at the root of the "black-
ening" of American popular culture.[11]

The actual cover design of *Arkansas Traveler* that substitutes for the artist's original intention, while making much the same point about "origins,"
fails to bring out this racially inflected history. The mixed-media cover pho-
to features the real Michelle Shocked in a cartoon-like mise-en-scène à la Li'l
Abner. Dressed contemporarily in a black leotard and foregrounded against
the cultural markers of country life—a split rail fence, a ramshackle cabin,
Ma and Pa rocking on the front porch—the artist soaks her bare feet in a tin
washpan, holding a hobo's stick across her lap. Like the intended cover design, this one acknowledges the "real 'roots'" of this music as always already
commodified. Missing from the album cover, though, is any explicit reference to the racial history in which Shocked's performance takes part. Given
that racial history—the social and economic oppression of blacks and poor
southern whites, and the legal and commercial theft of black property in this
country—one could hardly deny that Shocked's decision (if, indeed, it was
hers) to abandon the original cover design was an ethically and politically
responsible one, if also a pragmatic one (playing it safe to protect sales). Yet
the absence of any reference to minstrelsy in effect disengages the music from
the social realities of its historical production and seems to indicate that the
"real" roots of her music are rural, white country music.[12] Whether or not
Michelle Shocked ever really intended to put on blackface, the phantasmatic image conjured up by her avowal works against the disavowal of that identification on the actual cover.

What emerges through Shocked's performance and defense of blackface
minstrelsy is an argument, however intuitive, much like Eric Lott's in *Love
and Theft*, his highly acclaimed analysis of the minstrel tradition. Even with-

Michelle Shocked, cover for *Arkansas Traveler,* Polygram Records, Inc., 1992.

out the explicit justification presented on the cover of *Arkansas Traveler,* songs like "Jump Jim Crow" and "Woody's Rag," a bluegrass jam interrupted by corny jokes in the fashion of the minstrel show, make explicit the heritage of the music Shocked performs—"the rural white tradition and its commercial issue in modern bluegrass inherited much from minstrelsy," writes Lott (5). Yet the songs, the humor, and the dances (like Jim Crow), as Lott says, "were so culturally mixed as to make their 'racial' origins quite undecidable" (94). Lott cites "Jump Jim Crow" as one example of an "impure" song taken as "authentic" (16). Michelle Shocked, one might say, has earned her right to perform this music by doing her homework, by learning the history of its "roots." That history of racial exchange, says Lott, makes it difficult to talk of "expropriation" in any simple terms, not only because minstrel tunes were impure mixtures to begin with and not the reproduction of actual slave songs as so often assumed, but because black performance itself, which blackface acts apparently appropriated, was first of all *performative,* a cultural construction and exhibition created in response to various social realities, not a signifier of an essence (Lott 39).[13] Blackface performance *stages* racial categories, and has kept blackness "on display and up for grabs" (36).

Blackface, like the social practice of passing, produces whiteness and blackness as racial identities to be assumed—in both senses of "put on" and "taken for granted." What this means has more profound implications than the rather pat conclusion that identity is a fiction, authenticity a drag.[14] It means a change in the kinds of questions we ask, the kinds of issues we pursue, and the kinds of imperatives we respond to in writing and teaching across boundaries of identities and identifications. As Lott says of minstrelsy, the issue is not what was really black in blackface and what mere racist typing; rather, the key issue is how and why such "impure" creations were circulated as "authentically" black (39–41) and how narratives of origins (or immaculate conceptions) are used to resolve ideological questions raised by minstrelsy (55). Narratives of origins reveal not *essences,* says Lott, but anxiety and guilt over the *fact* of cultural borrowing (57) and its implications for our identifications—the anxiety and guilt Shocked's blackface would confront, the anxiety and guilt still felt today over the cultural borrowing promoted under the rubric of border crossing.

I want to argue that passing, in its current cultural manifestation as I describe it here, must be understood in terms of a blackface tradition. What passing inherits from its roots in the racial history that made minstrelsy a defining practice of American popular culture is anxiety over the fact of cultural borrowing and the representation of such borrowing, as well as guilt over the economic issue of who profits from the marketing of certain representations and from the crossing of Sedgwick's "politically charged boundaries [of] group identification." But its heritage also means that passing is rooted in *performance* and serves to facilitate the racial exchange it seems merely to capitalize on. This is not to say that passing and the identities it seeks to engage or promote are only a matter of artifice. Rather, identities are the product of public practices and social relations that seem to precede them.[15] Lott conceives a blackface tradition as "a visible sign of cultural interaction" that safely facilitated "an exchange of energies between two otherwise rigidly bounded" cultures and that eventually "transmogrified" due to its own success in crossing cultural boundaries (6). I want to suggest that one form this transmogrification took is what I am calling, straight-faced, passing.

"Passing" and "Passing as"

> There is passing and then there is passing.
> —Judith Butler, *Bodies That Matter*

> It is possible to use a term in a new way, but it is not possible to escape the term's past.
> —Thomas McLaughlin, "Introduction."

The word never forgets where it has been, Mikhail Bakhtin reputedly has written.[16] The word "passing" has a history, or rather many histories, and thus my use of this term is neither innocent nor naïve. It is an appropriation, to be sure, but the fact of cultural appropriation, as Lott says of minstrelsy, is only a starting point, not the last word on the political and social implications of the practice (234). I would like to think of my deployment of passing as a "pragmatic appropriation" in that I treat the practice and its history as a "resignifiable narrative," which has a historical and political usefulness.[17]

"Passing" in its most traditional usage refers to the practice of assuming the identity of another type or class of persons in order to pass oneself off as a member of that group, for social, economic, or political reasons. In this country, passing has historically denoted the social practice of light-skinned people of African descent assuming a white identity, though the term is not limited to this specific use. "Passing" is generally implicated in a racist social organization. Although the identity issues I address in this book are not specifically an American phenomenon, nor are they limited to race, my use of passing as a central cultural figure for these identity issues *is* rooted in the racial history and politics of the United States. That's why a 1996 book on passing published in Italian couldn't translate the term, because the phenomenon is so very American in the anxieties it arouses and in the behaviors that define it.[18]

In its literal or first cultural sense, "passing" carries certain pejorative connotations of deception, dishonesty, fraudulence, or betrayal. It designates an effort to disguise or suppress one's racial heritage, racially marked body, or sexual orientation.[19] The painful psychic consequences of passing attested to in so many narratives are memorably and corporeally depicted in Agnieszka Holland's 1991 film *Europa Europa,* based on Solomon Perel's autobiography, where the protagonist, a German Jew, conceals his identity from his Nazi companions by pulling what remains of his foreskin over the tip of his circumcised penis and tying it in place with a piece of thread.

When used as a metaphor, with the operative "as" (passing as a), "passing" can apply to a variety of situations whereby one impersonates or represents another, speaking as or for a class of people, a practice not without its ethical problems. Whereas "passing," in both its metaphoric and literal usage, implies, at least initially, a conscious choice, passing may actually be conscious or unconscious.[20] In either case, to be successful, the passer must come to *be* that identity for a great many others, if not also for him- or herself. To the extent that that identity is *assumed,* at once taken on and taken for granted, passing always entails risks. In the nonmetaphoric sense, the passer runs the risk of disclosure, the exposure of his or her "real" identity (as a black, a Jew, a homosexual). In the metaphoric sense, the passer runs the risk of a slip or an indiscretion that threatens to expose his or her infelicitous performance (as a near-native speaker), true nature (a closet racist or homophobe), or inevitable implication in the very structures of identity passing was an effort to escape or disavow.

"Passing" in these usages depends on a binary logic of identity, the logic that says if A is white, A cannot be not white. In its most traditional sense, the practice presupposes a distinction between essence and appearance, authenticity and fraudulence, the real person and the persona—a distinction the passer must uphold if he or she is to be successful while also calling it into question through that very success. Thus, passing at once reinforces and disrupts the binary logic of identity that gives rise to the practice to begin with. As a social practice, passing can be reactionary (maintaining a normative whiteness or compulsory heterosexuality) or subversive (challenging the very assumptions on which such normative identifications rest), and even both at once.[21]

However much their experience of subjectivity in postmodern culture and in a multicultural classroom might give the lie to this logic, students often internalize the binary logic of identity in responding to narratives of passing. In a recent African American literature course, my students responded along racial lines to the passing protagonist in James Weldon Johnson's novel *The Autobiography of an Ex-Coloured Man.* White-identified students saw the tragedy as his need to choose between two identities; nonwhite students saw the tragedy as his belief that he has a choice. Although the first response conceives identity as a matter of individual will and the second as a matter of racial politics, both uphold the binary logic of identity: he must be either black or white.[22] Nonwhite students felt he had betrayed the race, white students sympathized with his ontological or existential dilemma, but all saw the protagonist as a fraud.

Contemporary literary and cultural critics who write about passing as a social practice and as a literary genre critique precisely this binary logic on which its original use depends. Passing conceived as fraudulence, betrayal, or "selling out" upholds this logic of identity and endorses both a politics of race that insists on authenticity and a politics of identity that conceives the subject as discrete and autonomous, having control over his or her identity and destiny. Alternatively, contemporary critics have come to reconceive passing as a performative practice. The passer does not relinquish one pre-existing identity to move into another, more highly valued one; rather passing participates in the cultural production of whiteness as "racially pure," ethnicity as "origin," and heterosexuality as "normative." The conception of passing as dishonesty, deception, or betrayal is produced by the very problem of identity to which the practice of passing is the solution.[23] There would be no need to pass if identity were not a problem, yet the passer must insist that identity is not a problem if he or she is to pass. Thus, while the *concept* of passing is understood within a binary logic of identity, the *practice* actually functions in terms of a double logic: it is both the problem and the solution. The passer adopts an identity that the act of passing in part constitutes. Herein lies the connection with blackface. Contemporary analyses of blackface minstrelsy emphasize not simply the appropriation of the cultural markers of another's racial identity but the way the public performance functions to produce the signs of racial difference it is seen to re-present. This is what is meant by a performative notion of identity.[24]

Reconceiving the social practice of passing as strategic intervention rather than as self-denial, as performativity not inauthenticity, has been imperative in efforts to undermine systems of racial and sexual oppression that make passing necessary to begin with. Passing as a social practice can be used to undermine the reliability and the political necessity of the binary logic of identity that subtends laws such as the one-drop rule and the rule of hypo-descent and the reliability of the visual field as a guarantee of racial and even sexual identity.[25] But here is the problem I see in recent efforts to reconceptualize passing. While using the social practice of passing to disrupt hegemonic concepts of identity that depend on a binary logic, many literary and cultural critics, when referring to passing in its figurative sense, seem compelled to maintain the binary logic they undermine in their reading of the social practice. The fact that social passing exposes "the actual fluidity of ostensibly rigid racial boundaries" (Mullen 74) and thereby disrupts the cultural production of whiteness as the norm and of blackness as (self-)denial, also gives rise to the fear that this notion of fluid racial boundaries can, if taken too far, suggest that anyone can change one's racial or sexual identification at will.[26] That is, many cultural critics fear that the fluidity of identity categories will necessarily lead to the collapse of categories, to the leveling of distinctions, and thus to the "disappearing" of actual black people, as many critics argue has happened in the "marketing of marginality" in popular entertainment or in the morphing that characterizes media representations of the future face of America.[27] Whites impersonating blacks, men professing feminism, straights becoming queer—all these forms of passing can potentially gloss over real material differences, so that passing as manifested in popular entertainment (and, I would add, in academic writing) serves to make a spectacle out of difference and ignores the history of oppressions that marks those differences (V. Smith 51).[28]

For example, Valerie Smith points out that narratives of passing always entail the potential for conflating differences between as well as within social groups (47). It is this potential that makes it imperative, in Smith's view, that passing as a cultural performance, as distinguished from passing as a social practice, be assessed in terms of an authenticity that, theoretically, is not necessarily tied to the performer's identity but politically most often is. In a reading of the film *The Commitments,* Philip Brian Harper argues that the fact that a cultural expression or aesthetic style can be taught and learned is what gives art its moral and political force, but it is also what allows for its co-optation. Because the signifiers of difference can be so easily appropriated, they can be exploited by the culture industry for purposes not necessarily beneficial to the social group (*Framing* 27, 188). This, in Harper's reading, is what happens in *The Commitments.* The working-class Irish musicians who form the eponymous band in the film identify *with* American blacks as an oppressed group and identify themselves *as* the blacks of Dublin. Their identification is both political and psychic insofar as they strive to *be* black, "to remake their personae" through the music they perform (189–90). Yet that identification is ultimately emptied of both psychic and political import, Harper argues, becoming "a merely cultural phenomenon" (192). Whether as a means of representing one's sense of cultural dislocation, as the Irish group does in performing soul music, or a means of representing the fluidity of identity categories, such identification, as a cultural phenomenon, masks the specificity of a group's oppression (192) and becomes, in Susan Willis's words, "hollowed of social meanings" (190). Conceived in this way, Michelle Shocked's blackface would signal the loss of any meaningful social distinctions, what Harper terms "the categorical collapse that always potentially characterizes the postmodern era" (192).[29]

However, like Shocked's performance, the rock group's identification has historical roots that are obscured when their performance is seen only as whites adopting a blackface mask, for the Irish were considered black, even called "Black Irish," and the stock characters Pat and Bridget competed for laughs with Jim Crow and Zip Coon on the minstrel stage (Ignatiev 2). "Category crisis," the concept by which Marjorie Garber designates "a failure of definitional distinction, a borderline that becomes permeable, that permits of border crossings from one (apparently distinct) category to another" (*Vested Interests* 16), always risks Harper's "categorical collapse." That risk gives rise to the fear that the destabilizing of identity categories means the loss of any distinctions. Barbara Herrnstein Smith writes in another context: "It seems that whenever systems of more or less strictly segregated hierarchical strata begin to break down and *differentiations* become more numerous, rapid, complex, less predictable, and less controllable, the resulting emergences, mixtures, and minglings will look . . . like flattenings, falls, and collapses—in short, like *losses* of *distinctions*" (77). It is the fear that "crisis" really means "collapse" that leads us to look for guarantees of meaning and import. "Passing" as I use it here means learning to live and act without such guarantees.

Conceiving passing in the metaphoric sense (passing as a) as simply the assumption of a mask or persona, or the appropriation or theft of another group's identity papers, ends up reinforcing the very binary logic of identity that reconceptualizations of passing as a social practice challenge, maintaining the belief (politically if not theoretically) that there is a "true" or "given" identity beneath or behind the performance of the (in)authenticity. Thus, the concept of the *performative,* so crucial in the refiguring of passing as a social practice, becomes conflated with *performance* as a theatrical production in discussions of metaphoric passing.[30] Questions of legitimacy and authenticity (who's real and who's a fraud, who has a right to certain cultural expressions and who appropriates them), which always entail the maintenance of certain power relations and identity boundaries, return. In other words, whereas in instances of social passing it is crucial to *undermine* the notion of identities as genuine or fraudulent, authentic or inauthentic, in order to rework a logic of identity that reproduces and reinforces normative categories and oppressive social structures, in cases of metaphoric passing it has been crucial for many critics to *retain* the untenable privileged identities in order to know the "real thing." I am arguing in response that we need to assuage the fear of *collapse* to sustain the productive possibilities in the notion of *crisis.*

Just as it has been a decisive political act to reconceive "passing" in its first cultural sense in terms of "passing as" in its figurative sense to focus on the production of racial and sexual identities taken to be "given," so it is crucial, I argue, to reconceive "passing as," in the figurative sense, in terms of "passing" (without the as), not to return to the binary logic that structures the originary use of the term, but precisely to avoid reinscribing such a logic. In its first cultural sense, "passing" didn't need the "as"; one didn't pass *as* a white person, one simply passed. To pass was literally to assume another's identity, "to go from one quality, state, or form to another" (*Webster's Ninth Collegiate*). Making "as" the operative word, as contemporary theorists do, is to understand social passing not as the co-optation of an already existing identity but as precisely the act by which identities are established and legitimized in the first place. Similarly, conceiving "passing as" in the metaphoric sense in terms of "passing" (without the "as") is to push to the limit the performative process by which identities are (re)produced, to keep "as" from becoming a safeguard, a fixed reference point, an originary origin to which one can always return, or be returned. Insofar as passing depends on the polarity of inside/outside, it is, even in its first cultural sense as a social practice, nonetheless a *figure* of speech. My use of "passing" serves to remind us that analogies work both ways, as J. Hillis Miller remarks, and a concept, including a concept of identity, can be "modeled on that for which it is the model" (22). The figure of passing serves to allegorize "the slippage between . . . mimesis and . . . performativity" (Butler, "Lana's 'Imitation'" 3). "Passing" in my use, without the "as," names a practice in which an original model or presence can be neither presumed nor assumed. Instead of attempting to (re)claim the real thing, I am arguing, we can (re)claim the act of passing as itself an ethical practice.[31] My purpose, then, in choosing passing as a figure for the performativity of subjectivity is to recall and remind my readers of the full potential of the performative and so to be able to exploit in turn the full ethical potential of the dynamics of passing.

As I use it, "passing" necessarily figures that always slippery difference between standing *for* something (having a firm position) and passing *as* something (having no position or a fraudulent one), between the strategic adoption of a politically empowered identity (as when blacks pass as white or homosexuals pass as heterosexual) and the disempowering appropriation of a potentially threatening difference (as when men pass as feminist or whites represent blacks), and between what one professes as a writer or teacher (the positions one assumes in an article or a classroom, often as spokesperson for another's position) and how one is actually positioned in a society, institution, discourse, or classroom. Marked by a discrepancy between what one professes to be (and what one professes) and how one is positioned, passing is risky business, whether one risks being *exposed* as passing or being *accused* of passing. Such risks, this book professes, are unavoidable, perhaps inevitable, for there is no occupying a position without passing.

In any effort to perform across identificatory boundaries, for which the story of Michelle Shocked's album cover has served as an exemplum, the crucial distinction is commonly seen to be between the politically effective and the culturally appropriative, between those acts that benefit others and those that serve only one's own interests. In other words, passing has come to be thought of in one of two ways: either positively, as an index of our culturally constructed, multiply positioned, and infinitely changeable identities; or negatively, as the politically problematic appropriation of another group's difference. The important distinction as I see it, however, and one crucial to my resignification of passing, is between those who insist on such distinctions and those who act without such guarantees. The phantasmatic figure conjured up by Shocked's intended cover design is, in essence, a *refusal* of the fantasy of a safe position, one insulated from the practices it would decry. No matter how sincere our efforts, how well earned our right to participate, how open our self-critique, how frank our confessions, our forays across politically charged boundaries of identity and identification can never guarantee that we will pass. Or, put differently, in our efforts to identify with and to represent others—including the "other" that is "self"—and to participate in "impure" cultural forms thought to be "authentic," we cannot help but pass.

"Passing" in my use is at once the condition of subjectivity in postmodernity and the cultural practices that (re)produce, respond to, and sustain that condition. Questions of legitimacy do not drop out, but they no longer structure the logic of passing. Legitimacy is raised as an issue at different registers, it "does not govern the entire scene" (Derrida, *Limited Inc.* 18). I am not arguing for the legitimacy of passing as an identity or a practice, but I do want to argue for its ethics.

Speaking "as" and Speaking "for"

> Why would the problem of identification not be, in general,
> the essential problem of the political?
> —Philippe Lacoue-Labarthe, qtd. in Fuss, *Identification
> Papers*

We have acknowledged that subjectivity is passing for some time now. The deconstruction of the "I" as an effect of language (Lacan), writing (Derrida), or discourse (Althusser, Foucault) has led to the exploration of gender, race, and sexuality as the performative effects of social practices, not the essential attributes of individuals. The term "subject" itself is linguistic, indicating that any "I" exists in and through, not prior to, language and social relations. "There can be no 'I' without a 'you,'" writes Carole-Anne Tyler in a 1994 essay on passing. "The subject is the effect of impersonation or mimicry, the assumption of an alienating signifier ('I' or 'you'). . . . All subjects therefore are *passing* through the signifiers which represent them for an other" (221). We are always performing our identities even or especially when we would present ourselves sincerely to others. This is not to say that the subject is reduced to its linguistic performance, only to recognize, as Susan David Bernstein says, that "the dimensions of language structure the representation of any epistemological claims about an 'I'" (142). I need not rehearse this history of the subject yet again. This deconstructive insight has now entered the public consciousness as the word "deconstruction" now pervades public discourse. From the *performance* (not the pretense) of sincerity that Michelle Shocked's blackface signifies, to the title of Sandra Bernhard's film, *Without You I'm Nothing*, to Anna Deavere Smith's dramas of "identity in motion," we live in the era of "the passing of *passing* [in its original sense] as a politically viable response to oppression" (Tyler 212)—and, I am suggesting, its emergence as the dynamics of responsibility.[32]

Yet we forget this deconstructive insight again and again in writing and teaching, even when writing and teaching about this very insight, and the reason we forget is inscribed in the structure of that forgetting. There is, in other words, a structure to this forgetting that one can notice, a structure I will elaborate in terms of the slippage passing always entails. Without the moment of slippage, without the possibility of making a mistake or running the risk of exposure, passing in popular culture and in cultural criticism becomes simply one more *position* to be advocated, safeguarded, or repudiated, not a *dynamics* to be negotiated. Without the understanding of passing as the slippage that we risk forgetting in our efforts to get it right, "passing" in its other uses is not passing all the way down. Or, put another way, without the slippage, passing is merely a performance, not performative. Some examples follow of the slippage and the anxiety it produces that can undermine the dynamics of passing.

Anxiety over the slippage is evident in the very terms we use to negotiate the dynamics I call "passing." Rarely do we refer to the kinds of identifications we make in our crossing of identity categories as instances of "passing." More commonly debates over issues of identification and representation are presented in terms of speaking "as" and speaking "for." The desire to resist these forms of speaking coupled with the temptation to conflate them, or the always-present possibility for conflating them, gives rise to the anxiety that undermines the potentially positive impulses of the practices. I begin with two examples. Lane's *The Mask of Benevolence* and Krupat's *Ethnocriticism*, both published in 1992, provide a powerful defense of the need to maintain the right to speak on behalf of certain social or cultural groups if we are not to relinquish the right to advocacy. Each argues the necessity of a double perspective that comes from self-consciously positioning oneself on both sides of a cultural divide.

In *The Mask of Benevolence*, Lane, a psychologist, seeks to make a discursive intervention in the representation of the deaf community by hearing professionals. Currently, psychologists and sociologists represent the deaf as "disabled," an ethnocentric representation Lane calls "audism" insofar as it privileges orality and judges the deaf as lacking in relation to what hearing people possess and value (43–47). Drawing on Foucault and Rorty, Lane argues that our ways of talking about the deaf are historical, the product of social and institutional forces, and therefore also political. The model of disability is a form of paternalism in that it allows hearing professionals to speak for a social group perceived to be unable to speak for themselves. Lane proposes instead that the deaf be seen as a "linguistic and cultural minority." His vocabulary is no more "true" than the others, Lane concedes, but the alternative conceptualization he offers carries powerfully positive social, political, and ethical implications.

Although skeptical of the kind of cultural relativism Lane endorses and critical of postmodern theorists, whom Lane draws on, Krupat's project in *Ethnocriticism* has much in common with Lane's. As a practitioner of ethnocriticism, Krupat places himself on the frontier where two cultures, Anglo-American and Native American, meet in order to "materializ[e] their [Indian] values on the sociopolitical level" (4). The self-positioning he advocates, like Lane's self-critical perspective, acknowledges its own complicity in the structures it critiques and offers in response a new, more self-conscious, and humbled, perspective. Lane's attentive listener is Krupat's frontiersman who tests "[his] own largely Western assumptions or origins" in relation to "otherness and difference" (27, 23).

Yet even the most innocent forms of identifying with and speaking on behalf of others, where one represents a certain subject position or cultural group in terms meant to empower the other, puts the writer at risk of being *accused* of "passing"—that is, of being misidentified. This risk requires in turn the kind of caveat Lane provides in his preface in response to the deaf person who criticized Lane for making pronouncements about the deaf, in effect accusing Lane himself of the very paternalism his book seeks to expose in other hearing professionals. In response to this criticism, Lane acknowledges that his position as cultural outsider limits the kinds of claims he can make about and on behalf of the deaf. There are two ways of knowing a culture, Lane explains to his correspondent (redoubling the sin of paternalism): from the outside as a trained professional and attentive listener, and from the inside as a "native speaker." In making pronouncements, Lane insists that he is neither speaking "as," engaging in the kind of mimicry that would suggest he could know the deaf community from the "inside," nor speaking "for," which would be to engage in the kind of paternalism he resists. Yet the very fact that this charge of paternalism has arisen, requiring the caveat Lane gives in response, points to the always slippery distinction between mimicry and paternalism, on the one hand, and advocacy, on the other.

Becoming aware of the structure of paternalism, as Lane would have us do, can enable us to self-consciously examine the representations that structure our relations to others, but it can also lead, Lane fears, to resentment, guilt, and even "collective indifference" (99)—and, I would add, to the caveat. Because paternalism is structural, not individual (47), those who try not to be paternalistic, Lane says, can be only partially successful (87). The truth of this is born out in Lane's preface, where he is painfully aware of and anxious about the possibility of that slippage.[33]

Krupat faces a similar problem. Insisting, like Lane, that he is not speaking for the other—in this case, the Indian—and rejecting what he characterizes as the "postmodern" logic that says, "we must either imperialistically 'tell our own story' *as* the other's, or imperialistically speak *for* the other" (9), Krupat concedes that the danger of silencing the native speaker is one the ethnocritic must risk if he or she is not to remain silent (30–31). The passage is worth quoting at length.

> In every case, the danger the would-be practitioner of ethnocriticism must try to avoid is . . . to speak *for* the "Indian" . . . This is a danger both for those (like myself) who can claim no experiential authority (i.e., they/we have no personal experience of being Indian), and also in some measure as well for those who have that experience. That is, it is always possible, as T. S. Eliot's Gerontion discovered, to have had the experience but missed the meaning— or to have provided a meaning that the experience cannot bear. Unwilling to speak *for* the Indian, and unable to speak *as* an Indian (although, as I have just said, simply to be an Indian speaking of Indians guarantees nothing), the danger *I* run as an ethnocritic is the danger of leaving the Indian silent entirely in my discourse. I don't know of any way securely to avoid this danger, for all that I hope it may somewhat be mitigated by a certain self-conscious awareness. (30)

Not only does such self-authorization muddle the notion of "experiential authority" that plays so keen a role in the political arguments Krupat makes on behalf of ethnocriticism, but it also positions the self-consciously Western observer (Robinson's "exceptional white person") as the figure most capable of residing on both sides of the cultural divide and, moreover, understanding the meaning of such residence.[34] As self-conscious as Krupat would like to be of the slippages his activity entails, his defense of himself in terms of "positionality" forecloses on the epistemological dangers and the ethical and political risks he describes as worthwhile.

The truth of Lane's statement that our representations of others determine the outcome of our ethical judgments (238) is nowhere more apparent. Krupat's and Lane's representation of their practices in terms of positionality and the inside/outside dichotomy and the need, as a result, to guard against speaking as and speaking for give rise to the nervous defensiveness in the passages cited above. Each goes to great lengths in his prefatory material to explain a difference that is always in danger of collapsing; and that always present possibility of slippage leads to what I call the "caveat syndrome," an effort to protect ourselves from being accused of doing precisely what we *are* doing and with which we should be willing to go all the way. Indeed, the caveat, an explanation meant to prevent misinterpretation, or (more pressingly) misidentification, conspicuously characterizes most academic instances of "passing." The inevitable—indeed, compulsory—self-justification made in response to hostile readers (whether real or imagined), the caveat structurally mimes that which the text overtly rejects. What we dismantle in theory—a clearly positioned, fixed, and ultimately stereotyped subject whose desires and beliefs we can read reductively from his or her place of origin or external features—we resurrect in practice by constructing, through the caveat, an imaginary reader that is itself an expression of our anxiety over the presumed impropriety of the theory. While I congratulate these critics for the risks they take in "boundary crossing," I regret the caveat they feel compelled to offer in an effort to save themselves from the implications of their own ethical practices. *It is precisely the ethical, pedagogical, and conceptual costs of efforts to justify or save ourselves in this way that my book brings out and seeks to make us accountable for through its reconceptualization of "passing."*

Krupat writes: "For all the difficulties of the ethnocritical position, I continue to think that boundary-crossing with care, self-positioning, as I have said, at the various frontiers of historical and cultural encounter, in the interest of questioning the culture that constitutes one's 'self,' remains foremost among nontrivial options for cultural critics today" (37). I agree. It is not the practice but the desire to protect ourselves from its unsettling implications that I am questioning. Gould's understanding of what Austin calls the Descriptive Fallacy—"the assumption of philosophers that the business

of a 'statement' can only be to 'describe' some state of affairs" (Austin 1)—
can help to explain what I mean by the caveat syndrome. "If Austin is right
about the nature and importance of this fallacy," Gould writes, "it makes a
certain kind of sense that the assumption that he is resisting should itself have
certain powers of resistance and obfuscation at its disposal" (22). If the Descriptive Fallacy is as widely held as Austin says, if it is "natural" to think of
language in this way, then "the fallacy in question does not vanish merely
upon the adoption of a terminology of speech-acts—not even when the terminology was specifically designed to repudiate that fallacy" (22–23). The
same could be said of efforts to repudiate what we might call the Identification Fallacy (the notion that one can speak for another or that the Indian
necessarily speaks as an Indian). Beliefs about the subject and about our responsibility to others that undergird enthocriticism and that also give rise
to the caveat syndrome do not vanish when we adopt a new vocabulary,
whether "positionality," "performativity," or "passing."

One advantage I see in using the term "passing" is that the distinction
between passing as a conscious practice and passing as an inevitable condition of subjectivity in postmodernity is never sure; for to fix that distinction
would be to insist on a kind of control and certainty that my reconceptualization of "passing" is meant to call into question. There is a constant slippage between conscious and unconscious passing and between passing as a
deliberate practice and passing as the experience of subjectivity. Gould goes
on to point out that Austin's objective was not to substitute the felicitious/
infelicitious dichotomy of performatives for the true/false fetish of the Descriptive Fallacy. (That is, if language is descriptive, we should be able to say
whether it is true or false; if passing is a performance, we should be able to
say whether it works or doesn't.) "His stragegy was rather to drag the fetish
of true and false into the same swamp of assessment and judgment . . . that
afflicts our performative utterances" (23). We don't simply give up true/false
distinctions as passé; rather, we now must confront what it means to give up
that fetish. And what it often means is falling back on the fetish and the Descriptive Fallacy to protect ourselves from the implications of giving them up.

"Passing" may seem to be an unfair description of what Lane and Krupat
are doing given that each goes to such lengths to assure us he is not identifying *as* a native speaker. In fact, passing in Lane's book is reserved for the practice of deaf people who present themselves as "oral," an exhausting performance structured by the oppositional logic of oppression (hearing/lack of
hearing, abled/disabled). Yet to the extent that in the dynamics of our engagement with others, "identifying with" and "identifying as" always risk sliding

into one another (an unconscious process we cannot fully control),[35] and to the extent that the threat of exposure Lane and Krupat defensively guard themselves against always faces the passer, passing can provide an alternative conceptualization of the slips and risks their writing entails, an alternative to the notion of positionality that inhibits their writing and to the rhetoric of "speaking as" and "speaking for," which entails thinking in terms of subject positions and the binary logic of the "other." To clarify the difference between these two ways of conceptualizing the problem, I want to discuss another 1992 publication that confronts the same issues and impasses as Lane's and Krupat's: Linda Alcoff's essay "The Problem of Speaking for Others."

The concept of positionality, as Krupat notes, comes from Alcoff, who, in an earlier essay, defines it, in Krupat's words, as "a strategy of self-conscious self-displacement within the epistemological and discursive frames any critic cannot help but inhabit" (23). By defining the subject in terms of social locations, its external contexts, and historical experiences, rather than in terms of its essential attributes, Alcoff's positionality, like Krupat's ethnocriticism, mediates between two opposing views: a humanist view of the subject as an autonomous, rational agent and a poststructuralist view of the subject as a linguistic performance; or between humanism's universal subject and poststructuralism's depersonalized subject.[36] The problem of speaking for others, writes Alcoff, arises from the recognition that the social location of the speaker "bears on" the meaning and truth of what the speaker says and that some privileged locations are "discursively dangerous" no matter what the speaker says and no matter what her or his intentions ("Problem" 6–7). A materialist focus on specific locations calls into question the legitimacy of speaking "for," but also the "mediated character of all representations" (9) calls into question the authenticity of speaking "as." As Alcoff puts it, even when one speaks for oneself, one represents (rather than inhabits) a position, creates "a public discursive self" that has an effect on "the self experienced as interiority" (10). Not even the Indian can speak as/for an Indian.

This problem of "speaking for" can lead to two equally objectionable responses, says Alcoff, the very responses Lane and Krupat defend themselves against: an unself-conscious appropriation of another's position (what Lane calls "paternalism" and Krupat "imperialism"), which comes from the speaker's desire for mastery, and a guilty retreat from the practice of "speaking for" (Lane's "collective indifference" and Krupat's "silence"), which comes from the speaker's desire to be immune to criticism. Although sometimes warranted by the politics of the situation (and Alcoff's essay opens with some examples), the retreat from speaking for (as when Joyce Trebilcot, a self-identified lesbian, refuses to speak for lesbians [Alcoff, "Problem" 19–20]) entails the faulty assumption "that one *can* retreat into one's discrete location" (20). In an effort to mediate between these two responses, Alcoff offers criteria for determining the validity of efforts to speak for others, which she presents in the form of imperatives. The first imperative is to resist the impulse to speak for another; and if one does speak, the second imperative is to interrogate the effect of one's location on what one says, as well as the effect of what one says on one's location and on the material and discursive contexts of the speech situation (24–26).

Alcoff's insistence on self-critique, central to her notion of positionality, depends on an understanding of the discursive character of subjectivity, the "mediated character of all representations" (9). Yet the forgetting of this insight leads Alcoff to slip, as evident in two sentences that appear on the same page of her essay:

> When I speak for myself, I am constructing a possible self, a way to be in the world, and am offering that to others, whether I intend to or not, as one possible way to be.

> When I "speak for myself" I am participating in the creation and reproduction of discourses through which my own and other selves are constituted. (21)

Alcoff seems to be saying much the same thing in these two sentences, yet the quotation marks around "speak for myself" in the second make the (dia)critical difference. In the first sentence, "I" takes for granted that it *can* speak for itself, assumes it can occupy a subject position, that there even *are* subject positions one can occupy, however self-consciously. In the second sentence, "I" is performative, constituted in and through the practice of speaking, the act of invoking an "I." The second sentence reveals the "I" of the first, and the subject of Alcoff's imperatives, to be a seduction of grammar (Butler, *Bodies* 6). The one who writes the first sentence forgets the "I" of the second, as if one could be immune to the effects of performance.

The impasse that emerges in the conflict between Alcoff's two sentences gives rise to the structural dynamics that I term "passing." It is the slippage between these two positions on the subject—the volitional and the performative—that makes passing inevitable whenever any "I" claims to speak for itself. Even if, as activists and theorists, writers and teachers, we acknowledge our social locations as multiple and unstable, shaped by specific histories and subject to various representational technologies, whenever we talk of subject positions and self-critique, we talk as if we were immune to performance and thereby resuscitate in practice (in grammar) the very subject we dismantle in theory.[37]

If postmodern theorists resist the practice of "speaking for," it may not reflect an abnegation of social responsibility and accountability, as Alcoff thinks, or a commitment to a radical relativism, as Krupat fears, but a rejection of a certain philosophical discourse that conceives representation (speaking for) in terms of "receptive listening," as Alcoff and Lane do, or "recognition" of the other, as Krupat does, and that assumes the other *has* a specific location. Such language suggests that representation is a matter of bridging the gap between social locations. It assumes that the speaker can give an honest account of him- or herself, if not also of the other.

But how, for example, can a white feminist like Alcoff ever be sure that her defense of a black feminist like Barbara Christian is not motivated by the kind of apologetics her male friend noted when he suggested to Alcoff that her defense of "The Race for Theory" revealed her desire "to valorize African American writing against all odds" (16)? I agree with Alcoff when she rejects "reductionist theories" that evaluate what a speaker says in terms of the speaker's location, reducing evaluation to a matter of the race, gender, sexuality, or ethnicity of the speaker. However, when is labeling her friend's charge "reductionism" accurate and when is it a resistance to interrogating the racial desires motivating any feminist practice? Missing in Alcoff's essay is any account of the kind of discursive practice that would promote the kind of accountability she calls for. It is such an account that I seek to provide in this and the chapters to follow.

However perverse "passing" (and I do not use that term pejoratively) may seem when applied to the projects of Alcoff, Krupat, and Lane, it would seem to be more than apt when applied to Nancy K. Miller's *Getting Personal,* for she articulates this "crisis of representativity," with its rhetorics of "speaking as" and "speaking for" (ix–x), in terms of a "poetics of passing" (50). The personal criticism Miller advocates and practices here is a response to "the anxiety over speaking *as* and speaking *for*" (20) that emerges with the passing of grand narratives and the deconstruction of the grounds of any authority. Personal criticism is not so much an alternative to, or retreat from, the kind of ethnocriticism Krupat and Lane offer in response to the same crisis as it is an expansion of its terms to include the personal as cultural material (21). But rather than offering, as Jane Tompkins says of the New Historicism, "occasional side glances at how the author's 'situatedness' affects his writing" (qtd. in Miller, *Getting Personal* 13), which Lane and Krupat could be said to do, in personal criticism the author's situatedness *is* the writing. That is, the "personal" in "personal criticism" is not the personal as such, Miller explains, but a performance, a rhetorical self-figuring that, "however self-fictional," is an effort to write in relation to lived experience and to resist the temptation to "the grandiosity of abstraction that inhabits . . . the crisis of representativity" (xiii). The "I" who practices personal criticism moves toward self-disclosure (1), making a spectacle of its authorial voice to theorize the stakes of its own performance (24). In such autobiographical acts, says Miller, the body functions as a brake on rhetoric and allows for the emergence of something unpredictable, something for Miller "not foreclosed by [her] own (rhetorically predictable) feminist discourse" (xii)—that is, the expectations that always accompany "speaking as" a feminist.

The stakes of performance become clear in her chapter 4 on the "poetics of passing." "Passing"—in Miller's case, as a professor of French—means mastering not just the grammar of another language but its characteristic gestures and intonation so that one can perform as a "near native speaker" (50). Passing is the acquisition of linguistic and rhetorical skills, not the assumption of another's identity. The threat to the passer, then, is not being detected but being corrected, being exposed as a fraud not because of who she really is but because of what she is professing to be—a skilled speaker, the consummate impersonator. The ultimate test of passing, as Alasdair MacIntyre points out in his elaboration of a narrative ethics, is being able to pull off a comic improvisation, to toss off a joke, as it were, in passing.[38] Miller narrates an amusing incident, the "French mistake" of the chapter title, in which she failed to pull off the joke, exposing the infelicity of her performed identity. Accompanying a visitor from France to an elegant restroom on campus, Miller announced "la plus belle toilette," inadvertently commenting on the woman's "frumpy" outfit rather than on the beautifully appointed lounge. Yet just as MacIntyre believes that a native speaker can perform without such slips, can speak in the first person without performing, so Miller believes that by getting out of the French department and relocating in her "native" English department, she can avoid being exposed as passing; as if by returning to her "true origin" (50) she could move into an identity as a professor and scholar that would not open her to the possibility of being betrayed by slips, improvisations, or passing comments.

Miller writes of passing as a near-native speaker as if it were a transgression to be confessed, as if this confessing "I" were not already passing in the very act of confessing, as if passing were not at issue when a "native" speaker is in the subject position, professing feminism or teaching literature in her "native" language. Insofar as she perceives her own gender, racial, and national credentials to function "a little like a passport" (4), identifying where she comes from (and, I might add, where she can return when things get messy), Miller assumes there is a position from which one can speak with an authority rooted in one's own history and marked body, as if that history and that body were not already shot through with representational technologies. As Anne Callahan noted in a provocative 1992 MMLA paper, "Critical Personae: The Face Value of the Paglia Phenomenon": "The question Miller's use of the term 'passing' raises is whether it is ever possible to come any closer than 'near' when speaking in the voice of *any* of the diverse critical positions from which we teach and write." Facing up to this possibility leads Miller to despair: "What chance does any 'I' have of undercutting its customary self-representations in the face of the expectations accompanying an 'as a': the burden of 'speaking for'?" (xiv). Miller assumes her autobiographical acts will save her from accusations of "speaking as" and "speaking for," from the rhetorical predictability of her own fraudulence. The problem, once again, is that the very notions of "position" and "true origin" foreclose on the ethical possibilities opened up by the practice.[39] Miller wants to get back to the safety of being herself, a "native" speaker.

Given this emphasis on positionality, what haunts Miller in *Getting Personal* is "the specter of recuperation" (3)—not just the possibility of her own recuperation to a "rhetorically predictable" feminist discourse, but also the recuperation of the practice she advocates. The worry she has about the personal criticism she promotes is, What if everyone were to do it? What if everyone were to practice personal criticism and it became (as many say it has become) just another "academic fashion"? Would personal criticism then become simply a writing style, the "personal" another form of impersonation? Would the strategic intervention that personal criticism is meant to bring about become merely a performance? If all criticism were personal, a resistance to collectivities and the predictability of "speaking as," what would happen to social activism and ethics?

But given the ethics of Miller's practice, shouldn't what she fears might come about be the very goal of her project, namely, to get everyone doing autobiographical acts so that no one presumes to speak from an unmarked position or to perform "a masquerade of self-effacement" (24)? So that everyone must "theorize the stakes of [his or her] own performance" (24) in the process of writing? But if everyone were to do it, if there were no more passers, only marked bodies speaking from specific positions, then where would the inducement to writing lie? How could we ever experience not just the superiority and the authority but the exhilaration that comes from exposing another?[40] And why (to turn a common criticism of deconstruction back on itself), just when others are beginning to expose the pretensions of critics who have long spoken unself-consciously as representatives of certain positions, do we decide that any such pretensions are wrong, or embarrassing, and rush to find a mode of critical inquiry such as the personal that can save us from such exposure, and then try to keep that critical position to ourselves out of fear of its dissemination? Miller's return to her native English department already gives up on the possibility that passing might itself have ethical and political implications. The worry Miller has that the personal (what is an act to begin with) might *become* impersonation, and the political become merely a performance, is yet another expression of the fear that "crisis" (of representativity) means "collapse" (of representation, in the political sense of that term).

In all these efforts to speak and write across "politically charged boundaries" of identity and identification, efforts that I term "passing," we return again and again to discomforting questions of who has the right to speak, who can represent or identify with another, and to our necessary implication in the very practices we critique. Again and again we offer in response solutions, disclaimers, imperatives, and caveats in a hopeless effort to save ourselves from criticism, or at least to get the jump on it so that our accusers can't accuse us of anything we don't already know.[41] The very fact that oppositions are breaking down, due in part to the cultural realities these writers negotiate and the critical practices they engage in, leads those committed to such a task to shore up oppositions all the more for fear that without them, anything goes. In other words, we not only rely on the very oppositions our theories call into question (e.g., between the genuine and the fraudulent, the experiential and the discursive), but we also put limits on the very self-displacements our forages across identity lines are supposed to foster.

The problem as I see it is that we want to control our identifications and the effects of performativity, neither of which, by definition, we can control. Sedgwick, whose writing has provided a powerful impetus for the kinds of practices I call "passing," sees clearly that the performance cannot be controlled. Raising the question in *Epistemology of the Closet* of her right, as a woman and a feminist, to write about male homosexuality and on behalf of gay men, Sedgwick argues that the problem the question would address lies in the very phrasing of the question. Asking who has the right to speak assumes one know in advance what identities, identifications, and political commitments are and should be. Such questions "obscure the way political commitments and identifications actually work" (59). Yet she insists that her resistance to addressing this question and to justifying herself in its terms should not be taken to mean that she is endorsing anyone's right to make such identifications "across politically charged boundaries" (the relativism of "anything goes"); rather, it is to call for a narrative explanation that can "unknot" the overdeterminations that structure any defense of one's right to speak (59–60). When Sedgwick "identifies" as a gay man, she passes in the ethical sense that I give that term: she doesn't pass *as* a gay man, she doesn't write from the *position* of a gay man, and therefore she doesn't need to defend or confess a transgression. She writes through an identification whose meaning and value lie in the writing itself. The value of one's practice lies in the contributions it makes, Sedgwick says, not in the claims one makes for it. Although we cannot control the reception of our writing any more than we can control the trajectory of our identifications, our writing does carry an implicit ethics in its performance. In this book, I want to locate ethics in the very practices we engage in as writers, readers, and teachers—more explicitly, in a performative practice that negotiates these anxious questions of identity and identification without rushing to formulate a means to explain and control them.

If authenticity now means owning up to the fact that no one occupies a privileged place of insight, as John Caputo puts it (258), then the question is no longer "Who can speak?"[42] Nor does it mean abandoning such moral and political concerns. Rather, it requires a different way of responding to such concerns, one that gets us out of the initially defining situation that would say, without some kind of categorical imperative, without some kind of standards for adjudicating between forms of passing, anything goes. This is not to say that there are no differences among the many practices I call "passing," but rather that there are many and various kinds of differences (cf. B. H. Smith 90).

The fear that "category crisis" will become "category collapse," that giving up clear-cut distinctions will mean we can make no distinctions, that disseminating the figure of passing will mean anyone can pass—this fear is generated by the very binary thinking, the all-or-nothing logic, that informs the originary meaning of "passing" (you're either white or black). The fear constantly held in check by the insistence that not just anything goes (not just anyone can pass, not just anyone can do personal criticism or cross identificatory boundaries) is the fear of the collapse of standards, the leveling of differences, the loss of identity and representativity. Yet the very kind of cultural critique the writers I have been discussing have participated in has already reconfigured those "originary" terms of reference. The fear that all distinctions will be lost is only a real worry within the very structure of debate that these critics, *courageously and responsibly,* have already moved out of. The real contribution to a politics of difference is to push to the limit the ethical practices these critics engage in. That means getting rid of the "as" in "passing as." The ethics of passing lies in the dissemination of the rhetorical figure, eliminating the need for the "as" that keeps us safe by functioning as a caveat.

The loss of distinctions on which our authority as critics and teachers has traditionally rested leads to the fear of losing a safe place to go home to, whether that place is the no-place of the Enlightenment subject or the private residence of one's own body.[43] Without such a space, the *economy* of the culture of identity, in which we have invested so heavily of late, would collapse and there would be no *interest,* neither economic gain nor intellectual stimulation nor professional advantage, in the political and intellectual projects we engage in.[44] The collapse of this economy, stimulated by the cultural realities and the deconstructive theories we are negotiating under the rubric of "postmodernism," is now coming about, not through the loss of a safe place, but, perversely, through the very need to shore it up. Instead of attempting to shore up this economy, we need to act from the loss of the safety of our own identity. "It is precisely here, with the breakdown of resting points, from the dissemination of principles that we begin to act" (Caputo 238).

I offer "passing" not as a solution to the double bind I elaborate above but as a descriptive theory of its *dynamics.* "Passing" is neither something one does (as in performing a role) nor something one is (a subject position one must account for) but a way of naming and conceptualizing the interpersonal, psychopolitical dynamics that structure, for many of us, the experience of reading, teaching, and writing about literature today. To the extent that questions of the political, ethical, and theoretical positioning of a person who "crosses over" lines of cultural, racial, and sexual identity are endemic to the dynamics of passing, its practitioners cannot pronounce on these issues, cannot justify or save themselves by taking a position; for, to repeat, there is no taking a position without passing. Passing is not always and only a volitional act that an already positioned subject chooses to engage in, nor is passing always and everywhere a risk. Passing happens, and it happens despite, more often because of, our sincere efforts to get it right.

More Shocking Performances

> I feel real.
> —Sandra Bernhard, *Without You I'm Nothing*

It would be a mistake to think that it is the imaginary which
is mortal and the real which is the living.
  —Jacques Lacan, Seminar of 21 January 1975

I want to end this chapter where I began, with an example of passing from popular culture. Sandra Bernhard may not don blackface in *Without You I'm Nothing,* but her campy performances produce an effect closely related to that intended by Michelle Shocked's imagined cover design. In the film as in the off-Broadway show on which it is based, Bernhard impersonates female singers, from the 1960s and 1970s in particular, with performances that invoke Diana Ross, Barbra Streisand, and Patti Smith. In the first number, Bernhard, dressed in African batik, sings Nina Simone's "Four Women." "My skin is black," she croons. Although Bernhard's controversial racial crossings have been praised as a genuine tribute to a tradition of female performers, as Jean Walton writes in a wonderful essay on this film, "it is difficult, . . . given the racial history of the U.S., for a white comedian to 'pay tribute' to a black performer by impersonating her without also being, in effect, in blackface" (249). Blackface minstrelsy *is* the racial history of popular entertainment and music in the United States. "From 'Oh! Susanna' to Elvis Presley," writes Lott, "from circus clowns to Saturday morning cartoons, blackface acts and words have figured significantly in the white Imaginary of the United States" (4–5). Bernhard's impersonations, like Shocked's blackface, call attention to the racial history of the music she performs. Her personae are composite characters processed by the mass media nostalgia mill through which authenticity is produced for popular consumption. The white Imaginary, not black people, would seem to be the target of Bernhard's mimicry.

Even from this brief description it is not hard to see why this film is controversial. What disturbs critics is not only Bernhard's impersonation of black performers for the entertainment of whites but her self-conscious critique of her own performances by setting the film version of her act in a black nightclub in Los Angeles. Lines that strike the mainly white movie and theater audiences as funny evoke a different reaction from the mostly black nightclub audience for whom Sandra performs in the film.[45] (I follow Walton in distinguishing between Sandra, Bernhard's persona in the film, and Bernhard, the filmmaker.) That audience is baffled, bored, and put off by the impersonations. The reefer-smoking emcee politely, methodically asks the audience to give *Sarah* Bernhard their support. In the final scene, Bernhard stands on stage, literally exposed in her pasties and G-string, looking pleadingly at the only remaining member of the audience, who writes "Fuck Sandra Bernhard" in lipstick on the tablecloth.

Sandra Bernhard as Nina Simone, in *Without You I'm Nothing,* directed by John Boscovich and Sandra Bernhard, Electric/M.C.E.G. Productions, 1990.

Such blatant self-critique by Bernhard has been interpreted by critics as an effort to save herself from criticism. "It could be suggested," Walton writes, that Bernhard's representation of race "forecloses on a serious exploration" of the cultural construction of whiteness implicit in its blackface performances by "too easily ironizing it" through her inclusion of the black audience (254). But at least the irony and self-critique saves her, in Walton's view, from the kind of criticism Madonna invites by her unself-conscious voguing that becomes "a universal affirmation" in "apparent obliviousness to the mechanism of appropriation" that structures any such crossover identification (255). Bernhard's performance flaunts the mechanism of appropriation. The fantasies of cross-racial identification operate guiltily, Walton argues, and thus the black audience, created and directed by Bernhard, plays the role of superego, punishing Sandra for her desires (255).

Walton would seem to affirm Bernhard's film for the very thing to which Marlon Riggs, director of *Ethnic Notions: Black People in White Minds* and *Tongues Untied,* attributes its failure: the fact that the film acknowledges its appropriation. Riggs would like to argue that black people are bored by Bernhard's "overt tribute to black people" because they know they are getting "an adulterated version of their culture—a version processed and diluted by a white artist, who was achieving success and notoriety on the basis of so-called originality, bravery, courage, and insight," but Bernhard has already beat him to such criticism by structuring self-critique into the very performance of the cross-over identity (Riggs 10, qtd. in Walton 250). Whereas Walton locates the effort to "speak for" black people in Sandra's impersonations (249), Riggs locates the effort to articulate black subjectivity in Bernhard's representation of a black audience. By including an imaginary hostile audience in the film, Bernhard may punish Sandra, but she does so by creating a fixed, stereotypical black response, Riggs says, one that is free of any ambivalence (11, qtd. in Walton 258). As I have argued, this is one problem with the caveat syndrome: it belies the theory of subjectivity informing the practice by imagining a hostile reader that is fixed and stereotyped in its anticipated response. In other words, the subject is performative, the "other" is not. In Riggs's reading, Bernhard's self-conscious critique cannot save her any more than the critic's caveat can, for the appropriation is redoubled in the effort. In the end, Riggs insists, the film fails and must fail because for all her self-conscious impersonations Bernhard cannot "articulate the experience of black people" even in the interest of "cultural healing," the title of Riggs's review (11, qtd. in Walton 258). What Riggs seems to have missed is that his own effort to speak for blacks by telling us how bored they are with such tributes would also not allow much room for ambivalence.

Bernhard's representation of a black audience *is* disturbing but not necessarily because she presents a reductive view of black people's responses, a caricatured portrait, but because she exposes efforts to do precisely that. Even Marlon Riggs thinks he can tell us how black people respond to the film. What he doesn't like is that Bernhard beat him to it and that *her* representation is unsuccessful; what he doesn't consider is whether his response would have been reductive as well, another caricature. What disturbs Riggs, I suggest, is the discomfort of the self-recognition, not in the audience, but in the artist's effort to represent that audience.

My interest in this film and in these readings of it is less with determining whether Bernhard's performance is appropriately self-aware or shamelessly appropriative than with establishing the linkages between academic crossover performances and Bernhard's own. Riggs's comment on the white artist who gains notoriety for courageously crossing boundaries of identification could pertain to cultural critics for whom, as bell hooks says, race or ethnicity is a new frontier. This is one reason, I think, that many academics, and not just white critics, anxiously distance their own crossover performances from those in the popular domain by criticizing the crass appropriation and commodification of differences in mass media productions. I am interested instead in what academics might learn from the performance artist about their own forms of passing.

One problem with criticisms of Bernhard for her portrayal of black subjectivity, as Walton points out, is that they often ignore her performances as a gay man, as a white woman, as a lesbian, and as a Jew—the latter three identities one might call her own. The nightclub audience is no more responsive when Sandra performs as Buffy, the jock-like daughter of the culturally dominant if illusionary WASP family, than they are when she performs Nina Simone. When Sandra invites the mostly black audience to join her in singing Israeli folksongs, she is answered with a chilling silence. The identifications are overdetermined. To say the film fails in its critique of racial identity is to assume that that critique can be separated from the exploration of the construction of "WASPness," "femaleness" and "heterosexuality" (Walton 251). It is hard to assess Bernhard's film solely in terms of her efforts to "speak for" blacks or in terms of her "coming out" as lesbian, as viewers tend to do, because the film reveals whiteness and straightness as themselves forms of passing. "I feel real," yells Sandra in the voice of a straight white male having his first gay experience. In its "relentlessly deconstructive approach" to identities and identifications, Walton writes, the film suggests the "ambiguity of *any* starting point" (245, 253; my emphasis). Noting the multiple crossings that inform Bernhard's drag performance as a black lesbian lounge singer, Walton queries: "Although I just suggested that Bernhard could not 'come out' as black [in the same way she could be said to "come out" as lesbian in this film], the 'obviousness' of that suggestion is perhaps called into question by the multiple and simultaneous 'crossings' of her performance: might it be possible, in other words, to consider racial identity [like feminine or lesbian identity] as much a matter of drag as of skin color?" (251–52) "Yes," I am tempted to respond, "it's passing all the way down."[46]

What makes this film so controversial, I suggest, is not that Bernhard impersonates blacks before a black audience for the entertainment of whites, nor even that she attempts to profit from while also spoofing just that kind of entertainment, but that she pushes passing to the limit. By this I mean that she does not fall back on the notion of a subject position to save herself from being misunderstood or misidentified. Bernhard mocks such efforts in the closing scene when she appears on stage, wrapped in the American flag, and apologizes to her audience for being a fraud. The desire to expose the other or one's self as a fraud keeps the subject intact, whereas the point of passing is to shift attention from the identity of the subject and the integrity of her actions to the dynamics of the social relations in which we act and to which we are accountable. Passing can be a transformative, and responsible, practice only if we do not hold on to a notion of the subject's integrity.

Bernhard's performance not only brings to mind our own forms of passing insofar as she acts within and acts out the psychic and social dynamics, and the racial history, that structure any such crossover identification, but it also makes no effort to disavow the practice. She performs without any safeguards, and thus without fostering the belief that the desires and motivations informing such border crossings can be controlled.[47] By resisting the caveat as a disavowed identification, Bernhard refuses to let herself off the hook of her own desires. Those desires may operate guiltily in this film, but the guilt is endemic to the practice, systemic not personal, and thus not something she can save herself from. Rather than exposing herself as a fraud, Bernhard exposes herself *to* the unruliness of the desires and identifications that motivate the performances, and to the unruliness of the discursive practices through which we attempt to control them. The film resists the critical tendency to draw boundaries around good and bad instances of passing, as if one could distinguish between those crossover performances that are appropriately self-aware and those that are shamelessly appropriative. That would be to promote the belief that by identifying all the shameful instances of passing we could safely engage in crossover practices without incurring guilt or blame; that we could find a mode of practice that would not implicate us in the very structures that have made it necessary for us to act to begin with.

To say that Bernhard's performance does not offer moral guidelines in this way as, say, Alcoff's essay does, is not to say that it is devoid of ethical implications. On the contrary, Bernhard's performances remind us that in the same instance one can be sincerely expressing one's conscious intention (whether that intention is to pay genuine tribute to another social group or to critique one's own position in doing so) and unconsciously revealing disavowed desires and motivations. That is, they remind us of the intentionality of cultural practices and institutionalized rhetorics themselves. We resist this insight insofar as we read her campy performances "straight." The resistance to a model of language as something other than the expression of a conscious intention, that is, resistance to the intentionality of discourse itself, is the same as the resistance to recognizing passing as inevitable, a matter of cultural practices, not personal choice.[48] The real contribution Bernhard makes to a theory of passing is to push passing to the limit.

Yet there is a limit, and that limit is figured in Roxanne. Roxanne (as her name appears in the credits) is a black woman who appears in brief vignettes throughout the film that are interspersed with the action of the nightclub performances.[49] These vignettes are presented as mimetic, that is, as imitating acts occurring in real time outside the film's frame. Yet they also subtly and increasingly intrude on the film's narrative space. In one vignette, Roxanne stands before a mirror, clipping the ends of her hair as Bernhard does in the opening sequence of the film. In another, she is shown reading a book in a laboratory, turning a page at the same moment Sandra on stage says "history turned a page." During one monologue, Sandra, complaining about her boyfriend, Joe, imagines a scene of the two of them having sex, yet the long hair and slim black body of the lover could be (and, I believe, is supposed to be) initially mistaken by the viewer for Roxanne. In the final scene, Roxanne sits at a table in the nightclub where Sandra performs. Her presence there reminds us how unreal that supposedly real black audience is. We think the nightclub audience represents a real black perspective in this film, at least as Bernhard sees it. Then it becomes clear that they're not real but set up by Bernhard to pass as real. But then this person Roxanne, who gets by as real because she is outside the film's frame, comes into the audience and we realize that we've fallen for it again. It's passing all the way down.

Roxanne is neither an autonomously existing black woman outside the film's frame nor the black audience constituted as the film's frame nor the black personae who are the subject of Sandra's impersonations. She resists all efforts to conceptualize her, to speak as or for her. A ghostly presence, like Beloved in Toni Morrison's novel of that name, neither a real body nor a disembodied spirit, Roxanne is the materialization of the psychic and social history Diana Fuss defines as "identification."[50] In this sense, Bernhard's inclusion of Roxanne recalls Jane Gallop's confession that black women now occupy the place in her imagination previously held by French men; whereas she used to write to please these men, she now writes to please black women.[51] Bernhard mocks her ostensibly male critics in the closing scene—"the critics are right," she says, "I am just a petty bilious girl"—but she does not mock Roxanne, her toughest critic, the one who writes "Fuck Sandra Bernhard" on the tablecloth.

Roxanne puts the breaks on the seemingly endless impersonations in the film, not because she is the "real thing," but because she functions as the limit.[52] That limit is the real, which in Lacan's formulation is inextricably bound up with the imaginary (the realm of identifications) and the symbolic (the order of language and cultural discourses). Jacqueline Rose defines the real as "the moment of impossibility" onto which the imaginary and the symbolic are grafted, "the point of that moment's endless return" (in Lacan, *Feminine Sexuality* 31). There *is* a limit to passing, though that limit is not to be found in the subject as already "there," an origin or reference point; rather, the limit is what resists efforts to conceive passing as either the masking and unmasking of the real thing or as the idealism that would say there is nothing but language, performance, or discourse—that is, what resists efforts to give either language or the body or the imaginary *priority* in our readings (Rose, in Lacan, *Feminine Sexuality* 171n6; Gallop, *Reading Lacan* 162). Roxanne's function as the limit, which is not an end, is most evident in the enigmatic closing sequence. When Roxanne passes out of the film's frame into a flood of golden light that closes the film, the scene suggests a near-death experience that marks the limit of any reality.

The point of passing is not simply to say there is no origin, no presence, no ground, no body but rather to continually pose the question of the limit. Thus, the question of responsibility is linked to one's practice rather than one's position, to the *practice* of writing in the poststructuralist sense of that term: not writing as communication or expression but as dissemination. Dissemination opens a gap between the writing and the meaning, between the performance and the reception, between the critical practice and its intended effects. In the endless return of that gap lies the ethical significance of passing. Writing on Austin's "performative," Gould says a gap opens up between the successful performance of the performative utterance and the achievement of the desired effects (33). Attention to that gap, to the force of the performative, works against notions of the performative as simply a verbal act that brings into being what it names (Gould 24–25; Butler, *Bodies* 2). One way to experience that gap, what I have been calling the slippage between positions or the crisis that is not a collapse, is by risking "exposure to language," by being willing to take responsibility for the writing, that is, for the gap between "the possibility of utterance" and "the possibility of the tyranny of sense" (Gould 38, 41). What this means is that in passing we cannot expose ourselves or others to get to a sense, or presence, that would eliminate the need for passing.[53] This is what I mean by "it's passing all the way down." We can learn this lesson only by yielding to the performative, giving up the desire for a guarantee of meaning and "positional correctness." The desire for a guarantee produces the caveat as a categorical imperative.

What disturbs critics, I suggest, is not just that Bernhard's performance brings to mind our own forms of passing but that it makes no effort to disavow them. Bernhard neither apologizes for nor defends her identifications across racial boundaries; instead, she acts within and acts out the psychic and social dynamics and the racial history that structures any such crossover identifications. The laughter the film evokes only reinforces this structural similarity, for Bernhard becomes the scapegoat for our own unruly desires, the traditional role of the stand-up comic. What we might learn from the performance artist is how to teach and write within these dynamics, how to prolong the moment when a gap opens between the performance and the meaning, how to resist too quickly closing the gap by looking for "a guarantee of sense and relevance" (Gould) and how to move our students from the relatively safe space of pronouncements about the risks and benefits of crossover performances to the riskier moment of actually engaging in them. Barbara Johnson calls that moment "the surprise of otherness," the moment when our ignorance "is suddenly activated as an imperative" (*World* 16).

The lesson implicit in Bernhard's performance, as in Shocked's blackface, is that in writing about issues of identity and identification we cannot help but pass in the ethical sense that I give that term. I understand Toni Morrison to be making a similar point in *Playing in the Dark*. Bernhard's film brings to mind Morrison's book not just because Bernhard discloses the Africanist presence at the heart of American popular culture, without whom the white artist is nothing, but, more important, because Bernhard's function as a performance artist is analogous to Morrison's task as a writer. In "Black Matters," the opening chapter of *Playing in the Dark,* Morrison says:

> as a writer . . . I have to place enormous trust in my ability to imagine others and my willingness to project consciously into the danger zones such others may represent for me. . . .
>
> I am interested in what prompts and makes possible this process of entering what one is estranged from—and in what disables the foray, for purposes of fiction, into corners of the consciousness held off and away from the reach of the writer's imagination. My work requires me to think about how free I can be as an African-American woman writer in my genderized, sexualized, wholly racialized world. To think about (and wrestle with) the full implications of my situation leads me to consider what happens when other writers work in a highly and historically racialized society. For them, as for me, imagining is not merely looking or looking at; nor is it taking oneself intact into the other. It is, for the purposes of the work, *becoming.* (4–5)

This is where I locate the ethics of their practices: in confronting the difficulties of one's own performance as a way of understanding the difficulties of others. Posing the question of the limit is what Rajchman sees as the ethics of Foucault's practice as well. The ethical crisis for Foucault, Rajchman says, was "a crisis in the limits of the work of which he was capable" (14)—not a moral failing to be confessed, not an error to be cleared up, not a neurosis to be cured, not a casting off of a false identity for a more authentic one, but a recalling to mind of what he had been unable to see in his writing and coming to see the difficulties others face in terms of his own difficulties as a writer (14, 27). "The question of ethics," writes Rajchman, "arises with the discovery of something that would be irreducible to the 'constitution of the subject' in the order of language, or in historical systems of thought, and so to the symbolic or discursive 'idealism' that says we are only what a culture makes us be" (143). To locate ethics in the performance or practice, not in the position posited by that practice, and in a notion of subjectivity as performativity, not in the caveat that restores the notion of the subject as already constituted and legitimized, is to attend to those moments when we refuse what we are, as Foucault puts it, to those moments, in Rajchman's words, "when our self-identifications seem contingent and violent in ways we hadn't realized" (13). In such moments, "it is no longer a matter of 'discovering' ourselves, but of 'crossing the line' to a new and improbable identity" (13). Responsibility, for Foucault as for Morrison and Bernhard, lies in the imperative to struggle with one's identity as historically constituted.[54]

If contemporary performance artists are not anxious or guilty about their crossover identifications, if they perform without caveats, it is not necessarily because they are uncritical or naïve or crassly appropriative (though, of course, they can be) but because they get "it"—that is, the performativity of subjectivity that many academics promote in theory but resist in practice. We can learn from performance artists like Bernhard how to act without the security of a safe haven but with increased awareness of the insecurity to which we are exposed (Caputo 239).[55] These performances can teach us about the performativity of critical discourse and can help us to conceive the pedagogical relation as the privileged cite of its revelation, if only we aren't too anxious to see it.

One point of the related explorations that make up this book is to move "passing" from its negative associations with disguise, impersonation, appropriation, and fraudulence and to refigure it as a potentially ethical practice. This means yielding to, rather than resisting, the ways in which we are passing in the classroom and in our writing. Facing up to our own implication in the structure of "passing" means being willing to risk a misperformance, for it is precisely the positive potentialities of a misperformance that can transform the dynamics of the pedagogical exchange into an ethics of passing.

NOTES

1. Anne Callahan sees this as an example of the troubadour effect in contemporary theory. See "The Voice of Pleasure."

2. This explicit formulation comes from Barbara Herrnstein Smith (38); however, others writing on postmetaphysical philosophy and postmodern theories make a similar charge (e.g., Caputo).

3. Three important works that treat passing as a theme in literature and popular culture and as a literary genre whose popularity has recently been revived all appeared in summer 1994: Amy Robinson's "It Takes One to Know One: Passing and Communities of Common Interest," Valerie Smith's "Reading the Intersection of Race and Gender in Narratives of Passing," and Harryette Mullen's "Optic White: Blackness and the Production of Whiteness." All refigure "passing" in ways that complement my own use of the term. That these, like my own project, were likely begun years before suggests that many of us were coming to a realization, around 1991, that passing—whether as a theme, a genre, a practice, or a metaphor—provides a useful framework, as Robinson says, for rethinking issues of identity and identity politics.

There are, of course, other related studies that treat passing in its various guises, most obviously Marjorie Garber's *Vested Interests* and less obviously Rosi Braidotti's *Nomadic Subjects*. The latter, also published in 1994, presents the nomadic subject as a "political fiction" that functions like Garber's transvestite to blur category distinctions and to cross the boundaries of identity categories. Braidotti's nomadic subject "designate[s] . . . a creative sort of becoming; a performative metaphor that allows for otherwise unlikely encounters and unsuspected sources of interaction of experience and of knowledge" (6). However, the proliferation of scholarship that creates new political myths or new figures for post-poststructuralist subjectivity is less a deterrent than a motivation for a study such as mine. My objective is not, or not only, to offer yet another metaphor for subjectivity in postmodern culture but rather to name and conceptualize the kinds of cultural practices, both academic and popular, that such subjectivity has engendered.

4. For this definition of catachresis, see B. Johnson (*World* 53) and Miller (*Ethics* 21). Alice Kaplan provides an excellent definition of this figure in her memoir, *French Lessons:* "De Man was working on the rhetorical figure known as 'catechresis' (I kept thinking about it in my mind as 'catechism'). It was the key to the whole way we students tried to think about language. A figure of speech is usually a substitute for the 'real' 'proper' meaning. Metaphor, for example, means 'jumping over' the basic meaning of a word to get to the poetic meaning. When you call dawn 'rosy fingered,' you're making the sun into a hand and its rays into fingers. Metonymy works with another kind of substitution: you identify a person or thing by some part of them, you call the man with the red hair 'Red.' Metonymy is the figure of selection and desire: you nickname your friend after the part of them that you like and notice most. But sometimes substitutions break down. Certain words don't have a meaning of their own; they borrow their meaning from another realm. Like 'leaf' for a page of a book (from the world of trees) or 'leg' for a table (from the human body). 'Table leg' and 'book leaf' are both instances of 'catechresis.' With catechresis, the substitute figure (leg, borrowed from the human anatomy; leaf, borrowed from nature) is the only word available: there is no proper meaning underneath, no foundation for the figure, no literal meaning. That was a deconstructive insight" (149–50).

5. On performativity, see Butler's introduction to *Bodies That Matter*. Performativity does not refer to constructionism, the notion that discourses determine identities, for it does not presume a prior subject to be acted upon. As Andrew Parker and Eve Kosofsky Sedgwick write in their introduction to *Performativity and Performance,* the concept of performativity opens up "more nuanced understandings of

the relations between what have been blandly, confidently, distinguished as 'text' and 'context'" (15), or "subject" and "discourse."

6. For the definition of postmodern culture offered here, I draw on a number of sources, including Harper (*Framing* 12); Poovey ("Feminism" 39); Rajchman (8); and Tyler (221). Kwame Anthony Appiah reminds us that the changes that take place in our conception of ourselves as subjects will not take place simply because we, professors and cultural critics, "pronounce on the matter in theory" but "will happen out of the changing everyday practices of . . . cultural life" (356).

7. Diana Fuss discusses identification as a political problem in *Identification Papers*. See the introduction, especially 7–10, and chapter 5.

8. See, for example, Alcoff "Problem"; Awkward; Fuss (*Essentially Speaking*); hooks ("Essentialism and Experience" in *Teaching* and *Yearning*); Jardine and Smith; Miller ("Feminist Confessions" in *Getting Personal*); Roof and Wiegman; S. Ruddick; Sedgwick (introduction to *Epistemology*, axiom 7, 59–63). My phrasing in this sentence alludes to Barbara Christian's "But What Do We Think We're Doing Anyway?"

9. On this notion of the miscegenated history of U.S. popular culture, see Lott and Mullen.

10. The phrase is Tania Modleski's (119), but many others, including Harper (*Framing*), Mullen, and Willis, make much the same point as Modleski about the disappearing of real black people in white cultural productions that appropriate black cultural forms.

11. Not simply whites' impersonation of blacks but, more complexly, whites' and blacks' impersonation of an image of blackness or black culture created in and through the performance. In her discussion of Fanon's and Bhabha's writings on mimesis and colonialism, Fuss notes that the colonized were made to "mime alterity" for the Imperial Subject, "to impersonate the image the colonizer offers them of themselves" (*Identification* 146). On Jimi Hendrix's minstrel mask, see Gilroy (chap. 3); on Michael Jackson and blackface, see Willis (188–93).

12. Compare Harper's reading of the film *The Commitments* (*Framing* esp. 194–95).

13. Lott provides several telling examples. The black minstrel troupe Gavitt's Original Ethiopian Serenaders used burnt cork to "blacken up." The important point, Lott says, is that "blackness" here is a matter of display or theater, a cultural construction. In his reading of Frederick Douglass's review of this troupe, Lott points out that this particular blackface performance inverts the racist logic of minstrelsy (for blackface conventions were used to *disguise* blackness) and locates its actual function in the staging of racial categories, boundaries, and types (36). Another example is the black Shakespearian actor Ira Aldridge. British actor Charles Mathews parodied Aldridge, incorporating minstrel songs into his act. Audiences then began to ask Aldridge for one of the songs Mathews made famous. Aldridge eventually incorporated it into his act, thereby, Lott says, making himself what he had been made (46).

14. On authenticity as drag, see Sawhney. Gilroy points out that it is not enough to say that "representing authenticity always involves artifice," however true that may be (99). He, like Lott, argues for a more refined political and critical language that can break free of the (supposedly) opposing views that dominate much cultural criticism: for Gilroy, essentialism vs. constructionism; for Lott, resistance vs. assimilation. On passing and the production of racial identities, see Mullen.

15. This insight, drawn from the work of Derrida and Foucault, is elaborated by Butler, most particularly in *Bodies That Matter*. Cf. Gilroy (99, 102n63).

16. Jennifer Ash attributed this quotation to Bakhtin in a discussion at a 1995 MMLA session.

17. Butler uses "pragmatic appropriation" in reference to Gilroy's appropriation of the narrative of modernity in *The Black Atlantic* ("Careful Reading" 128). Compare Gilroy's discussion of the appropriation of the term "diaspora" as used in black cultural studies from Jewish thought and his acknowledgment of the appropriation as in itself politically significant despite the difficulties that arise from using one history as an analogical means to explore another (205–6). Many others have resisted the charge of appropriation. Barbara Herrnstein Smith argues, in her defense of her use of economic metaphors to describe verbal transactions, that the usefulness of a figure need not be restricted to the historical site of its production or to the circumstances it originally described (114–15). Sedgwick says of her use of "the briar patch," the value of the fable does not "stand or fall with its history of racist uses" (*Epistemology* 11). Elaine Marks uses "Marrano" as a metaphor for Jewish identity despite the risks entailed given the term's historic meaning (xvii–xviii).

18. The book I'm referring to is *Dissolvere le identità, superare le differenze* by my former colleague Anna Camaiti Hostert. After reading and discussing my work on passing, Hostert reconceived her book on Italian feminism and technology as a book about passing.

19. See Robinson (*To Pass*) for a discussion of the "formal differences" between passing for white and passing for straight. She writes: "Passing for straight can only be conceptualized in tandem with passing for white in the binary terms of gender which the sexologists, among others, used in an effort to make sexuality 'readable' at all. In this sense, to equate race and sexuality as objects of recognition is not only to acquiesce to a gendered field of vision, but also to accept an analogy predicated on the manifest 'truth' of race as a self-evident object of knowledge" (8).

20. Mullen says that passing for white may be either self-conscious or unconscious, in the sense that the one who passes may actually become white. "Masquerade" is the term commonly used to refer to the unconscious adoption of an identity through mimesis. But passing can be unconscious in the sense that a light-skinned African American may find him- or herself taken for white without initially being aware of the (mis)identification. See Piper ("Passing") for examples of unconscious passing in this sense.

21. Cf. Robinson (*To Pass* xi–xii), V. Smith (43–45), and Mullen (73–74). Valerie Smith, for example, considers how passing may be disruptive of structures of racial oppression but may reinforce structures of gender and class oppression. "Normative whiteness" comes from Barbara Johnson's lecture "No Passing." "Compulsory heterosexuality" is Adrienne Rich's celebrated phrase from her essay "Compulsory Heterosexuality and Lesbian Existence." See the discussion of Rich's "lesbian continuum" in note 29. Johnson defines binary versus supplementary logic in "Writing."

22. Valerie Smith notes that this way of thinking internalizes the "one-drop" and "hypo-descent" laws that participate in the cultural production of whiteness as, in Mullen's words, "racially pure." See V. Smith (44) and Mullen (72).

23. Cf. Mullen (73–74). Passing, says Robinson, owes its very possibility to the

problem of identity, to identity conceived as a problem, and this problem is linking appearance and essence, providing the subject with "an epistemological guarantee" ("It Takes One" 716).

24. On the distinction between a performative notion of identity and a radical constructionist or pluralist position, see Butler (*Bodies* 6–7); Gilroy (chap. 3, esp. 96–110); Gallop (*Pedagogy* 14–15) and Jay ("Multiculturalism").

25. On the one-drop rule, see V. Smith (44). On the primacy of the visual, see Tyler (219–220) and Robinson (*To Pass*, introduction).

26. On changing racial identification at will, see V. Smith (44, 47) and Mullen (72, 86).

27. The "marketing of marginality" is Harper's phrase (*Framing* 143), though the point is made by many cultural critics. See, for example, Harper (*Framing*, coda), Willis, V. Smith, and Mullen. The cover of *Time* magazine for its special fall 1993 issue is one example of the morphing I refer to here.

28. This kind of practice in popular culture is linked to contemporary cultural criticism by bell hooks: "Separated from a political and historical context, *ethnicity* is being reconstituted as the new frontier, accessible to all, no passes or permits necessary" (*Yearning* 52).

29. The fear expressed by Harper, Modleski, Mullen, V. Smith, and Willis (among others) in their readings of passing in popular culture is the same kind of fear that led Rich to take back her invitation to women who identify as heterosexual to place themselves on the lesbian continuum. She worried that the lesbian continuum might provide "women who have not yet begun to examine the privileges and soplisisms of heterosexuality . . . a *safe* way to describe their felt connections with women, without having to share in the risks and threats of lesbian existence" (afterword; my emphasis). However, as Callahan writes, "In her fear that someone who has not paid their dues in risk-taking might 'pass,' Rich ignores the fact that to identify with the 'lesbian continuum' is itself a risk-taking change of subject position for heterosexual-defined women" ("Voice," introduction).

30. See especially V. Smith, who explicitly links passing as a performance with "discussions of the performativity of race and gender" in terms of the same logic (51).

31. Butler argues that to see drag as degrading to women is to falsely presume that imitation is derisive ("that structures of imitation and derision are indissolubly linked" [*Bodies* 1]); to assume "a drag performance is insulting or appropriative implies that there is a gender *improperly* expropriated in and through that imitation" (1). The important distinction, as Butler says, is not between drag as derivative and gender as original but between "those drag performances that pass as the original and those that do not" (1). That is, the question is one of legitimacy rather than originality.

32. Tyler's proclamation of the passing of "passing" may be a bit premature. Many gay and lesbian teenagers in particular still feel the need to pass. In the African American literature class I referred to earlier, one of my students dropped the course because the contempt many students voiced for the ex-colored man caused him acute pain as he struggled with the decision of whether or not to "come out," and to whom.

In *Fires in the Mirror*, Anna Deavere Smith writes: "There is an inevitable tension in America. It is the tension of identity in motion, the tension of identity which is in contest with an old idea, but a resonant idea of America. It was developed initially, or so we are told, by men, by White men, but an idea which has in fact been adapted by women and people of color. Can we guide the tension so that it is, in fact, identity in motion . . . ?" (xxxiv).

33. The truth is also born out in the first chapter where Lane presents a revealing anecdote meant to illustrate the danger of trying to understand another culture by extrapolating from one's own (that is, of being paternalistic or ethnocentric). He tells the story of watching the Miss Deaf Massachusetts pageant at the annual convention of the Massachusetts State Association of the Deaf. When a deaf person asks him what he thinks of the pageant, Lane responds that he is "uneasy" at the display of female flesh "like so many pounds of beef on the hoof" (10). His interlocutor exclaims, "'You've got a lot to learn about deaf culture. I think it's just fine!'" (10). And if that vote of approval isn't enough to teach us not to make pronouncements on the apparent sexism of this deaf community, Lane then drops the other shoe: his interlocutor was a woman. Lane would seem to ask, as Woolf's persona facetiously does in *A Room of One's Own* (18), was it for a guest, a stranger, an outsider like himself, a hearing person, and a man to boot to say the pageant was not good?

34. I am grateful to Steve Venturino for this formulation of the problem with Krupat's ethnocritical stance and for initially reviewing Krupat's book for this project. I also want to thank Peter Novak for introducing me to Lane's book.

35. See Fuss (*Identification* 8–10) and Sedgwick (*Epistemology* 61). Identification, writes Fuss, is "the point where the psychical/social distinction becomes . . . untenable" (*Identification* 10); and, "The meaning of a particular identification critically exceeds the limits of its social, historical, and political determinations" (8).

36. "Positionality" conceives the subject's position as "a place from where meaning is constructed, rather than simply the place where a meaning can be *discovered*" (Alcoff, "Cultural Feminism" 434).

37. For a related critique of Alcoff's notion of postitionality, see Caren Kaplan (178–79).

38. MacIntyre elaborates his concept of narrative ethics in *After Virtue* and *Whose Justice? Which Rationality?* Rejecting both foundationalist arguments, which seek to secure justice and rationality in self-evident truths, and objectivist arguments, which appeal to facts as separate from any theory, MacIntyre argues for the "historically and socially context-bound character" of morality, rationality, and justice (*Whose Justice?* 345). There is no rationality and no way to talk about justice and ethics apart from some tradition. As opposed to the modern view from nowhere and the liberal view from everywhere, his is a "situated" ethics. Situating the self in terms of some one tradition better enables us to understand other traditions and rationalities and the disagreements among them. MacIntyre employs the figure of passing to describe this understanding of another tradition. Passing requires "conceptual imagination" (395) and "poetic competence" or (paraphrasing Wittgenstein) knowing how to go on and go further (382). By learning how to go on, one can become, "so far as is possible," an adherent of another tradition or culture. No matter how successful the pass, however, one can speak that language or inhabit that tradition only as an "impersonator" (395).

MacIntyre's use of passing, however, necessitates the caveat. In the first chapter of *Whose Justice?* he explains his neglect of Jewish tradition by saying that that history "must be written by its own adherents" (10). For him, an outsider, to speak for them would be "a gross impertinence" (11). Yet in terms of his own narrative ethics, to understand another tradition, even to be an adherent of a tradition, means being able to give "the kind of account which an adherent would give" (11). It seems MacIntyre would mitigate the gross impertinence of speaking for (the Jew) with the lesser sin of speaking as (a Christian).

39. For differing assessments of Miller's confessional discourse, see Bauer ("Personal Criticism"), MacDonald, Probyn, and S. D. Bernstein.

40. The case of the Australian writer Helen Darville is an example. Darville won all kinds of literary honors for an ostensibly autobiographical novel that turned out to be a sham. She wasn't who she claimed to be; the experiences she narrated weren't true. Yet the awards were given to her in part for her exposure of a hitherto unknown immigrant experience. Now that the fraud has been revealed, critics worry that having been duped could undermine the authority of Australia's literary establishment. Those who opposed the awards all along because they found the book anti-Semitic or just plain pedestrian feel exonerated. Her exposure, they believe, proves their claims that the literary establishment has caved into political correctness, making ethnicity rather than quality the standard. On Darville's story, see Shenon.

41. I cannot avoid criticizing Krupat for scapegoating postmodernism. Krupat presents a caricature of postmodern theory, attributing to the theory the very oppositional logic he uses to define it and, as a result, making some rather odd claims about postmodernism. In other words, he saves himself from the politically problematic implications of his own practice by distancing himself from the very theories that inform it. Yet Krupat later acknowledges that it is not possible to "proceed 'neutrally'" and to avoid "scapegoating" and the "moral and political implications of any situated discourse" (21), in effect saving himself from my criticism of him. But saving himself comes at the cost of his exploring the full potential of the theory.

42. For a fascinating exploration of this problem, see Roof and Wiegman's *Who Can Speak? Authority and Critical Identity,* especially Andrew Lakritz's essay that opens the volume and the essays in part 4. The volume also includes a later version of Alcoff's essay "The Problem of Speaking for Others."

43. Tyler writes: "The wish for one's own terms and one's proper identity, perhaps the most deeply private property of all, is an impossible desire since both are held in common with others in the community as an effect of the symbolic" (215). Later she adds: "no matter how self-consciously we deconstruct identities, no matter how self-reflexively we perform our selves, we are still 'doing' them. What's more, we demand that the Other recognize both our identities and our 'cynicism' about them—the Other is at once our credulous dupe and the 'subject supposed to know' that we know better" (222). If, as MacIntyre says, "it was Freud's achievement to discover that unmasking arbitrariness in others may always be a defense against uncovering it in ourselves" (*After Virtue* 69), then it seems unmasking our own complicity, if not our "cynicism," may be a defense against being exposed by others, allowing them the agency we claim to be giving them.

44. My thanks to Anne Callahan, who suggested this economic metaphor to me.

45. Bernhard's representation of a primarily black audience *within* the film implies her assumption of a primarily white audience *for* the film, as Michelle Shocked's defense of blackface implies a white audience for her album. Blackface minstrelsy

was, after all, entertainment for white audiences, and there would be little need for Bernhard to represent black viewers' responses to her impersonations if she felt they would be amply represented in the audiences of her film. Both times I saw Bernhard's film at the Fine Arts Theater in Chicago the audience was mainly white. But in specifying the audience's racial identity, I am constructing the white audience as a homogeneous collectivity that stands in opposition to the black audience in the film, which is also constructed as a homogeneous collectivity. This is what Tyler refers to as "'passing' others into whiteness or blackness" (220), in effect disavowing their difference.

46. Gallop's reading of Indira Karamcheti's contribution to *Pedagogy: The Question of Impersonation* makes a similar point. In her introduction to the volume, Gallop says that Karamcheti moves beyond "the traditional opposition between the personal as authentic and impersonation as false performance" to "a more postmodern understanding in which the minority teacher playing a minority teacher would herself be in 'racial drag.'" She continues: "This 'neo-blackface' performance involves performers whose 'real faces' are not presumptively white. Yet the 'real black person' underneath does not make the 'blackface' any less a performance" (7). Realness, as Butler puts it, is not the subject of the impersonation but the standard against which the performance is measured. For realness to pass as real, it must "compel belief," and it can only do so by miming, and naturalizing, racial norms (*Bodies* 129).

47. Tyler's reading of Kobena Mercer's famous article on black hairstyles could apply to Bernhard's impersonations as well: "The object of 'love and theft' (Lott), African-American signifiers are themselves subject to the reappropriation from which Mercer at times seems to want to 'save' them. Their resignification may be a depoliticization of a style (if such a thing is possible), but it may be simply a different politicization of it" (227).

48. Barbara Johnson writes in *The Wake of Deconstruction:* "The resistance to recognizing misogyny as institutional is the *same* resistance as the resistance to questioning individual intention and control in language. This is perhaps where deconstruction and political critique come together" (46–47).

49. Walton offers an excellent discussion of Roxanne (255–58). If I cover some of the same ground here, it is to lay a different emphasis on Walton's insight: "Roxanne occupies a curious middle ground between the explicitly mimicked blackness in Sandra's personas and the apparently autonomous black audience" (255).

50. In *Identification Papers,* Fuss defines identifications as "ghosts from the past," "the phantasmal relics of our complicated psychical histories" (2). She writes that identification is always inscribed within a particular history (165), yet, "the meaning of a particular identification critically exceeds the limits of its social, historical, and political determinations" (8). The political is located within those psychical identifications, but the trajectory of those identifications cannot be controlled or foretold in advance (8).

51. Gallop writes: "I realize that the set of feelings that I used to have about French men I now have about African-American women. Those are the people I feel inadequate in relation to and try to please in my writing" (Gallop et al. 363–64).

52. My discussion of Roxanne's function as the limit is indebted to Cornell's discussion of deconstruction as the philosophy of the limit: "Deconstruction more accurately described by the notion of limit is related to what Charles Peirce . . . called

secondness. By secondness Peirce indicates the materiality that persists *beyond* any attempt to conceptualize it. Secondness, in other words, is what resists" (*Philosophy* 1).

53. Cf. B. Johnson's point about writing as dissemination ("Writing" 44–45).

54. See Foucault ("What Is Enlightenment?" 43), Rajchman (103).

55. For a corroboration of this argument that cultural critics and literature teachers can learn from popular culture, see Friedman.

TWO

Pedagogy at Risk

In 1975, I looked in at a homoerotic world, trying to imagine
my future place. How would I pass? In 1977, having
"passed," I was trying to imagine being an academic speaker *as a woman.*
  —Jane Gallop, *Thinking through the Body*

In those days, those of us from marginal groups who were
allowed to enter prestigious, predominantly white colleges
were made to feel that we were there not to learn but to
prove that we were the equal of whites. We were . . . to prove
this by showing how well we could become clones of our
peers.
  —bell hooks, *Teaching to Transgress*

Passing is the end of education. The goal toward which students strive, passing marks the completion of a course of study. At once a terminus, "the point
or line beyond which [one] does not or cannot pass" (*Webster's Ninth Collegiate*), and a threshold, a crossing over into something new, passing is bit-
tersweet. In the academic world, passing is everything. For professors and
students alike, the desire to pass structures our identifications, motivates our
performances, and defines our relations to others in the classroom and in the
profession. Passing confers authority, not only on the one who passes, but
also on the one who awards the passing grade, for no single act shores up the
authority of the professor and reaffirms the status of the discipline more than
the act of determining who passes. The one who passes presumably has
mastered, to varying degrees, a body of knowledge or a methodology, which
actually entails mastery of the rhetorical and stylistic conventions of mastery that constitute the discourse of a discipline. With passing come new

anxieties about performing as "the one supposed to know" (Lacan), which always entails the possibility of being exposed as a fraud. More, then, than a homonymic relation links passing as a social practice and passing as an academic event.

As the epigraphs to this chapter make clear, passing in the figurative sense has long been an implicit requirement of the educational experience, especially for those individuals for whom authority, historically a white male prerogative, does not come naturally, that is, by virtue of who they are. As a student, bell hooks understood that she could pass for smart only by passing as white, modeling her performance on that of white students to demonstrate to those professors who had the authority to pass her that any nonconformity on her part was not a sign of racial inferiority (*Teaching* 5). In graduate school, Jane Gallop worried about whether or not she would be able to pass, how as a woman she could assume the male prerogative in a world where "mimetic desire" (Girard) circulated only among white men.[1] For both women, the problem in the end was not achieving the mastery assumed to be a white male prerogative but where to go afterward. The fact that Gallop puts quotation marks around the more common academic meaning of "passing," in effect defamiliarizing that term, serves to normalize passing (in the figurative sense) as a performative practice within the academy. Those diacritical marks make apparent the extent to which "passing" as the mastery of knowledge depends on "passing" as the ability to be regarded as or to accept identification as a certain type of person (an authority)—that is, being able to perform a certain social role. The standard academic meaning of "passing" is to move into an unmarked subject position, reinforcing the belief that passing has nothing to do with who we are, nothing to do with our bodies. At one time in the academy, as the epigraphs suggest, we were all white men.

Jane Tompkins, writing as a professor, not as a student, has argued that the fear of being exposed as a fraud, which always accompanies passing in the sense of assuming an identity that is not by rights one's own, motivates our classroom performances no matter who occupies the position of authority. The roots of this fear lie not in the individual who performs in the classroom—hooks or Gallop, for example—but in the performance model of pedagogy itself. That model, as Tompkins defines it in her essay "Pedagogy of the Distressed," is based on the notion that the professor is the expert, the authority who has mastered all the knowledge relevant to the course content and whose job it is to pass this knowledge and expertise on to others, which also means passing on the performance model of pedagogy itself (655). The student masters the material by modeling his or her performance of content mastery after the professor, giving rise to the fear that the professor really has the knowledge that the student has only learned to mime. Passing in this sense is a matter of role playing and works much like transference. The problem is not so much that passing is based on a false belief in the subject presumed to know but rather that a belief in "the illusion of a consciousness transparent to itself" (Felman, "Psychoanalysis" 34) constitutes the pedagogical relation. Not conforming to the illusion means not making the grade. In other words, for Tompkins, the fraudulence derives from the pedagogical dynamic itself, though for many it feels as if it has to do with their "persons," with the body of the one who inhabits that position. In the dynamics of passing, an inevitable slippage occurs between the position and the person. If white men have not as often voiced the same anxiety about passing as women like Gallop and hooks do, it is because the subject position into which they too must pass feels comfortable and fitting to them. When Nancy K. Miller moves from the French department back to her "native" English department, she believes that the safe haven of her native tongue will protect her from the risk of being exposed for "passing," eliding the inevitability of passing in the classroom. A safe subject position allows you to forget that you are passing.

This is the point of Adrian Piper's video installation exhibit entitled "Cornered," part of the permanent collection at the Museum of Contemporary Art in Chicago. The exhibit confronts the viewer with a series of double binds, beginning with the artist's, who is light-skinned but identifies as black. The video opens with Piper sitting behind a wooden desk (the kind found in many classrooms) facing the viewer. "I'm black," she begins, asking the viewers (positioned as white and as students) how that declaration makes them feel. She then brings the lesson home: "If someone who looks and sounds like me is black," she says, "then no one is safely, unquestionably white."

In an academic milieu where identity politics, political correctness, multiculturalism, and cultural studies respond to, or in some views give rise to, a deep ambivalence about the teaching of Western culture and traditional subject matter, and also signal a loss of consensus on the teaching of literature and the mission of the university, what can it mean to pass? What happens to passing when standards are challenged, when disciplinary boundaries are crossed, when one judges, as Jean-François Lyotard says we do today, without criteria? (*Differend*) Although in one sense (transference), we are always passing in the classroom, "passing" as I deploy the term is not just being that authority; it can also be understood as a recent phenomenon, a response to precisely these kinds of questions.

Exploring the relation of passing to pedagogy, and the multiplicity of ways in which that relation puts pedagogy at risk, is the subject of this chapter.

Specifically, I will argue that not just students and professors, curricula and methodologies are at risk in the university today—pedagogy itself is at risk. By this I mean that the kind of crisis produced in literary studies by the structuralist turn, the onset of theory in the academy, was not only concurrent with the crisis brought about by the diversifying of the academy and the curriculum but the two phenomena have mutually sustained each other. Rather than confront what the convergence of these powerful forces for change has meant for pedagogy, many have sought to blame either theory or diversity (or both) for the loss of core values, shared standards, codified methodologies, and even a common vocabulary thought necessary to sustain pedagogy. Understanding the structural dynamics of passing as central to the pedagogical relation, I will argue, provides a means of responding to the "crisis" signified by the phrase "at risk."

Risking Who We Are

> Does the quality of risk . . . *surround* language like a kind of *ditch* or external place of perdition which speech could never hope to leave, but which it can escape by remaining "at home," by and in itself, in the shelter of its essence or *telos*? Or, on the contrary, is the risk rather its internal and positive condition of possibility? Is that outside its inside, the very force and law of its emergence?
> —Jacques Derrida, "Signature Event Context"

Today, in the aftermath of postmodern theories and various challenges to the hegemony of Western canons and culture, we commonly speak of teaching in terms of risks—risking oneself, taking risks, putting students at risk.[2] We are on the edge, intellectually (the cutting edge) and emotionally (anxious). Safety, the notion of being at home, feeling comfortable in our protected space, secure in our knowledge and in ourselves, is now seen by many to be inimical to pedagogy, if not downright dangerous to intellectual inquiry and academic freedom. "We should regard knowledge as something for which to risk identity," intones Edward Said, "and we should think of academic freedom as an invitation to give up on identity in the hope of understanding and perhaps even assuming more than one" ("Identity" 16–17). No single word recurs as often in contemporary writing about identity, epistemology, and pedagogy as the word "risk." Risk, always shadowed by the possibility of loss, is now a value. Today, writes philosopher John Caputo, "the metaphysical desire to make things safe and secure has become consummately dangerous" (7).

But what exactly do we mean by "risk"? What are the *teacher*'s notions of risk and safety?[3] Many writing on pedagogy today understand risk taking in terms of the demands made on students. "Unlike the stereotypical feminist model that suggests women best come to voice in an atmosphere of safety," writes bell hooks, "I encourage students to work . . . in an atmosphere where they may be afraid or see themselves at risk" (*Talking Back* 53). Students do not choose to be at risk; rather, professors impose risk on students. We ask students to take the risk of interrogating received models for the study of literature in order to understand the history and legitimation of those models and to question the values implicit in them. By asking students to read literature not just for its content and form but for the ways in which it reproduces cultural identities and social hierarchies, we ask them to risk their notions of literary studies as a safe domain, outside or above the fray, as well as their notions of themselves as discrete, rational individuals. Students risk feelings of guilt and shame as we urge them to examine the cultural production of knowledge and identities by deconstructing race, interrogating whiteness, exposing heterosexism, decolonizing their minds. What makes learning about diversity so risky, as Spivak, hooks, and others have pointed out, is the imperative it brings to unlearn our own forms of privilege (hooks, *Yearning;* Lakritz 16). In unlearning forms of privilege, in responding to the challenge of their own ignorance, students, it is generally assumed, must be willing to take the risk of uncertainty and to suspend their desire for mastery. Asking them not to pass as authorities, we ask them to take the ultimate risk of not passing at all.

For teachers of literature, the risks presented in much of the writing on pedagogy are different but related. We share with students the risk to our sense of self and our own forms of privilege that comes with teaching multicultural literatures, deconstructing received forms of knowledge, and interrogating disciplinary practices. Yet, in shifting our tasks from literary criticism focused on the interpretation of individual works, to cultural criticism focused on the analysis of the symbolic and material systems that produce them, we risk charges that we no longer teach literature but use it as a document to study history, politics, or sociology, or as an occasion for consciousness raising. Teaching noncanonical and even nonliterary texts, we risk accusations by colleagues, students, administrators, and the public of being trendy, lacking depth, and promoting politics. As we respond to calls for cross-disciplinary and multicultural scholarship, we risk running up against the limits of our own disciplinary education, teaching texts and subjects we may not have been trained in, making claims our disciplinary methodologies may not sustain. Student evaluations may show resistance to the risk taking being asked of them, confusion over the shift from textual interpretation to cultural critique, or anger at having wasted their time on noncanonical authors; thus, professors may risk institutional progress toward tenure, promotion, and renewal. Diversifying our syllabi opens us to the risk of being confused with the subject position we are teaching (the woman professor and the woman writer, for example) or being accused of not having the authority to speak from that subject position (the white professor teaching race theory, for example, or the male professor of feminist studies). "Maybe there was some safety in teaching the 'old' curriculum," writes Cheryl Johnson, "because we could place some distance between us and the text; our participation was not personal" ("Participatory Rhetoric" 417).

Johnson's remark gets at an important difference between teaching literature in the university today and teaching literature before the theory revolution and the culture wars of the past three decades that can help to clarify what is at stake in all the talk about risks. Issues of representation in the canon are now bound up with issues of representation in the classroom. If thirty years ago we were all white men, the diversifying of the academy and the curriculum has made us all representative bodies, signifying our difference before we open our mouths. Teaching today is something we cannot help but take personally. That is, on the one hand, risk seems to be an intellectual and moral choice anyone can and everyone should make, a situation we can bring about through our own volition; on the other hand, risk is something that befalls us, a condition we are exposed to by virtue of where and who we are. Risk in this latter sense has the character of an event.

Confusion over what we mean by risk stems in part from the fact that the notion of risking ourselves is nothing new to literary studies. In fact, I would say that risking oneself has long been a value, if not *the* value, of literary studies. The idea that knowledge changes us justifies the study of literature as a crucial component of a liberal arts education. Sedgwick writes, "It was from [Allan] Bloom, as much as from more explicitly literary and deconstructive theorists or from more leftist ones, that I and some others of that late-sixties generation learned the urgencies and pleasures of reading against the visible grain of any influential text . . . the lesson that the true sins against the holy ghost would be to read without risking oneself" (*Epistemology* 55). Writing on the "risky fraying" of logic and the boundaries of the self that reading literature brings, Spivak argues that such "experiences of fraying can produce new, more-capacious modes of apprehension" without which "we remain safe" (*Outside* 180). Susan Rubin Suleiman values the study of contemporary novels because "they are . . . less 'safe' to write about than works of the past. They bring the critic's self into play, and into risk" (6). The "sur-

prise of otherness" (B. Johnson, *World* 16) and "the suspension of intellectual mastery and psychological defense" (Martin 17) are risks both traditional
(Bloom, the newly reformed Lentricchia) and more radical (Sedgwick, Spivak, Suleiman) critics can endorse. In other words, if today we are talking a
lot about the risks to ourselves posed by literary studies, such talk is nothing
new. From modernist exile writers to that monument of modernist criticism,
Erich Auerbach's *Mimesis,* highly valued writing has been produced out of
the experience of *not* being at home, safe and secure.[4] In narratives of passing and in narrative transvestism (the authorial adoption of the persona or
perspective of someone of a different gender or race), literature has long been
the realm in which we attempt to imaginatively experience other lives, to
consciously alter our personae, to fray identity boundaries through the crossing of cultural boundaries.[5] "The shame of being a man," Gilles Deleuze
offers, "is there any better reason to write?" (225)

The conflation of these different notions of risks that I have been rehearsing, the way we use the same term to push very different pedagogical agendas, has served to obscure the real source of the "crisis" that recent writing
on pedagogy and the profession attempts to address. We commonly think
of risk as opposed to safety, but the moral imperative to risk ourselves has
long been the safety clause in teaching literature, for the very specialness of
literary language that allows us to risk ourselves in the experience of reading serves as well to contain the risk by confining it to the experience of reading. What has made pedagogy possible in literary studies, I argue, has been
precisely the unacknowledged tension between, and the uneasy alliance of,
two competing notions of risk and safety. On the one hand, we have a notion of literary studies as itself risky insofar as literature's specialness rests
on its ability to defamiliarize the familiar, to make the strangeness of the other
our own, thereby taking us out of ourselves, so to speak—the "shame of being
a man" idea. On the other hand, we have a notion of literary studies as safe
insofar as literature is seen to sustain a common culture, to imaginatively
expand our knowledge of other lives and experiences, and to resist on the level
of language the kind of reductive rhetoric that serves political and commercial ends.[6] It is the disruption of these particular notions of risk and safety,
not the content of what we teach or even the theories by which we teach, that
puts pedagogy at risk today. As long as the notion of risk has a certain familiarity in literary studies, critics and theories that rely on this term to signify
their difference from traditional pedagogies fail to create the very crisis their
language calls for.

However familiar the notion of risk may be to the experience of reading
and writing literature, the notion of "pedagogy" as risk taking comes into

conflict with its more traditional definition as the passing on of knowledge, information, and skills. If real teaching, like real art, as Susan Sontag describes it in "Against Interpretation" (99) has the capacity to make us nervous, or to put us at risk, pedagogy, like interpretation, has traditionally tried to comfort us by making the subject matter and the classroom experience manageable. Pedagogy, often defined as the "art" of teaching, functions more like interpretation; it provides students with the means to accomplish something. The purpose of pedagogy is to make things clear; risk taking means throwing everything into doubt. Even if, following John Dewey, we conceive pedagogy as teaching inquiry, not knowledge, as process-oriented rather than content-centered, and even if we resist its reduction to a set of rules or methodology, still pedagogy is largely conceived in humanist terms; it is supposed to be comforting by providing guidance, enabling students to become part of an academic community and to see themselves as members of a broader social community, responsive and responsible to it. In fact, precisely because reading literature necessitates intellectual and emotional risks, pedagogy in literary studies has sought to contain the risks through arguments for literature's specialness and value and by assuring students they can control the experience of reading through critical methodologies meant to guide interpretation.

Although literary and cultural critics talk much about the *recent* turn to pedagogy, pedagogy has long been a focus of our professional interests. Take, for example, two classic works, I. A. Richards's *Practical Criticism* (1929) and Cleanth Brooks Jr. and Robert Penn Warren's *Understanding Poetry* (1938). What's new is not our professional interest in pedagogy but the kind of pedagogy we are interested in. Where pedagogy used to boost our confidence by offering us methodologies derived from particular kinds of texts (e.g., modernist poetry) that were then generalized and applied to other kinds of texts, now pedagogy makes us anxious. Barbara Johnson's edited collection *The Pedagogical Imperative* was a major move in this direction. A special 1982 issue of *Yale French Studies,* it shifted the focus from pedagogy as statements about teaching to pedagogy as a literary genre or a mode of writing. Pedagogy in this collection is not about the application of theory to classroom practices but about the implications of theory emerging in the teaching situation itself. The deconstructive and psychoanalytic theories that inform the essays in this volume give authority, in Shoshana Felman's words, "to the teaching of a knowledge which does not know its own meaning" ("Psychoanalysis" 41), thereby undermining the notion that pedagogy is something we can control through codified practices. Pedagogy, understood as the passing on of knowledge, is necessarily implicated as well in the teaching of ignorance, to borrow the title of Johnson's contribution to this collection. "To teach ignorance is, for Socrates, to teach to *un*-know, to become conscious of the fact that what one thinks is knowledge is really an array of received ideas, prejudices, and opinions—a way of *not* knowing that one does not know" (*Pedagogical Imperative* 181). These essays reconceive pedagogy as a mode of writing and as the site of the cultural reproduction and regulation of identities (Gallop, *Around 1981* 3).[7] This move has been a decisive one in putting pedagogy at risk. However, insofar as many of the essays in the Johnson volume offer primarily close readings of texts (Molière, Lacan, de Sade), pedagogy remains confined to the experience of reading and is taken out of the classroom. Indeed, that is the objective of the volume as stated in the "Editor's Preface": "While discussions of pedagogy generally deal with classroom procedures for the teaching of texts, this volume studies the ways in which the texts themselves dramatize the problematics of teaching" (iii).

Pedagogy is about more than reading or skills, though; it is about vocation. Vocation, in Cornel West's words, entails "what we are about, who we are, and why we do what we do" (30). The kind of risk taking valued today at once contributes to and responds to the notion of a *profession* at risk. "At risk" is a phrase often used as well by conservative educators and politicians, such as William Bennett, who worry that education is under siege by advocates of theory, proponents of multiculturalism, and leftist critics who together have brought about the collapse of standards, the end of methodological debate, and the politicization of literary studies—a situation the late Allan Bloom termed the "closing of the American mind." If we can no longer agree on the skills to be imparted, the knowledge to be secured, the goals to be accomplished—indeed, if "we" can no longer say "we" (Caputo 209)—then pedagogy itself would indeed seem to be at risk. It is no wonder that pedagogy has become the focus of inquiry and the site of an identity crisis within the profession of literary studies (Faigley 112; cf. Guillory, "Preprofessionalism"). Yet those who call for a return to the teaching of critical methods, which they see as having been displaced by the teaching of theory, and for a renewed commitment to standards to ward off the threat of relativism, fail to understand the nature of this crisis.[8] Rather than confront the end of pedagogy as we have known it, recent debates have focused on placing blame for its demise.

The shift to a cultural studies paradigm over the past two decades has often been targeted as a major source of that identity crisis and as a risk to literary studies, among other disciplines.[9] And I agree, not because cultural studies has politicized the academy for the worse, but because its institutionalization has served to expose a contradiction that has always been at the heart of literary pedagogy: that literary pedagogy at once values risk and seeks to contain it. It is precisely the convergence of forces giving rise to the emergence of cultural studies in the U.S. academy today that has led, on the one hand, to the promotion of risk taking as a value in the classroom and, on the other hand, to worry that our profession is at risk. But that convergence, I argue, has also led us to conflate different notions of risk, thereby obscuring the real issue. The end of literary studies as we have known it is upon us. The humanist project is over, with all its ramifications for ethics, politics, pedagogy, and our profession. The subject at the heart of that pedagogy has been brought into question. The risk is not confined to the individual person (the professor or student, the white man or black woman) but is indeed more pervasive: the very category of the person is at risk in the classroom today. Yet even those who promote this risk to the subject do not accept, in my view, what this really means for our vocation. Pedagogy can no longer be the arena in which we debate the desirability and consequences of such a loss, for the classroom is the very site where we experience the effects of this loss most intensely. In this book, I understand pedagogy not as a method but as an event. Pedagogy is the site in which the implications of this shift from a humanist to a post-humanist subject are being felt and worked through, not resolved but confronted. In the dynamics of our engagement with others, we come face to face with what Ihab Hassan once humorously described as the unseemly spectacle of our posthumous selves.

While I agree that pedagogy is at risk in literature and composition studies today, and in ways other than those acknowledged by the claims we make for risk taking in the classroom, in this chapter, as in chapter 1, I want to retain the notion of crisis conveyed by the phrase "at risk" without giving in to the fear that crisis means collapse. Whether we understand risk as a danger to be avoided by staying at home (within traditional curricula and familiar methodologies) or as a boundary to be crossed to promote change (such as disciplinary boundaries and cultural boundaries), risk is conceived as surrounding us like a ditch. Risk has always been situated somewhere within the parameters of our familiar experience: in the texts we read, in the methodologies we employ, in the theories we promote, in the standards we uphold. In "Signature Event Context," Derrida offers an alternative notion of risk as structurally integral to the communicative exchange, and thus by extension to the pedagogical relation. Pushing Austin's theory of the performative to the limit, Derrida shows how the risk of meaning misfiring, of intentions going astray, is internal to the very structure of communication, not a fate that may befall it from the outside. Although Austin recognizes that "infelicity is an ill to which . . . all *conventional* acts" are subject (19), Derrida notes that "Austin does not ponder the consequences issuing from the fact that a possibility—a possible risk—is *always* possible, and is in some sense a necessary possibility" (*Limited Inc.* 15). Understood in this way, risk in pedagogy today is neither something to be achieved (a value to be promoted through claims to be doing it) nor a situation to be remedied (by coming to consensus on standards and methods). Risk does not lie "out there" in the new territories we enter or the new texts we teach; risk is internal, giving rise to the very possibility of teaching. Today, pedagogy is always, permanently, at risk. This has profound implications for what it means to pass. Traditionally conceived as a rite of passage, passing is no longer the end of pedagogy but, as Derrida says of risk, "the very force and law of its emergence" (17).

Let me give one brief example here of the kind of conceptual shift I am talking about when I say passing is the possibility of pedagogy and the kind of shift I will pursue in subsequent chapters. Passing judgment, in the classroom as in a court of law, has long been thought to require neutral standards or principles of justice. Today, with the impact of critical race theory on legal studies, some legal scholars argue that at times it may be not only appropriate but imperative to find a defendant "not guilty" on the basis of his or her race. While such action is commonly seen as a threat to neutral principles, the real issue is not whether we will have disinterested or interested legal standards. The conflict opened up by such decisions is between, on the one hand, supposedly impartial decisions that ignore social and historical conditions, and, on the other hand, avowedly partial decisions that respond to the moral imperative to take such conditions into consideration. Whether or not we agree with the verdict, the point is that the verdict no longer serves to ratify the principles on which justice is based but to open them to deliberation and contestation. Passing judgment in such cases is not the end of justice but, in Derrida's words, "the very force and law of its emergence."[10]

Passing would introduce the question of who we are into the heart of pedagogy rather than seek to resolve the question to get on with the business of teaching literature and without reducing that question to, in Rajchman's words, the "'constitution of the subject' in the order of language . . . and so to the symbolic or discursive 'idealism' that says we are only what a culture makes us be" (143). To clarify further the relation of passing to pedagogy, I will review the history of how the subject of pedagogy, and pedagogy itself, came to be at risk. I will then look at the ways in which those most responsible for bringing this situation about are foreclosing on the possibilities it opens up. In the end, as throughout this book, I will argue that pedagogy can occur only when and if we open ourselves to the inevitable slip that exposes us to the ethical implications of our own theoretical and disciplinary agendas.

Dead Subjects

The day of high theory is passing.
—*Chronicle of Higher Education,* 13 October 1993

We are all familiar by now with the story of the death of the subject. Structuralist and poststructuralist theories of the 1950s and 1960s proclaimed the subject's demise in terms of language, signifying systems, and the unconscious. As Foucault explains it, "The researches of psychoanalysis, of linguistics, of anthropology have 'decentered' the subject in relation to the laws of its desire, the forms of its language, the rules of its actions, or the play of its mythical and imaginative discourse" (qtd. in Culler 93). Feminist, postcolonial, and critical race theories of the 1970s and 1980s undermined the humanist subject by exposing its masculinist, colonialist, white Western agenda. Often contrasted as textualist (the first group) and materialist (the second group) practices, these various theories are seen by some to offer competing explanations for the death of the autonomous, rational subject of humanism: namely, psycholinguistic and historical-political ones. Others lump these theories together under the rubric of multiculturalism or political correctness. While neither the critique of the humanist subject in poststructuralist and multicultural theories nor the challenge to traditional authority brought about by the diversifying of the academy and the curriculum has led to the current crisis in pedagogy, the historical conjunction of theory and diversity, coming into the academy at roughly the same time, has. That crisis has opened up the opportunities for what I call "passing." At the same time that theory has deconstructed the subject, displaced its authority, and called into question any ultimate signified for terms of identity, we have been faced with demands made by others to account for our subject positions. For example, at the same time we are told that there is no such thing as "Woman," we are asked to account for ourselves as women. This situation, in my view, has been all for the good. But rather than working in the space opened up by this convergence, in the dynamics I call "passing," pedagogy is the site where we attempt to reclaim an identity at risk—at risk in both senses of being subject to deconstruction and being under seige. The untold story is the survival in pedagogy of the subject that has been put to rest in theory.

The coincidence of the institutionalization of studies programs and the institutionalization of theory courses in the 1970s and 1980s, which I argue (in chapters 1 and 5) gave rise to cultural studies, intensified the conflict between two notions of literary pedagogy seen to be opposing but which co-existed more or less peacefully in literary studies for a long time, in effect reinforcing and sustaining each other. On the one hand, the proliferation of studies programs and the challenges to the canon and Western culture they present have been undertaken as a moral and political imperative. "Students ought to base at least part of their study on the perception and consequences of *difference*," Paul Lauter, for one, has argued; "indeed, responsibly preparing students for the future involves educating them in and about diversity" (2).[11] Teaching for diversity in this view promotes critical and cultural literacy and makes the study of literature more relevant to our contemporary world and to our students' everyday lives. To teach diverse literatures because the world or the academy is more diverse is to remain committed to pedagogical assumptions based on a mimetic or expressivist concept of literature: literature is "about" life; literature represents characteristic experiences and conveys knowledge about others living in a world apart; literature expresses the author's experiences, ideas, values, and feelings. These notions, which have long informed the teaching of literature, may be challenged in theory—even by the very theory that informs the courses—but they commonly inform a *pedagogical* defense for teaching "marginal" literatures.

On the other hand, studies programs, such as women's studies, black studies, gay/lesbian studies, and cultural studies, are often criticized as having more to do with ideology and politics than with literature and criticism. This argument is grounded in the tenets of the New Criticism, a formalism that remains, despite recent theories, the other dominant literary pedagogy in the academy. With its assumption of literature's autonomy and its adoption of modernist impersonality, this pedagogy depends on a belief that the literature we read is not affected in any essential way by who and where we are when we read but that we stand in some kind of transcendental relation to the texts we study. In other words, our participation is not personal. In this view, literature is not "about" life, in the sense of being a reflection of it, but rather, as a specific kind of language, literature bears a certain special relation to life that distinguishes it from other forms of writing (e.g., scientific treatises, memoirs, histories). The purpose of literary studies is to sensitize us to the experience of the writing itself, not to interpret the writing in terms of the experience it represents. Teaching literature means learning to analyze "words, images, and symbols rather than character, thought, and plot" (Abrams 223). A pedagogy based on New Critical assumptions seeks to isolate literature from other disciplines, such as philosophy, anthropology, so-

ciology, communications, and history, the very disciplines that studies programs seek to bring together.

We could sum up these two prevailing pedagogies by saying, no doubt
reductively, that literature is either that which represents its kind (expressivist)
or that which transcends its time (formalist). However various our critical
methodologies and theoretical paradigms have become, *pedagogy* in literary
studies traditionally has been (and still is) based on a liberation politics, on
the one hand, and a New Critical formalism, on the other.[12] Far from competing with each other, these two views actually have long served to sustain
a certain notion of liberal education. Liberal education both promotes the
social and political values of a democracy (and thus its attention to diversity
and personal experience) and transmits the universal moral truths on which
that democratic society is based (and thus its concern with a common canon, shared standards, codified methodologies, and impersonal inquiry)—the
traditional modernist enterprise. The *integrity* of our vocation, its moral
rectitude as well as its cohesiveness, has depended on the compatibility of
these competing pedagogies. Both expressivist and formalist pedagogies
know where to locate truth, however complex or ambiguous it may be, however differently located, and both assure us of the bond between language and
meaning, between the self and the words that are its expression.[13]

The metaphor of the tourist has been used to conceptualize the subject
in each of these models, thereby revealing the relation between these apparently conflicting pedagogies. Henry Louis Gates Jr., who has said that black
students have felt like tourists in a traditional canon and curriculum that have
neglected their cultural heritage, is one of the first to use this metaphor. As
Elizabeth Fox-Genovese puts it, "attacks on the canon derive primarily from
the perception that it does not adequately represent the experiences and identities of most of those who are expected to study it" (132). Studies programs
designed to promote diversity and to challenge various forms of cultural
hegemony, then, are meant to make students feel more at home in the curriculum, recognizing themselves in its literary representations, expressing
themselves through the personal essay, and understanding their former sense
of alienation. Of particular importance is the way Gates's position here illustrates the difference between theoretical and pedagogical arguments.
Gates's theoretical writings on African American literature work against the
notion that literature represents its kind. On the contrary, he has argued, it
is precisely that notion which historically has kept the study of African American literature focused primarily on black experience to the exclusion of black
cultural forms of expression. This conflict between theoretical assumptions
and pedagogical agendas helps to account for the risk I am exploring here.

Just as new literatures are being added to the curriculum to make students feel more at home in literature departments, new theories are working to make us uncomfortable with the notion of being at home anywhere.

Such pedagogical objectives in turn give rise to the worry that teaching for diversity might create, in the words of Linda Nicholson, "an attitude towards difference suggested by the experience of tourism: where diversity is experienced in its most superficial manifestations" (14).[14] Multiculturalism in this view means nothing more than taking students on a tour of other cultures, suggesting that a little exposure to otherness can make students more tolerant, if not more knowledgeable. Whereas for Gates the tourist is the outsider, the one who is not at home here (the subject various studies programs address), for Nicholson the tourist is the imperialist who makes him- or herself at home everywhere (the subject formalism presupposes). On the one hand, the metaphor of tourism evokes a certain intellectual experience of estrangement; on the other hand, it connotes a sense of entitlement associated with economic exchange and the history of colonialism. "The relentless celebration of 'difference' and 'otherness' can . . . be seen as an ominous trend," writes Edward Said. "It suggests not only . . . spectacularization . . . but also the heedless appropriation and translation of the world by a process that . . . cannot easily be distinguished from the process of empire" ("Representing" 213–14).[15]

The metaphor of the subject as tourist has been used at once to promote the notion that teaching for diversity is essentially disruptive (challenging pedagogy grounded in the New Criticism that ignores social and cultural differences and that would make us all white men) and to forestall that pedagogical agenda by suggesting that teaching for diversity essentially reinforces the assumptions behind a formalism developed within a particular historical and economic context. In either case, the metaphor of the tourist suggests a stable, unitary subject who interacts with the world from "a fixed point of departure or arrival" (De Lauretis 159), one who has a home to which to return. Whether literary texts are seen as representing specific cultures and experiences or as monuments of enduring intellect, whether one argues that reading great books produces a consensus on value and meaning that excludes other perspectives or that the process of interpretation learned from those great books is what keeps consensus from forming and thus makes the canon timeless and inclusive, pedagogy itself can create the experience of tourism.[16] Teaching students different cultures may not be fundamentally different from teaching students their own cultural heritage *if* we teach literature as representing its kind or transcending its time. The difference between the kind of disinterested study of literature that characterizes formalism and the kind of interested teaching that characterizes expressivism is not simply arbitrary but moot, purely academic, insofar as they sustain a common concept of the subject at the core of liberal education.

Peter Weir's 1989 film *Dead Poets Society* appeals nostalgically to this tension between formalist and expressivist pedagogies at a time (the 1980s) when that debate had been put to rest in criticism. Set in 1959 on the campus of an all-male prep school, the film pits the inspired (expressivist) pedagogy of John Keating (Robin Williams) against the formalist analytics of the headmaster, Mr. Nolan (Norman Lloyd), and Prichard's poetry textbook. Keating's unconventional teaching style, which takes the students outside the classroom and roots authority and truth in themselves, opposes the professionalism of literary studies which, by the 1950s, had been solidified through the success of New Critical methodologies that sought to make the study of poetry more rigorous and disciplined.[17] The climax of the film centers on the death of one of Keating's students. Inspired by Keating's romantic philosophy, Neal commits suicide rather than deny his artistic aspirations by giving in to his father's demand that he attend a military academy and medical school. Although this event forces Keating to take responsibility for his teaching, the film in no way blames Keating's pedagogy for Neal's tragedy (nor should it). In fact, far from undermining the authority of their teacher, Neal's death only reaffirms the students' faith in their Captain (as they call Keating, after Whitman's "Oh Captain, My Captain") and his philosophy of the Self and further sentimentalizes the tension between the two competing pedagogies. Despite the apparent victory of formalist pedagogy in Keating's dismissal (he is drummed out of the institution by his formalist opponent, the headmaster, a former English teacher who takes over Keating's class), the melodramatic classroom scene at the end, where the students stand on their desks and chant romantic platitudes to their departing Captain, attests to the continuing appeal of an expressivist pedagogy rooted in liberal humanist notions of literature and the subject. *This* is what teaching should be, the film suggests—not dry analysis, not politicized debates, but heroic acts of inspiration. No wonder Frank Lentricchia has turned rhapsodic!

Historically accurate in depicting the defeat of expressivist pedagogy by the 1950s and in anticipating the challenges to institutional authority to come in the next decade, the film nonetheless looks back nostalgically to a time when the most significant debate in literary pedagogy was between whether to read Whitman through the apparatus of New Criticism or to read Whitman as the spontaneous outburst of powerful feelings. At the very time when both formalist and expressivist paradigms are under stress by the forces of multiculturalism, feminism, and poststructuralism, the popularity of Weir's film suggests that we really cannot let that liberal pedagogy pass. That this mundane and predictable film could win such acclaim (its screenplay won an Oscar) suggests to me the public's urgent need to return to the familiarity and safety of that debate in the face of new theories, new literatures, and new demographics that were giving the lie to its appeal. But more than that, the film reveals nostalgia to be the very basis of a liberal education.

This nostalgia (which, Garber points out in "'Greatness'" comes from the Greek *nostos*, return home) explains one of the film's most salient features. The maleness and whiteness of the academy depicted in the film not only dates the story but also serves to delimit the parameters of its pedagogical debate. Significantly, Keating is a product of the academy in which he teaches; the current headmaster taught at the prep school when he was a student there. Although the film portrays Keating as a radical teacher who defies conventions and flaunts decorum, Keating is no outsider to the authority of the institution. He may have his students rip out Prichard's formalist introduction to their poetry textbook, but his pedagogy depends on its canon of texts. (Like Mortimer Adler, whose "Great Books" series was being published in the 1950s, Keating believes that great books need no critical apparatus.) It is not just that the debate represented in the film is between men (women are essentially out of it, appearing only as romantic objects or muses); it is that the debate is hermetic, inbred, attesting to the essentially conservative nature of literary pedagogy no matter how unconventional the methods. As Catherine Belsey wrote in 1980, "Only by closing the doors of the English department against theoretical [and political] challenges from outside can we continue to ignore the 'Copernican' revolution which is currently taking place, and which is radically undermining traditional ways of perceiving both the world and the text" (130).

In the 1960s and 1970s, educational institutions in the United States felt pressure from without, and the demographics as well as the content of the English classroom changed dramatically.[18] By 1989, when *Dead Poets Society* was released, formalism as a mode of criticism was enough a relic of the past that it could be gently satirized as an aging white man in a gray suit. Yet already in 1959, when the film is set, formalism's reign was coming to an end; in 1961, even René Wellek could foresee its inevitable demise (Belsey 20). Outside the hermetically sealed classroom represented in Weir's film, in new social movements in the United States and in the new critical practices in France, the forces of defeat were gathering.

The Copernican revolution Belsey refers to is, of course, the theory—or, more precisely, the structuralist—revolution. As Lacan points out, Freud compared his discovery of the unconscious with the Copernican revolution because it so profoundly altered man's place in the universe ("Insistence" 311). Lacan attributed a "revolution in knowledge" to $\frac{S}{s}$, Saussure's formula for the sign: "No meaning is sustained by anything other than reference to another meaning" (292). Rereading Freud through Saussure in the 1950s, Lacan wrote "What the psychoanalytic experience discovers in the unconscious is the whole structure of language" (289), where language is roughly equivalent with culture.[19] Both Freud and Saussure, structuralists *avant la lettre,* provide a new mode of explanation in terms of the relation among elements in a system rather than in terms of the thing itself. That the unconscious produces effects apart from the conscious intentions of the speaking subject is not the most revolutionary aspect of Freud's theory. Unconscious slips do not reveal the truth about the subject that he would rather keep hidden; rather, the unconscious reveals "the place of the subject in the search for the truth" (Lacan, "Insistence" 299). As Roland Barthes puts it in "Change the Object Itself," an essay on semiology (the science of signs derived from Saussurean linguistics), "the problem is not to reveal the (latent) meaning of an utterance . . . but to fissure the very representation of meaning, . . . to challenge the symbolic itself" (167). Freud displaces the subject from the center of our epistemological and moral universe: where consciousness was, there the unconscious shall be. Revising Freudian theory through Saussurean linguistics, Lacan reformulates Freud's statement: where consciousness was, there language shall be. Language, for Saussure, is a system of differential relations, not a medium of communication. Where "a difference bears meaning for members of a culture," explains Jonathan Culler, there is a sign (63). This, quite simply, explains why the word "race" has been put in quotation marks, most famously by Henry Louis Gates Jr. in his edited collection *"Race," Writing, and Difference.* As a sign, "race" doesn't name any*thing;* it signifies a system of conventional and arbitrary (thus changeable) distinctions.

The revolution produced by structuralism is a shift in the *locus* of explanation, from the nature of the subject or the nature of meaning to the place of the subject or the place of the signifier in a system of differential relations. Derrida asks, "If we refer, once again, to the semiological difference, of what does Saussure, in particular, remind us?" He answers:

That "language [which only consists of differences] is not a function of the speaking subject." This implies that the subject (in its identity with itself, or eventually in its consciousness of its identity with itself, its self-consciousness) is inscribed in language, is a "function" of language, becomes a *speaking* subject only by making its speech conform—even in so-called "creation," or in so-called "transgression"—to the system of the rules of language as a system of differences. ("Différance" 15)[20]

The notion that language precedes us, even speaks us, as Lacan says, has become a critical commonplace. The death of the subject is commonly taught in precisely these terms. But whether we put the cart before the horse or the horse before the cart, we still have a cart and a horse. What often gets elided in these formulations is that we are not simply choosing between two notions of the subject (as the agent of language or its product) or two concepts of language (referential or differential). The conceptual revolution demands a different response and a new responsibility, for the "semiological difference" is an *ethical-political* difference.[21] "The slightest alteration in the relation between man and the signifier, *in this case in the procedures of exegesis*," writes Lacan, "changes the whole course of history by modifying the lines which anchor his being. . . . everything involving not just the human sciences, but the destiny of man, politics, metaphysics, literature, advertising, propaganda, and through these even the economy, everything has been affected" ("Insistence" 321–22; my emphasis). The truth of structualist analysis "demands that we bestir ourselves" (316); it presents us with a moral imperative to give up the subject of metaphysics and Enlightenment humanism that "renders modern man so sure of being himself even in his uncertainties about himself" (311). This is what I mean by "risk." This displacement of the (self-)conscious, autonomous individual disrupts the very economy of the pedagogical exchange, putting us literally and figuratively beside ourselves. "It is not a question of knowing whether I speak of myself in a way that conforms to what I am, but rather of knowing whether I am the same as that of which I speak" (Lacan, "Insistence" 311). "I" am not identical to the identity "I" assume, for identity is a function of differences.

Austin's theory of the performative, developed in his 1955 lectures at Harvard University, has also disrupted the integrity of the subject and profoundly changed contemporary thinking about identity formation. When Austin introduces the category of the performative in *How to Do Things with Words,* he does so to challenge the Descriptive Fallacy, the assumption that the primary function of language is to describe some state of affairs (1). Performatives do something rather than refer to something: "the issuing of the utterance is the performing of an action" (6). Performatives, Austin says, cannot be evaluated in terms of their truth or accuracy; instead, they either succeed or fail. A performative statement like "I now pronounce you man and wife" (Austin's most famous example of the performative) works only because it is a reiteration of what other justices have said. The legal discourse, not the speaker's intentions, give these words their force.

Although a common understanding of performatives is that they bring into being something that does not exist prior to the utterance itself, what

Austin's theory does, far more radically, is to undercut the "solid moralist" who believes that, in Austin's words, "accuracy and morality are alike on the side of the plain saying that *our word is our bond*" (10). To reiterate my point in my prefacing remarks, Austin's performative decouples the copula, for a performative statement does not belong to the speaker. A performative act, like promising, does not refer to or express some idea in the speaker's head but is accomplished in the words themselves uttered within certain circumstances. By introducing a category of statements that are not capable of being evaluated in terms of truth or accuracy (what Austin terms the true/false fetish of the Descriptive Fallacy), and then suggesting that all speech acts, insofar as they are conventional, are performatives, Austin drives a wedge between word and bond, undercutting our tendency to attribute positions to the speaker alone and thwarting our desire for a guarantee that the speaker means what she or he says. The necessary connection between word and bond (between truth and fidelity to the thing itself, between accuracy and morality) can no longer be assumed—not because there is nothing against which to measure the truth or falsity of a statement, but because assessing the truth or falsity of a statement can never be done "outside" the performative dimension of language.[22]

This is Derrida's point in his essay on Austin cited earlier. Derived from Austin's performative, Derrida's concept of iterability (a sign can carry meaning only by being reiterated, thereby calling into question the notion of an original presence or meaning) opens a space of mediation between the person of the author and the one who signs the text and thus takes responsibility for it. Where Austin tries to set aside special instances in which performatives are merely being cited, not performed (as when an actor speaks the line "I now pronounce you husband and wife" on stage, for example), Derrida recognizes citationality as that which makes the performative possible. "Iterability" is the necessary repetition that makes any sign recognizable *as* a sign.[23] The possibility of being repeated or cited is not something that befalls an utterance; rather, it is the condition that defines any utterance or sign, including the sign of the writer, the pronoun "I" or the signature. By virtue of his definition, Austin makes citationality intrinsic to the functioning of the performative. "I now pronounce you husband and wife" would mean nothing if spoken only once. As Derrida recognizes, Austin's performative challenges the concept of speech and writing as the "'communication of consciousnesses'" (*Limited Inc.* 20), the transference of meaning, every bit as much as Saussure's sign.

Although the New Criticism also rejected the Descriptive Fallacy along with the Intentionalist Fallacy, and shared with Derrida the notion that "Writing is 'read,' it is not the site . . . of . . . the decoding of a meaning or truth" (*Limited Inc.* 21) that exists prior to the act of writing, it did not disrupt the integrity of the subject. Its scrutiny of the formal properties of the poem discloses "the moral quality of the meaning expressed by the poem itself" (Wimsatt, qtd. in Belsey 18). Language, for New Critics, may not convey a meaning apart from the poem itself, but language still serves to bond word and meaning, the poem and its truth. The guarantee of meaning keeps the integrity of the subject (the poem, the poet, the critic) intact. In post-Saussurean linguistics, "what is put into question is precisely the quest for a rightful beginning, an absolute point of departure, a principal responsibility" (Derrida, "Différance" 6). What is irresponsible in this view is not the dislodging of language from the writer's conscious control but the failure to pursue the implications of such a loss.

Foucault pursues this ethical difference in "What Is an Author?" which ends with the well-known question, "What difference does it make who's speaking?" Often read as saying it makes no difference who's speaking, Foucault's question differs subtly but significantly from the modernist-formalist question with which he begins his essay, "What does it matter who's speaking?"—a question he attributes to Beckett. In that indifference to who's speaking, says Foucault, "appears one of the fundamental ethical principles of contemporary writing" (141), an ethics "immanent" in formalism insofar as it eliminates the author as individual from analysis of the work or text and thus "has freed itself from the dimension of expression" (142). Yet, Foucault argues, formalism preserves the "privileges of the author" by relocating the site of its authority in the "work" or "writing" itself.[24] He locates meaning and value not in some entity (the writer, the text, the reading) but in the dynamics of an economic system: "These aspects of an individual which we designate as making him an author [such as possessing "a 'deep' motive, a 'creative' power, or a 'design'"] are only a projection . . . of the operations that we force texts to undergo, the connections that we make, the traits that we establish as pertinent, the continuities we recognize, or the exclusions that we practice" ("What Is" 150). "In short," Foucault says, "it's a matter of depriving the subject (or its substitute) of its role as originator, and of analyzing the subject as a variable and complex function of discourse" (158). Rejecting formalism along with expressivism, Foucault's question implies a different ethics than Beckett's. "What difference does it make who's speaking?" insists on the difference without presupposing that the difference resides in the author, whose name refers to some "real and exterior individual" who produced the text (147). "Who speaks?" matters once again, but its significance is neither personal (as in expressivism) nor impersonal (as in formalism); rather, it is structural, relational not referential.

If all this is what we mean by the death of the subject, if theory *is* responsible for its demise, I would respond, citing Foucault, that "it is not enough to repeat the empty affirmation that the [subject] has disappeared. . . . we must locate the space left empty by the [subject's] disappearance" ("What Is" 145). Coming into the academy at the same time various studies programs were being justified in terms of expressivist pedagogy, structuralist and post-structuralist theory came to occupy the place of the New Criticism, both conceptually and pedagogically. Conceptually, theory was accused of depersonalizing the subject as formalism had, making language primary and ignoring experience. Pedagogically, theory courses came to be taught like methods courses, through casebooks providing different theoretical readings of the same text and through textbooks that reduced each theory to a set of axioms. Theory is commonly taught, sometimes even read, but its ethical implications—and what it means for the pedagogical relation itself—have generally been considered suspect rather than pursued.

Despite new theories and new modes of explanation, the tension between formalist and expressivist *pedagogies* has continued to structure debates in literary studies, though now focused less on the content of the canon than on the status of the profession.[25] That debate has long been a productive one, enabling us to go on professing literature not *despite* the conflict between a liberation politics and a New Critical formalism but *because* of it. Displace that conflict from the object of study (the literary text or the critical methodology) to the subject who studies it (the professor or student) and pedagogy loses its basis of support in a notion of the subject as tourist, whether that notion conveys a sense of estrangement or entitlement. Yet as teachers we are loathe to give it up.

This continued interest in maintaining an expressivist pedagogy is apparent even in the writings of those most responsible for undermining it. In the introduction to *Tendencies,* for example, Sedgwick discusses a course in gay/lesbian studies that she designed with gay and lesbian students in mind, hoping that "the course material would address them where they live" (4), would "hit home," so to speak. In making her intended audience explicit, Sedgwick outraged many nongay students who felt entitled to study this literature despite their sexuality. The controversy was not, as before, over the material being taught but over who had a right to study that material. This is a significant change, a consequence of the co-institutionalization of theory and diversity that we have been exploring here. Sedgwick's response to her students' outburst makes explicit the assumptions undergirding these students' notion of literary studies through the analogy of tourism:

> Their sense of entitlement as straight-defined students was so strong that they considered it an inalienable right to have all kinds of different lives, histories, cultures unfolded as if anthropologically in formats specifically designed—designed from the ground up—for maximum legibility to themselves: they felt they shouldn't so much as have to slow down the Mercedes to read the historical markers on the battlefield. That it was a field where the actual survival of other people in the class might at the very moment be at stake—where, indeed, in a variety of ways so might their own be—was hard to make notable to them among the permitted assumptions of their liberal arts education. (*Tendencies* 5)

Sedgwick's analogy may erroneously posit a class divide between the straight-identified and gay-identified students at Amherst, where the straight students are the moneyed imperialists and the gay students the impoverished natives, yet the reference to the Mercedes and the battlefield markers serves to emphasize the extent to which the structure of tourism continues to define literary pedagogy, even for a poststructuralist theorist like Sedgwick. She rightly links the straight-identified students' sense of entitlement to the assumptions of a liberal arts education; however, the assumptions behind her own teaching play out a related aspect of that liberal model: the notion that their experiences entitle the gay-identified students to claim this literature as their own. The tourist metaphor depends on a territorial concept of literature with a division between insider and outsider. Although Sedgwick insists that gay studies may be as essential to the survival of nongay students as it is to the survival of gay students, the structure she sets up would position the nongay student as the tourist or ethnographer who stands apart and witnesses other peoples and cultures to gain personally from that experience with little personal risk.[26] The quality of risk surrounds the literature classroom like a ditch; we are still teaching in the trenches.

Indeed, the subject of traditional pedagogy is becoming all the more entrenched despite theories of its displacement. The debates now being waged in the academy are no longer between critical methods but between persons and their social, cultural, and institutional positions; no longer over the content of our pedagogies but over the very possibility of pedagogy and thus over the survival of our profession. Writing on pedagogy has moved from how to teach what to who can teach whom. The profession itself is facing an identity crisis. Yet it is not because we have gotten off the track, distracted from our professional work by our politics; rather, it is because the convergence of theory and diversity has in effect deconstructed the grounds of our literary pedagogies, leaving us with literally no place to which we can return—which characterizes the experience I call "passing." The deconstruction of the subject of liberal education marks the site where passing enters pedagogy. To take seriously the challenge posed by the convergence of (post)structuralism and multiculturalism would mean learning to teach beside—even despite—ourselves. While the day of high theory may indeed be passing, theory has made the inevitability of passing visible, and that illumination is not going to pass. There's no going back.

Teaching beside Ourselves

> In the teaching situation, nobody should anywhere be in his place.
> —Roland Barthes, "Writers, Intellectuals, Teachers"

It is one thing to theorize the subject's displacement and another to experience it. As far as pedagogy is concerned, that experience of being nonidentical with oneself has come about with the diversifying of the academy, among other social and cultural changes we have come to associate with postmodernity. Today the subject-as-tourist central to liberal education and at the heart of these debates over the profession has been decentered, displaced, and decultured, essentially rendered homeless, not just by poststructuralist theories, but in postmodern culture as well. The various demographic, cultural, economic, and technological changes over the past three decades summed up by the shorthand "postmodernity" have had a profound effect on how we experience and think about identity. As a result of such displacement, nomadism has become a more compelling metaphor for our postmodern era than tourism. While one strain of postmodernism invokes tourism to conceptualize the notion that the real has been replaced by the simulacrum (the tourist as the Baudrillardian traveler in America), others offer the nomad as a new metaphor for the subject, insofar as the subject in poststructuralist theory and postmodern culture is conceived as continually displaced and relocated. Where the tourist is at home somewhere, or everywhere, the nomad is at home in no *one* place. In contemporary discourses such as Deleuze and Guattari's *Thousand Plateaus,* Lyotard's *Pacific Wall,* and Braidotti's *Nomadic Subjects,* the metaphor serves to reimagine the contours of personal and social space and to produce new sites of subjectivity and new forms of identity and identification.[27] Nomadism in these writings suggests the situ-

ation of everyone in a world so diverse and destabilized that no one is anywhere in his or her rightful place. "Marginality," writes Michel de Certeau
in *The Practice of Everyday Life*, "is today no longer limited to minority
groups, but is rather massive and pervasive" (xvii). Certeau's statement characterizes the social and psychic condition of postmodernity, a shared sense
of displacement and dislocation often attributed to the rapid technological,
economic, social, and cultural changes that have taken place over the past few
decades. In *Yearning,* hooks echoes Certeau's remark: "The overall impact of
postmodernism is that many other groups now share with black folks a sense
of deep alienation, despair, uncertainty, loss of a sense of grounding even if
it is not informed by shared circumstance" (27).[28]

One consequence of this constant displacement is that displacement has
become not just a shared condition but a value. As the epigraph from Barthes
attests, it is good *not* to be in one's place, whether in one's classroom or in
one's writing. In "Writers, Intellectuals, Teachers," Barthes is "comforted"
by this constant displacement: "were I to *find my place,* I would not even go
on pretending to teach" (*Image/Music/Text* 206). Spivak literalizes the metaphor when she refuses the seat at the seminar table that her students always
leave open for her (*In Other Worlds* 98). Ironically and oxymoronically, displacement becomes a *privileged position* as well as a dominant trope in postmodern discourses.

Yet, as Caren Kaplan argues in *Questions of Travel,* "displacement is not
universally available or desirable for many subjects, nor is it evenly experienced" (1). Displacement functions as a psychological and aesthetic experience for some, as a collective historical experience for others (4, 28). Thus,
"simply destabilizing the notion of home [or of the subject]," Kaplan insists,
"can no longer answer the historical question of accountability" (7). Far from
resolving the problem discussed in the previous section by providing an alternative to the subject of liberal education, the metaphor of the nomad
merely displaces the problem.

For psychoanalytic and deconstructive theorists, as we have seen, the
subject's displacement comes about through the effects of language and the
unconscious. One of Freud's laws of the unconscious, displacement (the
process that transcribes the latent content of the dream into its manifest
content through a series of substitutions) names the effect produced by language and desire in the constitution of the subject. Structures of representations and processes of identification are not expressive of individual attitudes
and positions but constitutive of the subject itself, its desires and drives.
"Identification," writes Diana Fuss, "is the point where the psychical/social
distinction becomes impossibly confused and finally untenable" (*Identifica-*

tion 11). Lacan's famous anecdote of the boy and girl on the train illustrates not only the sliding of the signified under the signifier but the importance of how one is positioned in language, the place from which one speaks ("Insistence" 294–95). In Seminar 20 Lacan writes, "The question, first and foremost, for each subject, is how to situate *the place from which he himself addresses* the subject presumed to know" (qtd. in Felman, "Psychoanalysis" 35). Yet that place can never be fixed or located in that the subject is constituted by the effects of splitting. The dynamic of the unconscious lies not in the self but in the space between self and other (Kearney 260). Thus Lacan rewrites Descartes's cogito: "I think where I am not, therefore I am where I do not think" ("Insistence" 312).

Thinking in terms of place in a structure works against the tendency of subjects like "I" and "you" to solidify, says Fuss ("Reading" 105); these pronouns signify structural positions rather than identify personal referents. Identity and difference, self and other, are "structure[s] of address"; no one (no "one") is free of the dynamics of exchange (Felman, "Psychoanalysis" 35). In the saying, "It's a black thing, you wouldn't understand," "you" is structurally, not essentially, white. The structure of address creates the illusion of mastery and authority that supposedly belongs by rights to the speaker. This does not mean that the speaker's interlocutor isn't really white; rather, to paraphrase Gates, you can believe the speaker is white without believing that white is something you can be ("White like Me" 78).

In various postcolonial and black cultural theories, displacement comes about through the historical experience of diaspora. Displacement in these theories is at once a reponse to the experience of rootlessness that marks the history of certain groups and that forms the basis of a new politics of alliance, and a response to interrogations of Western imperialism and Enlightenment discourse that historically constitute the subject as autonomous, unified, fixed, and freely choosing. For example, in his chapter on W. E. B. Du Bois in *The Black Atlantic,* Gilroy contends that homelessness and enforced exile are repossessed by black cultural critics and political theorists, "reconstructed as the basis of a privileged standpoint" (111). "DuBois's concern with the value of movement, relocation, and displacement," argues Gilroy, leads to his resistance to any essentialist understanding of the racial self and to his effort to escape "from the closed codes of *any* constricting or absolutist understanding of ethnicity" (138).

At the same time that various psychoanalytic, deconstructive, and cultural theories are shifting the focus of literary studies from "empathy" (liberalism) to "signification" (structuralism) to "identification" and "representation" (poststructuralism and multiculturalism), so that reading literature is no longer a safe participation in otherness but a way of understanding the very cultural formation of self and other, the changing demographics of the academy are making identification and representation political, not just aesthetic or theoretical, issues. In the 1970s and 1980s, the institutionalization of poststructuralist theory and multiculturalism brought the two notions of displacement into contact and into conflict. A theory of displacement came to require a politics of location. "The location and situation of the critic become crucial factors in the politics of theoretical production," Caren Kaplan writes (96). A "politics of location" (a term Adrienne Rich coined in the 1980s) seeks to make us accountable for what we say and thus, in Donna Haraway's words, "answerable for what we learn how to see" ("Situated Knowledges" 583). In her 1988 article, Haraway attempts to reconcile the kind of claims made by the standpoint theory Gilroy invokes—that incorporating the experiences and knowledges of others can produce more faithful accounts of the real—and the kinds of claims made by poststructuralist theories—that knowledge is always mediated, never guaranteed by reference to an extradiscursive reality. "The issue," she argues, "is one of ethics and politics perhaps more than epistemology" (579). Haraway insists that ethics and politics are the grounds of knowledge, or, rather, what passes as knowledge; that "moral and political discourse" should be the paradigm for epistemology (587). She understands all knowledge claims as "situated knowledges" or partial perspectives (581), thereby reversing "commonsense" notions of responsibility: irresponsible practices are ones that are *not* located or locatable, while specific and partial knowledge is responsible because it can be "called into account" (583, 589). Whereas the more traditional notion of objectivity emphasizes the need for "distance" if one is to act responsibly, Haraway's notion insists on being accountable for what and how we claim to know. As opposed to the view from nowhere that has traditionally defined objectivity in both science and ethics, Haraway's view from somewhere insists "*metaphorically* on the particularity and embodiment of all vision" (582; my emphasis).[29]

Such attention to the positionality of the one who writes or speaks has been crucial for understanding the imperialism of impersonal modes of criticism. Yet attention to positionality has also had the effect of making us account for ourselves in such personal ways that the position begins to slide into the person; the emphasis on metaphor in Haraway's argument gets lost. The more we feel under siege and vulnerable to criticism, and critique, the more we feel a need to account for ourselves as persons, to fall back on a notion of the person that post-Saussurean theories have already rendered untenable and to leave behind the notion of mediation central to the writings of poststructuralist theorists who have been so instrumental in the displacement of that subject. The historic conjunction of theory courses and studies programs threatens to resuscitate that humanist subject as a defense against the slippage between the "I" who writes and the "I" who is the subject of the writing.

The space created by the subject's displacement, what I call "passing," emerges in the difference between Sontag writing about "camp" and Sedgwick writing about the closet, between Barthes's semiology and Krupat's ethnocriticism. While the cultural criticism of Barthes and Sontag has contributed significantly to that practiced by Sedgwick and Krupat, Barthes and Sontag write without the anxiety that their subject position is implicated in what they write about. There is some safety in writing that is not perceived to be personal. The kind of slippage I identify as inevitable in passing is missing in these precursors. For how can you slip when what you are writing about has nothing to do with you personally? Sontag may claim to be personally attracted to camp, Barthes may project himself into his subjects, as Sontag says (443), but both are still writing about the other as a cultural double or metaphor, a literary device that recognizes mediation. When Sontag identifies camp with a gay subculture, she does not question her right to say this. When, at the opening of "The Death of the Author" (*Image/Music/Text*) Barthes quotes a passage from Balzac's "Sarrasine" and asks, "Who speaks thus?" that question, so central to contemporary cultural criticism, is still for Barthes one of mediation (Where do the writer's notions of femininity come from?) not identification (Who am I or who is Balzac to write about "woman"?). That "who" in "Who speaks thus?" opens up a rhetorical space to be explored; it does not refer to a preexisting subject. That is the point of Barthes's death of the author. The death of the author as a subject who exists prior to the writing and uses writing as a medium through which to communicate his or her experience gives way to the notion of writing as the performance of identity and the writer as coming into being with the act of writing. Writing within a traditional model of the cultural critic, these poststructuralist critics assume their distance from the other; contemporary cultural critics, in contrast, identify with the other and as a result write about the self.[30] In continually assessing its own interventionist potential, cultural studies, as Louis Simon put it, "serves as a mirror in which academics can examine themselves and their own social and political status" so that "recent American manifestations of [cultural studies] tell us more about the identity dilemma confronting intellectuals in the wake of poststructuralism and late capitalist postmodernism than about the 'culture' these writers analyze and examine."[31] That identity dilemma opened up by the historical convergence of theory and diversity within the academy is central to the phenomenon I term "passing." Rather than serving as another metaphor for the self, passing in this book figures the dynamics of that responsibility in terms of actual relationships. Passing is the effect of *institutional,* not just attitudinal or theoretical, change.

Theories of displacement, even or especially when coupled with a desire to displace one's own position and authority, can reproduce the experience of tourism, as hooks argues when she says that scholarship on African American culture by whites can treat that culture as if "it exists solely to suggest new aesthetic and political directions white folks might move in . . . seeing African-American culture as 'the starting point for white self-criticism'" (*Yearning* 21). Similarly, many feminists have critiqued the way male theorists move into the feminine position as a way of refiguring themselves, the way their writing may be "performatively feminine but politically masculine" (Morgan 6).[32] How different is this from Erich Auerbach's or David Denby's welcoming of Virginia Woolf's "feminine" (Auerbach) and "feminist" (Denby) writing into the canon of texts that attest to "the elementary things which men in general have in common" (Auerbach 552)?[33] When does the imperative to unlearn our own forms of privilege and to risk ourselves change the very nature of what we think we know (B. Johnson, *World*) and make us accountable for our ways of knowing (Haraway, "Situated"), and when does it reveal our desire for a "safe" participation in otherness, our willingness to risk ourselves only in the security of our privileged locations? That is the always slippery difference we can never know in advance.

Too often we feel we must answer this normative question before we can responsibly participate in a cultural criticism that demands to be taken personally. I am suggesting that responsibility lies neither solely in the subject position from which we speak nor in the subject position we would assume in speaking but in the positions we put into play in our teaching and writing. Any notion of the subject, whether displaced or located, rational or split, any notion of literature, whether expressive or formalist, as work or text, can relieve one of the responsibility that *is* pedagogy. In the rush to defend ourselves against accusations leveled by others, in the rush to formulate the consequences of theory for pedagogy, what gets lost is precisely the notion of pedagogy as the dynamics of responsibility. "We have . . . often engaged in a kind of 'position-taking' in which one defends against the claims of the other and refuses to learn what is at stake in the making of the claim," writes Butler ("Careful Reading" 128). Pedagogy is the site where we are confronted with the stakes of our claims. Passing in pedagogy recognizes that slippage as inevitable. In response to those who blame theory for destroying the grounds for methodological debate by rejecting normative criteria (nonarbitrary arbiters), in response to those who ask rhetorically how one can ground a pedagogy in difference, indeterminacy, undecidability, desire, differends, and performativity (to name the most familiar concepts of poststructuralist and postmodernist theories)—in short, in response to those who believe theory can never inform pedagogy without disastrous consequences—I would say that pedagogy is precisely the arena in which such theory can have public relevance.[34]

Taking Pedagogy Personally

> Our practice in the classroom doesn't often come very close
> to instantiating the values we preach.
> —Jane Tompkins, "Pedagogy of the Distressed"

Literary studies today is something we cannot help but take personally. The turn to pedagogy in literary and cultural studies, as Lynn Worsham has argued in "Emotion and Pedagogic Violence," is in part a response to the failure of various linguistic and cultural theories to seriously confront the ethical and political consequences of postmodernism. Given that ethics and politics are manifest in actions, in what we do, pedagogy has become both the site of and model for the ethical relation. Pedagogy—broadly conceived as dynamic interactions with others in actual face-to-face relationships—is precisely the means by which we travel our theories in person. In the pedagogical exchange, as one of my friends so baldly puts it, our faces are hanging out there. The personal cannot dissolve into the abstract idealism of either the universal reader or the constituted subject.

The turn to pedagogy is an effort to work through the ethics and politics of poststructuralist theories, and yet what ethics and politics are seen to demand (specifically, a bond between word and bond) comes into conflict with those theories. In making a case for the ethics and politics of so-called radical theory, we often fall back on notions of language and the subject that we have called into question (for example, in personal narratives meant to validate our integrity) or continually reiterate the point that identities are constructed in the disciplinary (and disciplining) structures of the academy. The problem with the second response is that it leaves us at an impasse, continually explaining but not enabling subject positions. The problem with the first response is the difficulty of resisting, in Linda Kauffman's words, "the temptation to view the personal as inherently paradigmatic, the individual . . . story as coherent, unified, morally inspiring" (133). The turn to pedagogy and to the personal reveals a desire for a mode of writing that will heal the split between linguistic and materialist theories, between a rhetorical analysis of symbolic systems and a materialist analysis of everyday life. It thus belies, as Kauffman says, "a nostalgia for a clear, transparent language," for "integration and unity," thereby ignoring the ways in which "we are always *beside ourselves*" (137–38).

Both the possibilities for pedagogy opened up by taking pedagogy personally and the risk of losing sight of those possibilities in the rush to the personal were brought home to me at a conference sponsored by the Center for Twentieth-Century Studies at the University of Wisconsin at Milwaukee in April 1993, entitled "Pedagogy: The Question of the Personal." It soon became apparent to many of us present that the "personal" in pedagogy was understood by the presenters to be a matter of performance (mediation). That the personal should be seen in this way is not surprising given that Jane Gallop, the conference organizer, had recently published an essay, "Knot a Love Story," in which she conceptualized "pedagogical positions as drag performance" (217). The moment that emblematized the conference as a performance of the personal occurred on the morning of the second day, when Madeleine Grumet presented her paper, "*Scholae Personae:* Masks for Meaning." Confronting, as did so many presenters, her resistance to "the personal," Grumet moved into that risky subject by talking about something she would rather not make public: the green robe she wears to write. "When I think about the personal, I think about my green robe. . . . When I think about [my green robe] I remember my body. . . . It is a robe I write in, not about. It is strange to see it move into the yellow letters on my screen. It is my robe, it has my smell, and as I present it to you, it becomes my costume" (36). At a signal from Grumet, Kathleen Woodward pulled the green robe out of a bag and displayed it on stage. At that moment, the auditorium was turned into a gigantic closet. After that, everyone could be read as "coming out." The personal became a matter of passing.[35]

I was not too surprised, then, though rather amused, when two years later a copy of the conference collection appeared with the title changed to *Pedagogy: The Question of Impersonation.* What did surprise me, though, were the double introductory narratives felt necessary to explain that change. Both the preface, written by one of Gallop's students, David Crane, and the introduction by Gallop tell the story of how "the personal" became "impersonation." Both stage the personal in pedagogy as a performance: Crane performs the classic role of the brown-noser who desires to please the teacher; Gallop concedes that as a teacher she plays to the students, trying to please them. In each narrative, the "narrative dyad" of teacher-student is "constitutive of the present attempt to think pedagogy at the place where the personal becomes impersonation" (Gallop, *Pedagogy* 2).

These introductory narratives suggest that the personal *became* impersonation at some point. Yet Gallop writes, "When the personal appears, it is always as a result of a process of im-personation, a process of performing the personal for a public" (*Pedagogy* 9), which is precisely what the presenters did. Defining "impersonation" as the act of performing as someone else and "im-personation" as the act of "appearing as a person" (9), Gallop suggests that the personal in pedagogy is always already an im-personation. Her reading of the conference papers persistently reveals the moment when the opposition between the two, between performing and appearing (between performance and performativity), breaks down. The moment when there is a hesitation (rather than an opposition) between the personal as authentic and the impersonation as fraudulent opens up the possibilities for what I call "passing." Any position is divided against itself as soon as it is presented, so that the pedagogical performance itself initiates an identity crisis, exposing the difference within the signification of any position (Cornell, *Beyond* 108). In other words, the personal, once represented, is always mediated. Even one's own person must be performed through discourses that define the terms of one's self-recognition.

So if the personal didn't exactly become im-personation at some point in the conference but was already understood as such, already divided against itself (as the hyphen in "im-personation" suggests) as soon as the first person appeared, what, then, is the point of these introductory narratives meant to explain the change in title? Why put that explanation in the form of personal stories? These stories give the conference a narrative coherence, not simply a theoretical one; they show that the personal (a question, after all, in the original conference title) emerges in a series of events rather than initiating that series. In other words, it seems one point of getting personal is to explain performativity.

Gallop uses Susan Miller's paper, which concluded the conference, to explain this theory. Miller's paper, as Gallop says, "turned on [the personal] and denounced it as a sham" (*Pedagogy* 13). (*Webster's Ninth Collegiate* defines sham as "a decorative piece of cloth made to simulate an article of personal linen and used in place of it," a "cheap falseness," a word choice that recalls Grumet's synthetic green robe that first exposed the personal to be a performance. Thus, Miller's denunciation of the personal comes as no revelation, for precisely the effect, if not the point, of the conference was to expose the personal as a sham.) Gallop distinguishes between Miller's understanding of performance as role playing and her own understanding of performance as im-personation. "Miller's critique [of the personal] presupposes a restricted and voluntaristic understanding of performance," Gallop writes (*Pedagogy* 15). Gallop quotes Butler to explain her different position: "'There is no volitional subject behind the mime who decides, as it were, which gender it will be today. . . . gender is not a performance that a prior subject elects to do, but gender is *performative*'" ("Imitation" 23–24, qtd. in *Pedagogy* 15). Significant to Gallop's purpose here is the shift that occurs in Butler's rhetoric of performativity in her more recent work, *Bodies That Matter*. In chapter 8, Butler clarifies her concept of performativity by switching metaphors, from gender as drag performance to gender as an assignment. "To the extent that gender is an assignment," she writes, "it is an assignment which is never quite carried out according to expectation, whose addressee never quite inhabits the ideal s/he is compelled to approximate" (231). The notion of gender—or race or sexuality—as an *assignment* rather than a performance makes the assumption of gender and racial identity a matter of *passing* and serves to reinforce my argument for the relation between passing as an academic event and passing as a social practice. If the assignment of identity is never fully carried out, then the question is not, How do we know when one has passed? (a normative question) but rather, What can it mean to pass? (an ethico-political question). What subject positions, if any, are available in the dynamics of passing? Passing, in this sense, is not the end but the very possibility of pedagogy.

Gallop's theory of im-personation calls into question the referentiality of the pronoun "I"; it confounds the opposition between the real thing and the fraud; and, it recognizes that psycholinguistic issues of fantasy, desire, and identification cannot be separated from disciplinary issues of reading, writing, and teaching. This understanding also motivates my use of "passing." However, I would push the ethical implications of performativity beyond the conventional morality of Gallop's introduction.

Gallop's claim to end the volume with Miller's paper because it presents a challenge to her own position is a common pedagogical tactic to create the illusion of objectivity and fairness. By ending with Miller, Gallop wants to take seriously "the gloomier side" of impersonation conceived as "motivated deception and exploitative strategy" (*Pedagogy* 14) that Miller's paper presents. Yet here we can see one ethical consequence of Gallop's theories. Miller's position cannot be taken seriously in the way Gallop professes to do without relying on the very logic of identity that Gallop's own writing resists. According to Gallop's theory of performativity, there would be no "gloomier side" to impersonation because there would be no prior subject to willfully engage in a fraudulent performance or strategic exploitation. To take Miller seriously would require a different logic from the one that structures Gallop's concession at the end.

The very narratives Gallop and Crane have constructed to explain how the personal became impersonation are themselves complicit with a certain "pedagogical moral technology" (S. Miller 162). Insofar as Miller's paper, in Gallop's words, "demonstrates . . . how 'personal' relations between teachers and students have historically been recommended as a mechanism of regulation" (*Pedagogy* 13), the point is not simply that the personal is a sham but that stories of the personal, whatever concept of the person we are working with, repeat the strategies of regulation we would resist by getting personal, and mask the mechanism of control that structures personal relations in pedagogy.[36] Performing the personal is no less a "pedagogical moral technology" than the impersonal, authoritative pedagogy it would resist. Gallop neatly turns Miller's challenge into a conflict between two concepts of the subject, the volitional and the performative, and thus turns from the ethical argument implicit in such challenges to performativity.

Gallop's last paragraph effectively forecloses on the ethical possibilities opened up by her concept of im-personation: "When I changed the book's title from 'the personal' to 'impersonation,' it was not to leave the personal behind" (17). How, I wonder, can you leave behind that which was never "there" before? Sensitive to the criticism that performativity, like some con artist's shell game, gets rid of the person(al), Gallop suppresses her ability to enjoy and to act on what she has so eloquently theorized in her writings: that the personal *in public* is already so highly mediated that it never appears as such. Her unwillingness to leave the personal behind implicitly concedes that performativity may do just that and allows her a safe place to return when things get messy, as they inevitably do in real life. After all, there is a certain safety in being yourself, even or especially when the personal is the persona of the bad girl. Gallop's concession here is another instance of the slippage I conceptualize through passing, the slippage that was performed again and again throughout the conference, the slippage that belies the public relevance of performative theory. That slippage is evident in Gallop's characterization of the pedagogical relation as the site where the personal becomes impersonation for the very notion of the personal *becoming* impersonation at some point implies some prior moment when the personal was something other than a performance. That slippage leads to the anxiety associated with impersonation, the fear of being a fraud (a real brown-noser, a *really* bad teacher), the fear that a risky practice may be merely risqué. Both her concession at the end and her concession to Miller signify a failure to take responsibility for the *practice* of im-personation by falling back on the personal. It is another instance of what I have called in chapter 1 the "caveat syndrome."

It is hard to resist reinvoking a certain notion of the personal precisely because the binary logic of inside/outside, embodied/disembodied has structured debates over the very theory meant to resist such a logic, debates that characterize the issue as a conflict between materialist and textualist theories. It is also not surprising that the very philosopher who gave us the concept of the performative should have been responsible for its confusion with performance. Austin's effort to distinguish between genuine (explicit) performatives and mere performances (citations) of the performative is largely responsible for the confusion of these terms. A contiguity (the two terms being brought together in Austin's writing) slides into a similarity; performance becomes a metaphor for performativity. My concept of passing is an effort to exploit this inevitable slippage. The distinctions we make for purposes of analysis—for instance, between the personal (expressivism), the impersonal (formalism), and the im-personation (performativity)—are, in actuality, not as separate as we would like to think. Slippage means that you cannot isolate any pure state. "A successful performative is necessarily an 'impure' performative," Derrida writes in "SEC" (*Limited Inc.* 17). Falling back on a concept of the personal or positional, whatever concept we uphold, can never save us from the slippage, can never guarantee that we won't, or that we will, pass.

I want to make it clear that I am not calling Gallop's theory of im-personation unethical, a cover for her own personal antics. And I am certainly not arguing for the "*intrinsic* amorality of French theory" (Paglia, "Academic Feminists" B4; my emphasis).[37] Indeed, it is the ethics of her position that I am trying to bring out. It has been Gallop's writings that have best enabled me to understand performativity because her writings *perform* the theory and the personal. For instance, what I admire in her book *Reading Lacan* is that she does precisely that: she *reads* Lacan. Although the book is based on her teaching of Lacan, she resists readers' expectations by refusing to present summaries and explanations and instead enacts the difference Lacanian theory makes in her very method of reading, even in the interchapters where she gets personal. Gallop may enrage or discomfort her interlocutors with personal confessions like the one she makes in a conversation with Nancy K. Miller and Marianne Hirsch: "I realize that the set of feelings that I used to have about French men I now have about African-American women. Those are the people I feel inadequate in relation to and try to please in my writing" (Gallop et al. 363). Such a statement, however, is neither perverse nor idiosyncratic but symptomatic of broader institutional and psychopolitical changes. It is so much more honest, in my view, than either the kind of hand-wringing over what to do as a white middle-class woman that informs Nancy K. Miller's response to Gallop (cited in chapter 5) or the kind of pontificating about what we all must do that informs so much cultural criticism in which the critic seems to think the right political disposition will relieve one of the implications of one's subject position, including the structural relation between self and other that is in part constitutive of the problem the critic seeks to resolve. While I argue throughout this book that we need to move from defending certain theoretical positions to taking responsibility for the positions we put into play in our practices, I resist any simple, causal relation between the theory and the practice. A (post)structuralist explanation has no predictive value (cf. Culler 88). It is the belief that we can, and must, find that causal link that leads to such silliness as Reed Way Dasenbrock's claim that the critique of liberal humanism found in poststructuralism (which he believes now dominates the academy) has led to the emergence of Newt Gingrich as a powerful political force (Caughie and Dasenbrock 551).

What I *am* arguing is that in her concession to Susan Miller and in her return to the personal at the end (playing to the students, perhaps), Gallop reneges on the ethical promise of her theory. That slip is not so much a sign of her own moral failure as it is an imperative to locate ethics in the public site of the pedagogical exchange. Another way to read Gallop's point about pedagogy as the site where the personal becomes impersonation is to say that pedagogy is the site where performative theory comes to have public relevance. It is not just the supposed enemy, the one who opposes our theories, that we fear; not the Allan Blooms and William Bennetts, not the residual formalists or the born-again rhapsodists, not the tenured radicals or P.C. advocates. It is ourselves, our posthumous selves, we fear. Like the risk-taker played by Stephen Rea in *The Crying Game* confronting the moment when he sees the penis on the woman he desires, we, as practitioners of a vocation, are retching at the implications of our own desire for the various masquerades we have exposed. It really is not what we expected. The temptation is to cover up the slip, to retreat to the safety of being ourselves. My use of "passing" is not just a matter of introducing or defending a concept of subjectivity; it is a matter of changing a certain pedagogical moral economy.

How this might be done is addressed in subsequent chapters, but let me offer one example here by way of conclusion to this chapter. In a February 1997 *New York Times* article, Margo Jefferson assailed the self-righteous posturing and flagrant self-representations that structured a Town Hall debate, "On Cultural Power," held in Manhattan on 27 January 1997. The event, moderated by Anna Deavere Smith, pitted the lofty impersonality of critic Robert Brustein, performing as the defender of Western culture, against the insistent particularity of playwright August Wilson, speaking as the embodiment of pan-African experience. What was missing, Jefferson laments, was any sense of the productive tension and unease that comes from the sense of not being identical with the position one represents. In contrast, a related discussion on the PBS special "Talk to Me: Americans in Conversation" was more satisfying to Jefferson because its "momentum was all toward intellectual and emotional risks, thinking not pontificating about 'your people' and other people as well." According to her, such risks made the taped special more "real" than the live debate. In closing, Jefferson asks: "When are our public conversations going to start living up to the complexities of actual lives?" (B1–2).

Jefferson acknowledges that in producing "Talk to Me," the director, Andrea Simon, had the advantage of photographs, film clips, music, and "a camera that could move when people's beliefs and imaginations were standing still" (B1–2). The use of such technologies has its own risks, Jefferson concedes, especially insofar as the program creates a seamless movement from analysis to personal testimony, from history to pop culture fantasies, that can suggest a certain glibness. But that technology also served to make the TV production more "real" than the staged debate insofar as it made apparent that the real is always mediated, discursive, whereas the debate gave the illusion of presence, where knowledge and experience are simply, self-evidently embodied. The different genres and media of the two events served to make Jefferson's point that the "how" (the medium) is as important as the "who" (the persons) when representing culture and identity. Simon's production compared with the staged debate shows that the complexities of our actual lives are in part an effect of the lived reality and the imaginative possibilities of new representational technologies and popular culture, an insight that raises pedagogical issues. What is it about the structures of our classrooms or public auditoriums, as well as our concepts of pedagogy, that limits the possibilities of passing—making the kind of performativity we advocate in theory difficult to sustain in practice? One way of changing those physical as well as conceptual structures is for teachers to become producers, not just consumers, of culture, making pedagogy the site and not just the subject of debate so that the subject matter of the course becomes enacted in and through the classroom dynamics, in and through the difficulties, challenges, and contradictions the classroom presents. What is learned is not just new information or new concepts but the *experience* of that new material, the way that material functions as an imperative that changes modes of interaction and thus the sense of ourselves and others.

Writing about her course on testimonies in literary, psychoanalyic, and historical narratives, Shoshana Felman provides an example of teaching as a performative act. Viewing tapes from the Holocaust video archive at Yale University, Felman's students experienced what the writings they had read throughout the course testified to: the loss of connectedness, the "anxiety of fragmentation," and the failure of language coupled with a strong need to speak that is the experience of trauma. Felman draws from this singular event a "generic lesson." "I would venture to propose, today," she writes, "that teaching in itself, teaching as such, takes place precisely only through a crisis: if teaching does not hit upon some sort of crisis . . . it has perhaps *not truly taught*" (Felman and Laub, *Testimony* 53).

In other words, crisis, what we hear so much about in writing on the profession today, is not the end of pedagogy but its condition of possibility. Teaching, Felman continues, must "make something happen." Like psychoanalysis as a clinical practice, teaching "is called upon to be *performative,* and not just *cognitive,* insofar as both strive to produce, and to enable, *change*" and insofar as both are concerned with "the capacity of their recipients to *transform themselves*" (Felman and Laub *Testimony* 53). Here the risks associated with psychoanalysis (Freud's self-analysis serves as a paradigmatic example) and with literature (in the form of testimonies) are extended to pedagogy.

Felman's narrative attempts to make "generic claims" on behalf of personal narratives of classroom experiences. Although pedagogy has long been thought to be precisely the making of generic claims based on particular subject matter and particular experiences, the difference between pedagogy as traditionally conceived and pedagogy conceived as crisis is that the latter has the character of an accident or event, as Felman says. Its outcome or lesson cannot be guaranteed, its methodology cannot be determined in advance. Too often today writing about pedagogy does not take the form of a generic story but remains personal, confessional, where the attention is directed more to the person who performs in the classroom than to the performative event itself, for we still, despite our theorizing against such views, seem to think that knowledge *derives from* experience rather than thinking of knowledge as having something to do with experience and as something to be transformed into an experience.[38] To give pedagogy the character of an event, as Felman urges, is to undermine the classical notion of competence that pedagogy is supposed to impart. "The classical concept of competence," writes Derrida, "supposes that one can rigorously disassociate knowledge (in its act or in its position) from the event that one is dealing with, and especially from the ambiguity of written or oral marks . . ." (*Reader* 580).[39] For all our theorizing, it is hard to resist thinking of teaching as making statements about knowledge and expressing our experience rather than as the medium through which we experience the complex historical, linguistic, and psychopolitical dynamics of knowing. The notion that pedagogy is at risk has led to writing about pedagogy that seeks to contain the risk, saving us from the slip.

The question then is not how to teach and write given the current "crisis of representativity," the danger of "speaking as a," as Nancy K. Miller expresses it in *Getting Personal* (see chapter 1); rather, the question is how to make that crisis something that we experience in our teaching and our writing. How do we give our classrooms the character of an event that allows students to experience what the crisis means in terms of how we act? Far from simply illustrating theoretical concepts, performativity of the kind Felman and Jefferson value offers a resistance to theory as a model that regulates practice and instead allows exposure to the cultural discourses, material practices, and lived realities that those theories attempt to negotiate. We are never going to win the debate over theory and diversity in the terms in which it has been cast (e.g., as a conflict between textualist and materialist approaches, or as a conflict between two concepts of the subject). Theory is not a matter of getting it right but rather, in Fuss's words, "a practice of accountability." "More than a disturbance, theory operates within its institutional confines as something of a pest—a vexing and nagging presence that continually calls one to account. How do we account for theory in the classroom? Perhaps precisely as a practice of accountability, a ceaseless calling to action that takes the form of a communal reckoning" (Fuss, "Accounting" 111). To paraphrase Walter Benjamin, the best theoretical tendency is wrong if it does not demonstrate the attitude with which it is to be followed (306), and that attitude the teacher can best demonstrate through her or his teaching practice.

For a theory to have any relevance, it must institutionalize its ways of proceeding. Yet the kind of performativity I have been discussing here cannot be codified as a model for pedagogy or offered as a solution to a crisis in the profession. It must be enacted. Its different logic, as Barbara Johnson says of supplementarity, cannot be held in the head but must be written or acted out. But there is a risk to performativity in pedagogy not often acknowledged by those (like me) who promote it. If you perform the theory, you risk that your students won't get it, and thus you may be seen to advocate or to inhabit the positions you are putting into play in the classroom. If instead you spell it out, telling the students what it is they should get, your practice goes against the very performativity you want to teach. That is, *you* are the one who doesn't get it. What makes performativity difficult to grasp as a practice or a pedagogy, however, is our insistence on the distinction between practice guided by principle and performance motivated by desire. On the contrary, I would argue that performativity is not opposed to practice but is itself a form of practice guided by the principle that one cannot control the slippage between precisely those concepts that some critics would keep distinct: a libidinal economy and a conceptual economy.

Our ethical failure as literature and composition professors is not to value *in our practice* the relation of subjectivity to practice. We close off the possibility of subjectivity to so many unless we reveal the inevitable absence of a secure position, the dislocation between the speaking subject and the grammatical "I." The kind of pedagogy I elaborate through the metaphor of passing is an effort to exploit, not to master, the slippage between psycholinguistic issues of identity and identification, on the one hand, and disciplinary issues of reading, writing, and teaching, on the other. The ethics of passing has to do with the practice, with the process, of teaching, not solely or even primarily with the question of character or positionality. It is an effort to further, rather than foreclose on, the possibilities opened up by the historical transformations we call postmodernity and the contradictions these have revealed in traditional pedagogies. "Passing" as I use the term seeks to institutionalize those crises as the permanent risk of pedagogy.[40]

Notes

1. Writing on her confrontation with a male student, Gallop explains that "fantasmatic sense of being in a role that was not by rights mine" in terms of gender hierarchy: "Here gender hierarchy crosses pedagogical position: teacher's power runs counter to male prerogative. The contradiction between the two hierarchies destabilizes the positions, makes each position seem, at least in part, playacting" ("Knot" 217, 215). Yet the Gallop epigraph I use to begin this chapter proves to be more complicated than this. Brilliant and campy, Gallop could easily pass as a gay white man in the "homoerotic world" of the academy. The real problem was how to pass as a heterosexual woman in the classroom. See Callahan ("Voice") on "vagabondage."

2. I borrow the heading for this section from Susan Rubin Suleiman's 1994 book on contemporary art and literature, *Risking Who One Is.*

3. Toni Morrison asks this question in relation to writers in *Playing in the Dark* (xi).

4. On Auerbach's *Mimesis* as a "politics of exile" and a "politics of nostalgia," see Garber's brilliant and witty analysis of the ideology of greatness ("'Greatness'"). Garber argues that Auerbach's exile of necessity became "a principle of pedagogy"

for U.S. scholars of the time with the publication of Mortimer Adler's Great Books series in the 1950s. Caren Kaplan associates exile with a modernist "ideology of artistic production," which emphasizes the artist alone, never at home, nostalgic (28).

5. I first encountered the phrase "narrative transvestism" in Marianna Torgovnick's discussion of the writings of D. H. Lawrence, where she uses it to refer to Lawrence's effort to write from a woman's perspective. More recently, in a call for papers, Joe Lockhard defines narrative transvestism as "the conscious authorial alteration of racial, ethnic, or gendered self-representation" (*PMLA*, January 1997: 154).

6. Thus, in *Great Books* David Denby can maintain that the study of literature should be kept separate from political happenings outside the classroom while praising the inclusion of Virginia Woolf in Columbia University's core literature requirement because, he says, Woolf privileges emotion, which has traditionally been excluded by male critics and male culture. I am grateful to Brenda Silver for bringing Denby's reading of Woolf and the canon to my attention in her paper "Retro-Anger and Baby Boomer Nostalgia." See also Peter Rabinowitz's "Against Close Reading" for an analysis of how close reading shores up the assumptions and values of a liberal arts education.

7. Examples of this institutional critique include essays by Barbara Johnson (*Pedagogical Imperative*), Michael Ryan, and Neil Hertz.

8. The crisis or turning point brought about by structuralist and poststructuralist criticism, the radical change these theories brought about in thinking about language, knowledge, and identity, was decisive. On teaching critical methods versus teaching theory, see Caughie and Dasenbrock.

9. See, for example, the March 1997 issue of *PMLA*, the most recent entry in this debate before this manuscript went to press. By "cultural studies" I do not mean a specific movement, such as the Birmingham school, or a specific manifesto, such as Cary Nelson's "Always Already Cultural Studies." Rather, I use "cultural studies" as Isaiah Smithson uses "culture studies" in his introduction to *English Studies/Culture Studies,* to designate less a distinct methodology and critical tradition than the state of the humanities in the aftermath of various theoretical and social upheavals of the past two decades that have had a profound effect on what we do as teachers of literature. In subsequent chapters, I will use "cultural criticism" as well as "cultural studies" to designate this new state of the humanities. I define my use of "cultural criticism" throughout, most explicitly in chapter 4.

10. For a similar argument, see Stanley Fish's op-ed piece on affirmative action, "When Principles Get in the Way." Rajchman sums up this kind of conceptual shift in his closing chapter (see esp. 147).

11. Avrom Fleishman, whose critical and pedagogical philosophy could not be farther from Lauter's concept of critical pedagogy, also holds the view that literary studies should prepare students "to go forth as well-informed participants in a national cultural community" (818), only Fleishman sees the study of diversity distracting from this goal, not contributing to it, as Lauter does.

12. See Carolyn Porter on the coexistence of these two prevailing views.

13. For a discussion of expressive realism and New Criticism, see Catherine Belsey (chap. 1). Others, most recently John Guillory (*Cultural Capital*), have argued that the survival of the profession of literary studies depends on the admission of scholars and texts from previously marginalized social groups, thereby perpetually repro-

ducing the system and assuring its survival. What is less commonly pointed out in writing on the profession (with the exception of Porter) is the codependence of expressivism and formalism often seen to be at odds in the culture wars. The presence of other texts matters little insofar as they become subject to the same process of reading as other great books. Denby justifies Woolf's presence in the core literature course at Columbia in these terms. Yet the inclusion of "other" texts, such as Woolf's, has been undertaken in response to the presence of "other" people, such as women, in the classroom. Expressivism and formalism are mutually sustaining, not competing, pedagogies.

14. See Nicholson's introduction to *Feminism/Postmodernism* for this representation of an argument by Elspeth Probyn.

15. Ironically, despite this warning, Said risks promoting the spectacularization of difference and otherness in *After the Last Sky* by trying to imagine seeing from a female perspective (see Torgovnick 255n35). Such empathetic identification with the feminine is a version of what Torgovnick calls "narrative transvestism."

16. In "Higher Education in the 1990s," Hartman argues that "advocacy teaching," which he seems to equate with teaching for diversity, is distinct from, and hostile to, an ethos of inquiry, which he equates with liberal education based on notions of conversation, tolerance, democratic exchange, freedom, and the pursuit of happiness (729, 730, 733, 739). He argues for teaching the classic or proven works of literature, not because they form a consensus opinion, but because their ethos of inquiry keeps authority hanging in the balance (735). Hartman's defense of an ethos of inquiry (based in liberalism) as existing in the processes of interpretation (that formalism reveals) not only would confine risk taking to the experience of reading but also makes clear the connection between these seemingly competing pedagogies. His commitment to a liberal paradigm is nowhere more apparent than in the question he raises about diversity. "One of the urgent questions for the university in the 1990s must be," he insists, "when does the insistence on ethnicity become productive, and when counterproductive?" (738). A normative question such as this implies we can and should set up standards for deciding between the two. It elides questions of who gets to determine what is productive and what is counterproductive and to say when ethnicity is being insisted on and when it is being evaded.

17. Key works of New Criticism were published in the 1940s and 1950s, including Cleanth Brooks, *The Well Wrought Urn* (1947), W. K. Wimsatt, *The Verbal Icon* (1954), and Northrop Frye, *Anatomy of Criticism* (1957).

18. Granted, U.S. classrooms changed dramatically after World War II as well, as detailed by Gerald Graff in his important book *Professing Literature: An Institutional History.* That diversification had much to do with the institutionalization of a New Critical pedagogy. In contrast, the racial, gender, and ethnic diversification that came in the 1960s and 1970s, and that I am focusing on here, strained that pedagogy to the breaking point.

19. Lacan writes: "the ethnographic duality of nature and culture is giving way to a ternary conception of the human condition: nature, society, and culture, the last term of which could well be equated to language" ("Insistence" 290).

20. "Semiology" sometimes goes by the name "mythology" (as in Barthes's 1957 book by that name), or "ideology" (as in Althusser's writings), or the human sciences (which Foucault defines in *The Order of Things* as the "analysis of unconscious pro-

cesses in terms of rules and signifying systems" [qtd. in Sheridan 84]). Belsey quotes a different version of this passage from "Différance" (59).

21. Spivak, in her reading of *Limited Inc.*, says Derrida calls his critique "ethico-political" rather than "ideological" ("Revolutions" 30). In "The Principle of Reason," Derrida calls for a new responsibility, one that cannot be justified in advance by appeal to principles but can only emerge in practice, by interrogating appeals to the principle of reason (16). Many others have emphasized the ethical implications of semiological or poststructuralist theories. For example, Mark Edmundson points out that what is at stake in Derrida's notion of *différance* are the *values* that ground humanistic practices and the institutions associated with these (628).

22. See Gould for an excellent analysis of Austin's performative. Felman's *Literary Speech Act* also pursues the implications of Austin's performative and its refusal of reference and, like Gould, corrects some misreadings of Austin, including Derrida's. I see Gould and Felman as more in line with Derrida than they may think, especially in the challenge all three pose to "commonsense" readings of Austin that would say, simply, that intention and expression are one and the same thing. See Searle and also Modleski (49–50) for examples of such commonsense readings.

23. "Iterative" in narrative theory refers to a repeated event that is presented only once in a narrative: for example, "he saw her every day" (see Wallace 124–26). Derrida may well have known this term from Gérard Gennette's *Narrative Discourse*. The term suggests a repetition of an act or event that always varies and yet always gives the impression of being the first time. An example of iterative narration occurs in part 3 of Virginia Woolf's *To the Lighthouse*, where Mr. Ramsay's boat trip to the lighthouse with his children, Cam and James, is narrated in the conditional tense: "Now they would sail on for hours like this, and Mr. Ramsay would ask old Macalister a question—about the great storm last winter probably—and old Macalister would answer it, and they would puff their pipes together, and Macalister would take a tarry rope in his fingers, tying or untying some knot, and the boy would fish, and never say a word to any one" (163). The narration suggests this action has occurred before, and yet supposedly this is their first trip to the lighthouse, the deferred fulfillment of the novel's opening promise: "'Yes, of course, if it's fine tomorrow,' said Mrs. Ramsay" (3). The effect created by the iterative is precisely what Derrida elaborates in "SEC": for an event to have significance, it must invoke a prior occasion. There is no first time. This significance is also evident in the use of "iteration" to refer to the choral repetition found in "communal music," such as spirituals. See, for example, James Weldon Johnson's preface to *The Book of American Negro Poetry*.

24. Foucault's critique of formalism is relevant to both New Criticism, with its concept of the "work," and structuralist textualism, with its concept of *écriture*, or "writing." As Gould points out, the notion that words themselves are the locus of authority is how the performative is often misunderstood, as in J. Hillis Miller's formulation: "A true performative brings something into existence that has no basis *except in the words*" (qtd. in Gould 25; my emphasis). Miller's statement shows the link Foucault's critique establishes between a certain version of poststructuralism and New Critical formalism.

25. The uneasy alliance of these views is evident in debates over the effect of theory, multiculturalism, and cultural studies on the teaching of literature. In *Profession 1996*, for example, Charles Muscatine argues that challenges to a literary canon

promoted by Theory (capitalized and singular) provide teachers with "a wider choice of materials and, from works that speak directly to the actual condition of a wide range of students, a chance to make a powerful initial case for the appeal of literature" (118). But Theory also undermines that appeal, according to Muscatine, by its failure to treat literature as a special type of language, dissolving "literature into a great congeries of other 'texts'," and by its failure to treat "our profession or our culture in peacefully unitive, consensual terms" (119). In other words, new literatures are not the problem. It makes little difference that the texts we teach now are different from the ones we taught before as long as the way we teach those texts reinforces the traditional values of a liberal arts education.

26. Lakritz writes: "I feel these suspicions [of those from privileged positions] come from a deep-seated belief that biology and experience are enough (and necessary) to earn authenticity for an individual and that biology and experience are . . . prior to all other forms of identification and identity making" (25). This belief in a primary identity informs the tourist metaphor, whether the tourist signifies the outsider who feels alien to the culture being studied or the imperialist who feels entitled to appropriate any culture. In this sense, Sedgwick's defense of the course seems at odds with what she says about identity and identification in her writings.

27. See Caren Kaplan for a thorough and compelling critique of modernist and postmodernist discourses of tourism, exile, and displacement. She establishes a continuity between tourism and nomadism as metaphors for the creative subject. See especially pages 85–88 on the metaphor of the nomad.

28. That last phrase, "even if . . . ," marks the difference between theories of marginality and postmodernity that begin, as Certeau does, with the general culture and those that begin, as hooks does, with the experiences of specific marginalized groups. That shared sense of marginality can provide "a base for solidarity and coalition," as hooks points out (*Yearning* 27), yet such pervasive marginality also threatens to homogenize social groups in the simulacra of cultural commodities, as Harper (*Framing*) argues.

29. Ironically, while Haraway warns against "romanticizing and/or appropriating" those who have been marginalized or subjugated (583–84), that is precisely what she herself has been accused of doing in "Ecce Homo," where she uses Sojourner Truth to embody a new, "nongeneric" figure of humanity; that is, to figure a postmodern theory of subjectivity. See my discussion of Homans's accusations against Haraway in chapter 5. For a recent discussion of Haraway's essay and her relation to standpoint theory, see Hekman.

30. Dale Bauer defines three modes of identification: as personal recognition ("I am like her"); as political alliance ("I speak for her"); and as rhetorical strategy ("If I were her") (58).

31. I quote with permission from Simon's paper for my 1994 graduate seminar in cultural studies.

32. Barbara Johnson writing on Derrida (*World* 2) and Callahan writing on Rorty ("Critical Personae") have made this point.

33. For a fuller discussion of Auerbach's reading of Woolf's feminine difference, see B. Johnson (*World* 165–66) and Reed (23).

34. For examples of the kinds of arguments against theory that I refer to here, see

Gertrude Himmelfarb, Muscatine, Dasenbrock, and Hartman. Suleiman argues, on the other hand, that we must be able to consider a postmodernist understanding of the self to have public relevance (234). Her discussion of ethical postmodernism is consonant with the argument I make about passing. So too is Fuss's concept of the "double take" used to describe "the intellectual drama of the act [of doing theory] itself": "Where theory does its work is in the temporal oscillation between knowledge and ignorance, belief and doubt, certainty and uncertainty, immediacy and interminability, seeing and knowing" ("Accounting" 110). In pedagogy, that oscillation is not simply an intellectual drama but a somatic, emotional experience.

35. Commenting on the undecidable difference between "playing teacher" and "really teaching," Gallop connects performance with passing: "The fantasmatic sense of being in a role that was not by rights mine made me feel very powerful" ("Knot" 217).

36. This was, in fact, the argument made by a group of students protesting the conference who saw the focus on the personal as a distraction from or coverup for Gallop's pending disciplinary action on charges of sexual harassment. For an extended treatment of Gallop's case and the issue of sexual harassment, see chapter 6.

37. Camille Paglia makes this claim in "Academic Feminists Must Begin to Fulfill Their Noble, Animating Ideal," though I am not sure whether that is a title or a homily. The fact that the article appeared in *The Chronicle of Higher Education* brought home to me the sad reality that academic journals no more than the tabloids can resist stalking those female perversions. Never before has such a vicious, mendacious piece of self-promotion succeeded in passing itself off (to the editors, at least) as a learned and thoughtful essay. Although I share with Paglia the belief that academics have much to learn from popular culture, I'm afraid that what we learn from Paglia are the perils of publicity seeking.

38. On the relation of knowledge to experience, see, for example, Fuss (*Essentially Speaking* chap. 7), hooks (*Teaching* chap. 6), Harding ("Who Knows?"), and Spack.

39. In his paper at the Ninth International James Joyce Symposium, Derrida elaborates the problem by noting the double bind in which Joyce's *Ulysses* puts scholars: the institution promotes the belief in expertise in Joyce scholarship, yet Joyce's writing promotes the aleatory, the "chance encounter of letters and languages," that gives the lie to expertise (Kamuf, in Derrida, *Reader* 570).

40. For arguments related to the one I make here, see Jay (*American*) and Poovey ("Feminism" 50).

Museums Do Have Walls:
A Performative Interlude

> The best political tendency is wrong if it does not demon-
> strate the attitude with which it is to be followed.
> —Walter Benjamin, "The Author as Producer"

The title of this interchapter alludes to André Malraux's 1965 book *Le Musée Imaginaire* (*Museum without Walls*). Malraux draws attention to the vital role "played by the art museum in our approach to works of art today." He writes: "[Museums] were so important to the artistic life of the nineteenth century and are so much a part of our lives today that we forget they have imposed on the spectator a wholly new attitude toward the work of art. They have tended to estrange the works they bring together from their original functions and to transform even portraits into 'pictures'" (9). What at first seems to be a forerunner of today's cultural criticism, presenting as it does a critique of the role of the museum as an institution in the production and preservation of a specifically Western concept of art, turns out to be an argument for art's universality. Malraux posits a museum without walls made possible by new technologies, such as photography, which have made more kinds of art accessible to larger numbers of people in a shorter space of time. In the age of mechanical reproduction, artists are no longer dependent on "techniques of illusion" and thus are freer to concentrate on art as form. The museum without walls is an ideal museum, where each artwork speaks to all others rather than representing a particular time and culture, speaks *to* us in the language of music, not *of* something in the language of representation. Far from doing away with high culture (as so many readers feared) by breaking down the museum walls and democratizing standards of taste, in a sense giving a free pass to everyone, Malraux's book turns the world into a museum that assures the universality of Art conceived as form. Thus, as a critique of the notion of unmediated art Malraux's book doesn't go far enough—or rather, it goes too far in positing a museum without walls where Art speaks for itself. In the end, the book is not about the production of art but about its preservation as form. Museum passes are never free.[1]

☺☺

The "Degenerate Art" exhibition at the Art Institute of Chicago in May 1991 crystalized my already growing awareness of the pedagogical double bind that moves through these chapters. In Gallery 6 of that exhibit, a video monitor displayed newsreel footage of the crowd at the original Munich exhibition of *Entartete Kunst* ("Degenerate Art") in 1937. An exhibit of 650 works of art confiscated by the Nazis and displayed publicly in an effort to defame the avant-garde, *Entartete Kunst* was a product of and testament to Nazi censorship and oppression. "Degenerate Art," first mounted in Los Angeles and later in Chicago and Washington, D.C., reassembled extant pieces from the original show, reinstating them in a "proper" exhibit context while documenting the "derisive intent" of the Nazi installation, reminding us, as the brochure says, of "the fragility of freedom."[2] The video exhibit in Gallery 6 allowed participants to watch throngs of earlier viewers pass by and pause to regard many of the same paintings we were seeing here for the first time under conditions very different from the oppressive climate captured by the newsreel. Yet as I stared at the black-and-white images on the monitor, I wondered to what extent my situation as a viewer replicated theirs. Was not this show, like its predecessor, attempting to move its audience to share a particular attitude toward the art on display by means of its very *method* of display?

Entartete Kunst justified its excessive commentary (in the form of graffiti slogans scrawled around the artworks and a vitriolic brochure denouncing them) by passing as a means of saving German culture from degenerates and their art. In contrast, "Degenerate Art" attempted to save art from politics by separating its historical and highly politicized introduction from its decontextualized exhibition of the artworks. Nonetheless, each show expects that its audience will come to share its organizers' opposition to a particular mode of cultural production—whether the modernist experimental art the Nazis decried or the fascist politicization of art the Chicago exhibition denounced. As I watched the newsreel, I became acutely aware of the double bind the spectator at "Degenerate Art" was in. One could not help accepting the moral and political position the show promoted, yet in accepting its truth, one succumbed to the strategies of manipulation that the exhibition moved one to oppose. While clearly the didactic messages of the two exhibits could not have differed more, their *pedagogy*, I will argue, was much the same.

My attendance at the "Degenerate Art" exhibition forced me to question my own moral position within a collectivity of like-minded people and the ways in which my adoption of a particular set of values in my teaching—whether as a feminist critic, a teacher of African American literature, or a practitioner of cultural studies—may implicate me in the very attitudes and practices I set out to oppose. This double bind, I suggest, is not specific to my personal experiences; rather, it is intrinsic to a cultural studies paradigm in which politics and values have come to displace truth and knowledge as the goals of literary pedagogy. Where interpretation—what and how a work means—once guided the study of literature, now production—how a work comes to acquire meaning and value within a particular historical and cultural matrix—has become the focus of critical inquiry. (This shift is discussed further in chapter 4.) The double bind engendered by cultural criticism's insistence on the need to interrogate the cultural institutions and practices in which we, as academics, necessarily participate forces us all into the position of "passing." As I define it in chapter 1, all passing is marked by the double bind that opens up a discrepancy between what one professes to be and how one is actually positioned in a society, institution, discourse, or classroom. Thus, the double bind cannot be resolved, theoretically or morally, by finding the right position but must be confronted performatively as well, through a performative practice that seeks to enact rather than to endorse certain positions.

The "Degenerate Art" exhibition serves as an example of this double bind to the extent that it created a discrepancy between what it said and what it did. What struck me most about this exhibition was the excessive amount of introductory material. By the time one got through the four introductory galleries meant to incite one's moral outrage by documenting Nazi atrocities—burning books, persecuting artists, purging museum curators—one could hardly view the extant works from *Entartete Kunst* "on their own merits," as the brochure promised. Despite the disclaimer by Frank O. Gehry, the architect who designed the original Los Angeles exhibition, that "what you don't want to do is to make a work of art important simply because of its associations" ("Degenerate"), that is precisely what "Degenerate Art" did. Indeed, the vast introduction to the main exhibition suggested that the organizers may have feared that without a great deal of interpretive assistance, the viewers might laugh at the milk cows by Emil Nolde, scoff at the crucifix by Max Beckmann, or protest the homosexuality of Karl Hofer's *Two Friends*, as the original audience was encouraged to do. The excessive commentary

Emil Nolde, *Kuhmelken* (Milk cows), 1913, from *"Degenerate Art": The Fate of the Avant-Garde in Nazi Germany,* Los Angeles County Museum of Art, 1991. (© Nolde-Stiftung Seebüll)

sought to create in the audience not so much an aesthetic appreciation as a shared moral sensibility.

I am not suggesting that art and politics can or should be separated, as if we could view artworks "on their own merits." In my view, this position was exposed as untenable by the very exhibition that professed to safeguard it. Nor am I suggesting that members of the original audience any more than the contemporary viewers were, in Stuart Hall's terms, "cultural dupes," easily manipulated by and unself-consciously buying into the politics of the exhibition's organizers. What I *am* asking is, In opposing a dominant discourse or cultural policy, do we necessarily engage in related efforts to press upon others a moral and political consensus? "Degenerate Art" raised for me the question of how one can oppose a political and cultural agenda without engaging in the kind of indoctrinating behavior one claims to resist. "Indoctrinate" means to imbue with partisan beliefs or propagandize and also to instruct in the fundamentals or teach. While most of us would insist that as

Max Beckmann, *Kreuzabnahme* (Deposition), 1917, from *"Degenerate Art": The Fate of the Avant-Garde in Nazi Germany,* Los Angeles County Museum of Art, 1991. (© 1999 Artists Rights Society (ARS), New York / VG Bild-Kunst, Bonn)

teachers we do not engage in the former, the exposure of humanist objectivity and art's apoliticality as myths by contemporary theorists and cultural critics renders the distinction between the two definitions all the more tenuous, giving rise to the double bind I see as intrinsic to a cultural studies model.

Like all double binds, this one calls for a deconstructive approach. Indeed, that monitor in Gallery 6 marked for me the moment when the contempo-

Karl Hofer, *Zwei Freunde* (Two friends), 1926, from *"Degenerate Art": The Fate of the Avant-Garde in Nazi Germany,* Los Angeles County Museum of Art, 1991. (Nachlaß Karl HOFER, Köln.)

rary exhibition began unself-consciously to deconstruct itself; for without the video screen "Degenerate Art" conveyed a straightforward lesson in the horrors of cultural oppression under fascism. With the video screen, however, the viewer potentially became aware of another kind of replication, not just the historical reconstruction of the content and context of the Nazi show, but the structural reproduction of its didactic strategies. My purpose here is not to make an argument for deconstruction; but that video display at least made a case for a performative pedagogy, one that would provide a safeguard against being manipulated even by the political discourse one endorses while at the same time acknowledging that no pedagogy can provide such a guarantee. The monitor, at least potentially, functioned as a deconstructive double gesture. Had a video camera and a second monitor been placed next to the newsreel monitor, allowing us to see images of ourselves viewing others viewing this art, Gallery 6 could have been transformed into a performative classroom.

Double monitors could potentially have turned "Degenerate Art" from a reproduction of and commentary on the Nazi effort to link art and politics into a reiteration (in Derrida's sense of that term) and interrogation of the very acts by which politics and art become complexly but intimately related, including the acts of exhibition, commentary, and critique.[3] The political difference between the original exhibition and its remounting would have remained apparent (the ideology of *Entartete Kunst* is clearly rejected by "Degenerate Art"), while the similar pedagogical structure, dramatically played out in the double vision before us, could have called attention to the museum's role in promoting a certain notion of artistic freedom. In the second monitor, we could have more readily seen ourselves caught up in the structure of opposition and consent—polarized by the choice of being "for" and "against"—that confronted the original Munich audience. This is not to say that the second camera would have solved the problem created by the first, providing a "corrective" to the exhibit's remounting of *Entartete Kunst*. Rather, the *mise-en-abyme* structure created by a second camera would have problematized the pedagogical assumptions of the Chicago exhibit—namely, that a "proper" mounting of the artworks would be unmediated and objective, allowing the artworks to speak for themselves. A performative pedagogy cannot be translated into a clear position in that way, for it seeks to shift attention from the intentions of individual subjects or texts to the intentionality of institutionalized practices. A performative pedagogy is not a solution to the double bind but the process by which we come to recognize the terms of our own implication.

Acknowledging the double bind through such a performative strategy need not result in political or moral paralysis or undecidability, as so often feared. One may be moved by such a pedagogy to abandon the kind of opposition thought necessary to sustain a shared moral sensibility without necessarily abandoning the values that initially motivated one's position. Indeed, the double vision produced by double monitors would have no more obscured the objective of the Chicago exhibition than our binocular vision that allows us to see both a duck and a rabbit in the same ink sketch distorts our vision; instead, double vision provides a different way of organizing and processing visual experience and, in the case of this exhibition, a different way of assessing our collaboration in the semiology of the art museum. Such a performative pedagogy, in my view, would have demonstrated not just the attitude but the *practice* by which the political tendency of "Degenerate Art"—the desire to preserve art from being pressed into the service of a political cause—can best be followed.

"Degenerate Art" functions as an allegory for the double bind intrinsic to a cultural studies model. To read allegorically in this way is not to say what a text or pedagogical performance means but to raise the question of the readability of any text or performance (B. Johnson, *Wake* 63). "'Allegories are always ethical,'" writes Paul de Man, "'the term ethical designating the structural interference of two distinct values systems'" (*Allegories of Reading;* qtd. in Johnson, *Wake* 68). What makes a cultural studies pedagogy difficult is not not knowing the best method of getting meaning across but the incompatibility of its epistemological and political imperatives. For a more explicit example of how a cultural studies pedagogy may work against the very politics it endorses, forcing cultural critics into the position of passing, I want to turn briefly to an essay by Paul Smith.

The coincidence of the publication of Smith's essay, "A Course in 'Cultural Studies,'" at the time of the "Degenerate Art" exhibition brought home to me the structural similarity of the pedagogical double bind that each in its own way creates. The spatial move from the introductory rooms of "Degenerate Art" to the exhibit of the actual artworks is structurally equivalent to the relation between the two main sections of Smith's essay: his description of the content, objectives, and pedagogy of his course ("What Is Cultural Studies?") and his narrative of what transpired in the classroom. The article begins with a series of disclaimers. Smith admits that no reportage is innocent, that any course is an intervention and any course description "an argument of a sort" (39). He acknowledges that his selections of readings are necessarily determined by his own "levels of knowledge, expertise, experience, and, indeed, willingness" (41). This introductory material establishes

Smith's reliability as a narrator in the same way the introductory material he provides his students establishes his reliability as a teacher. His syllabus also opens with a disclaimer: "Inevitably, in the space of one semester we shan't be able to answer fully the question that the course's title poses" (40), "What Is Cultural Studies?" Because of the impossibility of the task the course sets for the students, Smith begins to answer the question himself by providing a definition of cultural studies on his syllabus, even "at the risk of prejudicing [class] discussion" in advance (40). Like the video monitor in "Degenerate Art," Smith's disclaimers undermine his conscious desires, placing himself and his students in a double bind. Such disclaimers reveal the impossibility of leaving students "more or less to their own devices" (43) while at the same time providing some direction that must inevitably bias the discussion. But also like the video monitor, Smith's disclaimers reveal an *unconscious* desire that is pedagogically far more interesting.

What happens to Smith's course objectives and pedagogical values in the classroom? His narrative of the course suggests that, despite his effort to allow texts and students to argue with one another, despite his insistence on cultural studies as "a resistant operation," the course evoked little dissent. For example, Patrick Brantlinger's *Crusoe's Footprints* was dropped after three weeks and only two chapters. "*We* decided," Smith writes, "that Brantlinger's book would not be particularly useful in this course" because of the author's "antipathy to the political project of 'cultural studies'" (45; my emphasis). At the end of the course Dick Hebdige's *Hiding the Light,* which had served as a central text, elicited mutual criticism as well, "students being somewhat less convinced of the 'positive potentialities' of postmodernism than [Hebdige]" (Smith 47). Resistance may be claimed as a value in the course content but consensus structures the plot of Smith's narrative. If there were disagreements among the students, and between students and teacher, they went either unvoiced or unrecorded. Although Smith feels compelled to tell us the racial and gender configurations of his class (there were two African American students in a class of seventeen and "slightly more women than men" [43]), these make no significant difference in his narrative, as if all shared a common political and theoretical agenda with the professor.

Why might diverse students come to share resistance to a particular intellectual and political project? We should not be surprised to find that an answer lies in the professor's selections, emphases, and commitments. "I want to take some credit for the students' unwillingness in regard to the more optimistic views of the politics of 'postmodernism,'" Smith writes, "since we had spent a considerable amount of time discussing my own essay, 'Visiting the Banana Republic'—an essay which is by no manner of means a paean to 'postmodernism' or many of its theoretical discourses" (47). What may surprise us is that Smith takes *credit* for his students' *unwillingness* to entertain alternative "explanations of culture" (40). Moreover, he is not the least bit self-conscious about the ways his language here and his use of "we" *discredit* his reliability. For one so attuned to "the political functions of the academic" and to the ways in which subjects are "pulled into place" by cultural institutions and knowledges (44), Smith surprisingly ignores the ways in which institutional structures and, indeed, his own disclaimers shore up his authority and impel students to comply, even while theorizing a notion of resistance. Smith ignores "the dialectics of resistance and consent" (45) in his own classroom. Thus his pedagogy puts him in the position of the passer and puts into question the reliability of the one who would teach us.

Smith's unreliability, like that of the curators of "Degenerate Art," emerges in the disjunction between the intentions of his course and his pedagogy. In both the article and the exhibition the introductory material makes all the right statements, but the pedagogical performance works against the stated objectives, *paradoxically revealing an unconscious desire to do the right thing by putting authority in question.* That is, the article and the exhibition seem to say, "Question Authority," a command that places us in a double bind in that to obey it is to violate it.[4] Yet their performance puts into question the very authority they claim for their own positions, thereby playing out the double bind their stated objectives create. Lacking a performative pedagogy capable of calling attention to the double bind and thereby confronting their positions as passers, however, the professor and the curators are blind to their own unconscious desires. All are ignorant of the possibilities their unreliability holds for oppositional discourse and for the necessary yet interminable task of negotiating political and cultural differences.

Read as an allegory of the cultural studies professor's potential blindness to the workings of his or her own pedagogy, "Degenerate Art" allows us to see the way cultural studies passes as a pedagogy capable of serving the interests of diverse groups and of fostering an oppositional practice. Yet "passing" in my use of the term is not only inevitable but ethical. One might say, borrowing a statement attributed to W. B. Yeats, "'active virtue, as distinct from the passive acceptance of a current code, is the wearing of a mask'" (qtd. in Ellison 1546).[5] While passing is generally thought of in one of two ways—either negatively, as an appropriation of another's identity and experience, or more positively, as an expression of our culturally constructed and therefore changeable identities—is it not possible that passing can be conceived as a behavior especially suited to the double bind I have elaborated here, where the usual mode of resistance to dominant discourses and institution-

al structures is intellectually rigid and morally untenable? A truly oppositional practice, I argue, would displace the teacher's authority, making it impossible for students to identify with any one position.

The question arises, then, whether or not students and the general public can understand the deconstructive double gesture. Isn't the kind of
straightforward commentary "Degenerate Art" or Smith provides, however
complicit it may be in the pedagogy it resists, preferable to the "play of undecidability" so often associated with deconstruction and performativity? A
year before the mounting of "Degenerate Art," the Royal Ontario Museum
in Toronto organized an exhibition that attempted just such a deconstruction of its own authority. "Into the Heart of Africa" was an overtly political
exhibition whose intention was not to defame particular forms of art but
rather to "deconstruct the ideology of Empire" in which the museum, as a
modern institution, is complicit (Hutcheon 208).[6]

Linda Hutcheon's reading of "Into the Heart of Africa" raises the question of the accessibility or readability of a performative pedagogy as much
as the exhibition itself. "Into the Heart of Africa" displayed examples of African artifacts from the museum's permanent collection for the explicit purpose of critiquing colonialism. As Hutcheon explains in her introductory
remarks, the museum as a modern institution takes objects out of their contexts and histories, classifying and ordering them in a way that suggests an
ideal of "apolitical, detached objectivity" (206) and thereby embodying
"modernity's desire to make order and therefore meaning" (207). This is what
I argue "Degenerate Art" did by separating its historicized and politicized
introduction from its decontextualized display of the extant works from
Entartete Kunst. In contrast, the postmodern museum brings the "politics of
representation to the fore" (207) and seeks to expose the very historical processes and ideological assumptions through which such meaning is forged.
(Double monitors in Gallery 6 would have transformed "Degenerate Art"
from a modernist into a postmodernist exhibition, in Hutcheon's terms.)
"Over the last few decades," Hutcheon writes, "museums have begun to see
themselves as cultural 'texts' and have become increasingly self-reflexive
about their premises, identity, and mission" (206). Through its irony and
reflexivity the Toronto exhibition sought to expose the museum's own role
in the imperial ideology responsible for the collection on display.

For example, the title of the exhibition—"Into the Heart of Africa"—
invokes Joseph Conrad's *Heart of Darkness,* an ironic allusion the curator felt
would be sufficient to mark the critique of imperialism intended by the exhibit. Plaques at the entrance to each room called attention to the paternalistic attitudes and primitivist discourse evident in the visual and verbal mes-

sages on display. In addition, the Toronto museum took part in the "post-modern discourse of museums" by seeking greater community involvement (208). Rather than speak for the African Canadian community through the pedagogical device of the exhibition brochure, the organizers submitted the initial (and ultimately rejected) brochure to members of that community for evaluation. Despite such efforts to deconstruct a colonial legacy and to empower the wider community, the exhibition ended up offending not only members of the African Canadian community but audiences from across the political and cultural spectrum (216), culminating in charges of racism being leveled against the curator, a white woman known as an expert in African art (208).

What went wrong? Hutcheon suggests that the conflict between the political sensibility of the organizers and the political context of the viewers created a problem of reading. For example, the title of the exhibition intended by the curator as an ironic allusion to Conrad's novel and as an implicit critique of imperialism signified to others "an imperialistic perspective" (211). Similarly, the use of quotation marks around words such as "barbarous" and "primitive" to signal ironic distance functioned for some readers as citations, re-presenting the colonialist perspective the curator sought to ironize. Also, the effort to involve the wider community ended up obscuring the intended audience for the exhibition. "The first printed message at the entry to the exhibition," Hutcheon explains, "openly stated that *Canadians* (implicitly, white and British Canadians) were to be the focus, that their 'experience of Africa, as seen in this exhibition, was very different from the way Africans perceived themselves, their own cultures, and these events'" (212). Yet the brochure, revised with the input of African Canadians, suggested the exhibition was a celebration of Africa, which was more what the African Canadian community wanted to see, Hutcheon proposes, and what the general public would expect to see than the critique of imperialism the exhibition was originally intended to be and, in fact, still was.

In light of these problems, Hutcheon criticizes the Toronto show for the ways in which it seemed to be complicit with the colonialist assumptions it meant to critique, as I claim "Degenerate Art" was complicit with the politicizing of the art it claimed to deplore. For Hutcheon, the problem with the Toronto exhibition was not that the curator sought to deconstruct the museum's implication in colonialist practices; rather, the problem was in the pedagogy of that exercise, what she terms its "semiotic inattention" (214). The organizers relied on accompanying texts to bring out the irony and critique of its exhibitions, yet the actual displays—such as glass cases housing African artifacts and British military regalia and a wall-sized picture of a British officer stabbing a Zulu warrior—were, in the context of a museum, "un-ironized commonplaces" (214). "In an institution where the norm is that visual messages and verbal texts convey the *same* meaning," Hutcheon cautions, "the risks taken through ironic disjunction here are great" (218). Moreover, even if the irony were understood, it seemed to many, as one visitor put it, "'a pretty limp way to examine a subject as grave as racially motivated genocide'" (217). What the public wanted, it seems, was either unironized celebration or unequivocal denunciation.

Hutcheon's analysis of what went wrong in the Toronto exhibition makes some important observations about the use of irony for the purposes of oppositional discourse. As she points out, the effectiveness of a particular form of irony may well "depend on who is doing the interpreting" (218). A major shortcoming of the exhibit, in her view, was not so much its ironic commentary but that its irony was too elusive, directed to a limited audience (which Hutcheon identifies as "academics"), and worked against the expectations of most viewers. "Irony," she writes, "has always been risky," for it depends not just on context but on "the identity and position" of both the speaker and the interlocutor (222). Given the numerous discursive communities we all take part in, it's a wonder irony ever comes off. As Hutcheon says, "all ironies, in fact, might therefore be unstable ironies" (222). In some circumstances, such as the Toronto exhibition, irony is simply not worth the risk (219). Hutcheon attributes the exhibition's failed pedagogy to its postmodernist strategies, of which irony is one, or to the kind of performative pedagogy I am advocating here.

The broader point of Hutcheon's critique is that any rhetorical or pedagogical strategy we deploy presupposes an audience, a particular discursive community, and may misfire when the actual audience is not homogeneous. Her discussion of postmodern irony raises a crucial question for pedagogy: "The question is whether . . . you should ever assume that visitors [or students] will necessarily share the 'values, the assumptions and the intellectual preoccupations that have guided not only the choice and presentation of exhibitions [or readings], but also, more fundamentally, the selection and acquisition of objects'" (221).[7] Such an assumption, coupled with the desire to produce a shared moral sensibility, is what I criticize in the pedagogy of "Degenerate Art" and in Smith's essay. Rather than seeking a means of exploiting just this inevitability—that is, that not all students will share the same values—Hutcheon seems to fault the curator-professor for not controlling well enough the responses of the visitor-student, for not exercising the kind of social control she identifies, in the beginning of her essay, as a *modernist* legacy that implicates all academics:

> Those of us who are academics work within one of the major cultural in-
> stitutions of modernity and whatever our individual evaluation of the mod-
> ern project, and whatever our personal position (consensual support or op-
> positional resistance), we participate in what [Hooper-Greenhill] has . . . called
> the "exercise of social control through the meting out of learning, mediated
> and identified with the achievement of worth." . . . Both the museum and the
> academy in Europe and North America have traditionally shared an institu-
> tionalized faith in reason and method. (206)

Ironically, and perhaps inevitably, a pedagogy meant to expose such forms
of social control is seen to fail to the extent that it does not exercise such
control. Thus, it passes as pedagogy.

Behind Hutcheon's critique of the Toronto exhibition lies the anxiety felt
by other professionals (such as those I discuss in chapter 1) who are caught
in the structure of passing. Hutcheon must feel a bit awkward as a white
British Canadian woman exposing another white British Canadian woman
(the curator), both of whom speak with some authority on issues of cultural differences, for failing to get the politics right in the effort to expose the
political complicity of white British Canadians. After quoting one reviewer's list of the numerous groups who were offended by the exhibition, Hutcheon responds: "One might add to that list even liberal, white Canadians who
thought of themselves as multiculturally tolerant and even postcolonially
oppositional" (217). Precisely the point, I would think. Yet the charges of
racism and complicity leveled against the curator might well be enough to
obscure that message and to motivate Hutcheon (or anyone similarly positioned) to reject, as she puts it, the "postmodernly deconstructive" for the
"postcolonially oppositional" (222)—or, in my terms, the "performative
pedagogy" for the "clear position."

It is precisely such an impasse that calls for a performative pedagogy. In
Hutcheon's experience of "Into the Heart of Africa," as in my experience of
"Degenerate Art," the disjunction between what the exhibition said and what
it did, or between the verbal component of the exhibition, on the one hand,
and the visual and structural component, on the other, implicitly undercut
the exhibition's intended message. Yet our responses to this kind of discrepancy differ insofar as Hutcheon does not recognize—or at least does not seek
to exploit—the double bind created by the exhibition. Whereas the difficulty I had with the Art Institute's exhibition was its lack of self-consciousness
about its own implication in pedagogical strategies it sought to discredit,
Hutcheon's difficulty with the Toronto exhibition was precisely its self-conscious pedagogy that sought to expose the museum's implication in the
modernist project. In response to the disjunction between visual and verbal

texts, Hutcheon advocates not a performative practice but a more straight-forward commentary. Missing from the exhibition, she says, was the "very kind of overt statement of judgement" that would make the curator's intentions clear (221–22). Interpreting the organizers' irony and reflexivity as a refusal to take a stand and as a reveling in ambiguity, Hutcheon concludes that postmodern critique may be a liberal luxury, *saving* one from the need to *act* oppositionally. As an alternative model she offers an exhibition mounted by an African American artist, Fred Wilson, entitled "The Other Museum" (225). Like the Toronto exhibition, Wilson's presented a critique of colonialism through irony, relying on written texts such as the brochure to explain the irony to the viewers. Why, then, was his exhibition successful? Because, Hutcheon explains, while his techniques may have been too obvious (as were those in the Nazi exhibition), at least there was no mistaking the artist's intentions (225).

Hutcheon would seem to endorse not just the view of "Degenerate Art," which also presented an overt statement of judgement on the politics of the Nazi exhibition, but also the attitude of those who put on the original Munich exhibition in 1937. A main objective of the Nazi exhibition was to malign modernist works of art that were not easily accessible to the public, as if there were art forms that did not require some prior knowledge of the semiotics of artistic production.[8] Hutcheon suggests that pedagogy, if not art, should be readily accessible to the public; efforts to undercut viewers' expectations and to complicate their visual and ideological perspectives are seen as politically dangerous by both the Nazi curators and the postmodern theorist. My point in this comparison is to bring out the naïveté of assuming that artworks or artifacts can speak for themselves and the risks entailed in assuming that, to be effective, pedagogy must be straightforward: direct, intelligible, accessible, and undisguised. Not even the simplest language or image is transparent and therefore immune to misunderstanding.

Hutcheon repeatedly asks, What if the visitors did not read the texts? What if they missed the beginning or ending of the seven-minute slide show where the "cultural superiority and paternalism" of the voiceover was explicitly labeled and denigrated (218)? Hutcheon suggests that such framing devices are merely introductory, even incidental. Similarly, we might worry: What if our students come to class late or miss key classes? What if they fail to read the text? What if they come to classes in African American or Asian American literature "looking for [their] roots," as did one African Canadian visitor to the Toronto exhibition, only to find that the professor, trained in postmodern theories, questions the very notions of "roots," "origins," and "essence"? What if students think that by showing Marlon Riggs's *Ethnic*

Notions, their professor seeks to reinforce the racist representations on the screen because students' "semiotic inattention" may lead them to respond to the images without listening to the voices of those interviewed in the film? The *Ethnic Notions* example is particularly relevant given Hutcheon's rhetorical question: "Do the existing ironies [in the exhibit] implicitly rely too much on an audience that can be affectively and politically detached from the pain represented in the exhibition's visual images?" (219) Riggs's film creates pain in the audience, especially for those whose ethnicity is figured in the racist images on display. What if students cannot detach from those images enough to hear the critique presented in the verbal text?

But isn't such "semiotic inattention" precisely what we as cultural critics and teachers of literature seek to confront and to change, both in our students and in the institutions in which we work? While the semiotic inattention of the organizers comes in for criticism by Hutcheon, she suggests that the semiotic inattention of the visitor-student is something we must teach to rather than something we might change. Precisely what the museum and the academy as institutions do is to teach people how to read cultural texts. If such an "exercise in social control" is potentially exclusive and inevitably biased, why not change the expectations of the audience rather than clarify (or purify) the intentions of the pedagogue? If we can never assume that our audience shares our values, assumptions, and semiotic habits, as Hutcheon points out, then pedagogy no more than writing can ever deliver the control it promises, no matter how straightforward it may be. That in itself might be an important lesson for students and museum visitors.

I would say the lesson of the Toronto exhibition, and of Hutcheon's essay, is not that postmodern critique is an elitist practice available only to the privileged few but that no critique is ever free of the contradictory realities in which we teach, write, and act. There is no safe place from which to launch an oppositional critique. One person's ironic evasion is another's devastating attack. What Hutcheon sees as a postmodern refusal to pass judgment is for others a way of judging differently, outside the binary logic of opposition and consent and in recognition of what Lyotard calls the "differend," the situation that results when disputing parties do not agree on the relevant rules of judgment. When Hutcheon faults the Toronto exhibition for failing to include the "answering African voice" (224), she suggests that there is one such voice and that political and cultural critique and change occur only through the clash *between* voices (or cultures) rather than from the self-subverting differences *within.*

I am not suggesting that the Toronto exhibition should not be held accountable for how its message was received, any more than I would want to

say that visitors and students should not be held accountable for their reading practices. But I am suggesting that the Toronto exhibition might provide
a different lesson from the one Hutcheon has learned. She is right that the
museum cannot escape its implication simply by naming or representing it,
however ironically—precisely one point I make about passing. Where she
goes wrong, in my view, is in suggesting that "The Other Museum" (the show
mounted by the African American artist) *can.* Hutcheon fails to see any
significance in the instability of irony other than the lesson that one should
avoid irony if one is to present a clearly oppositional stance, or else make one's
intentions so obvious that there is no mistaking them. Yet the fact that all
ironies are unstable, or that frames are always enframed, as Derrida puts it
and as a second monitor in "Degenerate Art" would suggest, calls attention
to the instability of the clear-cut distinctions that structure oppositional discourse and thus to the ideological, political, and moral complicity of the
museum that the Toronto exhibition wished to bring out. The protests evoked
by the exhibition may well be a sign of its effectiveness in implicating itself.
That is, it may succeed in its critique of the modernist project precisely where
it is seen to fail, by not escaping criticism itself.

What Hutcheon ignores in her critique of postmodern irony is the "undecidable contamination" between intentional acts and citations that Derrida terms "iterability" (*Limited Inc.* 59). Where Hutcheon seeks a practice that
can guarantee its results by making its intentions clear, a performative pedagogy is based on the belief that establishing such a practice would be a denial of the ethical relation, or what I term the "dynamics of responsibility." If
there is a lesson to be learned here it is, as Kwame Anthony Appiah writes of
yet another museum exhibition, that in the "circulation of cultures," as he
puts it, "we are all already contaminated by each other" (354).[9] The invocation of *Heart of Darkness* in the title of the Toronto exhibition signals more
than a critique of imperialism; it implicates the modernist project itself in the
imperialist project. The big lie of Conrad's novel is the modernist illusion of
self-knowledge. As Patrick McGee writes in an essay on modernist fiction and
Derridean frames: "The lie of imperialism still survives, even in the most
radical deconstructions of Western culture like *The Waves* and *Finnegans
Wake,* in the belief that Western culture is able to know itself from the outside, is able to produce its own self-critique without entailing the exclusion
of the others who have traditionally suffered from the construction of Euro-
pean subjectivities" (648). "There is no simple way out of the historical contradictions that are the legacy of colonialism," he continues, except "the commitment to perpetual negotiation across the borders of [cultural] difference
without any appeal to universal grounds or authority" (649)—including the

authority of clear intentions. Hutcheon's faith in clear intentions and straight-forward pedagogy resists this insight. The kind of commitment that McGee invokes is, in my terms, a commitment to "passing."

෬෬

In this chapter, "Degenerate Art" has served as an allegory of what I mean by "passing as pedagogy," the way our practices may belie our intentions, the way evaluative conflicts are elided in the very effort to address them. Alternatively, a reading of Nella Larsen's *Passing* in the next chapter shows how that novel can serve as an allegory of the pedagogical situation we now find ourselves in and how it offers a possible way of reconceiving passing for pedagogy. Teaching *Passing* in my African American literature course was like putting a video camera next to the monitor in Gallery 6 of "Degenerate Art"; it provided the class with the opportunity to see our own "dialectics of resistance and consent" (Smith, "Course") played out in the text before us. *Passing* provides a lesson in how pedagogy might *exploit,* not *resolve,* the positive potentialities of its own unreliability.

NOTES

1. My thanks to Susan Cavallo and Anne Callahan for suggesting this Malraux connection to me. The line about museum passes is Anne's.

2. Quotations are from the brochure for "Degenerate Art," which was distributed free to museum visitors, and should be distinguished from the exhibition catalog, which was available for purchase.

3. Reiteration, the necessary repetition that enables something to be recognized as the same, renders intention impure insofar as intention is no longer originary but the effect of various performances. There is, in Derrida's terms, an "undecidable contamination" between the intentional act and its parasitical citations or reiterations (*Limited Inc.* 59). What reiteration allows for, then, is greater awareness of the intentionality of institutionalized practices themselves, such as the remounting of an art exhibition.

4. This popular bumper sticker ("Question Authority") has often been invoked as an example of the deconstructive double bind. I believe I first heard it used by Barbara Johnson.

5. The full citation reads: "There is a relation between discipline and the theatrical sense. If we cannot imagine ourselves as different from what we are and assume the second self, we cannot impose a discipline upon ourselves, though we may accept one from others. Active virtue, as distinct from the passive acceptance of a current code, is the wearing of a mask. It is the condition of an arduous full life."

6. My description of the exhibition comes from Linda Hutcheon's 1993 Routledge Lecture and its published version, "The Post Always Rings Twice: The Postmodern

and the Postcolonial." My thanks to Michele Troy for bringing this article to my attention.

7. Hutcheon quotes from Eilean Hooper-Greenhill's essay "Counting Visitors or Visitors Who Count?"

8. For a more detailed discussion of the views of the curators, see Sauerländer.

9. Appiah's essay begins with a reading of the 1987 show on African art at the Center for African Art in New York City.

THREE

"Not Entirely Strange . . . Not Entirely Friendly": Passing and Pedagogy

> *Outsider! Trespasser! You have no right to this subject!*
> *. . . Poacher! Pirate! We reject your authority. We know you,*
> *with your foreign language wrapped around you like a flag:*
> *speaking about us in your forked tongue, what can you tell but*
> *lies?*
> —Salman Rushdie, *Shame*

> Where in heaven's name do we Negroes stand? If we orga-
> nize separately for anything—"Jim Crow!" scream all the
> Disconsolate; if we organize with white people—"Traitors!"
> . . . yell all the suspicious.
> —W. E. B. Du Bois, *Crisis*

When I taught Mahasweta Devi's Bengali short story "Breast-Giver" for the first time several years ago, I casually referred to the scene where the master's son-in-law assaults the cook. A student objected to my use of the term "assaults." "She wanted it," he argued, citing textual evidence from the story. In defense of my word choice, I drew on my politics as a feminist reader and my skills as a poststructuralist theorist to explain the power dynamics of the gender and class relations in the text as well as in the larger social context. At the end of my detailed response the student remained unconvinced. But when, at the next class meeting, Glory Dhamaraj, an Indian graduate student whom I had previously invited to my class to discuss the cultural background of Mahasweta Devi's story, innocently remarked, "In the scene where the master's son-in-law assaults the cook . . . ," no one questioned her word choice or showed any signs that her reading had been a point of debate in the previous class. Now their response could have been a matter of discretion, a sign of respect for a visitor, a point I will return to later in this chapter. Or I could flatter myself by believing that my earlier theoretically sophisticated response had finally sunk in. But I am well aware that my students' acceptance of Glory's interpretation had more to do with her authority as a native speaker than with my skills as a literary theorist. I might add that Glory wore a sari that day.[1]

I begin with this anecdote to raise the larger issue that I want to address in this chapter: the authority of experience and the role it plays, as well as the limits it sets, in teaching for diversity. To put this larger issue slightly differently, as a feminist critic and teacher trained in a largely Eurocentric theoretical and literary tradition, I am interested in the relations between poststructuralist theories and multicultural literatures. In bringing my theoretical training to bear on African American or postcolonial fiction, am I seen by students as imposing an alien discourse on the texts we study? Will the authority derived from experience always be more convincing than the authority acquired through training when discussing indigenous literatures? Must my students and I play the role of either the colonizer or the tourist when we visit new literary territories? In her chapter "Essentialism in the Classroom," Diana Fuss writes: "It is the unspoken law of the classroom not to trust those who cannot cite experience as the indisputable grounds of their knowledge" (*Essentially Speaking* 116). Although Fuss refers to the classroom in general, she actually has in mind a particular classroom: namely, the "studies" classroom, where women and/or minorities—racial, ethnic, sexual—are the subject. In the formalist classroom of the "great books" course, for example, experience supposedly has little if anything to do with knowledge. In *Teaching to Transgress,* bell hooks offers a powerful critique of the way Fuss implicitly links "the authority of experience" with marginalized groups, "ignor[ing] the subtle and overt ways essentialism is expressed from a location of privilege" (81–82). Arguing from a different theoretical perspective from Fuss in her essay "The Social Construction of Black Feminist Thought," Patricia Hill Collins makes a similar observation: "For ordinary African-American women, those individuals who have lived through the experiences about which they claim to be experts are more believable and credible than those who have merely read or thought about such experiences" (759). The pedagogical issue raised here is who can speak, and with what kind of authority, in the multicultural classroom.[2] Or, to frame this question in riskier terms, How can we teach that which we do not know?

These were some of the questions I was grappling with when I was preparing to teach Nella Larsen's *Passing* for the first time. As a result, I came to read in this novel both an allegory of the pedagogical situation I have been describing and a possible way of reconceiving the practice of reading and teaching literature in a classroom focused on gender, racial, and ethnic differences. My analysis of *Passing* examines the implications of what we have come to term "postmodern theory"—particularly poststructuralist concepts of self and text—for a reading of realistic black women's fiction, a reading that does not treat the text solely as a representation of black women's experience but also does not simply ignore or aestheticize that experience. In this chapter, I want to confront these questions about how to teach for diversity without treating texts only in terms of their racial, ethnic, or gender identity while acknowledging that their identity as such is precisely why we are teaching them—that is, in response to our recognition of the racial, ethnic, and gender bias of our traditional curriculum.[3]

Unreliable Narrators

Larsen's *Passing,* first published in 1929, is a novel about the strained friendship between two women, Irene Redfield and Clare Kendry. Having known each other in childhood, the two women have not seen or heard from one another for twelve years. During that time each has married and had children. Irene has married a black doctor and lives in Harlem; Clare has married a white racist and passes in white society. The first part of the novel presents, by way of a flashback, a chance encounter in Chicago. Part 2 narrates their re-encounter two years later in New York and their growing intimacy, despite Irene's reluctance, as Clare becomes a frequent visitor to Harlem. The last part of the novel details the breakup of this relationship, first by Irene's suspicion of an affair between Clare and Irene's husband, Brian, and ultimately by Clare's death when she falls from a sixth-story window, more than likely with a push by Irene. The novel is narrated from Irene's point of view.

When Irene meets Clare after twelve years, through a chance encounter at the Drayton Hotel, she is herself passing temporarily. Shopping in Chicago, she has been overcome by the heat and a sympathetic cab driver, mistaking her for a white woman, has taken her to the Drayton Hotel for tea. As Irene is sitting at her table, she becomes aware of another woman staring at her. At first Irene thinks there must be something wrong with her appearance and she does what Barbara Johnson calls a narcissistic check ("No Passing"): Is my hair messy? Is my lipstick smudged? Is my blouse stained? Then, Larsen writes, "gradually there rose in Irene a small inner disturbance, odious and hatefully familiar. . . . Did that woman, could that woman, somehow know that here before her very eyes on the roof of the Drayton sat a Negro?" (150). That woman turns out to be Clare Kendry, who is herself passing.

As these two old friends catch up on their pasts, Irene tactfully avoids the issue of passing, for Clare's passing is more than a temporary convenience, as it is for Irene; it has become a way of life, a new identity, and thus it is much more threatening. Irene thinks:

> There were things that she wanted to ask Clare Kendry. She wished to find out about this hazardous business of "passing," this breaking away from all that was familiar and friendly to take one's chances in another environment, *not entirely strange, perhaps, but certainly not entirely friendly.* What, for example, one did about background, how one accounted for oneself. And how one felt when one came into contact with other Negroes. But she couldn't. She was unable to think of a single question that in its context or its phrasing was not too frankly curious, if not actually impertinent. (157; my emphasis)

When I first read this passage it struck me that Irene's reticence in this scene resembles the response of many students and teachers reading and discussing literature of a different racial or cultural heritage for the first time. For the teacher there is the question of background, both personal and scholarly, and the question of how to account for oneself as a member of a different race or culture—questions of *authority*. For the student there may be a frank curiosity about what it is like to live in "another environment" coupled with a discreet politeness. To ask about race or ethnicity is to risk being impertinent; not to ask is to remain, as Irene finds out, naïve and ignorant. When the relation of the other's world to one's own is "not entirely strange," it seems impertinent, even unnecessary, to ask about or to raise the issue of differences; yet when that relation is "not entirely friendly," it is both imperative that one ask and risky.[4]

I want to suggest that like Irene in her first meeting with Clare, we (members of the multicultural classroom) may be "frankly curious" about racial or ethnic differences but afraid to ask for fear of being "impertinent" or "indiscreet." But in this novel's reticence on the narrative level itself (the word "passing," for example, does not appear until the fourteenth page) and in the extent to which all communication in the novel is marked by reticence, suspicion, and misperceptions, *Passing* reveals much more than a desire not to offend; it also reveals a desire not to know. Irene's reticence in that early conversation with Clare, like my students' reticence in their discussion with Glory Dhamaraj, may be less a matter of discretion than of self-protection. A reading of *Passing*, then, can disclose the workings of what Gregory Jay calls the "pedagogical unconscious," what we *resist* knowing (*American*).

Of course, my allegorical reading makes much of the racial and social differences between Irene and Clare while downplaying their racial identity—both are African American—and their similar social situations—both pass. I downplay their similarities because, for Irene, their differences are crucial. Irene considers herself to be "race woman," one who works for the social betterment of her people; in contrast, Clare, by passing, seems to have forsaken her racial heritage and to act as if she has no racial past. Irene finds Clare's rashness and lack of race consciousness very different from her own personality and politics. Despite their similar backgrounds and family connections, to Irene, Clare is foreign, a curiosity, even exotic, because she lives otherwise, lives as an exile in an alien land that is yet not entirely strange. In their differences lie both the threat and the attraction Clare presents to Irene.

Critics have accounted for Clare's role as "exotic other" in several ways. The earliest and most common readings interpret Clare, "the passer," in terms of the African American literary tradition of the tragic mulatto (or mulatta) figure who functions, as Hazel Carby says, both thematically and symbolically to express the social tensions between the races (*Reconstructing* 171). In criticism of Harlem Renaissance literature in particular, Clare is discussed in terms of the dominant image of black sexuality at that time, the "primitive exotic stereotype" that was popularized in the literature of such writers as Carl Van Vechten, Larsen's friend to whom *Passing* is dedicated (McDowell xiv–xvi). More recent critics have focused explicitly on the sexual rather than the racial politics of this novel. Drawing on Simone de Beauvoir's *Second Sex,* Cheryl Wall discusses "the exotic female Other" as a "symbol of the unconscious, the unknowable, the erotic" and, in Clare's case, as "those aspects of the psyche Irene denies within herself," in particular, her own sexual desires ("Passing" 102, 108–9). Deborah McDowell shares this reading, arguing further that the issue of racial identity in *Passing* has served to disguise the issue of female sexuality and the suggestion of a sexual attraction between Irene and Clare (xxiii–xxxi). For McDowell, the significance of the ending lies less in the disclosure of Clare's race than in the sense of "'dis'-closure" caused by Larsen's inability to give full narrative expression to the sexual subplot (xxxi). More recently, Butler analyzes the historical formations by means of which race, gender, and sexuality are constituted in and through one another (*Bodies*). For her, the word "queer" provides a semantic link that discloses the convergence of the passing plot with the muted homosexual plot. These readings all find support in the text, for throughout the novel Clare is constantly linked with the word "desire," presented both as desiring other and as object of desire.

Although these readings account for Clare's thematic or symbolic role in the novel, with the exception of Butler's, they do not address her function within the dynamic, intersubjective exchange that motivates the narrative as well as classroom discussion. By situating my reading pedagogically—in terms of the kinds of positions we can and cannot assume in a classroom multiply divided along racial, gender, and ethnic lines—I want to address our situation in the text and in the classroom context; the emphasis on writing, reading, and teaching within the novel itself, as event and thematic component, forces us to analyze our own position within both the narrative and the pedagogical exchange. In trying to understand the pedagogical relation here, a poststructuralist understanding of the "other" can prove useful.

In "The Insistence of the Letter in the Unconscious," Lacan connects the other with the letter, with writing or style (319), as Gallop points out in her chapter on this essay (*Reading Lacan* 116). It is significant, then, that Clare is first introduced in the opening paragraph of *Passing* by means of a letter— a letter that expresses her "wild desire" to see Irene (145), a letter that is alien, marked by its style:

> It was the last letter in Irene Redfield's little pile of morning mail. After her other ordinary and clearly directed letters the long envelope of thin Italian paper with its almost illegible scrawl seemed out of place and alien. And there was, too, something mysterious and slightly furtive about it. A thin sly thing which bore no return address to betray the sender. Not that she hadn't immediately known who its sender was. Some two years ago she had one very like it in outward appearance. Furtive, but yet in some peculiar, determined way a little flaunting. Purple ink. Foreign paper of extraordinary size. (143)

Although the letter serves synecdochically to figure Clare's status in the text, it also functions metonymically to initiate a chain of connections that drives the plot forward and thus suggests not only aspects of Clare's identity, as Claudia Tate says ("Larsen's *Passing*"), but aspects of the text's status as well, particularly its furtiveness, protectiveness, reticence, and self-difference. Most striking about *Passing* are the many things that are *not* said, narrated, or verbalized.

This opening passage, presented in terms of Irene's consciousness, emphasizes the "alien" and "mysterious" quality of this letter, its difference, and its familiarity. The letter both flaunts itself and conceals its identity, yet to Irene that letter, in its effort not to be detected, is "immediately known." "Not

entirely strange" but "not entirely friendly," it arouses annoyance in its re-
ceiver. Irene's annoyance at what she doesn't yet know, the unknown con-
tents of the letter, is also a fear of what she already knows but resists acknowledging—namely, the other's similarity to herself. What disturbs Irene about
Clare's style and lifestyle is its otherness, specifically, the danger Clare faces
by living in an environment that is "not entirely friendly," by presuming to
be something other than herself, and by carelessly exposing herself to possible detection. The risk the passer runs is at once a risk of being detected
(identified) and mistaken (misidentified), of being read and misread. When
Irene tries to dissuade Clare from attending the Negro Welfare League dance,
she warns her that she may be detected as a passer and that she may be mistaken for a prostitute (199), unwittingly making a moral connection between
"racial promiscuity" and sexual promiscuity. What Irene resists knowing,
however, is the possibility that the danger lies not in the other's difference
but in the discovery that the other is "not entirely strange"—that is, in discovering that it may not be only the passer who is other than what she knows
herself to be. In poststructuralist terms, Irene's resistance to the otherness
Clare represents is a resistance to the concomitant knowledge of her own self-
difference. According to Lacan, one's concept of oneself is formed through
intersubjective relations and therefore through alienation. As Gallop points
out, Lacan's theory of subjectivity means that the subject is always divided
and precarious, yet the subject resists this knowledge to satisfy his or her
desire for an imaginary wholeness, a self-mastery he or she lacks (*Reading
Lacan* 142–45). This danger posed by the other helps to explain Irene's reticence in her first meeting with Clare. Her hesitancy to risk asking about
Clare's life as a passer, like the white student's hesitancy to talk about the
black student's difference, may be less a matter of discretion than of self-
protection.

However, the dynamic of this text reveals that the threat also lies elsewhere: in the very writing itself. If we take seriously Lacan's insistence on the
letter, as Gallop says we should (*Reading Lacan* 30), then we might see Irene's
annoyance as directed *literally* at the letter: not at what it represents (its con-
tents) but at its style, a writing that is neither "clearly directed" nor clearly
readable. The annoyance and the risk may be located in the difficulty of assuming the position of the text's interlocutor, a position that makes the reader
of this text (whether Clare's letter or Larsen's novel) feel "nonidentical with
herself as a reader" or "inadequate" to his or her task as a reader (*Reading
Lacan* 117). Gallop's point about the effects of Lacan's style describes, I suggest, the effects of multicultural literature on the nonnative reader or on the
resisting reader.[5]

If, in her initial meeting with Clare, talking with her "own kind," Irene feels impertinent asking about racial difference, later, in conversation with Hugh Wentworth, a white man, Irene is anything but reticent. In fact, during their conversation at the Negro Welfare League dance, Irene is the most frank she has yet been in the novel. As Hugh watches Clare dancing with Irene's husband, he becomes curious about who she is and what race she is. Discussing with Irene Clare's sexual attraction and ultimately mistaking Clare for white, Hugh presents a common argument of that time: white women are attracted to black men, finding them exotic, beautiful, erotic. Irene at first responds with her typical reserve, saying simply that white women like to dance with black men because black men are superior dancers. Not surprisingly, Hugh rejects this explanation, sensing that there is "something else, some other attraction" (205). In turn, Irene objects to what Hugh means by the word "attraction":

> "I think that what they feel is—well, a kind of emotional excitement. You know, the sort of thing you feel in the presence of something strange, and even, perhaps, a bit repugnant to you; something so different that it's really at the opposite end of the pole from all your accustomed notions of beauty."
> "Damned if I don't think you're half-way right."
> "I'm sure I am. Completely. . . ." (205)

I am less interested in the way Larsen uses this conversation to rehearse interracial sexual attraction, a common topic of discussion during the Harlem Renaissance, than I am in Irene's uncharacteristic frankness. Granted, her frankness may come from the fact that she and Hugh are discussing something "known" among the Harlem intelligentsia. A "safe" topic puts them on familiar ground, a place Irene likes to be, where the conventions for formulating questions and supplying answers are already established so that neither interlocutor risks being impertinent. (The safety of familiar ground is precisely what is violated in the multicultural classroom.) But Irene's frankness here is telling to the extent that her explanation touches on more than the ostensible topic at hand, the attraction between white women and black men. It pertains to her own relation to Clare, for the language of this passage reveals Irene's feelings when she is in Clare's presence, the emotional excitement Clare arouses due to her otherness. In the early chapters especially, the text repeatedly mentions how attractive, appealing, and seductive Irene finds Clare, yet her attraction is always juxtaposed with her insistence on Clare's strangeness, even repulsiveness (e.g., 172, 176). What appears in this conversation between Irene and Hugh to be a discussion about something *familiar* (sexual attraction between people of different races) is also, as Mc-

Dowell suggests, an expression of something *unspeakable* (sexual attraction between people of the same sex).

This confusion of racial and sexual relations (both heterosexual and lesbian) recurs throughout the novel. For example, Brian longs to escape racist America by emigrating to Brazil, a place at once strange in that it is foreign and yet familiar in that it is populated by blacks. Later, Irene interprets his desire for the unknown, which has always frightened her, as a desire for Clare (224). Likewise, the two arguments Brian and Irene have over what their sons should and should not be taught focus on race and sexuality. Brian wants them to know about sex and racism; Irene wants to keep them "safe" by keeping them ignorant. Issues of race and sex are brought together throughout the novel. To this extent, Irene's frankness can be read as an oblique reference to what remains unspoken in her initial conversation with Clare, where she feels curious but reticent.

Here is one example of how our assumptions about race and sex can mislead us. We might expect that similarity of race and sex (as between Irene and Clare) would facilitate communication while difference of race and sex (as between Irene and Hugh) would strain communication. Yet in the conversation at the dance we find that difference enables more frank discussion. Our initial assumption, however, may show our preoccupation with racial relations, where difference is a potential problem, rather than with sexual relations, where similarity may be seen as a potential problem. Thus, McDowell argues that the text misleads us into focusing on what is most obvious—racial difference—causing us to miss what is latent, sexual desire. However, if we are misled, it may not be by the text alone. Our own misplaced assumptions and unasked questions may lead us to focus on certain issues and not to notice other uncomfortable topics. The pedagogical issue raised here is one Barbara Johnson discusses in "Teaching Ignorance": "Could it be," she asks, "that our ways of teaching students to ask *some* questions are always correlative with our ways of teaching them *not to ask*—indeed to be unconscious—of others?" (*World* 76). Such a possibility, I suggest, is all the stronger and more difficult to confront when racial differences are at issue.

Privileging racial difference or lesbian desire in our reading of *Passing,* and in our reading of the metaphor of "passing," may prevent us from asking other questions about other kinds of relations. In particular, focusing on what seem to be essential, immutable, and persistent differences—whether of race or gender—may cause us not to notice differences that are accidental, acquired, or alterable, such as social and interlocutory positions. If Irene can talk frankly to Hugh, it may well be due to their similar class and social status, for Irene, as many commentators have noted, aspires to the values of the white bourgeoisie and mimics their lifestyle. (Of course, referring to Irene's lifestyle as that of the *white* middle class assumes black middle-class life can be described only in terms of white standards and values, that it is necessarily derivative, which is to subsume differences to similarities.) Nonetheless, while focusing on Irene's repressed sexuality or her middle-class aspirations may explain why Irene is frank with Hugh in a way that she is not with Clare, Irene's relation to Hugh is not as open or friendly as it seems at first, and what changes their relation is the intervention of race.

Irene and Hugh's conversation at the dance moves from the "safe" topic of interracial attraction to the issue of passing, that dangerous issue *not* brought up by Irene in her conversation with Clare. Irene points out to Hugh the instinctual ability of her own people to detect the difference between the races and the confirmed inability of whites to detect a passing Negro, which John Bellew, Clare's unsuspecting husband, most clearly attests to in the novel. Whites are incompetent when it comes to detecting passers, she says, because they look for tangible signs, such as physical features, when the telltale sign of race is something else (206, 150). As Irene puts it, what marks the difference between the races is a "thing that couldn't be registered" (206), something that cannot be recorded, verbalized, narrated, yet cannot fail to be detected. While Hugh agrees that there may be something other than appearance, speech, or gesture that enables one to detect racial difference, he still denies that one can always tell. "Yet lots of people 'pass' all the time," he remarks. Irene responds, "Not on our side, Hugh" (206).

Here a black woman draws on her experience to assert her authority over a white man, a well-known author and intellectual who is capable of discerning stupidity and self-deception in others and contemptuously revealing it in his writings. By making him see that what he thinks he sees from one position may not look the same from another, Irene exposes Hugh's lack of awareness, his self-deception, and thereby helps him to see more clearly, though what she helps him to see is "a thing that couldn't be registered"— not just racial difference, but the racism that makes passing a sign of racial difference in that only one race must pass. Thus, Irene forces on Hugh a more threatening insight. The passage continues:

> "It's easy for a Negro to 'pass' for white[, Irene says]. But I don't think it would
> be so simple for a white person to 'pass' for coloured."
> "Never thought of that."
> "No, you wouldn't. Why should you?" (206)

By making him see what he has never had to face—namely, the fact that as a white man Hugh has no need to think about passing, while for blacks the issue can be a matter of survival—Irene forces on him an awareness of his own failure of imagination ("Never thought of that") and his own implicit racism.

Hugh senses in this exchange that Irene has exposed the racial difference that their friendship has supposedly covered over: "Slippin' me, Irene?" he asks. He suspects that while they had appeared to have been talking frankly she may have been talking ironically, even sarcastically, misleading him rather than leading him to see more clearly. As in Irene and Clare's first meeting, to be frank whenever racial difference is at issue is, it seems, to risk being impertinent. Once difference is asserted, the possibility of misunderstanding and even deception intensifies: "Slippin' me, Irene?" If Hugh's question shows that he *has* detected his potential racism, it also suggests, in its very doubt and suspicion, his *resistance* to this knowledge, a knowledge that is so much at odds with his own self-concept as an intellectual and a friend of the black race.

Again, this exchange has implications for the teaching situation. In terms of the classroom dynamics, it suggests that even if we can overcome certain kinds of differences (race, gender) among our students by focusing on certain kinds of similarities (social, political)—that is, if we teach for diversity as a way of overcoming difference—those differences may still intervene in ways we are not even aware of, and once we do make them conscious, suspicions and resistances may be aroused. Focusing on racial difference in the classroom can arouse mistrust; downplaying it can result in ignorance and self-deception. Ignorance, says Shoshana Felman, is not a *lack* of information but a *desire* to ignore ("Psychoanalysis" 30). Where Irene earlier opted for silence to protect herself from knowledge she resists knowing, here Hugh protects his self-image by doubting the sincerity and distrusting the motives of the one who would teach him. Not only the unasked questions but the unacknowledged resistances can cause any communication to misfire. Reticence and resistance are not unique to the multicultural classroom, but they are intensified there. Where issues of racial, sexual, and cultural politics converge, communication may be destined to misfire.[6]

If Hugh's doubts and suspicions suggest that Irene may be "slippin'" him, later, at her tea party, she deliberately misleads him. In this scene Hugh proves quite discerning when he comes to understand what Irene has not yet allowed herself to face fully: namely, that Brian is having an affair with Clare. Yet that very insight is based on his initial misperception that Clare is white, which is in turn based on his prior assumption that white women are sexually attracted to black men. If he *does* suspect the affair (since the novel is written from Irene's point of view, we cannot be sure that his suspicion isn't her projection), then he has failed to learn the lesson Irene has tried to teach him:

that whites cannot detect those who pass. Further, what Hugh perceives may well be Irene's own fiction since, as McDowell suggests, Irene may well project her own sexual desire for Clare onto her husband in imagining an affair between them (xxviii). The possibility that what Hugh seems to detect is not fact but fiction is all the stronger given that this scene ends with Irene telling a story meant to mislead Hugh (as opposed to the earlier tea party scene at Clare's, where Irene is a passive accomplice in the rhetorics of misperception and Clare is the provocateur). If Hugh knows about Brian and Clare, Irene thinks, at least he won't know that she knows, and thus he won't share this scandalous secret, this intimacy, with her. Significantly, the story Irene tells misleads Hugh by focusing on racial difference (Hugh's family history of Confederate ancestors and Brian's family history of the underground railroad) rather than on sexual desire (Brian's affair with Clare).

Irene functions as McDowell says the novel's epigraph by Countee Cullen does, misleading Hugh and the reader to focus on "racial identity," inviting her interlocutors "to place race at the center of any critical interpretation" (xxiii).[7] Irene misleads her interlocutor not only as an unreliable narrator but also as a deliberate fabricator, even an ironist. With Hugh, the reader might ask, "Slippin' me, Irene?" Irene represents not only the contradictions of black female sexuality or the race problem, not only the psychological consequences of her own repressions, but the reticence, ambivalence, and deception of the narrative's own dynamic.

Positive Unreliability

All of this raises the question of just what kind of teacher Irene is and just what this novel can teach us.[8] *Passing* deals with both racial tensions and sexual desires, and to this extent it teaches us about social-historical and psychosexual conflicts, as criticism of the novel has revealed. But it also enacts the tensions involved in reading and teaching narratives that focus on multiple differences, and to this extent it can reveal the difficulties and resistances that ensue whenever we attempt to read, interpret, or teach in terms of *one* privileged reference point, whether sexual politics or racial politics, the authority of experience or the authority of theory. As Fuss has remarked, singling out a privileged category for investigation in and of itself is not a problem; "however," she says, "it becomes a problem when the central category of difference under consideration blinds us to other modes of difference" (*Essentially Speaking* 116). Fuss goes on to point to the related tendency "to see only one part of a subject's identity (usually the most visible part) and to make that part stand for the whole" (116). This is the very problem that Irene points out to Hugh at the dance: focusing on the visible signs of race leads him to miss the very difference he wants to know. If race is a thing that cannot be registered, as Irene says, it's not because it isn't important or "real" but that it isn't *apparent* because it isn't one thing but always "something else," and somewhere else. "Passing" as a metaphor suggests not simply deception or disguise but (dis)placement as well. The question of what we learn returns us to the difficulty of the reader's role in a text that is not identical with itself and, by analogy, the difficulty of the learner's role in the multicultural classroom. To understand the relation of passing to pedagogy is to come to terms with the politics of (dis)placement. In this way, *Passing* dramatizes the situation we find ourselves in as members of a classroom and an institution profoundly changed over the past two decades, in part as a result of changing canons and efforts to theorize notions of difference and resistance.

As an example of our plight as readers and learners, let me return to my earlier point where, drawing on McDowell's reading, I argued that the language Irene uses to describe interracial heterosexual attraction reveals her own intraracial homosexual attraction to Clare. The same language, I said, brings together very different relations. But how? By equating them? Or by subsuming one under the other? What is the nature of the relation between these issues of race and sexuality? Do we even have a choice between these positions?

As a way of beginning to answer these questions, let me return to another difficult position we as readers find ourselves in. (My return within a return here mimics the text's own repetitive dynamic in that the first part, entitled "Encounter," is really, as Johnson pointed out in her lecture on *Passing,* a "Re-encounter" between Irene and Clare, the title of the second part of the novel.) During their discussion of the issue of passing, Irene asks Brian why someone who finds passing repulsive, as she does, would nonetheless protect the passer's identity. Brian explains the contradictory emotions aroused by the passer in terms of the instinct of the race to survive. "Rot!" replies Irene, objecting that racial instinct cannot explain everything (186). In this scene, should the reader accept or reject Irene's response? If Irene represses knowledge of her sexual desires and her discomfort with her own racial identity, then we may be tempted to dismiss her rejection of Brian's explanation and agree with him that race relations are the real issue in this novel. But if so, we may well miss the alternative reading suggested by McDowell that would also dismiss the race argument, if not as "rot," then at least as a coverup. That is, we would end up reading as Johnson says readers of

African American literature do, looking for confrontational racial politics rather than sexual politics (*World* 167). To reject Irene's response is to risk being misled (by yielding to Brian's racial explanation); yet to accept it is to risk being deceived (by relying on an unreliable narrator). The reader faces an impossible choice because the issues brought together, those of race and sex, are not substitutable. Another way of putting this is to say that things brought into close proximity may be mistaken as similar, so that we are tempted to resolve the dilemma by conflating the two issues or by substituting one for the other as the real point of the story. That is, we may mistake a metonymy for a metaphor.

This is the insight brought out in both Johnson's *World of Difference* and Gallop's *Reading Lacan.* Johnson points to "the tendency of contiguity to become overlaid by similarity" so that things next to each other come to seem *like* each other, noting the preference given to similarity (seen as necessary) over contiguity (seen as chance) (*World* 157–58). It may not be entirely coincidental, then, that the plot of *Passing* is forwarded by chance: Irene first meets Clare by chance; Irene later runs into Clare's husband by chance; Clare falls out of the window by chance just as Irene arrives at her side. It is our "habit of discursive reading," as Gallop says (*Reading Lacan* 118), that leads us to expect some logical connection between scenes that will result in closure, unity, and wholeness and to resist discontinuities, divisions, and dis-closure. When Johnson discusses Zora Neale Hurston's "impossible position between two oppositions" (*World* 167), those of racial and sexual politics—a position that may seem similar to Larsen's plight as McDowell describes it—she insists on the necessity of holding these "incompatible forces" together while acknowledging that the desire for "some ultimate unity and peace" (164) structures narrative and, I would add, pedagogy, even though the result may be the displacement of the very differences that initiated that desire. The ending of *Passing,* then, which McDowell describes as a "dis-closure," or a failure of closure, given that it seems so contrived, is not a critical problem to be explained away but a *narrative necessity* in a text that deals with racial and sexual differences that can be neither resolved nor reconciled.

My point is that the problem of the ending of this novel comes as much from the reader's expectations and desires as from the author's conflicting identifications. The intersubjective relations in this narrative, and the roles played by race and sex in these exchanges, are analogous to the multicultural classroom situation where reticence, misperception, and distrust may structure the pedagogical exchange. In this sense *Passing* can teach us as much about classroom dynamics as about the ideological tensions an African American woman writer faced during the Harlem Renaissance. And if, as

Collins says, African American women students are likely to insist on the priority of experience, and to insist on knowing the lived experiences of those who teach them, we can accept this position without privileging experience. Instead, we can examine the position of authority as it is structured by the pedagogical exchange. That is, we can turn our attention from interpretation to transference.

As readers we may transfer authority to the text in the same way that as students we may transfer authority to the teacher (Gallop, *Reading Lacan* 27–28); when that teacher is presumed not to know because she or he lacks the authority of experience, we may be all the more ready to assume that the text knows what it is talking about. Yet the discovery of transference, as Gallop says, is the discovery that the teacher's (or the text's) authority is positional and not personal, the discovery that knowledge or authority is not someone's possession but something that happens between interlocutors. To analyze transference in the reading and teaching relation, as both Gallop and Jay urge us to do, is to risk the doubt and uncertainty that come from disrupting the illusion of authority, from exposing the "one presumed to know" as a structural position that is always taken up in relation to the other, the student. In this sense, not just the text of *Passing* but the teacher as well as the student is already in the position of an imposter, as Jay puts it (*American* 315). We are always "passing" in the classroom. Yet if we would learn the lesson Irene teaches Hugh, we must realize that "passing" functions differently for differently positioned subjects. If as teachers we are always "passing" in the classroom because our authority is positional, and if we are multiply positioned in the multicultural classroom, still, race may intervene in some of our classrooms to expose not simply the illusion of authority but the illusion of whiteness as well. If we are all "passing," Wall's question still pertains: "Passing for what?"

This in turn raises the question of just who is passing in this novel. As one who does not belong where he or she is, the passer is not only Clare, who at one point is described as being at home everywhere (208), not only Hugh, who as a white man does not obviously "belong" to Harlem, but also Irene, the "race woman" who in a sense passes as black. Ironically, Clare—the one who lacks race consciousness, passes in white society, and accepts the appellation "Nig" given to her by her racist husband—is more the "race woman" than Irene, who lives a bourgeois lifestyle, gives up her seat at a dance to a white man (Hugh), and clings to the security of her own place, unable or unwiling to see that her place—whether the Negro Welfare League dance, her middle-class marriage, or racist America—is already made vulnerable by the other.[9]

What I am suggesting is that if white teachers of nonwhite literature are in the structural position of authority, the ones presumed to know, but if they are presumed not to know because they lack the necessary personal experience, then the transference relation that structures authority may function differently whenever ethnic or racial difference is at issue. A student of a different racial or ethnic background may not confuse the structural position of (white) authority with the mastery of knowledge. Instead of a conflation of knowledge and authority (as in the conventional color-blind pedagogical situation, or the transference situation as Lacan presents it), there may be an oscillation between knowledge and ignorance, identification and alienation. *Passing* reveals more than the desire to ignore (that is, those repressions that form the pedagogical unconscious); it reveals as well the desire to keep the other ignorant. In *Mules and Men,* Hurston writes of the Negro's "feather-bed resistance" to white people's curiosity: "The theory behind our tactics: 'The white man is always trying to know into somebody else's business. All right, I'll set something outside the door of my mind for him to play with and handle. He can read my writing but he sho' can't read my mind'" (Gates and McKay 1033). In *The Signifying Monkey,* Gates, echoing Hurston, cites numerous examples of blacks signifying upon whites who come to them looking for "straight answers" to their questions about black culture, thereby keeping outsiders ignorant of certain information but also "schooling" them, Gates says, in difference and indirection. As readers we must learn the lesson Irene would teach Hugh: that we cannot always rely on tangible evidence or "straight answers," that our desire for certainty and full disclosure in our readings and our teachings about diversity may lead us to miss the very thing we want to know, that thing which cannot be registered.

Tate's essay on *Passing,* subtitled "A Problem of Interpretation," most clearly reflects the problems that arise from our positions as readers in this text and from our "habit of discursive reading." Like McDowell and Wall, Tate rejects early criticism of *Passing* that focuses on the racial conflict and focuses instead on the psychological conflict. Dismissing race as a mere "device" to forward the action, Tate stresses Larsen's skill in portraying Irene's psychological conflicts, particularly her increasing jealousy of Clare, through her use of deliberate ambiguity and her ironic undercutting of Irene's remarks. As her subtitle indicates, Tate's primary concern is interpretation, and her goal is to simplify problems of interpretation, as she says, by deciding just how far we can trust Irene (143). Yet in detailing Irene's misperceptions (144–45), Tate finds herself in an uncomfortable position. We cannot judge the truth or falsity of Irene's perceptions after all, she says, for we have "no tangible evidence" of their truth and thus "we cannot know with any certainty" (145). Without such evidence we cannot say for certain whether or not Irene pushes Clare out of the window; we cannot "arrive at a definite conclusion" (146) about the end of the novel. The long penultimate paragraph of her essay, in which Tate struggles with her own uncertainty, is revealing less for what it says about the novel than for what it suggests about the reader's position:

> *Passing*'s conclusion defies simple solution. I cannot resolve this problem by accepting a single explanation, since Larsen, on [the] one hand, deliberately withheld crucial information that would enable me to arrive at a definite conclusion, and on the other, she counter-balanced each possible interpretation with another of equal credibility. . . . my admission of uncertainty is my honest response to the work, given only after serious consideration of my position as a literary critic. In fact, my inability to arrive at a conclusion in and of itself attests to Larsen's consummate skill in dramatizing psychological ambiguity. (146)

Privileging interpretation and tangible evidence, Tate projects onto the story the very undecidability her approach creates, attributing discontinuities and dis-closure to the author's skillful craftsmanship rather than to her own possibly faulty or misplaced assumptions. Tate finds herself in a position similar to Hugh Wentworth, who also relies on "tangible evidence" to detect passers, attributing their success to their ability to disguise their race rather than to his misperceptions about race. Like Hugh, who in many ways figures as the white teacher of African American literature, Tate misses the very "lesson" Irene would teach us: that we cannot always rely on tangible evidence and that desiring certainty and coherence in our interpretations may lead us to project the absence of such traits onto the craft or craftiness of the other—the text, the passer, or the teacher or student who has had a different racial, ethnic, or gender experience. This unanalyzed transference assures us in our own self-ignorance.

If this *is* the lesson *Passing* would teach us, however, we can learn this lesson only by acknowledging Irene's resistance to knowing, by recognizing her insights as partial and her authority as vulnerable. That is, we can only learn the lesson of *Passing*—and passing—if we are willing to learn from someone who does not know.

A Novel with a Moral

Our impossible position as readers may provide insight into our position as learners, as one final example may show.[10] At the end of the novel, when Irene finally faces the sexual relationship between Brian and Clare that she has long resisted knowing, she finds that "knowing . . . had changed her" (218) and that she "didn't like changes" (188). In fact, Irene becomes bitter when she discovers that the unknown is really quite familiar: "What bitterness! That the one fear, the one uncertainty, that she had left, Brian's ache to go somewhere else, should have dwindled to a childish triviality [an affair]! . . . Desperately she tried to shut out the knowledge from which had risen this turmoil, which she had no power to moderate or still, within her" (223). Irene resists this knowledge and regains her control and her security by convincing herself that the affair is her own fabrication. After all, she has no tangible evidence to support her "unfounded suspicion," so she can assure herself that "she has no real knowledge" (223) and can remain secure in her own nonknowledge. If we accept, as McDowell suggests, that Irene has imagined this affair by projecting her feelings for Clare onto Brian, then we risk acquiescing in her own nonknowledge. But if we dismiss her rationalization here and accept the affair she shrinks from knowing, then we risk being misled by her own earlier suspicions and (mis)perceptions. We seem to be caught again in an impasse: between disbelieving in a real affair dismissed as a fabrication and misbelieving in a fabricated affair presented as real. In either case we face the uncomfortable awareness that we may have been misled, not only *by* Irene, but *like* Irene. We seem to be caught between denial and deception. This is our impossible position as readers of *Passing* and as teachers and students in the multicultural classroom.[11]

It is also our impossible situation as readers of realistic fiction, conceived as the representation of the lived experiences of certain individuals: namely, we are caught between the necessity and the error of taking it seriously or literally. We can neither trust the text to be "like life," given that it is a fabrication, nor dismiss the text as false, given that it is "like life." The fiction is significant only to the extent that it functions like a real event; the event is significant only to the extent that it is part of a narrative structure, an insight drawn as much from psychoanalysis as from narrative fiction. The danger fiction poses is that we may mistake it for life and come to live our lives according to the clichés of fiction—and, at the other extreme, that we may dismiss it as a representation of experience to focus on its textuality alone. However, we face a dilemma here only if we accept the relation of fiction to life as *the* defining relation of the novel, that is, only if we accept the prevailing assumptions of traditional pedagogies: a critical formalism that ignores experience and an expressive realism that privileges it. To assert the authority of experience is to privilege difference and thus to risk devaluing the experience of others; to subsume difference under similarity by discussing all literature in relation to the same "universal" model is still to risk devaluing the distinctively racial or sexual experience. *Passing* plays out this contradiction. Once we grasp the dynamics of the intersubjective relations acted out in this novel, once we give up the expectation of full disclosure or shared meaning, we are in a better position to grasp the dynamics of the multicultural classroom and the conditions that make it possible to learn about diversity.

What I have been attempting to demonstrate through my allegorical reading is the difficulty of the reader's role in a text that insists on its self-difference and, by analogy, the difficulty of the teacher's and student's positions in a classroom where we can take neither similarities nor differences for granted—which is to take them as "natural," as something that goes without saying, rather than as something constructed by the very dynamics of our engagement. The reticence, resistance, ambivalence, and deception that structure the reading and teaching situations make readers as well as learners feel nonidentical with themselves as they try to establish a position in this relation. Our desire to explain Irene's self-difference in terms of what she denies leads us to deny, along with Irene, that identity *is* self-difference. As Tate's and McDowell's readings reveal, the attempt to resolve the problem of dis-closure must always result in the coverup one meant to expose and in the insecurity one meant to relieve. This situation in turn gives rise to the caveat syndrome that I discuss in chapter 2. Similarly, Irene's resistance to being displaced, *by* Clare or *to* Brazil, leaves her clinging to a racist America that Brian would escape as well as the kind of loveless marriage that Clare wants to end. The security Irene clings to is menaced by the vulnerability and illusoriness of those ideals. It is this insecurity and self-difference, or dis-placement, that must be confronted in teaching for diversity.

At times we may have to accept the unsaid or unasked as the limits of our knowledge, not as the truth to be extracted by a closer reading or a more enlightened pedagogy. If knowledge and authority reside anywhere, it is in the undecidability of irresolvable differences, the place where meaning misfires, the place of our own displacement; for the fear that seems to drive pedagogy and criticism in this multicultural era is less the fear of appropriation (after all, interpretation *is* appropriation) than the fear of displacement, the fear that others may come to claim our institutional positions. For me, then, the moment of insight in *Passing* comes when Irene admits what "she had long known": "she was aware that, to her, security was the most important and desired thing in life" (235). This desire for "safety and permanence" informs readings of realistic novels and traditional pedagogy. The "menace of impermanence" (229), the possibility that our reading may not end in a shared understanding or a resolution of conflicts, the possibility that our institutional or theoretical positions may be lost to and through others, is what we must confront, and *theorize,* if we are to teach *for* diversity, not simply about it. For Irene, as for many teachers and students, security and certainty go together; what she resists knowing is that knowing may be associated with insecurity and vulnerability. Yet this is precisely what we learn in reading *Passing* and in reading poststructuralist theory. A poststructuralist reading need not impose a "foreign language" on indigenous literatures if it raises the questions at issue in teaching and reading those literatures: what kind of authority is at stake and at risk?

Still, while I set out to show that "postmodern theories" are not inimical to African American or multicultural literature, what I may have ended up doing is (re)casting the issues of an African American woman's novel in the terms of a theoretical position that is not entirely strange but certainly not entirely friendly. Acknowledging that my theoretical reading is alien in many ways to the text and its context produces in me a certain discomfort, a feeling of disclosure—disclosure of my own possible complicity with forms of domination, "wrapped around [me] like a flag," and dis-closure as the lack of closure, the vulnerability I feel in confronting what I do not know.

In his reading of *Passing,* Peter Rabinowitz presents this theoretical dilemma as a moral one. "'Betraying the Sender'" considers the possibility that "some theoretical positions may be incompatible with some texts—not because they don't expose the workings of the text, but precisely because they *do,* and in so doing, inflict significant damage" (206–7). In teaching and interpreting "fragile" texts (those whose performative effects depend on less than full disclosure), Rabinowitz asks, are we "giving our students interpretive keys to cultures that have been trying to counter precisely the cultural forces that the American academy represents?" (208) He raises important ethical questions about our reading and teaching of multicultural literature, confronting the guilt produced in the reader who, from a position of privilege, comes to understand the textual codes of a marginalized group (see, for example, his note 16 on page 211). But I would like to offer a slight modification in Rabinowitz's staging of the moral conflict here. The phrase "interpretive keys" and the metaphor of finding "keys" to the closet are themselves ethically problematic, as Rabinowitz says of the metaphor of "decoding" texts (209). Or, rather, they are ethically *inappropriate* for the kind of dynamics he describes and the kind of dynamics I have been exploring throughout this book. As Rabinowitz understands, the very process of negotiating the "legitimate, but competing, demands (including ethical demands)" (207) that texts make on us as readers and teachers is itself the reward of studying fragile texts, not the "secret" that we reveal. The metaphor of a privileged reader "outing" a fragile text relies on a traditional notion of passing, as if individuals and texts were either "in" or "out" of the closet, and a traditional notion of pedagogy, as if teaching students to read texts means giving them ever more knowledge, enabling them to master a method of reading or a field of study. In other words, the ethical problem Rabinowitz identifies—the concern with giving students the "keys" to the text—is itself a product of reigning pedagogies in the academy. These ethical questions are urgent, he says, because we teach multicultural literatures and deal with "culturally charged questions" (209). I would say these ethical issues *arise from* our teaching of multicultural literatures. That is, what the teaching of multicultural literatures and cultural criticism has brought to literary studies is a new ethical dynamic that could never have been conceptualized in terms of canonical literatures and the formalist and expressivist pedagogies discussed in chapter 2.

I admire Rabinowitz's willingness to confront the ethical implications of what we often do as teachers in the multicultural classroom in the name of a more enlightened pedagogy and a "self-congratulatory liberalism" (201). He observes that the literary academy "is organized around an unexamined commitment to the act of publication—in the broad sense of 'making public'" (209). "Is it possible," Rabinowitz asks, "that there's something unhealthy about the profession's devotion, not to secrets, but to *exposing* secrets?" (209). He reminds us of what we tend to forget in the game of "making public": to the extent that a novel like *Passing* "provides a certain kind of pleasure and support for a still-oppressed group," serving "some social or psychological or aesthetic function for actual readers," our teaching of the novel "has significant practical (as opposed to theoretical) consequences for flesh-and-blood readers" (207). Yet the double bind he articulates—namely, that we cannot *not* teach texts from other cultures but in doing so we ultimately "betray" them—is less a problem for the teacher to resolve than the very possibility of an ethical practice. "But even if we can never eliminate the risks involved," Rabinowitz writes, "it is still worth discussing how to articulate them, and how to confront them responsibly" (209). It is for this reason that I say *Passing* is a novel with a moral and that I suggest "passing" as a metaphor for the dynamics of responsibility. Sissela Bok offers an important insight in her book, *Secrets:* how one learns to deal with secrecy reveals much about how one becomes aware of "one's self among others" and thus about "the possibility of moral choice" (xvi).[12]

If we find reason for despair in all this talk of miscommunication and displacement, reticence and resistance, lack of closure and lack of knowledge, it may be because we have not yet learned to face or to theorize the "menace of impermanence" and the threat of displacement that *is* our contemporary condition. The pedagogical assumption that we must learn to resist if we are to teach for diversity is the assumption, as Barbara Eckstein says, that vulnerability, uncertainty, and inconclusiveness have no authority and are inimical to learning. To give up the certainty and security that traditionally have been associated with authority *is* to put ourselves in the place of the "other," the unauthorized, the disfranchised, who bears the burden of race (Fuss, *Essentially Speaking* 75). The despair or resistance we feel in giving up our security may be a measure of our own failure of imagination—and, as Gates has said, racism *is* a failure of the imagination ("Transforming").

NOTES

1. In a 1997 essay in *College English,* Ruth Spack criticizes my opening example: "Caughie does not acknowledge her own role in promoting the guest lecturer as the authority. Nor does she note the irony of allowing a person of privilege to present herself as an authority on the less privileged in her country" (13). Certainly I promoted Glory as an authority by inviting her to my class, but the point of my opening anecdote is that her authority to speak on matters of Indian culture and history (which I had asked her to address) transferred to her an authority to speak on gender and class politics. I did not invite Glory as an authority in feminist criticism yet her feminist reading of the story was accepted where mine was not *because* she was a native speaker. But I don't believe that by offering a critique of the class politics in the story Glory was presenting herself "as an authority on the less privileged in her country"; rather, she was presenting a reading of the story based on her training in feminist, poststructuralist, and postcolonial theories. Still, Spack's objections are yet another example of the anxiety my book confronts, the anxiety produced by efforts to speak "as" or "for."

2. As I mention in my prefacing remarks, certain terms slide into one another in this book and this is one example. By "multicultural" classroom I do not mean simply a classroom focused on non-Western or ethnic literatures, nor a classroom made up of students from diverse cultural groups, but, more important, a classroom that, no matter what its subject matter or demographics, is structured, explicitly or implicitly, by the concerns, assumptions, and methodologies of cultural criticism.

3. These were the issues I was exploring when I first drafted this chapter. Since then several essays relevant to this discussion have been published, including essays by Butler (*Bodies*), Rabinowitz ("'Betraying'"), and Martha Cutter. I have not reconceived the chapter in response to these and other recent articles on this novel, though I refer to some of them in passing. Given this spurt of publications, the plot of the novel is likely more familiar to my readers today than it was in 1992 when an earlier version of this chapter first appeared but retelling the plot is crucial to my reading.

4. In reference to this passage, Spack argues that I let white people "off the hook" by attributing their reluctance to talk about race to politeness. But I hope my point here is clear. I am not suggesting that politeness is a valid excuse for the failure to confront racial differences in the classroom. I am exposing the various feelings that make many students and teachers uncomfortable when it comes to discussing race,

not excusing them for those feelings. In this passage I assume the voice of students and teachers who consciously or unconsciously experience this conflict. It is precisely the dynamics structured by such feelings in which I hope to intervene. Spack seems to have missed the point I make later: namely, that "the white student's hesitancy to talk about the black student's difference may be less a matter of discretion [politeness] than of self-protection."

Spack's misreading is symptomatic. She begins her article by pitting my comment, based on my students' responses, against a comment from Toni Morrison's "Unspeakable Things Unspoken." Spack says I let white people off the hook whereas Morrison forces whites to confront "unspeakable things" such as "race" (9). Whose authority or self-perception is being anxiously protected, I ask, when a white woman uses a black woman to voice her disagreement with another white woman? For an analysis of this kind of dynamic, see the interlude and especially chapter 5.

5. The nonnative reader need not be a resisting reader, in Judith Fetterley's sense of that term, although the resisting reader is one who is positioned as an "outsider" to the text, whether in terms of her or his gender, race, sexuality, or ethnicity.

6. In light of Spack's misreading of my essay (discussed in note 4), I will reiterate what I believe should by now be obvious: I do not see the situation I describe here as a problem to be resolved but as the very possibility of a responsible and responsive pedagogy.

7. The epigraph reads: "One three centuries removed / From the scenes his fathers loved, / Spicy grove, cinnamon tree, / What is Africa to me?"

8. The section heading plays on Barbara Johnson's "Rigorous Unreliability," the title of chapter 2 in *A World of Difference.*

9. Butler articulates a connection between Irene's belief in racial uplift and her class status: "This moral notion of 'race' . . . also requires the idealization of bourgeois family life in which women retain their place in the family. The institution of the family also protexts black women from a public exposure of sexuality that would be rendered vulnerable to a racist construction and exploitation" (*Bodies* 178).

10. The section heading plays on the subtitle of Jessie Redmon Fauset's novel *Plum Bun: A Novel without a Moral* (1928). Ironically, Fauset's novel, not Larsen's more modernist one, is seen by critics to present a moral lesson.

11. This "impossible position" is not unlike what Walter Benjamin describes as the position of the intellectual in the class struggle: "Here it is quite palpable where the conception of the 'intellectual,' as a type defined by his opinions, attitudes, or dispositions, but not by his position in the process of production, leads. He must . . . find his place *beside* the proletariat. But what kind of place is that? That of a benefactor, of an ideological patron—an impossible place" (301–3).

12. On the one hand, Bok says, secrecy "guards central aspects of identity" (13) and thus "some control over secrecy and openness is needed in order to protect identity: the sense of what we identify ourselves as, through and with" (20). This is the view Rabinowitz would seem to hold. On the other hand, prolonged concealment can impair one's sense of identity, Bok points out, by depriving one of the "benefit of challenge and exposure" (25). That is, secrecy is not just a matter of being closeted, as the notion of betraying the text suggests. Although the defining trait of secrecy is intentional concealment, "one cannot always know what is and is not intentionally kept hidden," Bok writes (9). "Some things we believe we know; many we are con-

scious of not knowing; and in between are countless shadings of belief, vacillation, and guesswork" (10). Indeed, Bok is skeptical of the claim that any secret, no matter how carefully concealed, can be betrayed, for "secrecy will never be reducible to any one set of secrets, any more than to one stage of human development or figurative compartment of the self" (36). I return to Bok's *Secrets* in my closing remarks, "Coming Out."

FOUR

Teaching "Woman"

The shame of being a man—is there any better reason to write?
  —Gilles Deleuze, "Literature and Life"

"This was woman herself, with her sudden fears, her irrational whims, her in-stinctive worries, her impetuous boldness, her fussings, and her delicious sensi-bility." So begins Roland Barthes's influential 1968 essay "The Death of the Author" (*Image/Music/Text* 142). The quotation, from Honoré de Balzac's *Sarrasine,* gives rise to Barthes's provocative question that has changed the very nature of reading: "Who is speaking thus?" "Is it the hero of the story bent on remaining ignorant of the castrato hidden beneath the woman? Is it Balzac the individual, furnished by his personal experience with a philoso-phy of Woman? Is it Balzac the author professing 'literary' ideas on feminin-ity? Is it universal wisdom? Romantic psychology? We shall never know, for the good reason that writing is the destruction of every voice, of every point of origin" (142).

Barthes's reading of *Sarrasine,* published in *S/Z* (1970), is often said to mark the turning point from structuralism to poststructuralism in literary studies. I begin with Barthes because the concept of literature implicit in his notion of the "death of the author" has given rise to a form of cultural crit-icism that I engage throughout this book. In this chapter, perhaps the most explicit discussion of cultural criticism in the book, I take the reader through a particular teaching situation to suggest the possibilities of cultural criticism for what I call a "performative pedagogy." Specifically, the chapter focuses on my teaching of D. H. Lawrence in a Women in Literature course. The in-clusion of a male writer in such a course immediately arouses suspicion. For some students, his inclusion spoils the course by diluting what they thought would be an exclusive and celebratory focus on women writers; for others, his presence suggests that he will serve as the straw man, held up to contempt for his sexist representations of women. While I do not want to allay these suspicions too quickly, for I believe they have their place in a performative pedagogy, I also do not want to get stuck on the horns of that dilemma. Realistically, no amount of protestation on my part can or should keep such suspicions at bay, but, more important, the political and ideological concerns they raise are especially relevant to a cultural criticism approach in which the culture of the classroom will inevitably produce such concerns—*if* what I am calling the "dynamics of responsibility" are at work, as required by the very cultural criticism approach I employ in this course. For me, the presence of Lawrence on my syllabus makes Barthes's questions all the more salient and pressing. Where *do* a writer's notions of woman, femininity, and female sexuality come from? How, when, and why do gender ideologies get constituted, produced, and reproduced? How do gender ideologies relate to processes of racialization? Whose voice is speaking in the text? Does it matter who is speaking? And what does the question of voice have to do with "woman herself"? The title of this chapter, then, is deliberately ambiguous, referring both to the literary text that is its subject, Lawrence's novella "The Woman Who Rode Away" (hereafter abbreviated "Woman"), and to the topic of my Women in Literature course, the cultural construction of "woman" in early twentieth-century Anglo-American society. The title also obliquely and perversely refers to the subject writing this chapter—namely, me, a teaching woman.

Although the description of the pedagogy offered here may confirm some people's suspicions about cultural studies (e.g., that literature becomes merely the pretext for exploring, in Biddy Martin's words, "the discursive production of historical formations" [8], such as "woman") and perhaps dispel others (e.g., that literature is reduced to sociology), I offer it not as an argument for a particular approach to literature but as a specific example that enables us to consider some of the effects of passing, as I have refigured that concept, on the writing and reading of literature, and to consider the ways in which cultural criticism forces us to recognize and come to terms with passing. In discussing how I teach Lawrence's "Woman" in a Women in Literature course, I will return to issues raised in chapter 2, where I discuss the metaphors of the tourist and the nomad as figuring modernist and postmodernist concepts of displacement. In this chapter I return to those metaphors by way of a literary text that promotes displacement (through a change in physical locale as well as through a spiritual or psychic identification) as a characteristically modernist way of refiguring the self.

Lawrence wrote "The Woman Who Rode Away" in Taos, New Mexico, in the summer of 1924, and it was first published in *Dial* in 1925. Set in the Sierra Madre during the recession years following World War I, the story tells of a woman in her early thirties whose boredom with her isolated surroundings and conventional marriage, coupled with her romantic notions of Mexican Indians, leads her to seek out the Chilchui, "the sacred tribe of all the Indians" (42), who live in the mountains beyond her home. When her husband, Lederman, is away on business, the woman (unnamed) rides away from home and children on a spiritual quest to find these "mysterious savages" (42) who still practice the ancient religion of their ancestors. Discovered in the mountains by the Chilchui, the woman is taken hostage and spends several months in the village as the priests prepare for her sacrifice at the winter solstice. The story ends with the sacrificial knife poised above her naked body.

Not surprisingly, most students find the ending disturbing. Through reading Lawrence's essays on the Southwest and comparing them with passages such as, "She lived on, in a kind of daze, feeling her power ebbing more and more away from her, as if her will were leaving her, . . . as if she were diffusing out deliciously into the harmony of things" ("Woman" 62), students come to see that Lawrence wants to represent the sacrifice of the petty individualism and self-centeredness of Western culture for the cosmic harmony of the ancient religious sensibility. Many are sympathetic to what they perceive as Lawrence's celebration of Indian culture and values. Lawrence's essay "New Mexico" helps students to discern in his representation of the Indians the author's criticism of Western materialism and patriarchy as embodied in that "little dynamo of energy" ("Woman" 39), the husband, Lederman: "He loved work, work, work, and making things. His marriage, his children, were something he was making, part of his business, but with a sentimental income this time" ("Woman" 40). In "New Mexico," Lawrence criticizes Western tourists whose "foolish romanticism," as he puts it in "Woman" (42), leads them to accept a celluloid image of New Mexico proffered by the film industry. The red kerchief that figures the tourist in "New Mexico" reappears in "Woman" as the "pathetic bit of a red tie" (55) that makes up part of the woman's riding attire, which the Indians literally cut off her. The red scarf knotted around her neck becomes a metonym for western imperialism and commercialism, thereby linking the woman and the tourist.[1]

From the turn of the century through the 1920s, according to Desley Deacon, biographer of the anthropologist Elsie Clews Parsons, business leaders, amateur archaeologists, artists, writers, and wealthy patrons banded together to promote "a romantic mix of archeology, art, tourism, and politics" in the Southwest (220). Intent on countering the notion of Indians as a degenerate or dying race, such institutions as the School of American Research and "colonies" of eastern visitors gathering at the homes of wealthy people, most notably Mabel Dodge, sought to promote Native American culture and to "reinvent themselves" in this exotic, pristine, and "primitive" locale. While they looked for ways to incorporate native art and ritual into Western lives and culture "without patronizing, appropriating, or destroying" the indigenous peoples (Deacon 221–22), such a project was necessarily fraught with ambiguity. Cultural preservation depended on western tourism; spiritual renewal meant "going native." "The Southwest is the great playground of the White American," Lawrence wrote in 1924. "The desert isn't good for anything else. But it does make a fine national playground. And the Indian . . . he's a wonderful live toy to play with" (qtd. in Deacon 222). Lawrence's "Woman" clearly criticizes this national pastime and even reverses its spiritual trajectory by suggesting that Native Americans can reinvent or reclaim themselves only by destroying the patronizing western tourist. Even so, the story also depends on and contributes to the appeal of this pastime in its representation of the Chilchui.

Yet, however sympathetic students might be to Lawrence's promotion of Indian culture and to his criticism of western tourism, most cannot accept the ending of the story. What bothers them is not just the human sacrifice but the representation of the woman as a passive accomplice. Described throughout as already dead, lacking any "will of her own" (45), the woman is nonetheless seen by the narrator as well as the Indians as willing, indeed desiring, her own sacrifice. Lawrence writes, "She knew she was a victim: that all this elaborate work upon her was the work of victimising her. But she did not mind. She wanted it" (67). The language of the rape defense strikes home. Leo, a student in my class, responded to the sacrifice in a characteristic way: "The last sacrificial scene is supposed to show the cosmic unity and balance, but instead it becomes another scene of male dominance through its allusion to rape," he writes. "The nakedness of the woman, the dark sacrificial stone, the 'four men holding her by the outstretched arms and legs,' the sun's last rays touching the 'shaft of ice,' and the impending insertion of the sacrificial knife into her body all serve to show male sexual dominance over the woman."[2] Why must a woman be the victim, students complain, and why does she come to accept her impending death? She has no epiphany. She achieves no power, no insight. Indeed, during the ceremony that will end in her death, "no-one translated" ("Woman" 68). The woman "is only a means to an end," writes Jennifer, another student. "She has made the ultimate sacrifice for a man. Instead of making the sacrifice a noble action the woman agrees to submit to for the benefit of humanity, Lawrence uses the sacrifice as a power trip for men, proving that he is anything but a feminist." Such observations, which suggest that Lawrence might easily be dismissed as reactionary in his portrayal of women even if he is to be commended as liberal in his treatment of race, move us from interpreting the meaning of the story in terms of the author's notion of cosmic unity to interrogating the notion of womanhood that informs the writer's representation of that vision.

Here Mary Poovey's definition of "culture" as it is understood by poststructuralist cultural critics can help students to make this shift. According to Poovey, culture is "the ensemble of categories and signifying systems that provide the terms through which humans understand our world, from which we derive our identity, and in which we formulate and express desire" ("Cultural Criticism" 618). Poovey brings the critiques of identity (as stable) and reference (as given) derived from poststructuralism and feminism to cultural criticism's preoccupation with culture as the ground of human activity. The result, she says, is "something like the three-tiered enterprise" that she calls "cultural criticism": "the study of culture as an interdependent set of institutional and informal practices and discourses; the study of the traces this larger social formation produces in individual texts; the study of the role our own practice—in this case, teaching—plays in reproducing or subverting the dominant cultural formation" (620). The basic principle of cultural criticism thus defined is that "concepts we treat as if they were things are seen as the effects of representations and institutional practices, not their origins" (621). Tracing the effects of these practices in individual texts requires paying close attention to language.

Deliberately beginning with a passage that inevitably provokes anger in some students, I shift the focus of class discussion from Lawrence's beliefs to his language: "Her kind of womanhood, intensely personal and individual, was to be obliterated again, and the great primeval symbols were to tower once more over the fallen individual independence of woman. The sharpness and the quivering nervous consciousness of the highly-bred white woman was to be destroyed again, womanhood was to be cast once more into the great stream of impersonal sex and impersonal passion" ("Woman" 60). "Who is speaking here?" I ask my students, echoing Barthes. Is it the narrator expressing the views of the Indians who will eventually sacrifice the woman? Is it Lawrence the writer offering his hyper-individualist, materialist, and sex-conscious age a philosophy of sexual harmony? Is it Lawrence the man expressing his personal misogyny and what we might call today his "inverse racism"? Identifying where such notions of (white) womanhood come from is our task in reading this story.

Barthes's poststructuralist critique of the author as origin, as the intending subject behind the text, and of the classical notion of representation as the re-presentation of a pre-existing reality provides the theoretical under-pinnings for our investigation of these questions. For Barthes, writing is no longer conceived in terms of its meaning or content, to be explained by ref-erence to the Author. That humanist model ignores the signifying force of language and cultural discourses that, through disciplines and institutions, provide the terms through which we represent ourselves as subjects in rela-tion to others. Instead, according to Barthes, writing is a "tissue of quota-tions drawn from the innumerable centres of culture" (*Image/Music/Text* 146), a "neutral space" where identities and bodies are "lost" (142). To speak of the "death" of the Author is not to deny the reality of identities, bodies, and intending subjects; rather, the coinage refers to the *critique* of the con-cepts of author, individual, originality, and intentionality that have long been central to the teaching of literature. A *critique* does not repudiate or negate certain beliefs and values but interrogates the historical conditions of their emergence and the "nonconscious presuppositions" they carry with them.[3] To say, "it is language which speaks, not the author" (*Image/Music/Text* 143) is to open inquiry into those "innumerable centres of culture" that are the very precondition of the writer's agency and creativity.

By way of opening this kind of investigation, I ask my students, "What motivates this sacrificial narrative and the representation of the woman and the Indians upon which its emotional and ideological effects depend?"[4] To begin to answer this question (one we return to throughout the course as we study other texts from the 1920s and 1930s), we go through the story noting the adjectives and imagery used to describe the woman, the Indians, and the land, as well as the kinds of oppositions set up between the races and between the sexes. The woman is described as "dazed," "void," and "dead," that last adjective linking her to the stripmined land, the "thrice-dead little Spanish town" near her home, and the dead silver market (39). The woman's con-scious development, we are told, has been arrested since marriage; she is morally held down by her husband (40). Such characterizations suggest her passivity and powerlessness and provide evidence (as Freud's writings have been said to do) of the oppressive effects of patriarchy on the psychology and moral capacity of women. Like Freud's essays on female sexuality from the 1930s and Virginia Woolf's *Room of One's Own*, which are also covered in this course, Lawrence's "Woman" could be seen to critique the construction of "woman" in patriarchy.

Yet Lawrence's woman is also "assured," a word repeatedly used to de-scribe her and linked with other adjectives such as "proud," "spoilt," and "foolhardy." Such descriptive terms suggest that her character flaws are partly responsible for her fatal destiny. It is her assertion of her independence and her rebellion against her "invincible slavery" (40)—kept in a "walled-in" adobe house (39) as if womanhood were, as Woolf quips, a "protected occupation" (*Room* 40)—that initiates the action of the story. She "had *harassed* her husband into letting her go riding with him"; later she forces her male servant to *yield* to her "peculiar overbearing" insistence that she go out riding alone; and she *silences* her young son when he questions her defiance of conventional gender roles: "Am I *never* to be let alone?" ("Woman" 43). Although the narrative in no way defends those conventional roles of wife, mistress, and mother—in fact, it challenges them—the woman's triumph over the men in her life is itself an effect of the sexual imbalance that needs to be restored through her ritual sacrifice. "Her ordinary personal consciousness" eventually succumbs to the "passional cosmic consciousness" of the Indians' religious vision (64). In other words, "Woman" at once challenges certain conventional notions of gender difference (e.g., women are property, husbands are masters) and mobilizes others (e.g., women are passive, men are active) in the service of a new sexual philosophy.

The Indians are described variously as marvelous, mysterious, and timeless, but also as unsanitary, indecent, and cunning, depending on whether the romanticized or the racist view of the natives is being invoked. These opposing views are readily accounted for in that the descriptive terms are attributed to a specific character, as in Lederman's racist dismissal of the Indians as "lowdown and dirty," all of them "more or less alike," and the "peculiar vague enthusiasm" for this ancient and mysterious people expressed by the young visitor to the Lederman home ("Woman" 42). My students readily see that Lawrence resists both views. But what about other adjectives and attitudes that are not tied to a specifiable narrative voice? "Savage" is the most common adjective or appellation used for the Indians and serves to link the divergent views of Lederman and the young visitor as well as the narrator's descriptions of the Indians and their religious ceremonies. Along with "barbaric," "wild," "terrible," "fierce," "inhuman," and "impersonal," "savage" recurs obsessively throughout the narrative. Clearly the term functions oppositionally to establish a fundamental contrast between civilized and primitive man. For example, in contrast to the "civilized" men (the husband, son, and servant), the Indians never yield to the woman's demands. Their relentless nature, their calm self-assurance without self-consciousness, and their "powerful physical presence" without sex-consciousness establish their difference from and superiority to modern Westerners who are highly "self-conscious" and "sex-conscious" (58–59).[5] But whose perspective are we getting in such passages? Where do these notions of Indians come from?

The uncertainty over who is speaking in passages such as those cited above can lead students to accept these insistent, indeed obsessive, characterizations as neutral ones. While most students in my women's studies class are quick to pick up on any loaded representations of the woman, many take the descriptions of the Indians at face value. Adjectives such as "proud," "foolish," and "childish" used for the woman clearly represent to them a specific, and specifically sexist, attitude, yet the kinds of adjectives used for the Indians are often seen to be *merely* descriptive. For many, Indians *are* proud, whereas the woman's pride signals a particular point of view, a masculine point of view that needs to disparage independent-minded women. The challenge is to get the students to ask how certain representations of natives and women come about and to question how certain representations can become so ingrained in our cultural imagination that we take them for granted as natural.

An answer begins to emerge when we examine another pair of adjectives used to describe and contrast the woman and the Indians. The woman is frequently described as "white," the Indians as "dark," more particularly "black." Students commonly take these terms as *simply* physical descriptions, rarely noting their persistent and even peculiar use. For example, observing the young Indian who guards her, the woman thinks:

> He seemed to have no sex, as he sat there so still and gentle and apparently submissive, with his head bent a little forward, and the river of glistening black hair streaming maidenly over his shoulders.
>
> Yet when she looked again, she saw his shoulders broad and powerful, his eyebrows black and level, the short, curved, obstinate black lashes over his lowered eyes, the small, fur-like line of moustache above his blackish, heavy lips, and the strong chin, and she knew that in some other mysterious way he was darkly and powerfully male. (58)

Once the persistent use of "black" is pointed out to them, students pick up on the identification of blackness and maleness in this and other descriptive passages. Because maleness for Lawrence is an elemental force, not an individual attribute, blackness or darkness suggests not a racial category but a primal spiritual state.

As Hazel Carby asserts in a lecture based on her book *Race Men: The Body and Soul of Race, Nation, and Manhood,* one of the most persuasive artistic fictions of the modernist movement was the invention of an essential black masculinity that served as a trope for spiritual renewal and utopian possibilities ("Body and Soul"). Focusing on nude photographs of Paul Robeson taken in the 1920s, Carby argues that the desires of white men for cultural representations of an unconflicted, essential masculinity were located in a black body. The black man came to stand for an ideal of masculinity that was transindividual, transsocial, and transhistorical. An internal spiritual essence was invented from a bodily difference, she argues. Lawrence's "Woman" participates in the creation of such an aesthetic fiction. Yet those modernist appeals to a transcendent and individual ideal of nobility and spiritual beauty, Carby says, were removed from and actively repressed the history of exploitation, oppression, and violence that made up the very cultural icon that is seen to represent this ideal. As a creation of the modernist aesthetic, the black man no more than the white woman could be a political accomplice in the work for social change.[6]

The persuasiveness and persistence of this modernist fiction as Carby defines it is evident today in what I call the "born-again men's movement." Indeed, Lawrence's notion of race in this story and his use of the Indians invites comparison with Robert Bly's *Iron John,* a defining text of the men's movement and one with which many students are familiar. Bly's figure of the ancient "Wild Man" represents an atavistic masculinity that all men must reclaim. In response to the crisis of masculinity brought about by the modern family structure with its two working parents, by the alienation of modern corporate life, and by the feminist movement, men must get back in touch with their male psyche and "the nourishing dark[ness]" (Bly 6). Although decades earlier Lawrence expressed ambivalence toward the kind of healing process Bly endorses—one conducted through rural retreats and native rituals, such as drumming and dancing—he too associated a primal maleness with a nourishing darkness, figured as paternal, and attributed the crisis of masculinity in his day in part to women's self-assertion. Like Bly's mythopoetic men's movement, Lawrence's cosmography conceives new gender relations in terms of spiritual renewal, not social and material change.[7]

After noting how Lawrence uses blackness and darkness in "Woman," we turn to an earlier passage, also presenting the woman's observation of her Indian captors, that provides a telling example of how whiteness functions in the story:

> And the elder men, squatting on their haunches, looked up at her in the terrible paling dawn, and there was not even derision in their eyes. Only that intense, yet remote, inhuman glitter which was terrible to her. They were inaccessible. They could not see her as a woman at all. As if she *were* not a woman. As if, perhaps, her whiteness took away all her womanhood, and left her as some giant, female white ant. That was all they could see in her. (49)

Whiteness absorbs womanhood. The woman's race, or rather her complexion, is first noted at the moment she asserts herself against the Indian servant who would confine her to the home and to the social conventions that limited women's freedom of movement: "'I shall go alone,' repeated the large, placid-seeming, fair-complexioned woman" (43). Here the narrative perspective seems to be that of the Indian addressed. The next reference to the woman's whiteness comes when she confronts the Chilchui in the mountains and announces, with "arrogant confidence in her own female power," that she is a "lady" (46). Whiteness is linked not with a primal femaleness, as blackness represents a primal maleness, but with class and national differences that must be overcome in the name of cosmic unity: "'Adios!' she replied, in her assured, *American* woman's voice" (45; my emphasis). The assurance Lawrence obsessively identifies with the "new woman" in such essays as "Women Are So Cocksure" becomes a *racial* attribute. What we see in this story, as Butler notes in her reading of Larsen, is "the racialization of sexual conflict" (*Bodies* 174).

The woman is whiteness personified; the Indian is maleness personified. Coupled with adjectives linking the woman to the impoverished land exploited by the colonizing Westerners and the reference to the red tie linking the woman and the tourist, the woman's whiteness comes to stand for, and ultimately to be sacrificed for, conventional middle-class femininity and Western imperialism. As opposed to the more conventional distinctions between whiteness and blackness and between women and men, Lawrence establishes an opposition between whiteness (gendered as feminine) and maleness (racialized as black). Understanding Lawrence's sexual philosophy in racial terms can account for the troubling ending. The woman's body mediates cross-racial male desire. Her sacrifice guarantees, in the words of the last line of the story, "the mastery that man must hold, and that passes from race to race" (71). "This line is important," writes Leo. "Since the opinion of 'the woman' has been irrelevant throughout the story, it is Lawrence who is commenting on the needed distribution of power. Men *must* hold the 'mastery,' and the sacrifice of the woman serves as a blood bond between men." That blood bond is specifically between men *of different races, between* men and *across* races. If students rarely pick up on this point, it is due in part, I believe, to the nature of the course—*women's* studies—which leads them to focus on sexual rather than racial differences and in part to their tendency to see gender and race as separate, and separable, attributes. As Lisa Ruddick argued in the 1992 MLA paper that inspired me to teach Lawrence's novella in my women's studies course, the woman's sacrifice blames white womanhood for colonization and expiates the guilt of white men. "The shame of being a [white] man—is there any better reason to write?" (Deleuze 225)

The cultural criticism of poststructuralists such as Barthes and Poovey provides a useful way of approaching the teaching of D. H. Lawrence in a

women's studies classroom. Rather than assuming that Lawrence's representation of the woman and his sexual politics are simply *expressions* of his personal beliefs and values, and instead of seeking origins or culprits, we look
at the complex historical, cultural, and psychopolitical dynamics in which
certain ideas and representations of "woman" are produced, naturalized, and
contested. I ask my students to take seriously the kinds of questions Barthes
asks. The point is neither to save Lawrence from criticism nor to hold him
up to ridicule for his characterizations of women; the point is to understand
how Lawrence's characterization of "woman" in certain writings of the 1920s
came to produce and reproduce certain meanings and values, even as it contested other dominant cultural beliefs about "woman."

Before reading Lawrence, we have already begun this kind of investigation with Woolf's *Room of One's Own*, the first work I teach in the course. As
an example of a cultural criticism approach, *Room* not only supplies a wealth
of information about the times through its tissue of cultural references (e.g.,
the suffrage movement, the popularity of Freudian psychology, the education of women, the trial of Radclyffe Hall, the anthropology of Margaret
Mead); more important, it emphasizes the effects of material conditions,
including social institutions, on notions of "woman" and on writings by and
about women. "Here I am asking why women did not write poetry in the
Elizabethan age," the narrator remarks, "and I am not sure how they were
educated; whether they were taught to write; whether they had sitting-rooms
to themselves; how many women had children before they were twenty-one;
what, in short, they did from eight in the morning till eight at night" (*Room*
46). In its guise as a lecture in progress to be delivered to students at a woman's college, *Room* explicitly addresses the role teaching practices and educational institutions play in reinforcing and sustaining dominant notions of
"woman"; and its shifting and playful narrating "I" makes the persona of the
"teaching woman" at once highly self-conscious and highly relevant. It is
precisely because the narrator-lecturer is a woman that she has been invited
to speak to women about women, but it is also the "fact" of her sex that
motivates her research and her teaching. That is, the persona in this essay
speaks deliberately and flagrantly as a woman, a fact that (along with her
caricature of Professor von X) could well lead her to be dismissed as an "ar-
rant feminist" (*Room* 35). Yet after all her inquiries into the lives, education,
social position, desires, and writings of women, the narrating "I" writes the
first line of her lecture: "it is fatal for anyone who writes to think of their sex"
(104). If her injunction to women students to avoid "speak[ing] consciously
as a woman" (104) and to think of "things in themselves" (111) sounds like a
manifesto for a modernist-formalist aesthetics, with its theory of imperson-

ality and transcendent ideals, such a reading can be sustained only by removing these claims from the context of the essay and actively repressing its arguments for the importance of material conditions and ideologies of gender on the writing subject.[8]

Woolf's essay provides specific examples of narrative representations of women to show how culture—the material conditions, discursive practices, and grammatical rules that structure one's relation to others—produces gendered, and racialized, identities.[9] Although she does not address race explicitly in *Room,* as does Lawrence in "Woman," Woolf's essay nonetheless expresses certain unquestioned notions of race. For example, contrasting men's love of fame with women's desire for anonymity, Woolf's narrator says: "It is one of the great advantages of being a woman that one can pass even a very fine negress without wishing to make an Englishwoman of her" (50). Intended as a critique of colonialism and masculinity, this passing remark also reveals that, for Woolf, "woman" means white; or, in the language of contemporary cultural criticism, whiteness is the default identity in *Room.*[10] I use this passage to show students how a writer can consciously resist damaging cultural constructions of gender and still reinforce other "nonconscious presuppositions" (Marks xiv) about "woman." Although Woolf takes whiteness for granted when discussing women, her references to colonialism, psychoanalysis ("the desire to be veiled"), and patriarchy in this passage serve to undermine the notion of gender and race as natural attributes and to raise questions about their cultural deployment—questions my students and I take to our reading of "Woman."

However much Lawrence may criticize both racist and romantic views of natives, however much he may modify conventional notions of so-called primitive peoples, his story depends on primitivist tropes for its emotional force and import. To contextualize Lawrence's representation of the woman and the Indians in terms of other discourses and literature of the time, I have my students read selections from Marianna Torgovnick's *Gone Primitive.* In the first chapter, "Defining the Primitive," students reencounter Lawrence's descriptive terms for the Indians in the context of the ideology of primitivism, according to which natives are childlike, libidinous, violent, dangerous, timeless, mysterious, natural, and free. "The ensemble of these tropes—" writes Torgovnick, "however miscellaneous and contradictory—forms the basic grammar and vocabulary of what I call primitivist discourse, a discourse fundamental to the Western sense of self and Other" (8). Whereas the primitive conceived as childish, irrational, and libidinous, a "dark" force to be feared, was feminized in many cultural productions of the time (later in the course we discuss Freud's essays of the 1930s in which he refers to female sexuality as the "dark continent"), Torgovnick argues that Lawrence "masculinized" or "phallicized" the other dominant representation of the primitive as powerful and assured, a "noble savage" to be emulated (159). The phallicizing of the black body as a powerful, noble ideal is what Carby sees in the nude photographs of Robeson she anaylzes. White fascination with primitivism (the kind of "going native" that Lawrence criticizes) is integral to male modernists' efforts to reclaim, through an objectified black body, an essential masculinity thought to be lost, Carby says, to the modern industrializing world ("Body and Soul"). Indeed, that is Lawrence's point, that masculinity and male sexuality have become vitiated in modern society.

Primitivism as defined by Torgovnick is a concept we return to in the class with Freud's essays on female sexuality, Nella Larsen's 1928 novel *Quicksand,* Fannie Hurst's popular 1933 novel *Imitation of Life* and its 1934 screen adaptation by John Stahl, Cedric Gibbons's 1934 film *Tarzan and His Mate,* and "Chasing a Rainbow," a 1992 PBS documentary on Josephine Baker. The poster for "La Revue Nègre," the Paris show that launched Baker's career, and pictures of Baker naked in animal-like poses, her fingers curled like claws, in the documentary convey visually and powerfully the tropes of primitivism that Torgovnick discusses, just as the juxtaposition of those images on the screen with the British male voice-over that assures us, "Josephine saw nothing racist or degrading in these poses," confronts students with the cultural contradictions motivating these racialized and sexualized representations. The purpose of reading and viewing such works, as Torgovnick says of her objective in *Gone Primitive,* is not simply to document Anglo-American attitudes toward natives and women, nor to disprove these representations, showing how inaccurate they were by consulting the objects of study themselves (e.g., interviews with Baker), but rather to emphasize the "political and psychological cost of these conceptions" (Torgovnick 12). Posters, films, photographs, and cartoons of the time reveal that nakedness figures not just as the natural vesture of women, as Barthes says in *Mythologies* (85) but as the natural vesture of blacks and natives as well. In *Ways of Seeing,* John Berger contrasts nakedness, being without clothes, with nudity, the condition of being seen naked by others (54). Nudity is a way of seeing that a painting or image achieves through certain conventions, Berger says, such as having a naked woman hold a mirror and thereby "connive in treating herself as . . . a sight" (51). Lawrence's poem "Gloire de Dijon," in which the speaker watches a woman taking her bath, provides a striking example of how nudity is achieved artistically. Berger's analysis of how women can come to collude in their own objectification helps students to understand the complex relation of a performer such as Josephine Baker to the "ensemble of categories and signifying systems" from which she derives an identity (Poovey, "Cultural Criticism" 618). Tracing primitivist iconography through various cultural productions of the 1920s and 1930s also shows students how pervasive such representations were and enables them to see how Lawrence both reproduces and refigures these dominant cultural tropes.

For example, the tension in "Woman," like the thrill of a Tarzan movie, depends on the reader sharing with the protagonist the belief that natives are savages. While the inhuman, impersonal, and inaccessible qualities of the Indians in "Woman" are meant to represent primal qualities before the "fall" into self-consciousness and egocentrism, these terms, along with the incantatory "savages" and the references to the "wild creatures howling" ("Woman" 60), suggesting something "unspeakable" (57), depend for their emotional effect on the same primitivist tropes that structure the popular Tarzan films. The viewer's certainty that those painted Africans carrying spears who attack the safari will ritually murder and consume their victims creates the tension in *Tarzan and His Mate*. Likewise, the "icy pang of fear and certainty" experienced by the woman must be shared by the reader for the message of Lawrence's story to "strike home" ("Woman" 61, 71). Yet for all their reliance on primitivist tropes, both Edgar Rice Burroughs, author of the Tarzan novels, and Lawrence criticize colonialism and white men's exploitation of natives and the land (see, e.g., Torgovnick 57).

This is the slip that reveals the dynamics of passing. Despite its overt resistance to certain disparaging views of Indians, "Woman" reveals its own blindness to and implicit endorsement of damaging racial ideologies in its very method of presentation (its characterizations, descriptive phrases, and plot motivations). Similarly, and despite the fact that Lawrence promotes women's emancipation from their moral enslavement to men, "Woman" conveys the anxiety about changing gender roles evident in other works of that time and the need to reaffirm gender hierarchies in the face of such change.[11] Like the woman in Lawrence's story, for example, Jane (Maureen O'Sullivan) in *Tarzan and His Mate* is self-assured, defiant of conventional gender roles, and confident of "her own female power" ("Woman" 46). She too seeks a more thrilling and meaningful existence by experiencing another culture. In each case the threat of disrupting sexual roles is figured in terms of the crossing of racial and cultural boundaries; the only difference is that Jane is eroticized through such crossings whereas the woman in Lawrence's story is desexualized—an important difference in terms of Lawrence's sexual philosophy. If the truth of "woman" in popular culture is her sexuality, Lawrence's writing engages in the "desexualization of woman as truth" to restore "woman" to her proper place of complementarity in a cosmic har-

mony that will assure "the mastery that man must hold."[12] Lawrence's story, as Torgovnick says of the Tarzan series, "seems designed as a cautionary
tale in the wake of suffrage for . . . women" (67).[13]

The threat of economic and social disruption posed by white women
newly emerging in the workforce in large numbers is evident in other works
of the time, and not just male-authored texts. Bea Pullman, known in the
business world as "B. Pullman, business man," is a single working mother
who unwittingly becomes a celebrated icon of New Womanhood in Hurst's
popular novel *Imitation of Life.* Responding to the anxiety expressed in editorials from the 1920s and 1930s over the emergence of white women into the
workforce, an anxiety Woolf writes about in *Room,* Hurst's novel seems to
be another cautionary tale. The novel ends with the wildly successful B. Pullman losing the home she has built and the man she has loved to her daughter, a young woman with no higher ambition than to be taken care of by a
man. (I present a fuller discussion of Hurst's novel in chapter 6.)

Lawrence's 1928 editorial in the *Evening News,* retitled "Matriarchy" in
Bonnie Kime Scott's anthology *The Gender of Modernism,* captures the same
anxiety that motivates Hurst's plot. Lawrence describes working women as
the "silked-legged horde" who "settle like silky locusts on all the jobs" and
"occupy the offices and the playing-fields like immensely active ants" ("Matriarchy" 224). The word "ants" recalls the passage from "Woman" in which
the woman's whiteness reduces her to a gigantic ant in the eyes of the Indians. The semantic repetition serves to reinforce the yoking of the economic
exploitation of imperialism to the economic threat brought about by the independent and self-assertive women of the 1920s, the disfranchised "flapper,"
also known at the time as the "superfluous woman." Putting "Matriarchy"
in the context of other writings (such as those by Hurst and Burroughs) that
attest to and respond to the widespread fear over changing gender roles can
show students that whether one reads this editorial as sharing or mocking
such fears, it registers a pervasive cultural anxiety to which Lawrence is not
immune.

The anxiety over "superfluous women" in the 1920s is the subject of his-
torian Billie Melman's book *Women and the Popular Imagination of the
Twenties.* Melman examines the relation between changes in the material and
legal status of women in Britain in the early part of this century and the
emergence of popular genres for women, such as the girls' weeklies and the
Empire romance. Melman writes: "The war brought about structural changes in the material conditions of life which particularly affected women. At
precisely this time there took place important changes in the texture of popular culture, transforming its character and trajectory. This particular

combination . . . accounts for the rise of 'flapper' and the unprecedentedly wide discussion of the woman and of feminine sexuality" (4–5). "The major cause," Melman continues, "of the obsession with the modern woman was the fear aroused by the disparity between the sexes" (18). The disproportionate number of women to men in Britain in the decade following the war upset what was conceived to be the "natural" state of harmony and balance between the sexes. By 1921, Melman writes, "the adjective 'surplus' was superseded by 'superfluous,' . . . a conveniently equivocal epithet indicating something excessive or superabundant but also that which is unnecessary and, therefore, dispensable" (19). The surplus of women after the war and the scarcity of jobs for men sparked proposals, like Lady Bruton's in Woolf's *Mrs. Dalloway,* for British women's emigration to the colonies (Melman 18). The anxiety created by the number of newly independent women led to an obsessive concern with notions of a degenerate masculinity as figured in the effete intellectual, the homosexual, or the androgynously attired Sheik, as in the popular 1921 film with Rudolph Valentino.[14] The "new woman" or "flapper" was likewise androgynous, even boyish, with her short hair, her characteristic cigarette, and her air of insouciance. The exchange between Orlando and her lover in Woolf's 1928 novel at once invokes and deflates such anxiety over the blurring of gender identifications by dismissing the topic within a sentence: "'You're a woman, Shel!' she cried. 'You're a man, Orlando!' he cried" (*Orlando* 252).

On the one hand, as Melman points out, this blurring of distinctions between the sexes was alluring. It clearly signaled a modernist challenge to conventional gender roles. Lawrence's description of the Indian cited earlier suggests that his apparent effeminacy, signifed by his long hair and by adjectives conventionally associated with women ("gentle," "submissive," "maidenly"), somehow heightens his mysterious and powerful maleness. On the other hand, Melman says, "the effacement of gender seemed to be, and was interpreted as, a symptom of decay, an outward sign of an internal *racial* degeneracy and moral decline" (22; my emphasis). Much popular fiction of the time aroused, contained, or transformed these fears of sexual imbalance and racial degeneracy. In the genre of the desert romance, for example, the image of the androgynous flapper and emasculated man gave rise to a counter-representation in the hero and heroine who were characterized as "antipodal yet magnetic poles, drawn together solely by the power of sex" (Melman 89). Following up on Melman's passing reference to "The Woman Who Rode Away" in her chapter on this popular genre, I suggest to students that the desert romance may well have provided Lawrence with a generic model for his narrative of racial guilt and expiation. Both E. M. Hull's 1919 bestselling novel *The Sheik* and Lawrence's 1924 novella share preoccupations with racial identity and sexual difference.[15] As in the desert romance novel, the impetuous, independent, traveling woman in Lawrence's novella becomes a willing victim.

The desert romance narrative centers on a woman protagonist who is self-assured, economically secure, and socially independent, though typically the woman is a young unmarried virgin rather than a middle-aged wife and mother, as in Lawrence's story. (This is a significant difference that signals Lawrence's resistance to what he saw as the purely prurient plot motivations of the desert romance genre.) The heroine of the desert romance rides off alone into the desert, symbolizing her rejection of, or at least departure from, Western culture and values. She is taken captive by an Arab sheik, raped, and eventually won over by the man who violates her. Her sexual violation becomes her spiritual and sexual redemption; hereafter she is "truly" feminine, submissive and masochistic. Transformed by her encounter with the Arab male, who is masculinity incarnate, and by the mystical powers of the landscape, the heroine of this genre comes to recognize and accept sexual difference as sexual hierarchy: that is, she comes to accept masculine dominance and feminine passivity.[16]

In her discussion of *The Sheik,* Melman points to the similarity between the first riding scene in that novel and "the woman's solitary ride across the Mexican Sierra" in "Woman" (100). Riding becomes a metaphor not only for the new independence and social mobility of British women but also, as Caren Kaplan says of the metaphor of travel in contemporary theory, for the "cultural displacement and sense of unfamiliarity engendered by social change" (82). A more telling if less obvious similarity than the one Melman points out can be found between the scene in Hull's novel where the sheik strips the heroine, Diana Mayo, with his gaze and the scene in "Woman" where the Indians literally and ceremonially strip the protagonist. The woman is not just denuded in each of these scenes of "pretty pornography" (Lawrence's term for popular romances in his essay "Pornography and Obscenity" [*Phoenix* 178]); she is, as David Trotter suggests, "polarized" (208).[17] Sexual polarity is reinforced in the young Indian's story of the sun and moon, which, while defying Western notions of identity, relies on gendered notions of sexual difference ("Woman" 65). "In attempting to break from shallow conventions of gender," Aniko, one of my students, writes, "Lawrence reaffirms fundamental stereotypes. In the Indian's sun/moon story about how the world works, the hot active sun is male, the cold, passive moon female. The sun is supposed to be kept happy, the moon is supposed to be kept quiet." In both the novella and the romance, the women come to recognize sexual difference through sexual violation, and neither woman seeks to dominate again. Each has become, in Melman's words as well as my students', "a willing victim" (102).

The desert romance provides Lawrence with a generic model that enables him to allay racial guilt through the reaffirmation (however depersonalized) of sexual difference, for "the 'truth' of sexual polarity" (Trotter 215) transcends racial difference. Whereas sexual difference is (re)established in both the desert romance narratives and in "Woman," racial difference is problematized. Initially in each story the woman is haughty in the presence of an inferior who physically confirms the stereotype of the native: grossly physical, naked, dirty, and smelly. Yet Diana in *The Shiek* gains a new understanding of the Arab as the woman does of the Indian in "Woman" as these men come to behave and speak more like white men than "natives." Through the woman's consciousness and, ultimately, her sacrifice, Lawrence identifies masculinity with the "primal, integral *I*" of the Indians, seen to be "a *continuum* of all the rest of living things" (*Phoenix* 761). The notion of a continuum between you and me that Lawrence elaborates elsewhere in opposition to the social consciousness and self-consciousness of his day is reserved in this story for racial difference. In *The Sheik*, writes Trotter, "an unyielding description of the enforcement of sexual hierarchy secures a space for the blurring of cultural distinctions" as "a black man turns into a white man" (210). In the desert romance, this is a literal change in that the sheik is typically discovered to be the son of a degenerate British aristocrat who has "gone native" (and thus fear of miscegenation is at once aroused and alleviated in the desert romance, a kind of inverse of the "passing" novel popular in America at this time). In "Woman," this blurring of racial distinctions takes a figurative form: it is the white man as *writer* and narrative *agency* who becomes black. With the sacrifice of the woman, and through the writing of "Woman," "the mastery that man must hold . . . passes from race to race" ("Woman" 71).

Lawrence's "Woman" is, I am suggesting, a narrative of passing, where passing occurs not on the level of plot and theme but in the very dynamics of the narrative structure and its psychopolitical identifications. Lawrence's racial passing in this story clearly differs from the kind he criticizes in his writings on New Mexico. "Going native" in that conventional sense entails imitation or identification—that is, passing in the more conventional sense of a mimesis. In contrast, Lawrence creates through his writing what Gilles Deleuze calls "a zone of proximity," where one is "singularized out of a population rather than determined in a form" (225–26), or, as Barthes writes in "The Death of the Author," Lawrence creates "a neutral space" where *indi-*

vidual identities and bodies are "lost" (*Image/Music/Text* 142). Racial bonding is represented as transindividual, not personal. Yet that zone or space where racial and cultural boundaries are "undifferentiated" (Deleuze 225) depends on yet another form of passing.

"Woman," like the desert romance, is written from a woman's perspective, and this may be the most significant parallel between the two. In Lawrence's story this perspective creates an effect that Torgovnick terms "narrative transvestism" (172), which Leo picks up on in his remark about the irrelevance of the woman's opinion. Both the story and the desert romance reinforce notions of women's passivity and of female masochism through a woman's point of view that "ultimately celebrate[s] . . . an ideal of masculinity" as "'primitive,' . . . virile and priapic" (Melman 103). Melman contends that while it is tempting to see the popularity of the desert romance as a kind of backlash against the newly emancipated woman, such an argument fails to acknowledge that these were novels written by women for women. The genre represented a new form of erotic literature that was offensive to critics precisely, Melman suggests, because it was erotic literature *for women* (104). The anxiety it aroused was that "the modern, sexually emancipated woman can pursue pleasure without being punished for her presumption" (Melman 93). Given this argument, one might see any comparison between "Woman" and *The Sheik* as working in Lawrence's favor, saving him from the kind of criticism I offered earlier and revealing him to be, as Carol Siegel has argued, more resistant to conventional notions of sexual difference than even his feminist contemporaries insofar as he rejected a notion of sexual difference as opposition for a notion of sexual polarity as complementarity. Lawrence dismissed the desert romance genre as "pretty pornography," not because it presented women as sexual beings, but presumably because the sexual experience in the desert romance remained personal rather than becoming impersonal or transpersonal; it was erotic rather than aesthetic. But (and one might think this goes without saying) Lawrence's novella was not written by a woman. Here the question "Who speaks?" takes on a personal tone even or especially when the text in question promotes a modernist theory of impersonality. "What difference *does* it make who is speaking?" (Foucault, "What Is" 160; my emphasis).

In her introduction to *Men Writing the Feminine*, Thaïs Morgan asks: "What does it mean to say that a male author writes the feminine? Is he writing as (identifying with) a woman? Or writing like (mimicking, and perhaps mocking) a woman? Or writing through a woman (an Other that confirms his own identity as the Same)?" (1) The way I teach Lawrence's "Woman" seeks to situate these questions within a particular historical and cultural context as a way of suspending the rush to judgment, whether commending Lawrence's "narrative transvestism" or condemning it. To recapitulate, when I teach "The Woman Who Rode Away" I situate its representations of the woman and the Indians within a variety of discourses, media, and movements of the late nineteenth and early twentieth centuries: psychoanalysis, cultural anthropology, advertising, cinema, popular fiction, and suffrage, to name the most prominent. Freud's and the sexologists' accounts of female sexuality and homosexuality, the highly popular Tarzan stories and films, the desert romance genre, posters and cartoons depicting women as primitive savages, debates over the "flapper" vote, editorials expressing anxiety over the number of white middle-class women entering the workforce—all provide a historical and cultural matrix within which to read Lawrence's story for an understanding of how a literary work comes to be produced and to generate meanings in relation to other cultural productions. This approach enables students to understand literature as Barthes's "tissue of quotations" rather than as an original and autonomous object to be understood primarily through reference to the author and literary history. More important, this approach encourages students to see culture as Poovey defines it, not just as the creation of social groups, which then impacts on the experience of individuals, but as the very precondition of what it means to *be* an individual, a woman or a man ("Cultural Criticism" 617). We look at Lawrence as a "writer" (the term Barthes substitutes for "author"), producing his texts within this complex matrix of cultural discourses, "the matrix from which 'literature' is born" (Haraway, "Situated Knowledges" 595), not simply as a man expressing certain (sexist) beliefs. The object of study in this course is neither Lawrence's story nor his life and character nor even his British culture but the formal system of relations that makes possible the production of "Woman," both the story and the figure.

It is important to the dynamics of passing, however, that we situate "Woman" in a particular cultural matrix *without losing sight of the fact* that, in Morgan's words, "the interaction of writing and gender is complex and fraught with cultural significance when the author projects a voice from the imagined perspective of the opposite sex" (1). This approach has the effect of moving an analysis of Lawrence's "narrative transvestism" beyond voice "as a formal literary category to the psychosocial function of the speaking voice" (Kahane xiii).[18] Of course, as I have suggested, one could argue that, although told from a feminine perspective, "Woman" is not written by a man writing "as" a woman or even presuming to "speak for" women; rather, it might be more accurate to say that Lawrence is "becoming woman" by discovering the impersonal beneath the personal. Deleuze writes: "literature begins only when a third person is born in us that strips us of the power to say 'I' " (227). That stripping is represented in and through the woman in Lawrence's novella. In other words, it is not that a male writer is writing as a woman but that the woman figures the male *writer* as the Indian figures masculinity. Deleuze's comment on the writer could be applied to the woman: "all [the character's] individual traits elevate [her] to a vision that carries [her] off in an indefinite, like a becoming that is too powerful for [her]" (227). *The* woman becomes *a* woman, for even woman must become woman, says Deleuze and Guattari (25). In this sense, Lawrence's narrative transvestism is the process whereby the male writer is freed from masculine identification, the "empiricity" (Foucault's term ["What Is" 144]) and particularity of his identity.

If writing is the coming into being of an identity and not the expression of an already existing subject, as Barthes's concept of the "writer" and Deleuze and Guattari's notion of "becoming woman" signify, and even if such a becoming "ceaselessly slips away from [the writer]" (Deleuze 230) so that the writer never achieves that identity, still that becoming is figured as the performance of white male self-difference.[19] There is no becoming man, Deleuze says, "insofar as man presents himself as a dominant form of expression that claims to impose itself on all matter" (225). The man who writes must become something else—a woman, a Negro, an Indian, a giraffe, to cite a few possibilities mentioned in Deleuze's essay and in Lawrence's writings on which Deleuze draws (226–27). How then does the woman writer (or the Indian, or the Negro) engage in this performance of subjectivity as self-difference? Given that even the woman must become woman while for the man there is no possibility of becoming man (Deleuze 225), and given that the man must move out of the position of knowing subject while the woman must not move into it, the woman writer necessarily stands in a very different relation to becoming—to writing—than the man. Barthes figures the (white male) writer's performance of this move as a loss of identity, "beginning with the very identity of the body that writes" (*Image/Music/Text* 142). Thus, while Lawrence's adoption of a feminine perspective is not simply an effort to speak for women, as Siegel says certain writers, namely, Katherine Mansfield and Virginia Woolf, feared—indeed, it works against such identification—that move into the feminine position that represents the writer's subjectivity nonetheless depends on the reduction of the woman to her body, her difference, no less than does the eroticism of the desert romance. Barthes's question "Who speaks?" that inaugurates the form of cultural criticism I adopt in my teaching of "Woman" at once depends on the death of the author as origin, as knowing subject existing prior to the writing, and on the birth of writing as (white) male self-difference. Writing and identity are themselves rooted in sexual difference, a difference, Lawrence's story reveals, that is always already a racialized one. In the performance of identity we may all be passing, but the question still remains, Passing for what?[20]

If art is, as Lawrence says in "The Individual Consciousness v. the Social Consciousness," "the revelation of the *continuum* itself" (*Phoenix* 763), his moral allegory in "Woman" allows the male writer to be refigured by becoming woman or native but leaves no space for the woman or native to be refigured.[21] Lawrence's narrative transvestism as a form of passing seems decidedly one-way and depends on a certain figuration of femininity and race. There is no *inter*action, nor is the writer implicated personally in the process. Insofar as the story is meant to be read as an allegory, it takes the event out of the interpersonal realm and makes it impersonal, "everyone's spiritual quest rather than one individual's personal biography," as Donald Pease defines allegory (106). The absence of the personal distinguishes Lawrence's narrative transvestism from "passing" as I use the term throughout this book. I would agree with Siegel that it is not simply a matter of condemning Lawrence's "stale and limited concepts of gender" (98) or his brazen attempts to speak for women, appropriating their voices (88) and "encroaching on women's literary territory" (112). Rather, it is a matter of recognizing, to borrow Spivak's words, "that even the strongest personal goodwill on [Lawrence's] part cannot turn him quite free of the massive enclosure of the male appropriation of woman's voice" ("Displacement" 190).[22] My argument here looks back to chapter 1 and my critique of various scholars who seem to justify their acts of speaking as and speaking for in terms of their goodwill, *as if their attitudes were the basis on which to judge their actions.* In contrast, my use of "passing" insists that we can never guarantee that identification (speaking as or for) is not also appropriation; nor can we be sure that identification is always only appropriation. That is the false guarantee of purity or intentionality that Derrida resists. Lawrence may share with Woolf, as Siegel says, a notion of female essence "in opposition to femininity as constructed by male language and the social world it creates" (112), but Woolf's resistance to that notion of femininity is materialist and personal in *Room* while Lawrence's is spiritual and impersonal in "Woman." His writing is fabalistic, a matter of mythmaking, not identification (whether psychological or political), thereby effacing "the signs of his particular individuality" (Foucault, "What Is" 143).

The effacement of the author's individuality characterizes modernist impersonality. Writing is no longer conceived as expression: "The work should not give the person it affects anything that can be reduced to an idea of the author's person and thinking" (Valéry, qtd. in Sontag 444); and "The poet has, not a 'personality' to express, but a particular medium" (Eliot 42). As Sontag, Foucault, and Caren Kaplan argue, this modernist dictum underlies postmodernist and poststructuralist theories of writing. With the concept of *l'écriture*, Foucault says, the writing subject "disappears" into the writing, "effac[ing] the more visible marks of the author's empiricity" ("What Is" 142, 144). Such impersonality, Sontag argues, is "only another variation on the project of self-examination" (444)—and, I would add, self-transformation.

Deleuze's remark at the beginning of this chapter, taken from an essay that uses Lawrence's writings as an example of what Deleuze and Guattari mean by "becoming woman," focuses, as does Barthes, on writing as the site where subjectivity emerges and where the writer can move out of the constraints of socially and culturally prescribed identities and into that "neutral space" of writing. However, as we have seen, that supposedly neutral space is, in Deleuze's essay as in Lawrence's story, gendered and racialized. The cultural criticism approach that I have elaborated here would locate that notion of writing in a particular historical and cultural matrix of ideas and representations. Lawrence's "narrative transvestism"—not just the writer's assumption of a woman's perspective in this story, but Lawrence's effort to use writing as a means of refiguring his own gendered and racialized identity, itself a form of "passing"—must be understood in terms of that matrix of ideas. Lawrence would seem to contrast his transvestism with the woman's tourism (also a form of passing); or, more precisely, he would make his writing analogous to the Indian's ritual sacrifice, a way of defeating the egocentrism and ethnocentrism that tourism signifies. Yet Lawrence's laudable efforts to challenge and resist limiting notions of gendered and racialized identities, which he ties to a specific social and cultural economy and to the moral presuppositions that shore it up—efforts I promote through the concept of passing—implicate him all the more in the perpetuation of other gendered and racialized representations. To reiterate one of my main points about passing, the very effort to move into another's space, the effort to write or speak from or on behalf of another cultural group, or to "become" something else and thereby to mobilize new possibilities of subjectivity, can reinsert one back into the very structure of authority and privilege one would dismantle. As Poovey's "three-tiered enterprise" of cultural criticism ("Cultural Criticism" 620) encourages us to see, this happens not just in modernist fiction but in the teaching situation where certain cultural formations are reproduced.

The popularity of Freudian psychology, which Lawrence sometimes championed for its acknowledgment of the importance of sex in psychic development but more often repudiated for its insistence on "the egocentric absolute of the individual" (*Phoenix* 379), along with the writings of the sexologists, notably Havelock Ellis and Edward Carpenter, can help to explain how and why Lawrence might come to represent femininity as passivity in "Woman"; but, even more important, it can help us to understand the transmutation of the personal into the impersonal, the culturally specific into the structurally universal. In his essay on Lawrence and popular fiction, Trotter discusses Freud's 1919 essay "A Child Is Being Beaten," which deals with women's sadomasochistic fantasies, those that are acted out in the popular women's genre of the desert romance. "Guilt," writes Trotter, "transforms incipient sadism into full-blown masochism" (211) as Freud's analysand, feeling guilt over her desire for her father, fantasizes herself rather than another child as the object of the beating. Trotter traces these fantasies in Lawrence's women characters in *Women in Love*. I want to suggest that in "Woman" these fantasies of guilt and punishment are acted out on the level of the narrative itself and can be reproduced in the cultural criticism classroom, which seeks to expose the master narratives of modernity that survive in our collective unconscious.[23] Deleuze makes reference to this same essay by Freud in his discussion of Lawrence, arguing that whereas fantasy turns the impersonal into the personal ("a child" becomes "me"), literature does the opposite and "exists only when it discovers beneath apparent persons the power of an impersonal" (227). This is what Caren Kaplan means when, connecting modernist impersonality to postmodernist displacement, she writes that "becoming minor" depends on the "erasure of the site of [the writers'] own subject positions" (86). In his critique of individualism and his desire to move out of restrictive social meanings of sexual difference, Lawrence maintains a distinction between the impersonal and the personal, the masculine and the feminine, the individual and the social, the psychic and the political that reveals his roots in modernity. The conceptual oppositions themselves produce and affirm the notion of *natural* sexual difference that Lawrence believes is prior to them.

Teaching "Woman" in terms of contemporaneous writings on and representations of female sexuality, such as Freud's and Hull's, can lead students to dismiss Lawrence's views on sexuality as readily as they dismiss Freud's psychoanalysis and popular women's novels; such contextualization, however, can also move students from blaming Freud or Lawrence to understanding the cultural force of Freud's ideas and the cultural matrix within which Lawrence's writings on sexuality were produced. Despite his desire to break with conventional gender notions of his day, Lawrence writes within the cultural tropes available to him that necessarily uphold them, as Torgovnick argues in her reading of *The Plumed Serpent* (chap. 8). This in itself can be an important lesson for students who may too quickly label a writer like Lawrence or Hurst "racist" or "sexist," or celebrate a writer like Woolf as "feminist," without working through the complexities of the text's language and the cultural production of certain historical concepts like "woman" and "primitive." Therein lies the risk: to allow students their suspicions—of the writer or the teacher or one another—without allowing them to close off the process of negotiating these differences by thinking that they finally get it. For just when you think you've gotten it, there is yet another slip, another box to open, or another set of equations to pursue. Working through the complex and shifting relations between the personal and the impersonal, the individual and the cultural, as cultural studies enables us to do, can help students recognize and come to terms with their own forms of passing, not just in contemporary culture, but in a course in women and literature, where the relation of the women students and woman teacher to the material studied can be taken as a "given," that is, as unmediated.

In graduate school, where I first studied Lawrence seriously, I proclaimed *The Rainbow* the most beautiful novel in the English language. That comment put me at odds with many of my feminist peers who, with Kate Millet fresh in their minds, found my enthusiasm suspect if not perverse. I could not make such a comment today, not because it would be politically incorrect from a feminist perspective, nor because as a feminist critic I am no longer concerned with beauty, but because such a comment ignores Morgan's and other feminist critics' point that the relation of writing to gender has cultural significance and Foucault's insistence on the signficance of the social relations in which the writing is embedded. The beauty of the writing has not disappeared; rather, it can no longer be the single overriding standard by which to judge its value.

Precisely because it challenges institutionalized aesthetic values and reading practices, a cultural criticism approach can provoke resistance. Some students find the range of material they are asked to negotiate daunting, others object to studying noncanonical texts, such as Hurst's popular fiction and Gibbons's film, while still others resist reading literature in other than aesthetic terms. More than one student has complained that the approach I take neglects the beauty of Lawrence's prose, confirming the criticism often made of cultural studies that it ignores specifically literary concerns for sociological, political, or ideological ones. The worry many people have about cultural studies is that it finds the same knowledge (e.g., of power relations, of racial and sexual oppression, of homophobia) everywhere, so that students learn to read to a formula and to recite a mantra of race, gender, class, and sexual oppression. Nowadays, critics complain, we teach race and gender, not literature, making claims our disciplinary methodologies cannot support.[24]

I do not want to dismiss such criticism too quickly, for I cannot say I have never worried that such criticism might hit home in my case. However much I deliberately risk evoking such objections on course evaluations by asking students to face issues they may never have had to deal with, especially in a literature course, I cannot say that I always feel good about doing so. Yet resistance to an approach need not be seen as an argument against it, nor even as working against it; indeed, insofar as pedagogy today has become self-reflexive and self-critical, resistance is necessary precisely to keep any approach from becoming a formula.

Such resistance can provide yet another opportunity for presenting the insights of cultural criticism, for it requires teaching Lawrence with greater awareness of "the role our own practice plays—in this case, teaching—in reproducing or subverting the dominant cultural formation" (Poovey, "Cultural Criticism" 620). Lawrence's privileged place in the literary canon, from F. R. Leavis in the 1940s to the 1979 *Norton Anthology,* along with reigning formalist methodologies of that time, has contributed in no small way to the profound hold that gender hierarchy and processes of racialization have had in the Western imagination and in the conception of modernism. Gender and race as analytical categories frame questions that cannot even be conceptualized in terms of formalist and expressive approaches to literature. In other words, resistance to a cultural criticism approach comes from a particular model for literary studies that, as I argue in chapter 2, has been rendered untenable by the convergence of forces giving rise to cultural studies. This does not mean that we should stop teaching Lawrence or reject formalism, but it does mean that we should stop teaching as if disciplinary issues of reading and writing could be separated from political, ethical, and institutional issues of representation and identification. The relation of gender and race to writing and reading can be an important lesson to teach in a women's studies class. Speaking, writing, and teaching across gender and racial boundaries require the same kind of contextualization and the same suspension of control and of the rush to judgment as does the patient teasing out of connections that we undertake in our approach to "Woman."

Ferdinand de Saussure has said that "it is often easier to discover a truth than to assign it its rightful place" (qtd. in Culler 29). Teaching theory has brought home to me the truth of this insight. It is one thing to define Saussure's concept of the sign in terms of signifier and signified and to distinguish those concepts from word and meaning; it is quite another to determine precisely what this concept means, how it changes what we do, not just how we talk. And that difference can only be known in practice. Saussure's statement applies to the "truth" of cultural criticism as well. Too often we end with an assertion of its value rather than a demonstration of its consequences. That is why, throughout this book, I look to performative pedagogy as the site of ethical responsibility. The claim to be making issues more complex rather than to be advocating a particular position is not enough, for one person's complexity is another's reductiveness. The real testing ground for our ways of reading is the dynamics of the classroom exchange where our statements function not as constatives, passing on knowledge, but as performatives, producing effects. Teaching *is* advocacy, values advocacy, as many theorists have argued; yet those values do not lie in what we teach or in the claims we make for our teaching but emerge in the dynamic interaction in the classroom where the face-to-face relation to others and their responses is immediate, though not unmediated.

At least cultural criticism, as I understand it, seeks to account for the values we bring to our teaching, as well as the values a writer brings to his or her writing. If it seems to reduce reading to a formula, to deny agency to the author, or to leave the text behind (common complaints about poststructuralism and cultural criticism), it is not necessarily because political or sociological issues have displaced literary ones but because the convergence of poststructuralist theories with multicultural and feminist critiques has led many of us to understand, as Martin writes, that "our responsibility as teachers is less to the author or text than it is to the students' capacity to suspend control [and judgment] long enough and thoroughly enough to allow the text its agency" (10).

In the end, the important question this chapter raises for me is not how best to teach Lawrence, or even how useful cultural criticism is, but how to keep the example from becoming exemplary. That is commonly what happens in courses organized by topics—women writers, African American literature, modernism—where the individual text stands for a movement or discourse, or where a particular individual (Lawrence) can be seen to stand for all members of a class (white Western male writers). To allow the text, the student, or the teacher agency means resisting the very notion of exemplariness that also enables learning, for how can you learn what modernism was unless you can cite texts that exemplify the discourse? Exemplariness is at once intrinsic to pedagogy and a risk in writing about pedagogy, where the approach taken in the example can all too readily become simply a model for teaching in general. Exemplariness is a risk for the teaching woman as well, especially when, like Woolf's persona in *Room* and like me in the women's studies classroom, she addresses women on "woman." What can keep a particular lesson in cultural criticism from becoming a model for teaching in general is for the class to take on the character of an event, as Shoshana Felman says (*Testimony* 53); or, in my words, to produce a performative moment in which the lessons that seem to be confined to the text or the context being studied are suddenly activated in the dynamics of the classroom. This is what happened in my teaching of Fannie Hurst in another course, as I discuss in the next chapter.

NOTES

Thanks to my students Leo Dokshutsky, Jennifer Kostolansky, and Aniko Grandjean for their contributions to this essay and to the course on which it is based.

1. "Tourist" is deliberately ambiguous here, meant in both the literal sense of a visitor to a "foreign" locale and in the figurative sense used in chapter 2. Citing Manet and Cézanne, Malraux uses the figures of the tourist and the pioneer to distinguish between artists who imitate and those who innovate (68). The woman is figured as the imitator.

2. I quote from students' papers by permission. I have lightly edited their writing for coherence and clarity of reference. Their last names are given in the acknowledgments for this chapter. I use first names in the text to readily distinguish students' responses from the critics'.

3. In *Marrano as Metaphor*, Elaine Marks defines cultural studies, the paradigm for much cultural criticism in the United States today, by reference to Barthes. She writes: "I understand cultural studies through Roland Barthes's definition of myth as 'a chain of concepts widely accepted throughout culture, by which its members conceptualize and understand a particular topic or part of their social experience.' . . . In this sense cultural studies analyzes the nonconscious presuppositions that organize a text" (xiv). On Barthes's critique of the author, see B. Johnson (*Wake* 18); on deconstructive critique, see Butler ("Contingent" 15).

4. This question was raised by Lisa Ruddick in her 1992 MLA paper on Lawrence's novella. Drawing on the anthropologist Nancy Jay's theory of ritual sacrifice, Ruddick argues that "the sacrifice of the white woman is the act that magically cements the patrilineal bond between the Indian men and the white men."

5. Woolf also comments on her age as "stridently sex-conscious," a quality she attributes to the suffrage campaign, which aroused in men "an extraordinary desire for self-assertion" (*Room* 99). Lawrence, too, in this story connects the sex-consciousness of modern life with a desire for self-assertion, only women's rather than men's.

6. Since Carby's book was not available at the time I wrote this chapter, my summary of her argument comes from a rough transcription of her lecture. For that reason I am reluctant to quote her directly, although much of the language in this summary is Carby's.

7. On Lawrence's notion of primal maleness and its relation to the new woman, see, for example, "Indians and an Englishman" and "Autobiographical Fragment"

in *Phoenix;* on Bly's *Iron John* as a response to changing social and familiar structures, see Ross; and on Bly's movement as "mythopoetic," see McGann's response
to Robert J. Connors.

8. The familiar language of formalism in such passages allows Denby to applaud
the inclusion of *A Room of One's Own* in Columbia University's core literature course,
despite the fact that, as he admits, "Woolf was most assuredly a feminist" (445). As I
point out in chapter 2, much like Auerbach, who argued that Woolf subsumed the
trivial, minor, and feminine events in her writing to the universal or "elementary
things which men in general have in common" (552), Denby saves Woolf from charges
of being political by emphasizing the aesthetic, the formal, and the transcendent
qualities of her writing. Readings may change, readings may vary, Denby says, but
we all know a misreading when we see it, and current-day feminist "expropriation[s]"
of Woolf are misreadings that, Denby assures us, Woolf herself would have dismissed
scornfully, as "anyone who reads her carefully could prove" (446). That is, great books
speak for themselves. For Denby, as for Allan Bloom and Geoffrey Hartman, great
literature itself, in its very writing, works against the claims to authority attributed
to its canonization or attributed to it by critics.

9. As an example of the way grammatical rules structure concepts of "woman,"
consider Woolf's use of pronouns in *A Room of One's Own.* Her femininized "I" and
"one" refer neither to an individual person nor to a universal subject, avowedly neuter
yet implicitly male, nor even to women as an anonymous collectivity. Woolf's "I" and
"one" are not referential. The identity of the "I," she tells us, is immaterial, in both
senses of incorporeal ("'I' is only a convenient term for somebody who has no real
being" [4]) and unimportant (for who's speaking is "not a matter of any importance"
[5]). Woolf's "I" personifies the feminine subject position as a conceptual anonymity—"[women] remain even at this moment almost unclassified" (85)—and her use
of "one" jolts insofar as it is a decidedly feminine impersonal pronoun (see Caughie
and Callahan).

10. Mary Lou Emery first brought this passage and its racial implications to my
attention in "'Robbed of Meaning.'"

11. For arguments connecting changing roles for women with popular writing that
reinforces gender hierarchy, see Torgovnick's chapter "Taking Tarzan Seriously" (esp.
46 and 65) as well as her chapter on Lawrence, "'Oh Mexico!'" See also Melman's
Women in the Popular Imagination of the Twenties, discussed later in this chapter.

12. The phrase "desexualization of woman as truth," but not my particular argument, comes from Spivak's "Displacement and the Discourse of Woman," which I
return to later. "Woman as truth," like the notion of the nourishing darkness mentioned earlier, is a Nietzschean concept.

13. Writing on Malcolm Cowley's *Exile's Return,* Caren Kaplan argues that the
fantasy of escape from "bourgeois sexual norms" and "egalitarian impulses" in British
society of the 1920s brought together two powerful discourses: the exoticization of
another locale and "the exoticization of another gender, race, or culture" (45).

14. Melman writes that at this time "Arab garments, Arab cigarettes and Arab
motifs in decoration became the craze. In New York the sales of brilliantine and of
cosmestics and jewels for men boomed. . . . Such was the sheik mania that newspa-
pers in Britain and American pontificated that . . . [the fad] was a threat to the ideals of Western manhood" (91).

15. David Trotter also draws on this genre (in particular, E. M. Hull's novel *The Sheik*) and on Melman's book in a reading of *Women in Love*. Trotter's article, which I read only after I had incorporated Melman's analysis into my reading of "Woman," argues that modernist novels were not just parodic of popular fiction and ideologies, as commonly assumed, but also repeated them. "Their preoccupations—national and cultural identity, sexual difference—coincide to a striking degree" (194). My thanks to Michele Troy for drawing Trotter's essay to my attention.

16. My overview of this genre comes from Melman's chapter on the desert romance (see esp. 96 and 103).

17. In her MLA paper, Lisa Ruddick referred to the stripping scene in "Woman" as "soft porn."

18. Claire Kahane contends that the figure of the speaking woman, a particularly powerful and frightening *imago* and social reality of the late nineteenth and early twentieth centuries, came to embody the anxieties and desires of a historical era marked by rapid changes in the "geosocial landscape" and by a profound sense of "cultural transformation" (1). "Newly public women," as orators, preachers, doctors, reformers, and social workers, challenged the boundaries between private and public spheres and thus raised questions about "women's proper place" and men's as well (6). Kahane's readings extend the formal analysis of voice to a psychosocial analysis of women's increasing cultural influence and its representation in writing.

19. On this concept of male self-difference see Callahan's introduction to "The Voice of Pleasure," especially her concept of vagabondage.

20. This question comes from Wall's essay on Larsen's *Passing*, discussed in the previous chapter. As Butler argues in her reading of *Passing*, "the symbolic domain . . . is composed of *racializing norms*" that "exist not merely alongside gender norms, but are articulated through one another" (*Bodies* 182).

21. As Kaplan argues, modernist writers like Lawrence look elsewhere for "markers of . . . authenticity," to other cultures, purer lifestyles, or other voices (*Questions* 34–35). Poovey notes a similar tendency in recent films, where men appropriate traits associated with femininity to refigure themselves in response to the dehumanization threatened by postmodernity ("Feminism").

22. Spivak is commenting on both the affirmative and reactionary effects of Derrida's use of "woman" as "one of the important names for displacement, the special mark of deconstruction" (184).

23. This is Fredric Jameson's formulation cited in C. Kaplan (19). Kaplan goes on to argue that such master narratives have resurfaced in "ever more frightening versions" in anti-feminist backlash today (19)—and, I would add, in the born-again men's movement, whether Bly's, Louis Farrakhan's, or the Promise Keepers.

24. Catherine M. Cole, for one, makes this claim: "The traffic in theory within the academy in recent years has certainly opened new channels of communication among disciplines and stimulated some refreshing reconsiderations about the objects and methods of scholarly inquiry. However, theory has also led, in my opinion, to some rather unconvincing applications, particularly when scholars make interpretive claims for which their disciplines provide inadequate methodological grounding. For instance, while cultural studies transforms all the world into a 'text,' literary scholars may not have the methodological tools and evidentiary basis to make persuasive arguments about entire cultures or historical epochs" (214).

FIVE

Let It Pass: Changing the Subject, Once Again

> The "self" ultimately is the cognitive domain upon which
> the practice of writing . . . is grounded.
> —Mas'ud Zavarzadeh and Donald Morton

While the previous chapter attempted in part to illustrate the consequences of cultural criticism for teaching literature, this chapter attempts to work through its pedagogical dynamics. Specifically, it seeks to intervene, theoretically and pragmatically, at a critical moment in the profession when literary and composition studies in colleges and universities across the country increasingly are becoming cultural studies.[1] As I argue in chapters 1 and 2, this transformation over the past two decades in the social, philosophical, and political bases of what has been known traditionally as the humanities is due in part to the academy's efforts to acknowledge diversity by institutionalizing multiculturalism and various "studies programs" (women's studies, gay studies, ethnic studies, composition studies), in response to the influx of nontraditional students since the early 1970s, and in part to poststructuralism's efforts to theorize difference and to destabilize the categories of identity on which those studies programs are founded. On the one hand, studies programs, particularly composition studies and women's studies, traditionally have been devoted to a humanist concept of the subject as the "source and agent of conscious action or meaning" (P. Smith, *Discerning* xxxiii–xxxiv) and committed to opening this subject position to previously marginalized groups. On the other hand, poststructuralist theories, including some feminist and composition theories, reveal the humanist subject to be a sham insofar as it is the effect, not the origin, of representation. Cultural studies emerges in the clash between antifoundational theories that deconstruct the self and studies programs that revive it. To the extent that it makes issues of identity formation and subject positions central not only to its object of study but to its method of inquiry, cultural studies would seem to offer a pedagogy for working through the tensions between these two positions on the "subject."[2] Today scholars, especially in literature and composition studies, increasingly identify their work with the practices and objectives of a cultural studies paradigm.

Cultural studies in the United States is the institutionalized name given to an array of cross-disciplinary inquiries that make the construction of the subject in cultural institutions and social discourses central to their investigations. In doing so, these new methods challenge assumptions that inform traditional pedagogies within many studies programs: in women's studies, for example, a pedagogy of nurturance and consciousness-raising, where women learn to "come to voice" within the safe haven of the feminist classroom; in composition studies, a pedagogy of expressive realism, where the student writer learns to refine his or her language to express more clearly an extradiscursive self or position (Bauer and Jarratt 154–55; Faigley 112; Zavarzadeh and Morton 16; see also chapter 2). Given that the reading, writing, and teaching we do in the academy partially constitute the cultural formations it seeks to interrogate, cultural studies necessarily takes the work we do as teachers and scholars as one of its objects of scrutiny. Concerned with "the complex ways in which identity itself is articulated, experienced, and deployed" (Nelson et al. 9) and with the "politics of location" (Faigley 218), cultural studies (as opposed to literary studies) requires its practitioners "to include in their critical view the conditions of their own existence" at the same time it identifies itself "polemically with certain social constituencies," such as blacks, women, or workers (Bathrick 323–25). The classroom becomes both a site of cultural intervention and a practice of continual self-critique. To practice cultural studies, as Susan Rubin Suleiman writes in another context, "is to implicate yourself, your self, in what you write"—and in what you teach (2).

Yet however strong and however sincere our commitment as literature and composition professors to certain social constituencies and to continual self-critique, when ethnicity becomes "the new frontier, accessible to all" (hooks, *Yearning* 52); when men become feminists and straights become "queer"; when African American studies and women's studies become cultural studies; and when a prominent feminist, Nancy K. Miller, can write, "'I began to wonder whether there was any position from which a white middle-class feminist could say anything on the subject [of race] without sounding exactly like [a white middle-class feminist]. . . . In which case it might be better not to say anything'" (Gallop et al. 364)—something, it seems, has gone wrong. The shift from literary studies to cultural studies puts its practitioners in a double bind created by the tension between the desire—indeed, the imperative—to speak as or for members of a particular social group and the anxieties and risks such a practice evokes. The writer who deliberately assumes another's position risks being *accused* of unconsciously doing so.[3] Passing figures the dynamics of this double bind.

In this book, I have deployed the term "passing" to describe our subject positions in postmodern culture and, by extension, in a cultural studies paradigm. Defined most explicitly in chapter 1, my use of "passing" pushes to the limit the term's literal and figurative meanings. Literally, passing refers to the social practice of representing oneself as a member of a particular group not considered one's own. Used in a figurative sense, with the operative "as," passing can apply to a variety of situations in which one engages in impersonation for the purpose of fraud or parody. In both its literal and figurative meanings, passing may be conscious or unconscious, deliberate or accidental. As I deploy the term, however, passing (without the "as") figures the always slippery difference between these meanings, between, for example, standing *for* something and passing *as* something, or between the conscious adoption and the unconscious appropriation of a particular identity. Passing in the teaching situation signifies the slippage between, on the one hand, what a teacher or student professes, the positions one assumes in the classroom, and, on the other hand, what one does and how one is actually positioned in a society, institution, discourse, or classroom. In any and all of these senses, passing is risky business—but, I argue, unavoidable, for there is no occupying a subject position without passing.

Passing occurs in the inevitable slippage between the volitional and the performative subject whenever one attempts to speak for another or even oneself. In chapter 1, I clarify the difference between these two ways of conceptualizing the subject by comparing two sentences from Linda Alcoff's essay "The Problem of Speaking for Others." The slippage in her use of the first-person pronoun, from the volitional "I" in one sentence to the performative "I" in the other, illustrates how the structural dynamics I term "passing" emerges. In these sentences meant to clarify her concept of positionality, Alcoff tries at once to acknowledge the "truth" of the deconstruction of the "I" and to obviate it in the interests of a coalition politics, one premised on the fear that to disrupt categories of identity is to foreclose on political action. Alcoff's "positionality" attempts to resolve an implicit contradiction. My concept of passing, in contrast, is an effort to work within that contradiction by working through the radical implications of the postmodern theories and cultural transformations that have created this seeming impasse. I do not mean to deny that subjects are positioned but to deny that one acts from a discrete or prior position and to show how certain positions get elided in the process of acknowledging others. In place of the kind of self-critique Alcoff advocates, where one identifies oneself by race, gender, sexuality, class, age, and so on, *before* speaking or acting, passing offers a descriptive theory of the particular dynamics in which we can and must act. In the dynamics of passing one cannot worry about being exposed as either the real thing or the fraud, for passing contaminates the distinction between the two. Passing marks the delimitation of positionality, which is no more to abandon the notion of subject position altogether than Derrida's "iterability" abandons the category of intentionality. To repeat my argument from chapter 1, even if, as teachers and cultural critics, we acknowledge our social locations as multiple and unstable, shaped by specific histories and subject to various representational technologies, whenever we talk of subject positions and self-critique we talk as if we were immune to performance and thereby resuscitate in practice (in grammar) the very subject we dismantle in theory. In this sense, *the practice of writing itself,* as Zavarzadeh and Morton have argued (15–16), may resist the radical insights of postmodern theories, putting us all in the position of passing whenever we "speak for" ourselves and others.

Given that one condition of postmodernity is, as Caputo puts it, that "we" can no longer say "we" (209), the question no doubt arises of just whom I have in mind when I use the pronoun "we" and whether it is any longer responsible, if even possible, to invoke the first-person plural pronoun in discussing postmodern culture and the newly configured university. I use "we" deliberately to implicate myself and my readers in a cultural problematic that requires a shared structure of response. In the dynamics of passing I have been describing, "we" refers not to discrete identities that exist before engagement with others but signifies identities brought into being and into conflict through efforts to negotiate ever-proflierating subject positions. While feminist and African American critics have rightly questioned the imperial "we" in writing that takes white male experience as the norm, now critics who are by no means marginalized can mobilize that resistance to the use of "we" in their own interests, to escape their implication in the structural dynamics that I call "passing."[4] Without the ability to speak of "we," there is no possibility of ethics. This is why I feel it is important to differentiate between the "we" of disembodied truth and the "we" of a performative practice. But the issue is even more complicated than that. It would be all too easy to distinguish absolutely between the imperial "we" and the performative "we," but such a distinction ignores the inevitable slippage between the two, which has been the subject of this book.

Let me give a brief example of the kind of slippage I am talking about, which will serve to introduce the particular psychopolitical dynamics explored in this chapter. In a 1983 interview by Claudia Tate, Toni Morrison goes on at some length about the differences between black people and white people. Black people are "not too terrified . . . of being different," she says, "not too upset about divisions among . . . people. . . . Black people always see differences before they see similarities, which means they probably cannot lump people into groups as quickly as other kinds of people can" (qtd. in Tate, *Black Women* 123). When I read this, I was confused. Is Morrison saying that she's not black? That in generalizing about racial groups she's like other kinds of people, namely, whites? In other words, is she saying she's different (from other blacks) in not being different (from other people)?[5] Do her words come into conflict with her intended meaning, or does this assertion of difference confirm her point—namely, that as a black person she is not too terrified of being different, even from other black people? Tellingly, Morrison avoids using "we" to refer to black people in this particular response. The rhetorical slippage between difference and sameness, black and white, implicates Morrison in the structure I call "passing." Few academics, especially white academics, would challenge Morrison's right to use "we" when speaking about black people, but her assumption of an identity as a spokesperson on racial differences comes into conflict with that literal identity that many would take for granted. This impossible position between two oppositions (to employ a common deconstructive wording) is, at least for me, if not the space from which Morrison writes—the space of an authority that is not authorized—then the position in which her novels would put her readers. My point here is not to criticize Morrison for her position on black and white people. Rather, I am interested in how one enters the space opened up by her writing. Or, to draw on Morrison's language in *Playing in the Dark,* I am interested in "what prompts and makes possible this process of entering what one is estranged from," a process that Morrison calls *"becoming"* (4) and that I call "passing."

In this chapter, I want to engage performatively broader cultural and pedagogical debates over the nature of the subject by working though the dynamics of passing as exemplified in three specific and related contexts: in a particular exchange on the concept of the "subject" within feminist criticism; in two student responses to the 1934 film *Imitation of Life;* and in Fannie Hurst's novel that inspired the film. My purpose is not only to argue for a performative concept of the subject against those who would find such a

concept suspect but also, and more important, to show once again how taking a certain position on the subject—whether as feminists, cultural critics,
or literature teachers—is not the same as taking responsibility for the subject positions we assume and put into play in the classroom.

The Subject in Feminism

> The question of women as the subject of feminism raises
> the possibility that there may not be a subject who stands
> "before" the law, awaiting representation in or by the law.
> —Judith Butler, *Gender Trouble*

Two prominent debates among feminists in the 1990s have centered on the
viability of postmodern theories for feminist politics and on the political
implications of white feminists' use, in their writing and teaching, of black
women's writings. These debates are not unrelated, as black and white feminists alike have accused some white feminists of exploiting the "fractured
public identities" (Berlant 121) of African American women to promote a new
commodity of postmodern subjectivity. Where twenty years ago white feminists were fairly accused of ignoring the writings and experiences of black
women in their theories, today they are accused of turning to black wom-
en's writings and bodies to re-referentialize or rematerialize an increasingly
abstract and disengaged theoretical feminism. Twenty years ago, before the
convergence of forces instituting cultural studies in the U.S. academy, two responses to charges of neglect were prominent: to correct such an oversight
by adding the particular oppressions faced by black women to a universal and
liberationist theory of gender oppression; or to admit, as Patricia Meyer
Spacks does in *The Female Imagination,* that a white middle-class woman
could not theorize about experiences she had not had (see Carby, *Reconstructing* 9). In contrast, contemporary cultural critics, who problematize the very
boundaries of social identities upon which such responses rest, are more likely
to attend to "the operations of race in the feminine" (Abel 471). Today we
hear less about the failure of the (white) female imagination to project itself
into experiences it is estranged from than we do about the exposure of white
(female) desires in the very effort to imagine such experiences, to speak as
or for black women.

Two articles by white feminist critics published in the mid-1990s exemplify not only what cultural studies asks us to do (speak on behalf of certain
social constituencies while engaging in self-critique) but also the double bind
opened up by such an imperative. Margaret Homans in "'Women of Color'

Writers and Feminist Theory" and Elizabeth Abel in "Black Writing, White Reading: Race and the Politics of Feminist Interpretation" critique the positions assumed by white feminists in their use of black women's texts and are, to differing degrees, self-conscious about their own positions as white feminist critics writing on black women's texts. Together these essays serve well as a pretext for analyzing the dynamics of passing in cultural criticism and critical pedagogy.[6] Homans's and Abel's readings of other feminists, like my reading of their essays, are efforts to understand the complex and contradictory positions writers and teachers inhabit in cultural criticism and in postmodern culture.

Homans criticizes certain postmodern feminists (namely, Fuss, Haraway, and Butler) for the way they appropriate black women's writings: these theorists use texts by "women of color" (Homans's term) to embody a postmodern theory of subjectivity that critiques "bodily or biologically based theories of gender" and identity (82). In doing so they ignore the ways in which the works they appropriate position themselves on both sides of the identity debate, invoking a prior or natural, already existing identity while also revealing an awareness that such an identity is always "in the process of being made" (79). Citing only the postmodern aspects of the texts they appropriate, these theorists, Homans charges, downplay the texts' ambivalence (79). In response, Homans revalues these texts' naturalizing tendencies, the ways in which "women of color" reclaim themselves in their writings as embodied subjects. Their texts promote a concept of identity as embodiment; they construct the black female body as "natural" (86). To use their texts as examples of postmodern theories of the subject, which for Homans are theories of *dis*embodiment, is to deny their claim to the natural while *re*-embodying theories of dis-embodiment, making "women of color" do the cultural work they have always done—namely, embodying the body for white culture (73).

As an example, Homans contrasts Haraway's use of Sojourner Truth with Alice Walker's. Haraway urges us to be *like* Sojourner Truth, who becomes in her essay a figure for a "'nongeneric, nonoriginal humanity'" (qtd. in Homans 78). For Haraway, Homans says, the body of the black woman is a "resource for metaphor" (77). In contrast, Walker achieves a "personal identification" with Sojourner Truth; indeed, Walker claims to *be* her. Whereas Haraway's figurative language is "an alibi for de-materializing the [black] female body" (78), Walker's personal identification is, for Homans, a way of (re)claiming that body. In Homans's reading, Walker and Truth stand before the law (of representation) bearing an unmediated relation to the black female body—embodying it naturally, as if their identity were so close to nature that it did not pass through the filter of cultural discourses, those "powerful institutionalized rhetorics that provide the terms in which to represent the self as a subject in relation to others" (Brodkey, "Postmodern" 138). Yet the "ambivalence" Homans notes in black women's writings would also suggest these writers' awareness of the filter.

Abel's critique of Barbara Johnson follows the same lines as Homans's reading of Haraway. Johnson ignores in Zora Neale Hurston's writings "a possible belief in, or desire for belief in, a black identity," Abel argues, because she understands race as rhetorical rather than literal (480). As Johnson puts it in her essay on Hurston, representations of a black essence operate within "'specific interlocutionary situation[s]'" and are "'matters of strategy rather than truth'" (qtd. in Abel 480). By de-referentializing race, Abel says, Johnson displaces "a discourse on race" with "a discourse on positionality," a move that enables the white deconstructionist to write *as* the black novelist. By "as" Abel means not only "in the manner of" (for she has just compared Hurston's and Johnson's strategies of framing their essays) but also "in the subject position of"—for if race is only a matter of figuration, then a white critic can assume the position of a black writer. (This is what is commonly meant by "passing" when that term is used figuratively and pejoratively.) Drawing on Johnson's own critique of male philosophers who position themselves as women, Abel points out that Johnson, while capable of positioning herself philosophically as a black woman, cannot be positioned politically as black. Failing to make this distinction, Abel argues, Johnson risks "dislocating race from historically accreted differences in power" (482–83).

Homans and Abel demonstrate effectively that adopting a certain theoretical position on the subject (in this case, a reputedly postmodernist position) is not the same as taking responsibility for one's own subject position as enacted in one's writing, and to this extent they advance one argument I am also making about passing. Both reveal as well, to recall Abel's phrase, "the operations of race in the feminine" (471). But what interests me are the solutions Homans and Abel present to the problem of writing across racial differences, the ways in which they try to save themselves, as well as (white) feminist criticism, from exposure—that is, from passing.

The "cultural problematic" Homans uncovers in white feminist writings on black women's texts is, she says, "a problem of race relations in the academy" and a part of "the widespread debate over the uses of postmodernist theory for feminist political practice" (76). The troubling question, which she acknowledges, is whether this cultural problematic authorizes or invalidates (or authorizes *and* invalidates) her own position in this essay. While Homans never explicitly returns to this question, she implies an answer. She comes close to suggesting, as does Nancy K. Miller, that white feminists should have nothing to do with—or at least do nothing with—the writing of "women of color." Ironically, because she uses such writings herself, this argument would put Homans in the position of passing as a black feminist. But as Homans sees it, the difference between her work and that of the feminists she criticizes lies not in the *fact* that they use black women's writings to defend their positions on the subject but in the *positions* they take. As Abel points out, for Homans, all women share the cultural position of embodiment, which is devalued because the symbolic register (figuration) depends on the exclusion of "the female (maternal) body" (literalness) (484). Thus, it is precisely the construction of the black female body as natural that not only makes Walker's claim to (be) Truth tenable but also enables Homans to represent a theory of embodied subjectivity through Walker while at the same time saving herself from her own criticism of white feminists who use black women to embody their theories. Homans exonerates herself from the racially charged accusations she levels against others by claiming she uses black women's own figures of embodiment rather than making them figures for her position on embodiment (which just happens to coincide with theirs).

Yet Homans's effort to reclaim or reliteralize the black woman's body as she questions "the political utility of arguments that dissociate feminism from the body" (87) does not save her from charges of appropriation but actually implicates her in an instance of passing far more audacious than the examples she cites. Characterizing postmodern feminists as the exploitative white mistress using black women to do their work for them, Homans casts herself in the role of the domestic. As she puts it, black women in her essay "are working . . . for themselves at least as much as for me. Perhaps it could even be said that I am working for them" (88). The rhetoric of domestic service clearly serves Homans's interests in the very way she claims black women's historically constituted identities serve postmodern feminists' interests. The rhetorical gesture allows her to pass not only as the domestic (working for others) but as a black woman, speaking as and for black women in the pages of *New Literary History* and in this feminist debate over the subject. In the name of reclaiming an embodied position, Homans comes to embody another's position and then to use that figurative position to attack a theory of figuration. The rhetoric of her assertion is incompatible with its explicit meaning, and her performance (her assumption of an identity) comes into conflict with the literal identity she would assume—or take for granted.

Homans's use of Patricia J. Williams's work shows why her effort to save black women from misappropriation by white feminists is bound to fail. Homans chooses, appropriately, Williams's essay "Owning the Self in a Disowned World" in *The Alchemy of Race and Rights* to argue that Williams both celebrates her cyborgian split subjectivity and heals that painful split by identifying herself with her body, most dramatically in the dream Williams narrates at the end of the essay. What Homans ignores is Williams's *daydream* presented earlier in the essay. The daydream imagines race warfare in the form of "guerilla insemination," a vision of sperm banks infiltrated with black men's seeds to be introduced into the wombs of unsuspecting white women. The result of such guerilla warfare would be "the black-white child," "the impossible union of elements," who serves as "the icon of our entire civilization"—or at least of our postmodernist era, much as the androgyne served as the icon of the modernist era. Such "reproductive riot" evokes for Williams "the vision of white mothers rushing to remedy the depreciation of their offspring in suits about the lost property of their children's bodies" (189). The daydream of reproductive riot displaces the kind of oppositions (e.g., embodied/disembodied) that Homans's argument rests on and calls into question efforts to reclaim the body in an effort to unite women across race.

This is why, in my view, Williams's vision would be, as she says, "terrifying to so many women" (189)—not only to women who want to make our bodies our own, who believe "our destiny and our truth" are inscribed on our bodies, but also to white feminists who want to make other white feminists bear the burden of racism. If this vision, as Williams says, "squeezes racism out of the pores of people who deny they are racist" (189), the reproductive technologies that inspire the vision also trigger fears that the very nature of the body, like the nature of the humanist subject that depends on that body-in-nature, is at risk in postmodern culture.

Where Poovey argues that "responses to the postmodern condition are enlisting gendered meanings" ("Feminism" 40–41), Homans shows that they are enlisting racialized meanings as well. If, as Homans suggests, racialized traits are being appropriated by white feminists in an effort to promote a postmodern notion of subjectivity, it is also evident in essays like Homans's that racialized arguments are being mobilized to resist the social, material, and conceptual changes that go by the names "postmodernity" and "postmodernism." Yet to talk about the appropriation of feminized and racialized traits in this way is problematic insofar as the terms "feminized" and "racialized" mean that these traits belong not to bodies but to discourses of the body and thus are always already appropriated in the act of saying "I." The theorists Homans charges with "appropriation" have a different understanding of that term from Homans's. Racialized and feminized traits *must* be appropriated, or re-iterated, through what Butler terms a "compulsory citationality" (*Bodies* 232) for the subject to emerge in public. In this sense, even a woman must become woman, as Deleuze and Guatarri put it (see chapter 4); even a black must become black, as James Weldon Johnson's ex-colored man learns. "Paradoxically," writes Butler, "the discursive condition of social recognition precedes and conditions the formation of the subject: recognition is not conferred on a subject, but forms that subject" (*Bodies* 225). The constant slippage from the discursive to the embodied, from the represented to the real thing, is what my use of "passing" denotes.

I do not mean to deny the valuable insights provided by Homans's essay, especially in its attention to the writings of black feminist theorists. Rather, my point is that there is in her essay an incompatibility between her rhetoric and her meaning, her performance and her theory, and, moreover, that this incompatibility is a function of the dynamics that I have identified as inherent in the cultural problematic that Homans identifies as the problem to be resolved. Failing to interrogate how this cultural problematic inflects her own writing (the ways in which *she* may be passing), Homans displaces the general fear that the essence of feminism (not only a shared concept of woman but also the idea that women share the same positions) is at risk in postmodern culture with the more specific anxiety that "women of color" are being denied the opportunity to represent themselves because white feminists have unfair access to the means of representing theory in the academy and unfair access to "race" as, in hooks's words, "the new frontier."[7] I do not refute this specific claim, but I do question the effort to get out of this structure by reclaiming the body in the name of "women of color."

In calling for "thick descriptions" as a more viable feminist practice (496) and in engaging the writings of feminists of different theoretical persuasions, Abel at least potentially directs her attention to feminist criticism as an institution rather than to a particular kind of feminism. Analyzing the writings of Johnson, Homans, and Willis, she argues that no matter what theoretical positions they take, these readings across racial lines are marked by white desires. Comparing Johnson and Homans, Abel writes that where "privileging the figurative enables the white reader [Johnson] to achieve figurative blackness [i.e., to speak *as*], privileging the literal enables the white *woman* reader [Homans] to forge a gender alliance" across race (i.e., to speak *for*) (485). According to Abel, for Johnson black and white *writers* meet in shared figurality; for Homans, black and white *women* meet in shared literality. Both feminists, Abel argues, use black women to legitimate their own positions (486), and for both race is "a salient source of fantasies and allegiances" that shape white women's reading of black women's writing (497). All these efforts to read across racial lines are, for Abel, forms of "passing," and in the end all passing fails because "our inability to avoid inscribing racially inflected investments and agendas limits white feminism's capacity either to impersonate black feminism, and potentially render it expendable, or to counter its specific credibility" (497). Instead of deflecting these racial investments onto other feminists, Abel calls for a particular practice among white feminists reading black women's writing: to provide "thick descriptions" of black women's texts and to engage in continual self-critique.

In the opening of her essay, Abel practices self-critique, embarrassingly exposing her own "racially inflected investments" in her reading of Morrison's "Recitatif" (497). For Abel, self-critique depends on the confessional, and the confessional "I" is the guilty "I." This "I"—whether Abel's or Nancy K. Miller's or René Descartes's—responds to the anxiety of finding that "I" is not what it thought (i.e., that it is a fraud) by trying to master the self, hailing us right back to the Enlightenment notion of the subject before the law (see Worsham). The belief that we can and must rid ourselves of unruly (white) desires before we can write responsibly about others is not unlike the desire for an unmarked position that characterizes Enlightenment discourses—both presuppose the self-determining, rational subject of humanism. Abel's call for an alternative practice for feminist criticism assumes that honest individuals, who are coherent, comprehending subjects, can give an honest account of themselves (see Poovey, "Feminism" 37, 42). For Abel, as for Homans and Miller, the subject in feminism is already there, constituted by her (white) desires and exposing herself at every turn.

In Abel's and Homans's analyses, passing is a charge to be leveled against others, an illegitimate subject position, or a practice to be consciously avoided through persistent self-critique. Isolating certain categories of identity such as race and gender from other social determinants, as both Abel and Homans tend to do, does not invalidate the insights provided by their analyses, but it does mean that neither is capable of analyzing the way in which passing originates in the cultural problematic that Homans identifies as a problem of race relations in the academy and a consequence of postmodern theory and culture. Suffering feelings of guilt over prior exclusionary practices and deep anxiety about the precariousness of identity in postmodern culture, some white feminists seek comfort in these confessions aimed at reclaiming the subject in the name of those who have in part brought about this crisis of identity, in feminism as much as in the general culture.[8] Indeed, self-critique in the form of the confessional seems to intensify the tendency for white writers to use black people "as a way of talking about and policing matters of repression and meditations on ethics and accountability" (Morrison, *Playing* 7). For this reason, Abel, who connects her critical project in this essay with Morrison's in *Playing in the Dark,* cannot avoid participating in the very

practice she seeks to expose. Nor can I, or anyone else who is similarly positioned in the academy.

Failing to account for the postmodern context of her own analyses, Abel
misses the point of her call for thick descriptions of what Robyn Wiegman
refers to as "a cultural economy which constructs the feminine in the domain
of racial difference" ("Black Bodies" 323). If white feminists, in Wiegman's
words, tend "to circulate 'racial difference' as a commodity in our own discourses, pasting over the white bourgeois woman who occupies the center
of our theoretical paradigms with images of black women whose historical
and material specificity we thereby render indecipherable" (as Abel and
Homans argue), then "the future of feminism depends on revealing the in-
adequacies of its most privileged theoretical category"—woman (326). This
is precisely the task of postmodern feminism, insofar as postmodernism is
understood as a historical and cultural imperative, not narrowly conceived
as a theory of identity.

I have discussed this debate over the subject in feminism at some length
for two reasons. First, at least insofar as it gives rise to efforts to expose the
passer and to a form of self-critique that entails policing identities, this feminist debate can have the effect of making students unwilling to risk themselves in their writing (or in Suleiman's terms, to run the risk of being contemporary), thereby rendering them incapable of analyzing the import of
postmodernism for the multiple subject positions any one person can inhabit
and the multiplicity of subject positions that make up the body politic (see
Wicke 30; Harper, *Framing* 90–91). As in the composition studies known as
"current traditional rhetoric," which feminists have long opposed, these recent debates can make students feel they must get it right, say the right things,
make the right moves, and avoid revealing too much of themselves. Yet, con-
tradictorily, women's studies, African American studies, and composition
studies—as responses to the influx of nontraditional students into the academy—have historically sought to allow more exposure of the self in writing.
As forms of critical pedagogy, feminism and composition studies alike must
resist efforts to reclaim "a sovereign, self-aware consciousness at the center
of any composing act" (32), *in practice as much as in theory*, by shifting attention from the individual writer to the scene of writing, to the possibilities and constraints of the rhetorical and cultural situation in which we find
ourselves (see Crowley 32–34, 46). For passing—and this is my second
point—as "a politics of positioning" (not a new theory of identity but a *response* to the problem of identity in postmodern culture) is an effect of those
very institutional and cultural realities in which we teach and write. If cultural studies is about nothing else, it is about revealing the ways in which what

appears as natural, as a given, is actually a historical and cultural production. It is about questioning the legitimacy of any subject position taken to be secure, to be a safe space. In structuring our writing and reading assignments, we need to tap into those opportunities for passing that are made available in the current cultural studies climate. Cultural studies makes passing unavoidable, perhaps inevitable.

Class Notes: An Interlude

> Women have rarely been composers. But we do have one
> advantage. We're used to performing.
> —Laurie Anderson, qtd. in McClary

Midway through a writing-intensive core course in the Harlem Renaissance, I showed John Stahl's 1934 film *Imitation of Life,* a melodrama based on the popular novel by Fannie Hurst and remade by Douglas Sirk in 1959. I asked students to respond in their journals to the relationship between the two mothers in the film, Bea Pullman and her live-in domestic, Delilah. One woman, who asked me not to share her response with the class, clearly expresses the anxieties created when a humanist concept of the subject comes into conflict with a critical pedagogy:

> I am not even really sure if this is supposed to be an important part of the movie but it got me thinking. It's the "friendship" between Aunt D. and Miss B. The reason I am a bit confused is because I am not sure I am supposed to take it at face value. Here is the way I saw the friendship: I believe it was an honest to goodness one. For example, when Aunt D. was worried since her daughter didn't come home after she received a letter stating her daughter left school, Miss B. wanted to go with Aunt D. to help her find her. I saw Miss B. as someone who cared a great deal for Aunt D. Miss B. also let Peola know how disappointed she was in her by the way she was treating her mother.
> The confusion lies here. Being that this is a class on African Americans, I am not sure if I am not looking, or should be looking for hidden reasons (as far as color goes). Because Aunt D. did not move out and buy her own house after she came into some money, am I to think this had anything to do with color? See, I believe it does not. I myself am someone who enjoys taking care of others. It has always been a part of my nature. Did Aunt D. stay because this too was a part of her nature or because since she was black she felt she would not be in her "place" if she did not stay and take care of Miss B. and her daughter? Perhaps this was not a color issue. Just wondering.

The confusion, the hesitancy, the quotation marks as qualifiers all suggest that the student has learned that "an honest to goodness" response is not to be trusted, that what comes naturally to her may implicate her in racist language if not in racist social practices. But her language also reveals a strong desire to believe in that natural self, to assure herself that her desires belong to her and that they are "not a color issue."

In contrast, another woman, who was more than willing to share her response, shows that she has clearly learned the lesson of cultural criticism:

> The characteristics given to Delilah were many of the same characteristics attributed to the mammy stereotype. All of her tendencies were described as being "natural." For example, Delilah said that it was "natural" for her to raise children. This idea goes back to the notion that mammies have an overwhelming maternal instinct. It was also interesting to see how Delilah was made to be asexual or not involved in any sort of sexual relationship. Even though she at least had one intimate encounter [because she has a child], there was never any interest in her finding a man or love yet she was continually encouraging Mrs. Pullman to fall in love. In other words, Delilah's instincts were maternal not sexual.
>
> It was interesting to see how they portrayed Delilah as being the faithful servant. This stereotype, made up by white America, helps defend the ideology that African-Americans are perfectly satisfied in their subservient position. This is apparent when Mrs. Pullman tells Delilah that she could stop working and be fairly well off but Delilah cannot bear the thought of not taking care of Mrs. Pullman. We are to assume that Delilah cannot live independently of a white person. This was important because it made the audience more comfortable with the relationship between Delilah and Mrs. Pullman. This reassured them that Mrs. Pullman was not taking advantage of Delilah.

This student displays no anxieties in part because her own position in relation to the material she is writing about is not an issue for her. The first student risks putting herself—her "self"—into the text (something students in women's studies and African American studies are often encouraged to do) and, as a result, feels like a fraud. The second student blows the cover, as it were, on the first student's response, showing that those "natural" responses are "ready-made reflections which promise a false identity" (Lydon 248).

Yet however much these journal responses offer conflicting ways of reading the place of the "natural" in our concepts of the subject, these students hold similar notions of themselves as writing subjects. The first woman wants desperately to believe in her own authenticity and her authority to speak; the second simply assumes these. Indeed, although the second woman has mastered better than the first the lesson of reading and writing presented in a critical pedagogy, it was the first woman who came to change her notion of her self as a subject through her writing in this course. As her rhetoric so painfully reveals, she implicates herself, and her concept of self, in what she has written and, as a result, undermines the authenticity of that "I."

I am not saying that the first student was the better reader because she put herself into the text. Obviously, at this point in the course, the second student was reading with more sophistication. But I am saying that the first reader at least came to *experience* through *the act of writing itself* the kind of self-displacement that so many people writing on pedagogy advocate. In other words, there is more than one way of getting it right, or wrong. While intellectually and politically astute, the second student's argument does not require anything of her, makes no demands on her subjectivity, as does the first student's response. While the first student sought, and failed, to suppress her whiteness, which emerged through her writing as a category of analysis, the second implicitly suggests through her response that she can and must disavow her whiteness in analyzing whiteness as a racialized identity, thereby reinforcing the belief that knowing can be separate from experience (see Harding, "Who Knows?").

Changing the Subject

> Now I'm *loud*. . . . This is why I usually get along with African Americans. I mean, when we're together, "Whooo!" It's like I feel totally *myself*—we just let everything go!
> —Camille Paglia, qtd. in hooks, *Outlaw Culture*

Few white women have so repeatedly attracted charges of passing as has Fannie Hurst over some sixty years of criticism. What made Hurst's representation of black women so controversial, sparking a lengthy debate in the pages of *Opportunity* magazine in the 1930s, was that Hurst actively supported and promoted black artists, such as Zora Neale Hurston, her secretary and chauffeur for a time. Through her 1933 novel *Imitation of Life,* Hurst brought controversial issues of passing and racism to wide public attention. The film version of the novel was "one of the first screen dramas that linked issues of race, gender, and sexuality" (hooks, *Yearning* 3–4). Yet the racist representations of Delilah (the mammy) and Peola (the tragic mulatta) and their relationship to Bea (the mistress) fostered charges that Hurst was a closet racist, that her identity as a white liberal was a fraud. Hurst did not help to dispel this view when she responded to Sterling Brown's attack on the film, published in the March 1935 issue of *Opportunity*, with the patronizing suggestion that blacks should be grateful to her because the film "practically inaugurates into the important medium of the motion-picture a consideration of the Negro as part of the social pattern of American life" (Hurst, *Opportunity* 121), nor later when she wrote an editorial speculating "If I Were a Negro" ("Sure Way").[9] Not surprisingly, Brown expressed no more gratitude for the white woman's efforts than does bell hooks for Paglia's comment cited above: "Naturally, all black Americans were more than pleased to have Miss Camille give us this vote of confidence, since we live to make it possible for white girls like herself to have a place where they can be totally themselves" (*Outlaw Culture* 84).

The controversy surrounding Hurst's writing in the 1930s shares with feminist debates of the 1990s the question of whether white women write about black women to make their experiences and desires known to a white public or to become more comfortable with their own racial and gender identity at a time when many are suffering deep anxieties over the insecurity of that identity. Partly for this reason, I include *Imitation of Life* (the novel and the 1934 film) in my African American literature course on the Harlem Renaissance (from which the journal entries cited above were taken) as well as in my women's studies course on the construction of femininity in twentieth-century Anglo-American culture (discussed in the previous chapter). Written at a time of increasing anxiety over the number of white women entering the workforce and the number of black women leaving domestic service, especially as live-in domestics, *Imitation of Life* expresses the kind of ambivalence that attends systemic social change.[10] Working through the complex relations among race, gender, sexuality, and class in this novel can be a disconcerting experience, as the first student response quoted above reveals, but it can also provide a way of coming to terms with our own forms of passing in contemporary culture. As in Larsen's *Passing*, in *Imitation of Life* passing is the site where the often competing narratives of racial and gender oppression converge on the issue of sexuality.

Imitation of Life narrates the rise to fame of Bea Pullman, from daughter of a canvassing salesman in Atlantic City to founder of a national (and, by the end, multinational) corporation. Within a year of her mother's death, Bea, at age eighteen, marries the man of her father's choice, Benjamin Pullman, a salesman who boards with the family. Shortly thereafter, Bea's father suffers a series of strokes, leaving him confined to a wheelchair; her husband dies in a train accident on the way to Philadelphia to purchase life insurance; and Bea gives birth prematurely to a daughter, Jessie. Unskilled, Bea cannot find work at a time when opportunities for women are scarce (the year is 1914) and when white middle-class women simply did not work outside the home, unless, as Bea's mother once put it, they worked for "pin money." Desperate to feed her infant daughter and paralyzed father, Bea hits on the idea of assuming her deceased husband's identity to continue his side business of selling maple syrup to boardwalk establishments. But the demands of canvassing businesses by day, delivering maple syrup into the night, and caring for her infant daughter and invalid father leave Bea frantic and exhausted. She looks for help on the other side of the tracks, where she secures the services of Delilah, herself recently widowed with an infant daughter, Peola. Delilah and Peola move in with Bea and set up house, with Delilah caring for the house and Bea taking care of the business. Bea's break comes when she sets up a boardwalk concession, a diner modeled on a Pullman railroad car, and markets her syrup by selling waffles and maple sugar candy prepared by Delilah, whose down-home cooking and "Mammy to the world" appearance (103) are guaranteed to sell in America. Barely twenty years old, Bea has laid the foundation for her phenomenal success. Her chain of diners grows at a phenomenal pace over the next twenty years.

On the one hand, through the miraculous business success of Bea Pullman (who "passes" as "B. Pullman, business man" [124], the novel celebrates the mother's escape from domesticity into "a market economy where she can supposedly own her own labor" (Wiegman, "Black Bodies" 309). On the other hand, the novel appeals to the nostalgia for the lost mother and the security she represents (the novel opens with the death of Bea's mother), which is especially evident in the way Bea domesticates commercial space, fashioning her diners as wombs, kennels, and safe havens (134, 149, 161, 235–36). At the same time the novel appeals to the public's "racial nostalgia" (Berlant 122) for the lost mammy in the character of Delilah, it gives Delilah some of the most explicit statements about the operations of race and racism in American society. But the novel's great interest to me is that it makes clear (as the two film versions do not) that at times of increased anxiety over women's changing social roles and identities, as in Hurst's depression era or our own postmodern moment, the need for returning women to the (maternal) body becomes all the more urgent.

What is offbeat about Hurst's novel is that the maternal—traditionally assumed to be woman's natural role—is exposed as a cover for racism and sexism in American society precisely because the maternal is linked with the inability to pass. Like the 1934 film, Hurst's novel ostensibly suggests that racism can be overcome through women banding together on the basis of their shared condition of motherhood. As the second student understood in

her response, this proposed bond serves to sentimentalize racist social practices. But while the film's highly sentimentalized ending invites this reading,
the novel actually explodes it.

In the novel, the maternal is revealed to inhibit passing when we find out
that Peola, who passes as white and marries a white man, has had herself sterilized, a scene missing in the films. To pass, she must reject the possibility of
motherhood (which, if she gave birth to a dark-skinned child, could expose
her as a fraud), just as she must demand that her dark-skinned mother, Delilah, "unborn" her own child by disowning her. One cannot pass as a mother.
This lesson is reinforced at the end (another scene not in the films) when Bea,
whose business success has been driven by her desperate need for domestic
security, is deprived of the home she has spent a lifetime dreaming, planning,
building, and furnishing. That home is occupied by her daughter, who is now
married to Frank Flake, Bea's business manager, a man eight years her junior and the only man she has ever loved. This is a bitterly cruel punishment
for the working mother, making the novel seem complicit with a patriarchal
agenda. Yet the interdependence of the racial and maternal discourses suggests a different reading.

The novel actually exposes the nostalgia for the imaginary maternal for,
unlike both screen versions, in the novel Peola does not return home at the
end to throw herself on her mother's coffin. Instead, she "passes completely" in Bolivia with her white husband. The focus at Delilah's Harlem funeral is on Frank's discomfort in the presence of so many black people. "Didn't
know there were so many in the world," he says. "There can't be any darkies
left anywhere." "Except one," the narrator reminds us in a parenthetical aside.
"In her white man's jungle" (329). This reference to Peola (one of the few
narrative intrusions in the novel) reminds us that the passing and the maternal plotlines are chiasmatically linked. Bea, too, is living in the white man's
jungle, the world of business. By having Peola disappear from the novel, Hurst
leaves open the possibility that she has successfully disrupted cultural identities and identifications, eliding the effects of race on social relationships and
personal identity, which is so threatening in a highly racialized society (one
reason the film versions must have Peola return home to reclaim her racial
identity).

But the subversiveness of Hurst's novel actually turns on Peola's sterilization and the link between passing and motherhood. If Bea is punished at
the end as Peola is not, it is because Bea has tried to pass as a *mother*. Indeed,
her decision to pass occurs nearly simultaneously with the birth of her child.
Bea's parturition is presented as a dismemberment (72), recalling the opening scene of the novel where Bea's dead mother is described as a body in

pieces (1). Bea's "ether inspired corporeal dissolution in the pain of child-birth," as Lauren Berlant writes, enables her regendering not as a mother but as a businessman (118). In the next chapter, Bea finds her deceased husband's business cards embossed with the name "B. Pullman," the homophone of her husband's first initial enabling her to pass (73). Even the layout of these two chapters in the first edition of the novel—with the brief parturition chapter printed on the left-hand page, opposite the first page of the passing-as-businessman chapter—emphasizes the link between passing and moth-erhood that, like the mother's body, needs to be disavowed.

Insofar as the maternal stands for the origin—that idyllic period before the fall into the Symbolic, as Torgovnick writes (185, 187)—passing as a busi-nessman is a traitorous identification for a mother. However, by linking the passing and maternal plotlines, Hurst explodes that myth of the maternal as a natural origin. For me, a more compelling parallel between Bea's and Peo-lá's stories than the frequently discussed subplot of passing is the need felt by each daughter to renounce the maternal body. Hurst's novel opens with the passing of Bea's mother and Bea's obsession with her dead body: "It struck Bea . . . that quite the most physical thing she had ever connected with her mother was the fact of her having died" (1). The body in pieces repre-sents not only the mother's disavowed sexuality but also her lack of subjec-tivity in patriarchy. As Bea surveys her mother's body parts—arms, legs, breasts, loins, femurs—she identifies with the mother *as* body, as both sexu-al object and nurturing womb. It is this identification, according to the clas-sic psychoanalytic narrative of subjectivity, that the child must renounce, a move that is more difficult for girls because of their likeness to and intense identification with the mother.[11]

Peola too must disavow her mother and the social position she represents, "Mammy to the world," by insisting on her physical difference. Peola not only looks white, she insists she *is* white, an identification that eventually kills her mother. "I want you to let me pass," Peola tells Delilah and Bea. "I want your oath. Never so long as you live . . . to recognize or own me. I leave you no name. No address. . . . I'll have to learn to forget. You'll have to" (303–4). The pathos of the scene clearly lies in the severing of the maternal bond, but the language is that of repression, and what is being repressed *in both cases* (Peo-la's and Bea's) is not only maternal but also racial identification. The white woman who passes into the business world and the black woman who pass-es into the culturally sanctioned feminine role of the white middle class both imagine the maternal as black and abject. In a society stratified by race, be-coming a subject in the classic psychoanalytic model is here figured, for a woman, as "white slaughter of a black mother" (Morrison, *Playing* ix). Although Peola's sterilization may well imply that passing is unnatural, that a black woman passing as white will always only be a parody of white womanhood, the sterilization also allows female desire to be detached from maternal desire, opening up the possibility that the cultural production of femininity may proceed apart from the reproduction of mothering and the reproduction of mammies. In doing so, the novel undermines the "natural" basis of female identity (Poovey, "Abortion" 243) as well as the basis for female bonding across racial differences.[12] The novel's ending denies us any return home, or to the mother.

Hurst has let the black woman pass, which could, as Sterling Brown charges, reinforce the myth that all black people want to be white. Yet those very representations that Brown uses to argue that Hurst's novel is complicit with racism—and it is, in more ways than Brown imagined—function as well to locate racism in the cultural production of femininity rooted in the maternal. The first student's response to the film revealed this same connection, however unwittingly. Not only her whiteness but her femaleness implicated her in a racialized identity: "I myself am someone who enjoys taking care of others. It has always been part of my nature. . . . Perhaps this [is] not a color issue." Hurst's novel suggests that the idealization of the maternal is one way white patriarchal culture disavows the threat posed by passing women and that the racialization of the maternal may be a more pervasive phenomenon in the psychoanalytic narrative of subjectivity than the occlusion of women within the symbolic register (Homans's position). It is not a feminist project, Hurst suggests, to reclaim either the maternal or the black woman's body. You have to let it pass.

Let It Pass

> Louis: I'm not racist. Well, maybe I am.
> Belize: Oh, Louis, it's no fun picking on you; you're so
>   guilty.
>   —Chicago production of Tony Kushner's *Angels in
>   America*

Writing on the film *Imitation of Life,* the first student quoted above experienced the precariousness of identity that has come to characterize our postmodern moment. In the end, taking a certain position on the subject had fewer far-reaching consequences for writing than did changing her own subject position, for her doubts and hesitations meant that she could no longer take her self for granted as referent. She learned through her writing that the subject position from which one speaks and writes is never secure. Having no secure position to return to is precisely what distinguishes "passing" without the "as" from "passing as." Coming to terms with the precariousness of one's own identity opens up the possibilities of passing—or, in Morrison's words, "becoming," that "process of entering what one is estranged from" (4), which may not be those labeled "other" but rather the self that one has long thought to be one's own. Through her halting efforts to come to terms with gender identity as racially inflected, the first student came to work through (in both senses of that phrase) her personal identifications, something the second student, however savvy her response, was unable to do in her writing. The second student found a secure position from which to write; the first wrote through some precarious positions. Writing for the first student was a performative process that provided an *experience* of subjectivity as passing, something the second student's discourse rhetorically suppressed.

At the end of the semester, both students received an A in the course, but I believe the first student learned something more than the lesson of cultural criticism that the second student understood so well. The first student learned about the nature of writing, its supplementary logic. As Sharon Crowley explains: "writing never exactly substitutes for speech [for speaking for or as]. . . . But even more profoundly, writing never gets it exactly right; it never imitates or copies what would be said or thought exactly, but instead goes off under its own steam, does its own thing. Supplements never substitute exactly; they always differ from, and defer, realization of the 'real' thing" (14). If we are always already passing, even or especially when we seem to inhabit our "natural" position, it is not only because our social location is complex, multiple, and shifting, as Alcoff says ("The Problem")—although it is—it is also because, once represented, that subject position, the "real thing," is always to some degree an effect of the scene of writing. Many articles on the changing nature of literary studies, whether attacking or promoting this shift, reveal the desire to separate once again political issues of identity and identification from disciplinary issues of writing and reading, which is to separate "the 'messy' world of private fantasy and desire" from the sensible world of political action, communication, and interpretation (Cornell, "Wild" 315). Passing, as I reconceive it in this book, works against this separation; passing can neither be controlled as a politics or methodology, nor simply dismissed as a strategy of appropriation.

The point of all this for the teaching of literature and composition is that we need to provide our students with strategies and occasions for *working through* rather than *taking up*—in the sense of taking a stand on—certain subject positions. Such strategies and occasions are especially important whenever we make "whiteness" visible as a racial category, available for critique and open to delegitimation; whenever we reconceive concepts of essence and experience in the aftermath of poststructuralist theories; and whenever we engage the politics of identity in postmodern culture and in the (multi)cultural studies classroom.[13] The double bind created by the discrepancy between what we profess and how we are positioned, between the demands of a critical pedagogy and the constraints of postmodern culture, cannot be resolved only in the register of theory but must also be confronted performatively in literature and composition classrooms. My readings of the critical essays, the two student responses, and Hurst's novel are intended to alert us to those moments when passing is happening, in our classrooms and in our writing, so that we can exploit the analytical, political, and ethical possibilities it creates.

It is not that I would reject self-critique on the part of whites writing on race or men writing on feminism. On the contrary. But I would argue that self-critique can be effective only when we do not attempt to reclaim the body, or to revive the humanist subject, or to find appropriate figures for postmodern subjectivity. Self-critique without a postmodernist effort to free up concepts of identity from their metaphysical foundations leaves us with a choice between the confessional and the fraudulent, as the next chapter makes clear. The problem is not self-critique; rather, it is, as Poovey writes in another context, that the humanist subject continues to be produced as a solution to the cultural problematic that would place us all in the position of passing ("Feminism" 38). The more passing becomes the very real possibility opened up by our interrogation of subject positions, the more, it would seem, we need to defend ourselves against it by making it unnatural, illegitimate, or unethical. However, as I have tried to show, such a cultural problematic cannot be elided by seeking a more authentic position. We cannot get out of passing by attempting to reclaim the subject, the body, or the "real thing." We have to let it pass.

Notes

The subtitle was originally intended to allude to a 1985 paper by Nancy K. Miller, "Changing the Subject: Authorship, Writing, and the Reader" (in *Subject to Change*), in which she argues that a poststructuralist concept of the subject does not work for women, but I have since found other uses of this phrase. *Changing the Subject* is the title of a 1984 collection of essays integrating psychoanalytic theories of subjectivity with a Foucauldian practice concerned with the social discourses and technologies that regulate subjectivity (Henriques et al.). It is used by Linda Brodkey as the subtitle of a section on postmodern theories of subjectivity in her article, "On the Subjects of Class and Gender in 'The Literacy Letters.'" Gayle Greene and Coppélia Kahn play on this term in the title of their 1993 collection, *Changing Subjects: The Making of Feminist Criticism,* which reclaims the legitimacy of saying "I" and "we" for feminists by historicizing and theorizing the personal. One might say that "changing the subject" is not only a recurring trope but a defining one for feminism in the wake of poststructuralism.

1. In the *PMLA* version of this chapter, at the urging of the editors I substituted "culture studies," a term I borrowed from Isaiah Smithson, who in turn attributes it to Gayatri Chakravorty Spivak, for "cultural studies." I have restored "cultural studies" here to be consistent with the language in earlier chapters. See chapter 2, note 9 for an explanation of my use of "cultural studies."

2. On composition and women's studies courses as cultural studies, see Faigley, Schilb, Worsham, and Balsamo and Greer. On cultural studies, its relation to cultural criticism, and its institutionalization, see Poovey ("Cultural Criticism"), Graff and Robbins, essays in Berlin and Vivion and in Smithson and Ruff.

3. On the issue of who can speak in the classroom, see, for example, Fuss (*Essentially Speaking,* esp. chap. 7); hooks (*Yearning* and *Teaching to Transgress,* esp. chap. 6); and Roof and Wiegman.

4. The *PMLA* copy editor had difficulty with this statement. The phrase "critics who are by no means marginalized" could refer to white men, he pointed out. "Surely you don't mean that." He then rewrote the last clause to reflect the more common, predictable position he thought I wanted to argue: "now critics *formerly* marginalized can mobilize that resistance to the use of *we* in their own interests." I could cynically interpret this revision as yet another effort to let white men off the hook if it weren't for the fact that the copy editor feared *I* was doing precisely that. This is an excellent example of the problem of communicating given the intransigence of certain familiar positions. As a woman and a feminist, I was expected to argue for a political resistance to the "we" while at the same time being positioned in a "we," that is, in a collectivity of like-minded people called "feminists."

5. This particular formulation comes from Barbara Johnson's reading of Hurston's "How Does It Feel to Be Colored Me?" (*World* 174).

6. "Critical pedagogy," which refers generally to the activist nature of teaching, necessarily concerns itself with questions of subjectivity and agency in postmodern culture. See, for example, Aronowitz and Giroux 117–18, Giroux, George and Shoos 201–2, and Jarratt 107–17.

7. Poovey analyzes various defenses against the pervasive fear that the nature of the human is at risk in postmodern culture ("Feminism" 35–36). I borrow from her description to account for how postmodern feminist theory prompts defensive responses in some feminists who are afraid that it eliminates the body. As Robyn Wiegman similarly argues, certain rhetorical gestures "often allow us to claim perspectives of political noncomplicity" and to emphasize "the difficulty of extracting our critical gaze from the very relations we hope to expose" (*American Anatomies* 2). On the notion of identity at risk in postmodern culture, see Poovey ("Feminism"), Butler (*Bodies*), and Wicke.

8. The phrase "precariousness of identity" is, I believe, Butler's.

9. Hurst passed in other ways. To experience lives she wanted to write about, she would engage in impersonation. For example, she once took on the role of a shop girl in her father's factory so that she could portray such a lifestyle in one of her novels. To create a place for her, Hurst's father fired "the real thing." This example should be enough to warn us against the dangers of overgeneralizing about the ethics of passing. "There is passing and then there is passing" (Butler, *Bodies* 130).

10. Chafe writes that in the period between the wars, "magazines generally viewed [white] women's work as a threat to the family," and fiction of the time period often presented women rejecting work for marriage and family. "*This Freedom*—one of the most popular novels of 1922—attacked career women as traitors" (99). Headlines of the time asked what (white) women sacrifice for business careers (Kaplan, *Motherhood* 277).

11. From her first appearance in the novel, Delilah too is described, stereotypically, in terms of body parts: her large red mouth, Alpine bosom (91), crocodile hands (94), the upholstery of her lips (105). When her mother dies, Bea feels exposed: "With Mother gone," the narrator says in free indirect discourse, "life was much as if some one had left open a door to a warm room and strange bitter and alien winds were suddenly rushing into [that] security" (33). Delilah eventually breaks into the security of the white household, filling "every cranny and crevise" like the wind (96, 99). Alien and familiar, Delilah figures the return of the repressed.

12. Female bonding based on maternal identification is also betrayed in the film version when Delilah, in response to Peola's request that she disown her, says: "I can't unborn my own child. I'm no white mother." Of course, no white mother would have to unborn her child, disowning her so that she might pass. That line (which is not in the novel) suggests that white working mothers are less invested in their children than black domestics. In the beginning of the film, Delilah tells Bea that she's having trouble finding work because she refuses to be separated from Peola. By hiring Delilah to watch Jessie, Bea confirms for Delilah the difference between white and black mothers.

13. On the problems that can arise in the classroom whenever we engage in the interrogation of whiteness and other racialized identities, see Keating, especially her observation that students often conflate representations of "whiteness" with "white" people (908), as evident in the first student's reference to my course in African American literature as "a class on African Americans."

Sexual Harassment: A Pedagogical Problem

> Today, the question of values has reached the centre of the
> political and cultural agenda, with sexuality as the magnetic
> core.
>> —Jeffrey Weeks, *Invented Moralities*[1]

This chapter seeks to engage what Peter Baker refers to as the "ethical turn" in academic inquiry in terms of a particular social, legal, and, increasingly, pedagogical problem: sexual harassment.[2] Specifically, I want to address the ethical implications of postmodern ways of thinking, especially as these are elaborated in feminist political and legal theories, most prominently in the writings of Judith Butler, Drucilla Cornell, and Mary Poovey. Deconstruction, which, as David Harvey says, has provided a powerful impetus for postmodern ways of thinking (49), has contributed to the general shift in academic inquiry from questions of truth to questions of value, from what we *know* to what we *do*.[3] Yet in its critique of normative criteria and its alleged assault on the category of the person, deconstruction, according to its critics, denies truth, dismisses reality, and revels in undecidability, making a mockery of ethics and a shamble of politics. I do not want to debate the relation between feminism and deconstruction yet again, nor do I want to defend postmodern theory on ethical or political grounds.[4] Instead, I want to turn pragmatically from abstract arguments to particular cases—specifically, cases of sexual harassment—to consider why and how this ethical turn comes to be figured, as Jeffrey Weeks argues, in terms of sexuality. Here "sexuality" is meant in the broadest sense Weeks gives it, referring to sexual identities, sexual norms, and sexual behavior. Although, as Weeks concedes, sexuality has never been absent from political and cultural debates, today sexual identities and behavior provide the explicit focus for debates over communal values and public policies. If, as Lynn Worsham has argued, the turn to pedagogy in literary and cultural studies is in part a response to the failure of so-called radical theory to seriously confront the ethical and political consequences of postmodernism, those consequences, I suggest, are now being played out pedagogically in sexual harassment cases.

I begin with a classroom experience wherein the kind of critical responsibility demanded by deconstructive inquiry became paradigmatic of the kind of ethical and political responsibility called for today, not only by the increased visibility of newly empowered identities but also by feminist and postmodernist critiques of the discourses that shape the social emergence of any subject. Sexual harassment in particular has come to the fore recently in part because, as Cornell argues, women are breaking the bonds of traditional femininity. They are "out," she says, and this terrifies men (*Imaginary Domain* 220). That terror is linked to theory in recent academic cases of sexual harassment, which are the subject of part 2 of this chapter. These examples make urgent the need to reimagine the dynamics of responsibility in the newly reconfigured university.

"Is It Sexual Harassment Yet?"

> And remember, it's more than a storyline, it's a legacy.
> —Tag line for the daily recap of "All My Children" on a
> Chicago radio station

In the fall of 1991, I had on my syllabus for an introductory core-level course in narrative fiction a short story by Cris Mazza entitled "Is It Sexual Harassment Yet?"[5] I was teaching Mazza's story, published that year, for the first time, as a study in point of view. The story recounts events that lead a waitress, Michelle Rae, to file charges of sexual harassment against her supervisor, Terence Lovell. Printed in two columns, "Is It Sexual Harassment Yet?" presents Lovell's side of the story in the left-hand column using the third-person point of view, and Michelle Rae's version in the right-hand column in the first person. The two versions never quite fall into place; the question of just who is sexually harassing whom is never answered. Is Terence Lovell the innocent victim of a woman scorned? Or is Michelle Rae the emotion-racked survivor of a barroom sexual assault?

By one of those happy coincidences that likely come along only once in a teacher's career, my students and I began our discussion of this story the week Anita Hill's accusations against Clarence Thomas were leaked to the press. The uncanny parallels between the fictional story and the real-life drama (which were so intoxicating that one student delighted in pointing out that "Terence" rhymes with "Clarence") gave a different thrust to our discussions of Mazza's story during the next few weeks, transforming a lesson in the formal features of narrative fiction into a lesson in the social, political, and legal implications of forms of narrative discourse. Students who came to class prepared to dismiss Michelle Rae as a neurotic woman obsessed with Terence Lovell found themselves inadvertently mimicking press accounts of Anita Hill (a *U.S. News & World Report* story of 12 October 1992 cited "erotomania" as one explanation for Hill's charges against Thomas [Berger and Gest]);[6] and they heard Clarence Thomas during his testimony before the Senate Judiciary Committee repeating almost verbatim statements made by Terence Lovell (in his opening statement to the committee, Thomas remarked, "I cannot imagine anything that I said or did to Anita Hill that could have been mistaken for sexual harassment," echoing Terence's reported response to the charges against him, namely, that "he wasn't aware that anything he said or did could have possibly been so misunderstood" [201]).[7] The students became acutely aware of the structuring capacity of narrative—the power of narrative representation to structure our understanding of gender relations and social justice—and the social and political stakes of what we do as teachers of literature became clear to them, as did the implications of postmodern theory for the study of narrative fiction. I did not need to lecture the students about how identities are the product of representational technologies and discursive structures, using language they find alienating, to bring home to them the urgent implications of the theoretical inquiries that have produced that language.

The first issue we took up was the one I had intended to teach through this story, namely, point of view, or, more precisely, focalization—the relation between narrative agency (who supplies the narration) and point of view (whose vision determines what is narrated). Mazza's story opens in the left-hand column ("his" side) with the exposition: "Even before the Imperial Penthouse switched from a staff of exclusively male waiters and food handlers to a crew of fifteen waitresses, Terence Lovell was the floor captain" (197). The third-person narrator introduces us to Terence by means of his successful job and his ideal family life. In contrast, the right-hand column ("her" side) begins abruptly two and a half pages later: "I know they're going to ask about my previous sexual experiences" (199). We know Michelle only through her own words.

Students often think of point of view in commonsense terms, as some-body's perspective on something. Thus, like members of the Senate Judicia-ry Committee, students had thought, upon first reading this story, that their task was to chose between two points of view, two versions of the "same" story. Journal entries revealed that they initially saw Mazza's story in the same way *U.S. News & World Report*'s cover story of 12 October 1992 presented the Thomas hearings, "as a fierce and irreconcilable he-said, she-said battle" (33), although most of my students, like the majority of the public, found "his" version of what happened the more convincing one.

Reading the story alongside the hearings, however, made clear "what fo-calization achieves for narration": namely, "the textual inscription of a posi-tion for the reader or viewer in relation to the story," a position that is any-thing but value-neutral (Cohan and Shires 97). Significantly, in Terence Lovell's side of the story there is distance between the agent of the narration (an anonymous narrator) and the angle of vision (primarily Terence's). The left-hand column uses narrated dialogue, presenting Terence's comments indirectly while retaining some of his language: "Terence said his biggest fear [when purchasing a handgun] was that he might somehow, despite his pro-fessional, elegant manners, appear to the rest of the world like a cowboy swag-gering his way up to the bar" (199). This focalization implies a sympathy be-tween narrator and character, leading students to conflate the two at times and giving Terence's perspective the authority of a third-person (and thus seemingly objective) account. This focalization requires that the exposition be presented in his column, providing the reader with personal information about Terence that serves to establish his credibility as a witness or narrator.[8]

For the first two and a half pages of exposition Michelle's side of the text is blank. In her column, point of view is unmediated by narrative agency. She speaks directly to an interlocutor, sometimes addressing this person (who is not a character in the story) as "you." She seems at times to be answering questions, beginning a statement with "yes" or "no," so that her account reads like half of a conversation or interrogation. She goes off on tangents, juxta-poses seemingly unrelated comments, and at times responds as if she has been provoked. In comparison with Terence's story, hers sounds incoherent, even irrational, and it is emphatically personal and emotional: "But before all this happened, I wasn't a virgin, and I wasn't a virgin in so many ways. I never had an abortion, I never had VD, never went into a toilet stall with a wom-an, never castrated a guy at the moment of climax. But I know enough to know. As soon as you feel like *some*one, you're no one. Why am I doing this? *Why?*" (199–200)

Despite the textual clues throughout that suggest Michelle is in conversation with another, most students read the first-person account as confessional. Often they assume her references to "you" are direct addresses to them, the readers. Thus, her question "Why am I doing this?" was interpreted by many of my students as the soul-searching confession of a woman who doesn't know her own mind and isn't in control of her own actions. Michelle was seen to be implicated by her own words, by her own point of view.

Discussing how the different use of focalization in the two columns positions us differently as readers in relation to the story being narrated made many students aware that they could more easily believe Terence's side of the story because they had transferred the detached, objective, rational attributes of the third-person point of view to the male character. Because the law itself is characterized as rational, objective, and detached, their reading gave a kind of legal sanction not only to Terence's version of the story *but also to this kind of focalization,* which represents the apparent disinterestedness and impersonality of a judicial authority premised upon a concept of the subject as unmarked by attributes of cultural difference, such as gender (Bhabha 240). Moreover, because the confessional is characterized as the individual's exposure of the "truth" about him- or herself, Michelle was seen to indict herself through her first-person account of her feelings, experiences, desires, and fantasies.

Comparing the Thomas hearings with the story made students aware of point of view as a narrative convention and as a gendered concept. We noted that the exposition in Mazza's story functions as did Clarence Thomas's story of his family origins and his rise from poverty with which he began his testimony during his confirmation hearings. That narrative gave Thomas credibility. (The *People* magazine cover story of 12 November 1991 functioned similarly by presenting a picture of Thomas and his wife reading the Bible together.) Although Anita Hill also began her testimony before the Senate Judiciary Committee with her family history—a story similar in many ways to Thomas's, telling of her rural upbringing in poverty, of her strong family and church-centered childhood—this narrative (the narrative of upward mobility, of the self-made man) did not work for her.[9] Indeed, when I acquired the transcripts of the hearings a few months later, I was surprised to find that Hill had opened her testimony in much the same terms as Thomas had begun his, even though I had watched her testimony during the televised hearings. Her personal history carried so little weight, it was as if that testimony, as well as that *history,* had never happened. Instead, she was cast into the same roles as Michelle Rae—the vengeful woman, the erotomaniac, the tease, the liar, the fantasist, the bitch—however different Hill's intelligent,

poised, and reasoned testimony was from Michelle's racy, impassioned account.[10] Asking why two so very different women could be characterized in
the same ways, and why two so very similar personal histories did not carry
the same weight, students came to see what Kimberlé Crenshaw has since
argued in her essay on the hearings: "That perceptions of the credibility of
witnesses [or narrators] . . . are mediated by dominant narratives about the
ways men and women 'are,'" and once those "ideologically informed character assignments are made, 'the story' tells itself" (408–9). Our notions of
male and female behavior are the effects of cultural fictions and the power
relations implicit in narrative conventions, such as focalization, that structure our self-presentations in various institutional settings, such as hearing
rooms and classrooms. That the subject is the site of the reiteration of those
effects is what is meant by a performative concept of the subject.[11] Here we
can see the ethical and political implications of a postmodern theory of subjectivity: contexts in which gender and race are materialized may be altered
by interrogating and challenging the narrative and legal fictions that sustain
those character assignments.

Such character assignments functioned to the advantage of the men: both
Terence Lovell and Clarence Thomas could claim the role of victim in these
narratives. Terence loses his family and his prestigious position, and Thomas railed against the loss of his good name and his family's private life, ending his statement by saying, "I am a victim of this process." Initially, for many
of my students, as for Camille Paglia in her editorial on the Thomas hearings, this narrative of victimization supported the belief that sexual harassment "is not a gender issue" because men can be victims too ("Strange Case"
47).[12]

And so they can. But this claim of equity fails to consider the extent to
which the men, unlike the women, in both narratives are in a position to, and
find it desirable to, invoke the narrative of victimization. The plot of the self-
made, hardworking family man brought down by the vengeful, jealous, sex-
crazed woman is ready-made; it fits like a glove.[13] More to the point, if a
woman *is* "only as she is made to be by [her] victimization," as Cornell phrases Catharine MacKinnon's argument on femininity (*Beyond Accommodation*
10), then a woman cannot easily move into the role of victim, for she cannot
be the subject of a narrative she is already subjected to. Whether or not we
accept MacKinnon's view of women's essential victimization, we can see in
both women's stories what Hill explicitly testified to: the difficulty of going
public. Michelle and especially Hill appear to be less concerned with proving their personal victimization than with breaking silence. Hill concluded
her opening statement with: "I felt I had to tell the truth. I could not keep

silent." Michelle is incredulous when her interlocutor apparently asks why she is filing charges: "Why am I doing this? *Why?*" she asks, as if to say, How could I not press charges? If, as Donna Haraway states, "stories are means to ways of living" (*Primate Visions* 8), telling their stories is more important than proving their victimization insofar as to be a victim has long meant, for a woman, to be defeated, reduced to tears and pleading for help in the conventions of melodrama Roy Lichtenstein so humorously deflates in his art. This image of the victim has long worked against women seeking to make their claims heard in court (see Wicke 28–29).[14]

However, lest we respond, pace Paglia, that sexual harassment *is* a gender issue, pure and simple, we must not forget the way Thomas was able to tap into a far more public and recognizable narrative of victimization than the one he shares with Terence when he characterized the hearings as a "high-tech lynching"—a narrative of racism that was not, as many commentators have since pointed out, available to Anita Hill. Recognizing the way racism complicated the structural relations my class had been exploring in terms of gender alone served as an important reminder of "how a variety of forms of oppression intertwine systemically with each other; and especially how the person who is disabled through one set of oppressions may *by the same positioning* be enabled through others" (Sedgwick, *Epistemology* 32). Such awareness need not lead us to choose between racial and gender readings (the kind of choice that led Orlando Patterson to cast Hill as a "race traitor" and that led many white feminists to honor her as a heroine) or to choose between the essentialism of a radical feminism that would subsume differences between women to a metanarrative of victimization and the radical heterogeneity of a postmodern feminism, whose emphasis on difference and rejection of metanarratives would seem to belie efforts to establish women's collective oppression. Instead, understanding the relation between racism and sexual harassment could change the way we perceive the "reality" of sexual harassment, as a systemic problem—not as a misconstrued or misguided "social overture," but, as Crenshaw argues, as "an act of intentional discrimination that is insulting, threatening, and debilitating" (412). In this way, the narrative of sexual harassment just might be given the same truth-value as the narrative of racism that Thomas so successfully invoked.

This brings us back to the general question of the truth-value of narrative. In Mazza's story, there is no truth to be found because *there was no originary event*—nothing happened prior to this narrative. So when students believe their job is to determine who is telling the truth, I remind them that the characters and events are imaginary, that there never was an actual event, only the narrated versions. But in terms of the performative concept of subjectivity discussed earlier, this is no less true of the Thomas hearings. As Hayden White has written, "stories are not lived; there is no such thing as a 'real' story. . . . And as for the notion of a 'true' story, this is virtually a contradiction in terms. *All* stories are fictions, which means, of course, that they can be 'true' only in a metaphorical sense and in the sense in which a figure of speech is true." The relevant question, according to White, is: "Is this true enough?" (27). This is not to acquiesce in the naïve belief, so often attributed to postmodernists like White, that there is no difference between fictional stories and personal or legal testimonies; this is also not to say that there is no way to determine what happened (a conclusion that would risk doubly victimizing the victim of sexual harassment). Rather, this is to say that what happened, whether in fiction or in reality, will always *mean* only within a system of representations, in terms of "the narrative tropes available for representing our experience" (Crenshaw 403). Put simply, there is no unmediated relation to the truth. This is a performative insight, as Barbara Johnson makes clear: "The speaking subject is only a persona, an actor, not a person. But if one considers the conventionality of all performative utterances . . . , can it really be said that the chairman who opens a discussion or the priest who baptizes a baby or the judge who pronounces a verdict are persons rather than personae? . . . The performative utterance thus automatically fictionalizes its utterer when it makes him [or her] the mouth-piece of a conventionalized authority" (*Critical Difference* 60). It is in this sense that we can say, with the deconstructionist, that if people are judged and sentenced according to laws and not literature, it doesn't mean that the law is not also a fiction (*Critical Difference* 60).

Such an insight did not relieve my literature students any more than it would the Senate Judiciary Committee of responsibility for determining the truth, but it did change the nature of that task: from determining what really happened to making a certain kind of narrative accessible, and thus a certain kind of truth desirable. Truth is not to be determined by abstracting the stories from all vested interests but by situating the accounts within a larger cultural problematic and the systemic relations that structure them. It is in this sense that theory is, as Fuss says, a "practice of accountability" ("Accounting" 111). Studying literature in terms of postmodern theory can provide a more nuanced understanding of accountability as a linguistic and rhetorical concept. To give up the idea of establishing truth in the objectivist sense, as postmodernists do, does not mean we have to acquiesce in the belief that there is no truth or that all versions are equally true. It means instead that we must consider the discursive relations through which a certain truth is produced, maintained, reiterated, and lived as one's own. How does a narrative or discourse that claims the authority of being true come to compel belief? When is it "true enough"?

Mazza's story enabled us to see that it is not simply, as some members of the Senate Judiciary Committee liberally concluded, that Hill and Thomas were each remembering events differently but, more important, that "the interpretive structures we use to reconstruct events are thoroughly shaped by gender power" (Crenshaw 410), as well as by racial and class relations. For example, students wondered why they never noticed the lack of exposition in Michelle's version of the story or questioned the omission of her familial history, or why they never questioned the lack of any references to Terence's past sexual experiences, even when they read that his wife left him on grounds of "cruel and unusual adultery" (218). Likewise, the senators and the majority of the public never questioned why inquiry into Clarence Thomas's private life (testimony dealing with his consumption of pornography or speculations about his sexual fantasies) was off-limits, while speculations about Anita Hill's sexual fantasies and testimony by John Doggett about her personal relationships with men were deemed quite relevant.[15] If, in the end, certain members of the Senate Judiciary Committee were able to extricate themselves from an exceedingly uncomfortable situation by mimicking the parodic version of deconstruction—claiming there was no truth to be found, only competing interpretations—at least Thomas's account was "true enough" to earn him a seat on the Supreme Court.

Moral Implications

> I believe Anita Hill.
> —button slogan

What are the implications of this deconstruction of the boundaries between law and literature for social justice and ethical responsibility? If telling women's stories is not about getting at the "truth" of women's sexual and economic oppression instantiated in cases of sexual harassment, then how can women end the injustice of their "doctrinal exclusion" from the law, falling outside, in Crenshaw's words, "existing legal categories for recognizing injury" (404)? Commentaries in Toni Morrison's collection on the Thomas hearings, *Race-ing Justice, En-gender-ing Power,* argue that women's experiences in general, and black women's experiences in particular, go unnoticed by the law, keeping women's stories from being justified or even heard within the terms of legal discourse. To solve the problem of women's exclusion from legal discourse, argues Robin West, women must tell "true stories" of their lives so that the law, now premised upon a gender-neutral subjectivity, can come to reflect women's as well as men's experiences (70). This position advocates a normative ethics based on knowledge and premised upon an expressive view of language.[16] From this normative perspective, breaking silence, as Hill did, means telling the truth of women's experiences.

However, as the results of the hearings prove, breaking silence is not always sufficient and telling the truth is not always enough. What is true is not simply that which corresponds to what "really" happened; rather, what is true is what is accepted as being true within the terms of a given discourse. The law recognizes a certain kind of subject, allows certain kinds of evidence, and sanctions certain kinds of testimonies that establish what will count as the truth within the legal system. What is true and what is real are better thought of as standards used to judge an individual's performance or testimony within the terms of a particular discursive situation (Butler, *Bodies* 129).[17] Having faith that she would be heard within the system if she simply told the truth is what defeated Anita Hill. One of the best points bell hooks makes in her commentary on the hearings is that the problem with Hill's speaking out was that she had no strategy, no sense of an audience; that is, she had no understanding of discourse as a set of conventions (*Black Looks* 80). Of course, the absence of a strategy or agenda supposedly proves one's honesty and gives one credibility or the moral high ground. This assumption rests on the belief that individuals exist and are equal *before* the law, the belief that drives a normative ethics as well. Exposing Thomas, however, required more than exposing his "true character"; it also required exposing the mechanisms by which character assignments are made and sanctioned within dominant cultural discourses.[18]

Exposing is precisely what Mazza's story does. If Hill's truth seems to exist before the law, Michelle's story shows the extent to which truth is clearly subject to the law. To the extent that Michelle takes on the image of women shaped by the legal construction of sexual harassment, telling the truth in Mazza's story takes the form of playing out, and thereby bringing into strong relief, the system of gender representations that shapes our perception of women and our capacity to understand and respond to their suffering. Michelle's character is believable because she performs *in drag*, as defined by Butler ("Imitation" 23–24), thereby exposing the mechanisms by which gender is constituted in legal discourse. Mazza's choice of narrative for the woman plays out, and plays up, the "truth" of sexual harassment cases: that inquiry focuses on the character and conduct of the victim rather than the defendant, casting the defendant in the role of the mentally or emotionally unstable and drawing a connection—as Crenshaw says our legal system once drew a connection, as a matter of law—between lack of chastity and lack of veracity (412). That Michelle Rae knows this "truth" is revealed by her opening statement: "I know they're going to ask about my previous sexual experiences."

As Poovey points out, the reigning assumption in legal cases is that "true stories will be recognizable as true because they are coherent, comprehensive, and comprehensible" and that such coherent narratives are seen to be "generated by honest individuals because these persons are coherent, comprehending subjects." This assumption, however, has been challenged by psychological research that shows trauma victims surviving "precisely by losing their coherence and their ability to comprehend" ("Feminism" 42). The rambling, contradictory, incoherent account that Michelle provides, which was read by many students as evidence that she is either lying or mentally and emotionally unstable, attests to the truth of rape trauma victims, and thus what seems to prove her unreliability might well provide evidence of her victimization. This is not to say that we must choose between Michelle's victimization and her unreliability. Rather, Mazza's story requires us to take seriously Hayden White's question: "What wish is enacted, what desire is gratified, by the fantasy that real events are properly represented when they can be shown to display the formal coherency of a story?" (qtd. in De Lauretis 129).

As more of my students became sympathetic to Michelle Rae, and as more of the public came to believe Anita Hill, it was not because of any new evidence that convinced them of the truth of these women's actual experiences. Their changing attitudes had more to do with a change in the way they think about the relation between narrative tropes, legal constructions, and lived experience. That is, their changing attitudes stemmed from their training in textual analysis, which provided a more complex understanding of "accountability." Believing Michelle Rae and Anita Hill has more to do with affirming women's doctrinal exclusion in legal discourse than with confirming the truth of their stories. As Cornell writes, "believing women cannot be reduced, as MacKinnon would do, to believing their accounts of their oppression. Believing involves *believing in*. Believing in, allowing us credibility, includes the recognition of the legitimacy, not just the accuracy of our account" (*Beyond Accommodation* 136). The "I believe Anita Hill" button that I have since purchased does not mean that I now know that Hill was telling the truth; rather, it means that I now take seriously the question Poovey raises: "Why a black man was believed when he alleged racism, while a black woman was discredited when she alleged sexual harassment, is a question that cries out for serious attention" ("Feminism" 51).

The motive for telling women's stories need not be to ground the law in the truth of women's experiences but to make a certain kind of truth or justice desirable by imposing some order or meaning on events. Telling women's stories, as Homi Bhabha and Cornell both affirm, is like the process of metaphor, "a transformative act of the political imagination that makes new connections, breaks boundaries of sense, maps rare sources of sensibility, and embodies other, unsettling regimes of truth" (Bhabha 249). What would it mean for these women's narratives to be given credibility, and how might literary pedagogy contribute to such a change in our political imagination? To begin with, believing Michelle Rae and Anita Hill means changing our question from "Is this story true?" or "Did sexual harassment really occur?" to "When will we accept the 'truth' of stories of sexual harassment?" "Is it sexual harassment *yet*?" "Is this story 'true enough'?"

Pedagogical Imperatives

> The real moral knot . . . is . . . about falling into story.
> —Jane Gallop, "Knot a Love Story"

In a *New York Times* editorial on 25 September 1992, a year after the Thomas hearings, Michiko Kakutani presents a familiar argument that "these days [the] merging of reality and fiction has become . . . a common malady," citing exchanges between politicians and fictional characters, like Dan Quayle and Murphy Brown, and the confusion of the historical John F. Kennedy with Oliver Stone's filmic JFK as symptoms of this sickness. "No matter that [nonfiction novels] evade the strict responsibilities of both history and fiction, no matter that they make it impossible for the reader to distinguish between what is real and what is invented," Kakutani laments, we continue to mistake fiction for the truth (1). In their arguments over what *really* happened in Mazza's story, my students confirm Kakutani's point that readers/viewers do sometimes mistake fiction for reality. But more often than not my students insist that reality is real, not fictional, making a firm distinction, as Kakutani would have us do, between history and story. For many students, real is real, as MacKinnon is reputed to have said in response to deconstructionist critiques of representation (qtd. in Wicke 26n10). In my view, it is not that the confusion of reality and fiction is now epidemic but that the clear-cut distinction between them has always been *academic*. Or, to employ another play on words—specifically, MacKinnon's words about sexual harassment—the confusion is not epidemic but endemic to the functioning of power (qtd. in Bhabha 244). What is real is not what is "there" outside or prior to any story; rather, what is real is what is capable of taking on a believable form. What determines the effect of realness is the ability of a story to compel belief (see Butler, *Bodies* 129). To compel belief would be to institute some new system of law. "Where there is no rule of law," writes White, "there can be neither a subject nor the kind of event which lends itself to narrative representation. . . . And this raises the suspicion that narrative in general . . . has to do with the topics of law, legality, legitimacy, or, more generally, *authority*" (16–17).

To believe that our task as readers is to decide what really happened is to assume that all stories are re-presentational, that fiction gives us versions of real-life events so that we can exercise our moral judgment, hone our skills in making ethical and just decisions. It is to assume, as Robin West does, that truth and ethics exist before the law, and that what is just follows from what is true (Faigley 235). If fiction is the mirror of life, then we can judge characters the way we judge people, holding them to the same moral standards.

Once we grasp fiction as representational and conventional, structuring our sense of ourselves and others and our accounts of events, then understanding the effects produced by certain narrative tropes becomes more compelling than determining the truth of what happened. Put differently, textual analysis becomes an ethical imperative. If all stories—even those that are supposedly real or historical, based on actual events—are fictions, that is, are constructed within and according to cultural systems of representations with their own generic conventions and rhetorical strategies, then they cannot be assessed as if they were merely relating actual events in their temporal order. To believe that all stories are fictions is to learn to read people and events the way one reads characters and plots, taking into account the discursive structures, narrative conventions, and social contexts within which the stories operate.

These two views of fiction present two different ways of conceiving the ethics of pedagogy. The former view suggests that we learn to make ethical judgments by learning to sympathize with others' experiences as these are reflected in literature. We put ourselves in "their" place and thereby come to expand our notion of what it means to be a human being. Characters represent particular social positions, narrative events mirror actual experiences. Ethics lies in being able to bridge the gap between our position and theirs. Insisting that it is neither possible nor ethical "for men to invest in the pretense that they have successfully put themselves in women's shoes," Cornell says that we count on the "aesthetic realm" of narrative to help us cross these psychic and political barriers, though the barriers remain (*Imaginary Domain* 188). I am suggesting that we rethink this common notion of the aesthetic

realm in order to rethink where ethics takes place in the teaching of literature and in the dynamics of the classroom.

The second view, what might be called the ethical turn in literary studies, suggests that ethics takes place elsewhere, not solely in sympathetic identification with another but just as importantly in the deployment of certain
discursive conventions and rhetorical constructions in our efforts to negotiate the dynamics of responsibility in any particular situation. It makes questions of generic conventions and consideration of audience central to questions of ethical responsibility. That is, the postmodern view of narrative (if
we can even talk of such a thing) relocates ethics and justice in the "material
practices of reading and writing," as Faigley says Lyotard does in *The Differend* (237).

According to Lyotard, a differend arises whenever two parties do not agree
on rules of procedure, evidence, or justice. The differend is "the case where
the plaintiff is divested of the means to argue and becomes for that reason a
victim" (*Differend* 9). When Crenshaw writes of women's "doctrinal exclusion" in the law, falling as they do "between existing legal categories for recognizing injury" (404), she is naming a differend. Faigley cites the Thomas
hearings as an example of "silencing a differend" in that Hill was unable to
convince the senators "that a wrong had occurred" (234–35). Cornell also uses
sexual harassment to illustrate the differend, arguing that "the silencing of
women, because of *derelection,* can be understood as the *differend*" (*Beyond
Accommodation* 60–61).[19] Cornell has objected to the way the debate has focused on what is a "reasonable woman" rather than on "the essential injustice of . . . normative standards and the need to continually transform them"
(*Imaginary Domain* 16). The important point is not only, as Lyotard concludes, that the differend requires that justice be worked out on a case-by-
case basis and that we must not presume to know what justice is or should
be in advance of that process. Equally important is Lyotard's notion that
responsibility lies in one's choice of genre, which, for Lyotard, provides the
rules for linking phrases. Ethical responsibility lies "in detecting differends
and finding the (impossible) idiom for phrasing them" (*Differend* 142). The
point is not to advocate a particular genre or a particular conception of justice, not to replace a masculinist referential with a feminist one, but rather
"to consider the implications of [one's] linkages" (Faigley 238) in writing,
in reading, and in teaching. "*The Differend,*" writes Faigley, "can be read as
an argument for locating ethics within pedagogy. Lyotard would not have us
look to external discourses of the 'true' but to the discursive practices of the
classroom" (236). The Mazza lesson, for me, brought about this shift from
questions of truth to questions of value bound up with writing and reading

practices. It thereby enabled me to engage students in the pursuit of the differend so crucial to a deconstructive notion of ethics and justice rather than
to lecture to them about deconstructive theories and practices.

For a theory to be accepted, William James once said, it must meet certain conditions of acceptability, not correspond to the way things are. Telling a student that he or she is a narrative trope, the product of representational technologies, a persona not a person (in the language of postmodern
theory) hardly satisfies certain human needs. But the pragmatist's shift in
emphasis from truth as correspondence to truth as acceptability càn also serve
to make postmodern theory palatable. In a lesson such as this one, buying
into postmodernism does not mean accepting a certain theory of subjectivity so much as it means working through what "subject positioning" means
for any one individual by imagining the possible situations in which a certain understanding of the subject or a certain concept of truth will produce
desirable effects for certain individuals. It means not stopping with the postmodern "truth" of subjectivity as performativity, or as passing, but asking
what ethical and political possibilities are opened up by the self conceived
in these terms.

"He Said/She Said"

> This change in perspective is, precisely, a matter of ethics.
> —Luce Irigaray, *An Ethics of Sexual Difference*

A Gary Larsen "Far Side" cartoon I am particularly fond of illustrates a characteristic scene of miscommunication. On one side of the page, under the caption "What We Say," a woman is scolding a dog: "Bad dog, Fido. Never get into
the garbage. Bad, Fido, very bad." On the other side, under the caption "What
They Hear," the dog sits listening: "Blah blah, Fido. Blah blah blah blah, Fido,
blah blah." The cartoon encapsulates the failed communication between owner
and dog, parent and child, teacher and student, man and woman. Its structure is that of sexual harassment and date rape scenarios presented in terms
of the "he said/she said" paradigm of miscommunication that characterizes
the gender wars.[20] *They* just don't get it. *They* cannot grasp what *we* are saying. Might as well take a rolled up newspaper to their collective backside.

My subsequent efforts to teach Mazza's story have not been as successful
as they were in that initial class. Without the coincidence of events that allowed—indeed, compelled—a "postmodern" reading of the story, and without the powerful visual image of the African American woman being aggres-

sively questioned, even harassed, by a panel of older white men, students have found the "he said/she said" paradigm of failed communication and false accusation a far more familiar and comfortable scenario through which to make sense of sexual harassment cases. Substituting the transcript of the hearings for the live performance, and the Morrison collection *Race-ing Justice, En-gender-ing Power* for the media analyses, as I have in subsequent classes, has largely failed to convince students not already so inclined to *believe in* the legitimacy, if not the truth, of Anita Hill's and Michelle Rae's accounts. In fact, assigning Morrison's collection on the hearings has convinced some students that I have an agenda, a "side" to advance rather than a lesson to teach, while in that initial class, the uncanny coincidence of events was proof enough for most students that my motives were pure—even though my analysis of the story and the hearings questioned the very possibility of any "pure" motivation. This is not to say that the ethical and political import of postmodern theories can be taught only through a pedagogy conceived along the lines of "found art"—that is, only through a live, spontaneous, topically relevant media event. But it does make a case for the significance of what Houston Baker calls "local pedagogy," which compels us to take seriously students' demands for the relevance of literature to their everyday lives. This does not mean supplementing discussions of literature with discussions of topical events; nor does it mean substituting political analyses for formal analyses. The Thomas hearings provided instead an occasion for seeing the discourse of literary studies and the discourse of legal proceedings as, in Houston Baker's words, "coextensive interrogatives" ("Local Pedagogy" 404).

The coincidence of the fictional narrative and the real-life drama of sexual harassment provided, in that initial class, a means of making clear the social and political relevance of the kind of thinking about self, experience, fiction, and truth now identified as postmodern. The Mazza lesson illustrated the need to see sexual harassment in terms of broader theoretical and institutional issues, though neither the story nor the hearings were "about" those issues. The following academic year (1992–93), however, two cases of sexual harassment exploded in the media that were explicitly about theoretical and academic debates: David Mamet's *Oleanna* and Jane Gallop's sexual harassment case at the University of Wisconsin at Milwaukee. Another uncanny coincidence (charges of sexual harassment were filed against Gallop the same fall *Oleanna* came to the stage), the parallels between Mamet's play and Gallop's case and their shared preoccupations seem to suggest that sexual harassment on campus, insofar as it captures the public's interest, has more to do with theory in the academy than with sex or sexism in the classroom.[21] Both flash all kinds of warning lights about what happens when professors and students act on, and act out, the theoretical insights about power and authority, difference and identity, and politics and justice attributed to post-modern theory, and both present sexual harassment as a pedagogical prob-lem. I want to turn now from looking at how narratives of sexual harassment can bring home to students the implications of postmodern theory and look instead at how the consequences of theory are being played out in narratives of sexual harassment.

Gallop, a professor of feminist theory, was accused of sexual harassment by two female graduate students who claimed she made sexual advances and, when thwarted, retaliated with low grades or refusals to write letters of rec-ommendation. Although two students were involved, only the charges of one, Dana Beckelman, were taken seriously. In Beckelman's case, the relationship between student and teacher was intensely personal. Not only did they share a flamboyant style, they also shared, by all accounts, an intense kiss one evening, in the presence of other graduate students, as they were leaving a lesbian bar together. Gallop has since been cleared of the specific charge of sexual harassment, though she was officially reprimanded for violating the university's policy against "consensual amorous relations" when she kissed Beckelman in public.[22]

Oleanna, Mamet's play of three acts, stages an increasingly aggressive encounter between John, a professor of education who is about to receive tenure, and Carol, a student who is having a great deal of difficulty under-standing John's educational theory, which John attributes in part to her so-cioeconomic status being lower than that of the average student. All three acts take place in John's office, where the teacher-student conference is continu-ally interrupted by telephone conversations between John and his wife over their negotiations to buy a house, a symbol of the stability brought by John's imminent tenure. Carol brings charges against John in act 2, citing as evi-dence of sexual harassment statements and behavior we have witnessed in act 1. By act 3, John has been found guilty and dismissed, losing his tenure, his house, and possibly his freedom. The play ends with the enraged profes-sor's physical assault against the student he now belittles for her "political correctness."

Many reviewers insisted that *Oleanna* is merely passing as a play about sexual harassment, that it is really about something else: the indeterminacy of language, the relation between language and power, the gender wars, the Other as ultimately unknowable, the culture wars between advocates of di-versity and defenders of free speech, the politicization of the academy, and academic jargon. In his last speech, John finally hurls the epithet that char-acterizes for many viewers what the play boils down to, namely, a critique of political correctness: "You vicious little bitch," he cries. "You think you can come in here with your political correctness and destroy my life?" (Mamet 47). Mark Feingold offers the broadest assessment of what Mamet's play is about: "Versions of [*Oleanna*] . . . are being played out all over America these days. We live in a civilization that has lost its consensus—if indeed it ever really had one—and large segments of the social contract are in the process of being renegotiated. Mamet's play is a picture of the terrible things that can happen to a teacher and student when neither is wholly willing to admit the negotiations are going on" (109). Similarly, in Margaret Talbot's narrative, as well as in Gallop's defense of herself and her position on sexual harassment in "Feminism and Harassment Policy," Gallop's case has come to stand for the dangerous consequences of certain theoretical and political inquiries, especially when one takes them out of the relatively safe domain of the academic journal and into the messy terrain of the classroom. The lesson many read in these two cases is that those who politicize the academy will be undone by their own theories and practices.[23] Whether one cheers or fears this possible outcome typically depends on whose side one takes and whether one is "for" or "against" theory in the academy.

Yet what is missed by those who look beyond the ostensible subject matter (sexual harassment) for the real underlying issue (theory) is the way in which the common construction of sexual harassment as a "he said/she said" dispute provides the terms of debates over theory in the academy. Far from being a cover for academic debates, a "mere" plot device, sexual harassment provides a crucial structure for these debates. As Poovey says of the law in general, so I would say of sexual harassment in particular: it "stages the dynamics of social negotiation specifically in the form of contests and, therefore, makes these negotiations available to the public in the familiar, hence easily consumable, form of melodrama" ("Feminism" 42). To see *Oleanna* as a dramatization of themes in postmodern theory (the indeterminacy of meaning, the relation between language and power) or debates in academia (the culture wars, the hegemony of theory), or to see it simply as topically relevant, capitalizing on the Thomas hearings, is to miss the more significant question: Why are these particular themes and debates represented in terms of the sexual dynamics of this particular social and legal issue?[24] Far more compelling than the question of who is right or whose position is the more defensible is the question of why issues of political correctness, identity politics, cultural diversity, and theoretical inquiry are being played out in terms of the narrative dyads of sexual harassment.

To answer this question, we need to look more closely at the structural similarities among fictional (Mazza, Mamet) and actual (Hill-Thomas, Gallop-Beckelman) cases that reveal sexual harassment to be about systemic relations of power and status, not about individual actions and desires, undermining any clear-cut distinction between the real and the represented. Thus, the issue is "no longer limited to individual versions of the truth and specific cases," as Bhabha says of the Thomas hearings (245), or to efforts to distinguish misinterpretation or fantasy from the real meaning and intent of a statement or gesture. It is not a matter of what he said versus what she said, for to identify sexual harassment is not only to name prior actions but to produce a discourse with its own generic conventions, character assignments, and forms of knowledge and pleasure, as the Mazza lesson shows. That is, sexual harassment scenarios form a genre, as Lyotard uses that term, which produces a certain truth value. To better understand the specific academic issues relevant to Gallop's and Mamet's examples, we need to review the recurring features of sexual harassment narratives that reveal the extent to which sexual harassment laws do not simply carry "the force of a prohibition" against sex or discrimination but produce truth "understood as a system of ordered procedures for the production, regulation, distribution, circulation and operation of statements" (Foucault, *Power/Knowledge* 113).

To illustrate both the structural similarity and the pedagogical difference between Gallop's and Mamet's examples, on the one hand, and other sexual harassment narratives, on the other, I will add a third academic case to the examples discussed thus far, that of J. Donald Silva, a professor at the University of New Hampshire. According to the version presented by Richard Bernstein in the *New York Review of Books* on 13 January 1994, Silva was charged by eight women with sexual harassment for using sexually explicit analogies in class and for using sexual innuendos with women students outside of class. Although no physical contact, personal invitations, or threats against the students were involved, an internal inquiry found Silva guilty of creating a hostile academic environment and thereby violating the university's harassment policy. As in John's case, sexual harassment can occur with "mere words," as Bernstein puts it (13)—as if words had no material effects—and the verdict turns, as in Gallop's case, on what constitutes a hostile environment.

In each of these scenarios, the accused is commonly a more fully developed character than the accuser. Information about the family, career, and, where appropriate, the philosophy of the accused serves to bolster his or her credibility and contributes to the incredulity or the irony of the situation— that *this* particular person would be accused of such an act. For example, Bernstein begins his narrative of Silva's case with an exposition much like Mazza's: "J. Donald Silva, a tenured professor of English who has taught at

UNH for thirty years and, as it happens, is also the pastor of the Congregationalist Church on Great Island. . . . Silva is fifty-eight years old and the grandfather of four" (11). "As it happens" implies that this information is anything but incidental to the case. Likewise, we know that John and his wife are purchasing a home and that they have a young son in private school, and we learn about Gallop's family life through the *Lingua Franca* article (she watches "Star Trek" with her son, for example). In each case the personal information contributes to the irony that these particular professors are charged with this particular offense. In Silva's case, as in Clarence Thomas's, the irony rests on the character of the accused as a family man and a man of God. In Gallop's and John's cases, the irony depends less on their characters than on their pedagogical theories and their flamboyant teaching style, for both Gallop and John seek to expose as fraudulent the very institutional authority they are accused of using illegitimately. The aspects of their teaching that they thought were the most subversive of authority are the very aspects that open them to charges of sexual harassment. It is the implication of their theory and pedagogy, not just their persons, in charges of sexual harassment that makes Gallop's and John's cases the stuff of high drama, or melodrama, in contrast with Silva's offense, a point I will return to in the next section.

Correlatively, little or no personal information is provided about the accuser. We know less about Dana Beckelman and Carol than we do about Gallop and John, and we know nothing about Silva's accusers other than their names. In a court of law, such silence could be construed as an effort to protect the privacy of the accusers, who are perceived to be in a less-powerful position than the accused. Yet, as we saw in the Thomas hearings and in Mazza's story, it is the accused whose claims to privacy are respected more so than the alleged victim's. In contrast, going public with charges seems to imply, on the one hand, that the accuser has relinquished any right to privacy (as in Hill's case, where her own sexual desires were made the subject of speculation in the hearing room) and, on the other hand, that the sexual is the only aspect of the accuser's personal past that is at all relevant. Other than the fact that she is a talented writer, about all we know of Dana Beckelman, for example, is that she is a muscular lesbian from Texas.

The lack of information about the accuser makes it all the easier to typecast this character as an overzealous, paranoid ideologue with an agenda. This explains the ludicrous portrayal of the politically conservative Anita Hill as the purveyor of radical white feminism as well as the sudden and unconvincing change in Carol's character between acts 1 and 2 of *Oleanna*. In each of the cases considered here, the alleged victim is presented as unduly obsessed with the status of the accused, with her or his professional status, class status, income, family life, and, in some cases, fame. (Yet, as noted above, narratives of sexual harassment themselves seem to be obsessed with the accused in just these ways, given the nature of the exposition.) Many reviewers of Mamet's play point to Carol's resentment toward John for his status, security, and authority, leading more than one commentator to see the play as not really about sexual harassment but about envy and student revenge (see, e.g., Lahr and Morley). Yet John's own anger and resentment over the exploitative nature of pedagogical relations goes largely unexamined, not only by John but by most reviewers as well. Similarly, Hill was said to harbor resentment against Thomas, if not for his professional success, then for his marriage to a white woman.

A comment by Joseph Litvak, a professor of gay studies and a participant at Gallop's spring 1993 conference "Pedagogy: The Question of the Personal," makes this point explicit.[25] Responding to students who protested the conference by picketing and leafleting, Litvak argues: "'I think a lot of the aggression against Jane that seemed to be about sex was really about professional resentment. The leaflets played heavily on Jane's status as a distinguished professor, as though that were itself culpable. Her salary was mentioned also. It seemed like a lot of displaced status envy getting played out, like what was really behind it was the unhappiness of graduate students, their feelings of powerlessness, of abjectness'" (qtd. in Talbot 39). Of course, to the extent that sexual harassment is not about sex per se but about the abuse of power, the status of the accused *is* precisely the issue. Moreover, to see the accuser as unhappy, envious, and resentful, as Litvak does, fits the narrative of sexual harassment to a T. Explaining away the "real" (legal) charge of *sexual* harassment by focusing on the "real" (fundamental) issue of students' feelings of abjectness, such remarks tell us less about the state of mind of the individuals involved than about the conventional structure of sexual harassment narratives that construct the accuser as the abject. The relative lack of information about the accuser could suggest that her subjectivity is not only unrepresented or underrepresented but *unrepresentable*. In other words, it may be that charges of sexual harassment stem from the student's feelings of abjection, but it is also true that sexual harassment scenarios may produce the student subject as abject. The accuser, in Butler's words, "is constituted through the force of . . . abjection" (*Bodies* 3).[26] The problem with Litvak's defense of Gallop, and with sexual harassment narratives in general, is that they get the story all wrong by suggesting that the accuser's feelings of abjection are the student's problem to worry about rather than seeing that the accuser is abjected by the narrative itself.

Nonetheless, the feelings of the accuser become not just the focus of sexual harassment narratives but, as MacKinnon would have it, the "material reality" of sexual harassment (qtd. in Bhabha 244). The humiliation suffered by the accuser is an essential ingredient of sexual harassment scenarios. Under probing by Senator Joseph Biden, Anita Hill testified that she was humiliated and made extremely uncomfortable by Clarence Thomas's sexual banter. Silva's accusers said they felt embarrassed and "degraded" by his analogies, his vocabulary, and his insinuations in class (R. Bernstein 11). Carol claims she felt demeaned and humiliated by John's language and behavior. Sexual banter, however, is not the only, or even the primary, cause of such feelings. "There are so many ways to humiliate someone. Make someone so low they leave a snail-trail," says Mazza's character Michelle Rae. "Someone tells a story—a personal story, something that mattered—you don't listen, you aren't moved" (201). *Oleanna* dramatizes Michelle's point. At the end of act 1, John tries to comfort Carol, who is becoming increasingly agitated over her failure to understand anything he is saying. Acting on the belief that there is some personal reason for her failure to understand, some anger, embarrassment, or transference that is getting in the way, John urges Carol to confess.

Carol: I . . .
John: What? (Pause) What? *Tell* me.
Carol: I can't tell you.
John: No, you must.
Carol: I can't.
John: No. Tell me. (Pause)
Carol: I'm Bad. (26)

After hesitating further, Carol finally begins: "I always . . . all my life . . . I have never told anyone this . . . " and John coaxes, "Yes. Go on." Just then the phone rings. John hesitates, then answers and becomes so absorbed in the phone conversation that by the time he hangs up, he has forgotten entirely Carol's painful efforts at self-disclosure.

Gallop's case presents a similar example. Charges against her stemmed from a passing remark she made at a graduate student conference. Her statement that graduate students were her sexual preference "was taken as an instance of sexual harassment," Gallop writes, "because it was thought to indicate that I treated graduate students as objects, that I didn't respect them, that I didn't care about their minds and was only interested in their bodies" (*Feminist Accused* 88). Ignoring someone who craves one's attention, pretending to a sexual interest that one does not have—these are the humiliating, demeaning acts that, according to Michelle Rae, constitute sexual harassment. Humiliation can be experienced as a form of annihilation. "The Other exercises a constitutive power when he points you out," writes Alain Finkielkraut, "and an annihilating power when . . . he *passes* without giving you the benefit of the smallest glance" (171). Michelle feels a victim of this annihilating power: "As soon as you feel like *some*one, you're no one."

The prurient interest in the alleged victim's humiliation, a staple of sexual harassment narratives, creates the paradoxical situation in which the accuser's feelings are at once highly relevant and merely incidental to the key issue: What harm was done? Charging sexual harassment is not, as Carol says and as the Mazza lesson showed, simply a matter of validating the accuser's feelings, her sensitivity or jealousy or insecurity. It is a matter of giving them "a discursive, institutional reality" (Bhabha 244) so that one cannot be so easily annihilated. Mazza's story, Mamet's play, and commentaries on the Thomas hearings all suggest that sexual harassment is not about uncovering and acknowledging women's or students' personal feelings of resentment; rather, it is about the failure—indeed, the inability—to acknowledge the legitimacy of their claims within the dominant legal and narrative conventions that structure sexual harassment cases. In this sense, Carol speaks the truth when she tells John, "What I 'feel' is irrelevant" (31). It is this understanding of sexual harassment that makes Gallop's and John's theory and pedagogy so highly relevant to their cases, for each seeks to legitimize the claims of those who have been excluded by the dominant discourse of the academy.

On the level of plot, sexual harassment narratives rely on comparisons of different versions of the same events, the "he said/she said" structure of the date rape scenario. This narrative convention takes the form of "the accuser says X took place, the accused remembers it as Y." One of Silva's accusers claims that Silva said to her, when he saw her in the library on her hands and knees pulling out a floor-level drawer from the card catalog, "You look like you've had a lot of experience on your knees." Silva remembers his words as, "You look like you've had a lot of experience doing that" (R. Bernstein 11). "Beckelman says Gallop told her she had 'beautiful deltoids,'" Talbot writes. "[Gallop] says she kidded Beckelman about how she showed off her deltoids when she talked" (31). These "what we way/what they hear" scenarios are played out in act 2 of *Oleanna,* where John reads aloud the charges against him based in part on what he has said and done in act 1, for in this case (and this is what makes Mamet's play unique among sexual harassment scenarios) we have witnessed those prior events. That we are privy to this information, that we *know* what John has and has not done, is what makes the portrayal of Carol so disturbing and controversial. Our knowledge makes it seem that Mamet has stacked the deck against Carol, leading some members of the audience to bristle at Mamet's antifeminist characterization of Carol and others to cheer when John hits Carol at the end. We have heard John recount a tasteless anecdote, as Silva did; we have seen him touch his student, as Gallop did; we have heard him tell Carol he likes her—but we also see her misconstrual of his intentions. Yes, reviewers agree, John is sexist, racist, elitist, pedantic, and paternalistic, but he is no lecher. It was not his private fantasies that he was indulging by his behavior toward this student but his educational theories. A similar defense has been offered for Gallop. Her actions may have been inappropriate, reckless, even tasteless and offensive, but what *real* harm did they do? Talbot writes in Gallop's defense, "the kiss aside—it didn't sound like harassment" (25), though how, one wonders, could the kiss be put aside? The question of "real harm" is *the* question in sexual harassment cases (see, e.g., R. Bernstein 11, Paglia ["Strange Case"], and Mamet 30).

The fact that we do know what took place between Carol and John actually works against the "he said/she said" structure of miscommunication or false accusation, for the key question becomes not whether harm was done but how harm is defined, by whom, and at whose expense. This is the issue Carol articulates, the issue we miss if we dismiss Carol for wilfully misconstruing John's offensive but inculpable behavior. When John protests that his gesture of touching her shoulder "was devoid of sexual content," we can believe him while still *believing in* the truth of what she says in response: "I say it was not. I SAY IT WAS NOT. Don't you begin to *see* . . . ? Don't you begin to understand? IT'S NOT FOR YOU TO SAY" (43). Carol shifts the terms of the exchange from truth to power, from what we can know to what we can say and do, from personal intentions to performative effects. Gallop says of her statement at the graduate student conference, "The irony is that, whereas students heard my statement as demeaning, I had seldom felt so much respect for students. And I naively thought that in *this* context [a conference on gay/lesbian studies] a 'sexual preference' statement could be heard as an expression of admiration and esteem" (*Feminist Accused* 88). Dana Beckelman might well respond: "It's not for you to say."

The above exchange between Carol and John leads the reviewer Jeanne Silverthorne to label Carol a "deconstructionist," explicitly linking political correctness to the postmodern theory par excellence. "The gamelike nature of deconstruction," Silverthorne writes, "with its separation of 'meaning' from 'truth' or 'reality,' segues into Mamet's argument about the bankruptcy of language" (11). The familiar representation of deconstruction in the academy as the *destruction* of meaning, the *denial* of the real, and the *bankruptcy* of language, makes Carol's charges seem "tainted and venal." That is,

in Silverthorne's reading it is not Carol's feminist agenda or her "P.C." demand for "diversity" but her deconstructive critique that is the issue, as theory is made to be the issue in Gallop's case as well, though as much by Gallop as by others. Silverthorne writes that as the New Critical ironist, John "has
no comeback to Carol's quintessentially deconstructivist accusation: 'You
think . . . that these things . . . mean what you *said* they meant.'" (qtd. in
SIlverthorne 11). Never mind that Silverthorne gets New Criticism wrong, as
she does deconstruction (if John is the New Critical ironist, he is surely no
stranger to the notion that words do not mean what they apparently say).
For Silverthorne, as for many others, theory is seen to deny the obviousness
of intention, the transparency of meaning—which is to miss what is really
at issue here. The point of Carol's criticism is not to doubt whether meaning can be found but to show that nothing—not even discourses of rationality, truth, and freedom of speech—is free of power relations. When Carol accuses John of believing in nothing because he demystifies the educational
system that supports him, John counters by saying, "I believe in freedom of
thought." Carol retorts: "You believe *not* in 'freedom of thought,' but in an
elitist, in, in a protected hierarchy which rewards you" (Mamet 41). If Carol
is the deconstructor, it is because she comes to question how the authority
of meaning and the legitimacy of truth get established in the first place.

Insofar as Carol is blamed by many reviewers for politicizing knowledge
and truth, hers is the negative, nihilistic spin on this postmodern insight. This
parodic version of deconstruction, not the theory itself, relieves the subject
of responsibility every bit as much as a naïve belief in objective truth. The
shift in the framework by which we evaluate discursive practices brought
about by deconstruction is presented in sexual harassment narratives as a
conflict between truth and power, where truth seems to reside on the side of
the professor, power on the side of the student. Carol, like Hill's and Silva's
accusers, is seen to be used by feminist ideologues with an agenda. In Silva's
case, it is powerful women, like the director of affirmative action, the director of women's studies, and the head of the animal science program, and what
Bernstein refers to as "a campus advocacy group" called Sexual Harassment
and Rape Prevention Program (SHARPP), which, according to Bernstein,
incites the students to press charges (11). In Carol's case, it is the anonymous
group to which she refers in her second and final meetings with John: "Because I speak, yes, not for myself. But for the group; for those who suffer what
I suffer" (40). The power that creates Carol's position is anonymous and
hidden, *but this is no less true of John or Gallop or Thomas.* Indeed, this is
precisely what Carol's charges against John bring out (as do Beckelman's
against Gallop): namely, the extent to which the professor's position, for all

its radicalness, is produced by the powerful, elitist system that protects and rewards him or her. The fear that special interests groups are conniving against the individual professor fails to acknowledge the way the university—with its system of rankings, rewards, and recognition—functions as a special interest group as well. Its normative authority, as Barbara Herrnstein Smith writes, depends not only on "'standard-izing,' making a standard out of—not simply the preferences of the members of the group but more significantly and also more powerfully because more invisibly, *the particular contingencies that govern their preferences*" (41). John takes his own educational experiences as normative, assuming on the basis of that belief that he and Carol are alike, and he thereby ignores not only their differences (in gender, class, etc.) but also his own interpellation in systems of power, privilege, and status. It is on the basis of the "truth" of his experience that he dismisses Carol as politically correct and inhumane, inviting the audience to do the same. Gallop similarly elides her current position in the institution when she claims her own previous sexual experiences with professors (when she was in graduate school) were common among feminists of her generation and bolstered rather than threatened her sense of herself as a student. These experiences function for her as a norm by which we can judge not only sexual harassment policies that include prohibitions on consensual amorous relations but also those feminists who defend such policies.[27] Insofar as sexual harassment has to do with the failure to distinguish between sexual acts that occur in private and those that occur in a working relationship, where the power differential is potentially exploitative (Crenshaw 425), Gallop's defense—however accurate her argument that emphasizing the sexual in sexual harassment policies can obscure the real culprit, namely, sexist behavior—downplays the role institutional power plays in personal relationships.

The "truth" of Carol's charges against John lies not in her reduction of everything to power, making a mockery out of the truth, but rather in the way she opens up certain terms, assumptions, gestures, and preferences to "a redeployment that previously has not been authorized" (Butler, "Contingent" 15). Taking John's theories seriously, she questions the normative framework by which we evaluate the legitimacy of social practices, the very framework that puts "truth" on one side and "power" on the other. The point of Carol's critique, insofar as it is deconstructive, is not to believe in nothing but to believe in something that has not previously been acknowledged and legitimated. Such belief, however, takes on a sinister aspect in Mamet's play, and in the film based on it, in contrast to the utopianism of Cornell's or even Butler's writings. Public skepticism about theory is fueled, even justified, by staging theoretical disputes as sexual contests.

Yet Carol does not represent any one political or theoretical position any more than she represents any one class or sexuality. The characters are not allegorical figures for competing theoretical positions, as Silverthorne and others would have it. After all, the accusations made against deconstruction are leveled by Carol against John: "YOU BELIEVE IN NOTHING. YOU BELIEVE IN NOTHING AT ALL" (41). Carol voices the common resistance to deconstructive critique in the academy when she argues that John's exposure of the educational system as a myth mocks and destroys, as Carol puts it, the aspirations of his students and turns educational rituals rooted in social and material differences into a joke (33).[28]

Rather than accept Carol as a spokesperson for deconstruction to save feminism (as Silverthorne does), or deny that Carol has learned the lessons of deconstructive critique to save that theory—that is, rather than trying to decide who legitimately represents what theoretical positions in this play—I argue that a deconstructive reading enables us to respond to such contradictory positionings in the play. For me, Mamet's play, like Mazza's story, shows the need for and relevance of deconstructive inquiry. If truth and justice are not taken as given or normative foundations but are themselves produced within and by discursive relations of power, as Foucault has argued and as the Mazza lesson suggested, then the point is not to free John's truth from Carol's contestation of it on political grounds but to open up to questioning the framework of normativity by which claims of legitimacy are evaluated—that is, to detach, in Foucault's words, "the power of truth from the forms of hegemony, social, economic and cultural, within which it operates at the present time" (*Power/Knowledge* 133). This is what Carol has learned from John's critique of the education system: to take his pedagogy personally.

As Feingold's review suggests, Mamet's play illustrates starkly, if reductively, what sexual harassment in the academy today has come to signify—the fact that, as Herrnstein Smith remarks, certain institutionalized truths, rights, and preferences are threatened by those with a different set of truths, rights, and preferences (40). Here we can see why staging these complex theoretical and political debates in terms of sexual harassment is so compelling: the fear of acknowledging the claims of others and understanding what is at stake in making those claims can be defended against by structuring the issue as a matter of taking sides, drawing limits, defending a position, especially defending freedom of thought against the politicization of knowledge.

Questioning the limits of sexual harassment is what each of the narratives examined here is about. All three academic cases have been read as warnings against the terrible consequences of expansive definitions of sexual harassment. Bernstein quotes one of Silva's colleagues who opposes sexual harassment policies that limit freedom of speech. He cites the following example of the kind of statement that would be censored under more elastic sexual harassment policies: "'In the classroom, a faculty member repeatedly comments that women are not cut out to be scientists, because they do not have the motivation to succeed as men do.'" The colleague continues, "'That would be an opinion, . . . a very unpopular one, an incorrect one, but one whose expression should be protected by academic freedom'" (14). Gallop, who also opposes expansive definitions of sexual harassment because they would limit free intellectual inquiry, cites precisely this kind of speech— "the engineering professor who regularly tells his classes that women can't be engineers"—as a clear example of sexual harassment ("Feminism and Harassment Policy" 20). For Gallop, such behavior is not to be protected by freedom of speech but to be condemned as sexual harassment since it creates "a hostile environment" that "obstructs women from doing work" (16). That these two professors can both oppose broad interpretations of sexual harassment and yet want to draw the limits differently suggests that policing the line might not be the best approach.

Gallop argues against the slide from sexist into sexual in efforts to use harassment policies to restrict "consensual amorous relations" between teacher and student. Such an expansive definition, she argues, allows a conservative morality that deems sex bad, especially for women, to overshadow a feminist agenda ("Feminism and Harassment Policy" 20; Talbot 39). In his defense of Clarence Thomas, Orlando Patterson deploys a related argument by ridiculing Anita Hill for her conflation of sex and sexism. According to Patterson, it was Hill's puritan morality and her white feminist brainwashing that led her to turn a black male courting ritual into an actionable offense. Clearly sexual, Thomas's behavior was hardly sexist, Patterson insists, or sexist only insofar as black male heterosexuality is viewed as sexist by those outside the culture—as well as some within—who do not understand the sexual game played by black men and women (D15). If the slippage in meaning from sexual to sexist disturbs Gallop and Patterson, it is the slide from sexism into sex that outrages many viewers of Mamet's play, as it does Silva's colleague, and leads Carol to be dismissed as a politically correct ideologue, "some Maoist enforcer" (Lahr 124). John may have used a tasteless analogy, he may have made sexist remarks, the argument runs, but he did not engage in *sexual* harassment.

Given these competing views, one might well agree with Gallop that policing the line—whether between the sexual and the sexist, the erotic and the personal, the personal and the professional—is not only impossible but undesirable. To draw the line is to risk "sanitizing all the life out of pedagogy," writes Talbot. "There is something lost when we get too punctilious about defining teaching as a business relationship. And what's lost isn't trivial: It's the glimpses of the professor as a whole person" (40). I agree. But it does not follow that a more narrow definition of sexual harassment in the interests of freedom of speech, intellectual freedom, or cultural diversity will necessarily benefit professors and students. Such a definition always runs the risk of overlooking the way in which sexual discourse in the workplace "reflects a differential power relationship between men and women"(Crenshaw 429)—and teacher and student. Too narrow a definition of sexual harassment is the problem Michelle Rae confronts: "Isn't this sexual harassment *yet?*" On the one hand, women and students need a legal definition of sexual harassment to have their experiences recognized, their point of view legitimated, their feelings given material reality. On the other hand, the very effort to fix the limits of such a definition, whether broadly or narrowly, can end up causing suffering and damage to women and students, once again obstructing the work they can do.

The anxiety that comes from understanding that the grounds for arbitrating these disputes over definitions, policies, and standards are themselves being challenged can be defended against by claiming that what the others want is to destroy all grounds so that we are faced with moral anarchy. The melodrama of sexual harassment makes these theoretical debates seem tawdry and turns the anxiety of realizing that our secure positions are vulnerable on a number of fronts into the righteous indignation that requires us to take a stand against the barbarians at the gate. In the last act of *Oleanna,* after his dismissal from the university, John accuses Carol of having no feelings. Carol responds: "That's my point. You see? . . . I don't take your side, you question if I'm Human" (40). This exchange, which recalls the court case cited by Judith Resnik (see note 14), where the abused woman failed to make her story convincing because she did not display the proper emotions, plays out the terms in which critiques of normative standards are resisted. Without normative values, the argument goes, we are right back in the jungle. The worry that deconstructive theories have opened up a void that politics rushes to fill leads to calls for returning to traditional standards, methodology courses, and "free" (i.e., nonpoliticized) intellectual inquiry as the responsible path, the only way to diffuse the contestations opened up by replacing standards with "arbitrary arbiters" (see, e.g., Dasenbrock, Patai, and Hartman).

The point of deconstructive theory, however, is not to destroy all grounding claims but to ask what contingencies those grounding claims legitimate and what contingencies they prohibit or exclude. From this perspective, it is precisely the commitment to theory that is responsible by questioning the ethical and political implications of *non*arbitrary arbiters, normative criteria, and institutionalized preferences. We engage in theoretical debate not because we can now only agree to disagree (because, presumably, theory has done away with nonarbitrary arbiters, with agreed-upon principles for adjudicating disputes) but because we must not *only* agree to disagree (which is what a debate over whose evidence is worthy, whose testimony is true, whose point of view is reliable can lead to). The theoretical insight that truth can be grounded in nothing outside of some narrative of truth claims, that any ground for evidence can always be deconstructed to expose it as an arbitrary arbiter, need not lead to an infinite regress of critique and countercritique, but can lead to the transformation of our ways of describing, evaluating, valuing, and narrating our lives.

Yet, the very theory that potentially offers a way of negotiating the renegotiation of the social contract currently taking place in the academy as in the public sphere is rendered ineffectual and dangerous by these sexual harassment narratives. While in the Mazza lesson students came to understand sexual harassment cases in terms of the power of narrative discourse to produce certain forms of knowledge and truth, in the academic cases discussed here complex theoretical and institutional debates over the "truth" of that "postmodern" insight are reductively characterized in terms of the "he said/she said" (even in Gallop's case) dynamic of miscommunication and position taking that structures narratives of sexual harassment. (As Silverthorne puts it, "The shock of David Mamet's *Oleanna* . . . is the shock of the Hill/Thomas hearings: it astounds by revealing how many otherwise 'reasonable' people still don't get it" [10].) Indeed, one could argue that more recent public preoccupation with sexual harassment (Senator Packwood, President Clinton, Tailhook, and Captain Greene, to cite a few cases) says less about the success of feminists in naming women's oppression than about the failure of feminists and postmodernists alike to change the structure of debate. Challenges posed by critiques of normative constructions of truth and justice, rights and responsibilities, identities and identity politics can potentially change the terms of debate, yet that potential is being contained in sexual harassment narratives that figure such challenges in terms of a choice over whose point of view will prevail.

It is a mistake, I suggest, to see either Mamet's play or Gallop's case as *about* political correctness or theory in the academy. Instead, we would do better to approach each as really about sexual harassment insofar as that narrative provides the structure that makes these complex theoretical and cultural debates easily consumable. From this perspective, *Oleanna* is still disturbing, but less for the position Mamet takes in these debates (e.g., attacking feminism in the character of Carol, mocking academic jargon in the character of John) than for the extent to which his drama is symptomatic of the contestations that mark the site of theory in the academy. If *Oleanna* reveals the consequences of theory, it is not because either character represents a particular theoretical agenda (liberal, feminist, deconstructive). On the contrary, to the extent that we allow the play to seduce us into taking sides and into assigning each protagonist a position, as if each stands for some one thing, we fail to heed the consequences of the very theory that the play ostensibly indicts. Rather, *Oleanna* plays out the consequences of theory insofar as theory is understood as a form of harassment.

Taking Pedagogy Personally

> "I don't know how to do it, other than to be *personal.*"
> —John, *Oleanna*

If Silva's case has failed to capture the public imagination the way Gallop's case and Mamet's play have, it is because Silva's offense is not perceived to stem from his theoretical and pedagogical commitments. Both Mamet's play and Talbot's narrative of Gallop's case present the professors as, to paraphrase John, most vulnerable precisely where they would seem to be most unassailable: in taking pedagogy personally (29).[29] Talbot writes, "What bothered me was realizing that the trouble Gallop had gotten into was, in a way, inevitable. . . . it was the very aspects of her teaching she considers the most feminist, the most subversive, as she would put it, of 'phallic authority'—her emphasis on intimacy, on self-reflexivity, on rigorously working through the bonds of love that ensnare both teacher and student—that left her vulnerable to these charges" (26). Her teaching style is, Talbot continues, "by its nature—and hers—personal" in that Gallop teaches students to read symptomatically.[30] Similarly, John insists on working through the feelings of anger, resentment, humiliation, and unworthiness produced by those conventions of the educational system that seem to be most impersonal: lectures, tests, papers. Far from being neutral, objective measures of one's ability, such conventions, John argues, produce the student-subject presumed *not* to know. "Listen to this," John tells Carol. "If the young child is told he cannot understand. Then he takes it as a *description* of himself. What am I? I am *that which can not understand*" (15).

In their effort to expose the institution as, in Gallop's words, "a site of cultural reproduction, and an agency of cultural regulation" (*Around 1981* 3) and to work through the disavowed feelings and identifications endemic to the teacher-student relation, both professors get personal with their students: they confess to feelings of inadequacy and resentment (Mamet 15) and to private fantasies (Talbot 36); they divulge their personal relationships (emotional for John, sexual for Gallop) with their former teachers; and they drop the professorial pose, the "Artificial Strictures between 'Teacher' and 'Student'" (Mamet 17), and adopt the persona of the radical. Both John and Gallop masquerade as the "bad" teachers, the ones who question and transgress all the rules. In doing so, both greatly discompose their students, who want to know where they stand. When John tries to get Carol to see that the tests established by the academy to determine one's worth are "garbage," Carol disappoints him by responding, "I want to know about my grade" (19). Beckelman wants to know where she stands with Gallop, not only whether her performance on papers makes the grade but also where she stands in Gallop's affections: "'Are you coming on to me or just flirting?'" (qtd. in Talbot 32). For Carol, and for at least some of Gallop's students as well, the self-reflexive, rule-breaking, theory-wielding professor is all the more powerful and threatening.

If their actions produce discomfort in their students, this is precisely the point, both professors insist, of their pedagogy, the way they induce students to learn by breaking through the defenses, resistances, and transferences that structure the pedagogical relation. When Carol challenges John's argument that the desire for education is a prejudice, he responds: "Good. Good. *Good.* That's right! Speak up!" (21). He has made his student uncomfortable, and now real learning can begin; the anger Carol feels reveals the truth of what he says. Talbot quotes one of Gallop's students as saying, "'Jane makes you feel like your own position needs to be investigated. There has to be engagement, affect, discomfort sometimes. If those things aren't there, there's no learning'" (27). Gallop insists that when she kissed Beckelman in public, she was teaching a lesson: "'I wanted the other graduate students at the bar to think about the erotics of the relation between teacher and student'" (qtd. in Talbot 35). Since the legitimacy of Beckelman's charge of sexual harassment rests in part on the disputed meaning of this kiss, Gallop's explanation works to undermine Beckelman's case by putting her student in Carol's position, the one who just doesn't get it.

Defending the kiss on pedagogical grounds (a defense Talbot concedes few people find convincing), Gallop attributes the brouhaha over her behavior to her pedagogical style. "'People are beginning to interpret "hostile environment" as anything that makes students uncomfortable. Well, I have a problem, because I feel that part of my *job* as a teacher is to make students feel uncomfortable, to ask them questions they don't necessarily want to face'" (qtd. in Talbot 35). John shares Gallop's sense of pedagogical responsibility. He tells Carol, "that's my *job,* don't you know." "What is?" she asks. "To provoke you" (20). In both cases, their commitment to pedagogy, along with their radical critique and defiance of academic protocol, puts them at risk in an atmosphere increasingly charged with accusations of identity politics and in an institution that can no longer be considered a separate sphere or safe haven. It is their risk-taking pedagogy and their professorial personae that both of the accused see as the real issue rather than their personal behavior. For them, their kind of pedagogy is at risk.

Efforts to critique privileged positions that historically have constituted one's cultural identity and institutional authority put the professor in the position of passing, opening him or her to charges of fraudulence. The charges brought by both students are efforts to see through the pedagogical performance, to expose the professorial persona for the power ploy it is. When she kissed Beckelman, Gallop says, she was engaging in a performance, one that should not, it seems, have been taken personally. But Beckelman did take Gallop's pedagogy personally: "Are you coming on to me or just flirting?" Gallop responds that she is flirting "'theoretically, as a way of seducing students to learn'" (qtd. in Talbot 32). The performance leads Beckelman to accuse Gallop of "'playing with a kind of fashionable lesbianism, pretending to feel attraction to women when it was in fact a pose'" (qtd. in Talbot 36). Having read in the official complaint against him references to his "self-aggrandizing and theatrical *diversions,*" John admits to Carol that he loves "the aspect of *performance*" in teaching. "I think I must confess to that" (Mamet 28). As Carol puts it, John feels himself "empowered . . . To *strut.* To *posture.* To 'perform'" (33), that is, to use his position and his persona to secure his right "to do and say what [he] want[s] . . .—Testing, Questioning, *Flirting*" (40; my emphasis). (The sequence of actions makes the sexual one aspect of the professional.) Although in act 1 Carol desperately tries to "pass" in her paper by throwing around the empty rhetoric she thinks passes as theoretical sophistication in the academy, by act 2 she has come to expose John for passing: "If you possess one ounce of that inner honesty you describe in your book, you can look in yourself and see those things that I see. And you can find revulsion equal to my own" (33). Where the professor was opaque in act 1, now Carol easily sees through his pose, sees him for what he is (a fraud) rather than judging him by what he professes, in his teaching, and what he professes to be.

It is this disjunction between what one professes and how one is positioned that I have been exploring in terms of the dynamics of passing (see, e.g., chapter 1). When deconstructive critique is seen simply as self-reflexivity about one's positionality and one's complicity in hegemonic discursive practices, when its notion of performance is taken as theatrical, then what follows is the kind of guilt-ridden practice that I have examined in various instances of passing throughout this book, the kind of guilty response John makes to Carol's accusations that forecloses on any action, any change. Both Gallop and John are accused of selling out to the academy, valuing respectability and security, strutting their power, even to the betrayal of their own theories. But John responds guiltily, admitting to being elitist, pedantic, and paternalistic but not to doing any "real" harm. Carol has nothing but contempt for what she dismisses as his "silly weak guilt," his confession to desiring the security and status offered by the very system he exposes as a sham. John's only defense is to insist on being taken as a human being, an individual not a persona: "This is my *life*. I'm not a *bogeyman*. I don't 'stand' for something" (32). John throws off the professorial mask and pleads to be taken personally.

Gallop responds differently. She would accept the personal as a persona, an im-personation, which she defines as the effect of "the process of performing the personal for a public" (*Pedagogy* 9). She articulates this position most explicitly in her introduction to the collection of essays from her conference on pedagogy (see chapter 2). Gallop says that in talking about pedagogy as performance and the personal as an im-personation, she is not talking about the role-playing self. "It is this liberal understanding of pedagogical performance, that these are *just roles* we are playing, that blocks understanding of the situation" (*Pedagogy* 14–15). It is also this liberal understanding that John voices when he proposes he and Carol drop the "Artificial Strictures of 'Teacher' and 'Student',," as if these were roles they could "'individually' forego" (Susan Miller qtd. in Gallop, *Pedagogy* 14).

This kind of opposition between the "role" and the "real," the authentic and the inauthentic, and the private person and the public persona informs the common understanding of passing as fraudulence. Gallop challenges that understanding by admitting to passing. She concedes that "pedagogically I am an impersonator" because in taking pedagogy personally, her identity as a teacher is at once sincere (she really does believe in what she is doing) and a sham (the personal is always a persona); however, she argues that performative theory makes "this double realization less painfully contradictory" (*Pedagogy* 16–17)—at least, for her. A performative notion of identity such as she and others at the conference advocate means that there can be no meaningful opposition between the personal as authentic and the performative as inauthentic (7). If the personal relation between teacher and student is as contrived, conventional, historical, and linguistically and discursively mediated as is the professional relation it supposedly stands in opposition to, then to conceive pedagogy as the site where the personal is lived as im-personation, as Gallop does, is to guard against "a naive belief in bringing the authentic self into the institution," a belief that informs common conceptions of identity politics, studies programs, and process-oriented writing pedagogy. In the effort to "move beyond" this naïve belief, she uses im-personation to figure the "knot of pretense and reality" (16). Gallop's defense of herself in the *Lingua Franca* interview and in the *Academe* article can be read as an effort to salvage her reputation as a "bad girl" by reclaiming the mask *as* a mask.

But—and this is a point I have been making throughout—however much an adequate understanding of postmodern theory is necessary to appreciate Gallop's pedagogy, it is never sufficient as a defense of its performative effects. Beckelman, we can assume, understood the theory but felt its painful contradictions nonetheless. Even when we accept a performative notion of the subject, even when we come to understand performance as an insistent impersonation that passes as the real (Butler, *Gender Trouble* x), even when we reject notions of a volitional subject before the act and of the personal as authentic, the impulse to save the personal, and thus our "selves," is overwhelming. Gallop's friends, who defend her persona, offer support that inadvertently plays into Beckelman's accusations that Gallop is posing. What Gallop does in public, her friends say, "is precisely what she *wouldn't* do in private" (Talbot 35). Here the knot of pretense and reality is unraveled into a clear-cut distinction. The "stubborn tensions" between the personal and the positional are eased by ignoring the very "conflicts inhering in a collective situation" (Gallop, *Around 1981* 7). A similar unraveling occurs in Gallop's official written response to the students' charges that Beckelman once tried to show her a box of "sexual props" and that Gallop was "horrified" and told her that "her fantasies [were] and should remain a private thing between her and her lover" (32). Although sexual perversity and promiscuity are central to Gallop's "bad girl" persona, here Gallop seems to retreat to the moral high ground of sexual propriety to deflect any perversity onto the accuser. That this claim to privacy comes from a writer and teacher who has never shied away from publicly disclosing her own sexual fantasies, even to this particular student—a point never commented on by Talbot—raises the question of whether Gallop's defense or the alleged offense itself constitutes the real abuse of theory, which is what the case is supposedly about.[31] Talk of the performative always seems to raise this anxiety, the fear that one will be mistaken, that one will be seen to be "really" doing away with precisely what one *has,* intellectually, already done away with: namely, the self as present to itself. Personal disclosure may well be a way of cushioning the blow of finding your "self" undone by your own theory.

The very slippage in meaning at issue here, from one use of "performance" to the other, occurs over and over again in discussions of performativity and of pedagogy, not only because one's practice does not always live up to its precepts, but because we cannot help but take pedagogy, and ourselves, personally. It is this slippage that I have been exploring through the dynamics of passing. The deconstruction of the boundaries between the person and the persona, the private and the public, the ethical and the political, knowledge and power means not only that theoretical, cultural, and pedagogical debates are now taken personally but also that we cannot fall back on appeals to the personal, the intentional, to save us. We cannot draw absolute distinctions, but that does not mean we cannot draw any distinctions. This slippage, the dynamics that structures the teacher-student relation, marks an aporia, one that cannot be an impasse but must be worked through in terms of the kind of ethics that has come to be associated with postmodern theory.

The common response to accusations of fraudulence (the exposure of a gap between what one professes to be and what one really is) is to fall back on personal disclosure, the kind of writing that implies a self that is present to itself and that thereby refutes the very theory that has opened a gap between the "I" who writes and the "I" who is the subject of that writing. In other words, once you insist on a performative notion of the subject, you cannot fall back on self-identity to save yourself. Though critics of deconstruction might say that this is precisely the problem—that performativity works only in theory—I have argued throughout this book that, on the contrary, the loss of such a ground is what gives rise to the ethical imperative that Peter Baker describes: "The 'impossible' ethics of deconstruction demands that one continue to think about the issues involved in their full, abysslike complexity, a complexity that denies any firm ground upon which to maintain one's own lack of involvement in the very issues raised by the inquiry" (127). Ethical responsibility, according to Baker, Bauman, Caputo, Rajchman, Weeks, and others writing on postmodern ethics, lies in the effort to undertake that impossibility.

Coda

Two years after I wrote this chapter, Gallop published *Feminist Accused of Sexual Harassment,* a book about her case, thereby turning the accusations into an issue of scholarship. Reading it brought home to me the difficulty of assuming that ethical responsibility in practice. The writing in *Feminist Accused*, so different from Gallop's other writings, works against the theory and practice she is at pains to defend and illustrates the point I argued in chapter 2: namely, that to teach and write performatively is to risk that your audience won't get the point, yet to explain the performance is to elide the very difference you would have them get—and thus you are the one who doesn't get it. Gallop ends by saying she wrote the book to try to make herself understood, to explain the performative practice she is known for. The problem is that her explanation comes at the expense of the messiness she is typically willing to confront in her writing. Her book is an unconscious instance of *not* assuming the risks inherent in passing. What it ends up revealing, for me, is that the performative practice, once made explicit, no longer carries the same force. Indeed, it is no longer performative but constative.

Sexual harassment is about the "problem of definition" that Gallop so brilliantly analyzes in her essay by that title. In it she confronts the need for and the risks entailed in drawing boundaries around a concept or practice. Instead of choosing between being coherent but exclusive and vague but inclusive in defining feminist criticism (*Around 1981* 25), Gallop offers in this essay an alternative practice she terms (after Derrida) a "double discourse." Double discourse, or double practice, does not depend on the definitive distinction between two things but explores the contextual, historical, and rhetorical distinctions among things; it does not seek to define a practice or concept but to enact a way of proceeding. Herein lies a possible contribution of Gallop's writing and pedagogy to the issue of sexual harassment and its legal and ethical implications: namely, rethinking the ways in which we approach the task of definition and in which we read such narratives, thereby increasing our options for responding to the issues they raise. Rather than choosing between exclusive and inclusive definitions of sexual harassment, we can "think through the relation between the two positions" (*Around 1981* 26).

This kind of performative practice so crucial in working through these disputes is missing in *Feminist Accused*. With the exception of the closing pages (96–100), where she does a reading of an article about the case, Gallop eschews the kind of symptomatic textual analysis and language play that has made her such a powerful and provocative figure in the academy—at the very time when such a practice is most needed. Her book lacks the erotic charge of her earlier prose because in it she refuses to play with borders, to complicate, to deviate, and to implicate herself in the analysis. And that is where I locate its ethical failing—in the writing itself, in her choice of genre, in Lyotard's sense. As Peter Baker writes of Derrida's argument in *Of Grammatology*, all forms of violence, domination, and exploitation "need to be analysed as forms of 'writing'" (5). Eschewing that kind of analysis—the kind of deconstructive inquiry Gallop is known for—*Feminist Accused* fails to offer a way of understanding responsibility that is not grounded in the metaphysics of presence, normativity, intentionality, or intellectual freedom. Ironically, Gallop's defense of the erotic charge in pedagogical relations is de-sexualized by the writing itself. Her career, which has served as an example of passing at both the theoretical and pedagogical levels, is betrayed by her need to defend herself.

Writing against the misguided and ultimately futile attempts to de-sexualize teaching, Gallop says: "It is no more possible to really teach without at times eliciting powerful and troubling sensations than it is to write powerfully without producing some sort of sensation" (*Feminist Accused* 100). That is the point: a performative practice is risky, and I agree with Gallop that the risk should be run. Indeed, opening herself to the risk of misidentification, to the slippage between performativity and performance, is the ethical moment in her practice. But there are risks and there are risks. Where she slips up, for me, is in her effort to save herself from the slippage. In writing about the case as she does, Gallop ends up playing the game of sexual harassment, reinforcing its generic conventions. As with Mamet's John, the accuser's feelings, not the professor's behavior, become the key issue. Gallop attributes the charges to the students' feelings of abjection: when she criticized the student's work, Gallop explains, "the student felt let down, became outraged, and charged me with sexual harassment" (55). She defends her right to write about the case in the name of intellectual freedom, never questioning the power differential that gives her greater access to publication and that shores up the authority of her version. When her accusers sought to prohibit her from making this case "the subject of intellectual inquiry" (78), Gallop initially felt their motivation was to protect themselves from public exposure and only later came to see it as an effort to "police [her] thinking" (79). But that demand, it seems to me, had nothing to do with protecting their identities or censoring thought and everything to do with thwarting Gallop's power and reputation, which they perceived to depend on her exploitation of students. Gallop's conference on pedagogy may well have been seen by the students as an effort to put them in their place as objects of her intellectual work. Gallop occupies the *structural* position of the harasser by failing to legitimate the accusers' speech. In *Feminist Accused,* free intellectual inquiry becomes the ground to be defended at all costs, whereas in Gallop's other writings it becomes a terrain to be opened up to questioning and reconfiguration.

To the extent that Gallop seeks to exonerate herself, she falls into the same trap as Krupat, Homans, et al. (see chapters 1 and 5); her book is yet another example of the caveat syndrome. Gallop sanitizes her defense, reducing its complexity to the choice between narrow and expansive definitions of sexual harassment. The more relevant questions in her case than where or whether to draw a line between the personal and the professional are, What relations of power come into play when we take pedagogy personally? Whose interests are served when professors take on students in writing? In other words, Gallop elides the messiness of the case. Even the kiss comes up only toward the end. Granted, that structure works to decentralize the kiss as the key issue in this case, but it also keeps the defense offered earlier in the book in the realm of abstract theory and decontextualized practice. Gallop writes: "Seeing a relation between a student enamored of a teacher's work, a student who wanted to be like that teacher, and the teacher who responded deeply to the student's desire to work with her, who wanted profoundly to help her do what she desired, the university deemed such a connection, passionate and involving so many personal hopes and dreams, an amorous relation" (55–56). And it was amorous, Gallop admits. But then she goes on to explain why—theoretically, in terms of Freudian transference, eliding the kiss, of which the administration was aware.

I understand Gallop's *need* to write about the charges brought against her, that tremendous urge to save oneself from misunderstanding, to resist being exposed as a fraud. What I find troubling is her *reason* for writing about it. *Feminist Accused* strikes me as less a critique of sexual harassment policies (although it is that) or a defense of free intellectual inquiry (though it is that too) than a protestation of innocence. "I did nothing wrong" is its underlying refrain. In the face of criticism for our passing remarks, we turn to the personal writing to save us and expose ourselves all the more. Such a response fails to assume responsibility for our forms of passing. We can no more save ourselves from the effects of our passing remarks by getting personal, falling back on the personal defense, than we can guarantee the moral consequences of our actions.

Gallop complains: "The [sexual harassment] policies suggest there's no such thing as consensual amorous relations" (34). Well, in a sense, there isn't. That is, there is no *thing*, no relation there to be defined *outside* of institutional discourses and practices. That is a performative insight, one that perhaps it is hard to live by but, I would say, is crucial to the kind of social negotiations that sexual harassment has come to figure in the popular imagination. The question is not simply one of *intention* (Was the relation consensual?) but one of *relations* (What does consent mean within institutionalized relations of power?).

Gallop's case, like John's and unlike Silva's, reveals the dynamics of passing insofar as it shows that taking a certain theoretical position on the (student) subject is not the same as taking responsibility for the subject positions we assume and put into play in the classroom and in our writings. "A scholar's life is not the key to his or her work, nor the work the key to the life," writes Michael Bérubé (1067). That statement could be used in defense of Gallop if she didn't offer her work as a defense of her life. Theory and practice, intellectual inquiry and everyday life are never coterminous (though they are also not as discrete as critics of theory would have it). That's no reason to abandon the theory or the effort to put it into practice. On the contrary, the dynamics of responsibility means continuing to pursue that relation knowing that we will never finally get it right.

Notes

1. Homosexual marriage, adoptions by unmarried couples, teenage pregnancy, surrogate mothers, child pornography, genetic research, AIDS funding and treatment, the so-called abortion pill, cloning—"these and other topics," Weeks writes, "have become the focus of public agonizing and personal anguish, [and] the major theme of social policy debates" (4).

2. The "ethical turn" plays on the phrase "linguistic turn," a shorthand expression for structuralist and poststructuralist theories in which "language" displaces "man" as the organizing principle of the human sciences (P. Baker 1). Analyses of social formations take place in terms of signifying systems, not the rational, willing subject of Enlightenment discourses of knowledge.

3. On this shift from knowledge to values, see Harvey, Peter Baker, Davis and Schleifer, Caputo, and Jay ("Values and Deconstruction").

4. "Postmodern theory" has become a shorthand expression to designate, and more frequently to conflate, often for the purposes of dismissing, a range of contemporary theories that have converged to effect a profound change in notions of identity, subjectivity, representation, politics, and ethics. On postmodern theory (and specifically the relation between feminism and deconstruction), see Grosz, Poovey ("Feminism"), Flax, Alcoff ("Cultural Feminism"), Butler and Scott, Cornell (*Beyond Accommodation* and *Philosophy*), and Elam.

5. Cris Mazza teaches creative writing at the University of Illinois at Chicago. She is the author of four novels and three story collections. *Is It Sexual Harassment Yet?* (her second collection) was reissued in 1998.

6. In a *New York Times* interview, Phyllis Berry suggested that Anita Hill's accusations "'were a result of [her] disappointment and frustration that Mr. Thomas did not show any sexual interest in her'" (qtd. in "Ex-Colleagues" A21).

7. Terence's concluding statement, "I just want my life to get back to normal" (Mazza 221), is mimicked by Thomas in his concluding remark: "I want my life and my family's life back."

8. Taking point of view for granted, students often read the second sentence of the story as "straight" description, attributing the rhetorical flourishes to the author's style: "Wearing a starched ruffled shirt and black tails, he [Terence] embodied continental grace and elegance as he seated guests and, with a toreador's flourish, produced menus out of thin air" (Mazza 197). Once I point out to them that the language of this sentence is the language of the restaurant review, the kind of article Terence was featured in, they better understand point of view as an analytical rather than simply a classificatory concept (e.g., first-person, third-person), and they can see how point of view is mediated by social discourses.

9. In certain narratives or myths, explains Teresa De Lauretis, the hero must be male. The structural position is gendered, not the character. The mythical subject is constituted as male, as the active principle of culture, the establisher of distinction; female is what is not susceptible to transformation, to life or death (119)—or to the loss of one's good name and social position.

10. One role assigned to Anita Hill that could not have been assigned to Michelle Rae was that of "race traitor," which I will discuss shortly.

11. See chapter 1 and Butler's *Gender Trouble* and *Bodies That Matter,* especially the introduction, on this notion of performativity. For a related argument on how narratives structure our lives, see Sharon Marcus, who argues that understanding rape as a "cultural script" and deconstructing that discourse is, perhaps, the most effective way to change our "rape culture" (388–89). This kind of reading does not say that it doesn't matter that Hill is a real woman and not a fictional character, but it does say that what is significant—what signifies—within the structure of the sexual harassment narrative is Hill's status as an exemplum, and that her place in that narrative gives her the same ontological status as the fictional Michelle Rae (see P. Baker 14–16).

12. Gallop discusses this tendency to make sexual harassment a gender-neutral offense in *Feminist Accused,* specifically in reference to Michael Crichton's novel *Disclosure* (24).

13. This clichéd expression carries new meaning in the aftermath of the O. J. Simpson trial. Sometimes the glove doesn't fit. The Simpson trial is yet another example of the narrative of racial oppression being opposed to the narrative of gender oppression. O.J.'s case fit the wife-abuse narrative to a T, yet that story did not carry much weight. In the months following Simpson's acquittal, reports of sexual abuse to hotlines and women's shelters fell off significantly.

14. Judith Resnik writes of the 1989 trial of Evelyn Dixon, who was convicted of killing her abusive husband. Dixon's claim that she had killed in self-defense (her husband was attacking her at the time) was undermined by the fact that she never cried. The prosecutor reminded the jury several times that "'Ms. Dixon had not appeared teary, helpless, or fearful when she spoke to the police after her husband's death'" (qtd. in Heilbrun and Resnik 33).

15. What is deemed relevant as evidence has much to do with what is perceived to be the reality of sexual harassment, and as Robin West and Gallop both point out, sexual harassment continues to be seen as private, consensual, not discriminatory. This is born out no less by the incredulity shown by Senator Orrin Hatch and J. C. Alvarez when Anita Hill claimed she did not stop the harassment for fear of destroying her career than by Michelle Rae's characterization as a woman obsessed with Ter-

ence Lovell. Other commentators on the hearings, such as Crenshaw and Wahnee-ma Lubiano, have discussed the relevance of evidence.

16. "Normative feminism," according to Peter Baker, holds a normative view of language as expressive and nonalienated and advocates a normative ethics based on knowledge (84–89). Baker opposes this view, for which Sandra Gilbert and Susan Gubar serve as examples, to Julia Kristeva's position, which ties ethics to a textual practice. For a detailed discussion and critique of Robin West, see Cornell (*Beyond Accommodation,* chap. 1).

17. Philip Brian Harper makes a similar point in "'The Subversive Edge.'" Self-presentation in the juridical context necessarily partakes of and legitimates "socially sanctioned 'fantasies'" already active in the social-symbolic realm. "In other words," writes Harper, "juridical activity not only conforms to but actually helps to establish the terms of legitimacy that condition society as a whole" (97). Similarly, Cornell argues that what is admissible as evidence is not just that which meets "evidentiary standards and procedures . . . [that] define what is relevant" but is also dependent on "how one 'sees' women and sexual relations" (*Beyond Accommodation* 61). Whether or not the victim's attire is "relevant," whether or not it makes any difference to readers that Michelle Rae wears a dance leotard to work, depends on prior notions of what women are "really" like.

18. In other words, fraudulence is not willful but structural, and as such, it does not depend on an opposition between one's "true" character and one's social performance. To oppose the real and the role in this way is to ignore the performative power of language (see Cornell, *Beyond Accommodation* 3).

19. "Derelection," which is Irigaray's term, refers to the way in which "feminine difference cannot be expressed except as signified in the masculine imaginary or the masculine symbolic" (Cornell, *Beyond Accommodation* 7).

20. I use "date rape" rather than "rape" because, like sexual harassment, date rape is seen to be more a personal offense than a criminal assault, and thus the paradigm of miscommunication is frequently invoked when rape occurs in the context of dating.

21. My argument departs from but does not necessarily invalidate Gallop's argument in *Feminist Accused of Sexual Harassment:* that sexual harassment has ceased to be understood in terms of discrimination and has come to be thought of as having to do with sex.

22. The narrative of Gallop's case that I am drawing on comes primarily from Margaret Talbot's story in *Lingua Franca* which first brought this case to wide public attention. That version was constructed from interviews with Beckelman, Gallop, and other students and professors at the University of Wisconsin at Milwaukee. Gallop has published her own version and analysis of this case in *Feminist Accused of Sexual Harassment.* I have not revised this section of the chapter, written two years before Gallop's book was published, in response to Gallop's account, though I refer to and quote from the book in passing and address it directly in the concluding section of this chapter.

23. Of course, in the end Gallop was hardly "undone" by the charges. Not only has she retained her position, but she got another publication out of the painful ordeal.

24. This is not to deny that *Oleanna* does indeed profit, literally and thematically, from the public's preoccupation with the Thomas hearings. At first denying any relation between his play and the hearings, Mamet concedes in one interview that he

had abandoned the play and then decided to finish it when the hearings became a matter of public debate (Story 58). The play's financial success, grossing about $60,000 per week in its initial fifteenth-month run (Evans 63), proves producer Frederick Zollo's point: "'We were blessed with controversy'" (qtd. in Evans 65).

25. Gallop's conference, originally proposed as a conference on teacher-student sex in response to her university's harassment policy that barred such relations, met with protest from feminist colleagues and students. It was then reconceived as a conference on the personal in pedagogy, though it still stirred controversy since many saw it as a thinly veiled attempt to defend Gallop's personal relations with students, which were then being investigated as sexual harassment. As an invited discussant at that conference, I witnessed the petitions and protests, but not yet aware of the charges against Gallop, I understood the objections to be aimed at her particular brand of feminist theory. Thus, it was easy for me at that time to characterize the protestors as feminists of the "antipornography" type, or as critics of postmodern theory.

26. For a discussion of the ethical implications of Kristeva's work on abjection, see Peter Baker (chap. 5).

27. On the basis of her own experience, Gallop assumes that these feminists are covering up their own consensual relations with professors. That these feminists might never have had such relations never seems to occur to her; or if it does, such a possibility would only confirm her characterization of them as "antisex," as she labels those who defend harassment policies, and the policies themselves ("Feminism and Harassment Policy" 22; see also Talbot 39).

28. On this common resistance to deconstructive critique, see, for example, the citation to George Levine's "Real Trouble" in Fleishman (812).

29. This section heading, which I also use in chapter 2 to address a related problem, alludes to the title of Gregory Jay's presentation at Gallop's pedagogy conference, "Taking Multiculturalism Personally."

30. As Gallop explains in her book on academic feminism: "my goal has been to chip away at certain reigning myths. . . . Yet my hope is that what I uncover should be taken as not shameful but instructive. The necessary assumption for this is that we are all inevitably symptomatic, we are all subjects within a field of conflict" (*Around 1981* 7).

31. I am grateful to Marian Staats for this formulation of the ethical question raised by this case.

COMING OUT: ENVOI

I have passed. . . . What then remains, when I cannot pull
out my papers and make you believe by reading aloud my
credentials that I have passed? . . . There is always some-
body, when we come together, and the edges of meeting are
still sharp, who refuses to be submerged; whose identity
therefore one wishes to make crouch beneath one's own.
. . . I am merely "Neville" to you, who see the narrow limits
of my life and the line it cannot pass. But to myself I am im-
measurable; a net whose fibres pass imperceptibly beneath
the world.
  —Virginia Woolf, *The Waves*[1]

In September 1996, when all the tabloids were full of rumors about what
would happen in the upcoming season of the TV sitcom "Ellen," Rosie
O'Donnell invited Ellen DeGeneres to be her guest. Rosie wasted no time
getting to the point.

Rosie: All kinds of rumors are flying. Come on, out with it, what's going to
    happen on "Ellen."
Ellen: Well, for you. I don't know how this leaked out, we were trying to keep
    it quiet, but this season you're going to find out that Ellen is Lebanese.
Rosie: Really? [in mocked surprise] What, just like that? Have there been any
    clues?
Ellen: Oh yes. You've seen Ellen eating baba ganoush and hummus. She likes
    Casey Kasem.
Rosie: Wait a minute, *I* like Casey Kasem [she pushes a button and a voice
    says, "You go girl"]. Maybe *I'm* Lebanese?
Ellen: You could be Lebanese.[2]

Ellen and Rosie come out in this exchange, but as what? In coming out, Ellen passes into another subject position. The language play on Lebanese at once divulges and withholds the secret the public wants to know. The performance ultimately reveals that there is no subject to come out "as," an argument Eve Kosofsky Sedgwick makes in *Epistemology of the Closet*. Coming out is like the move to the personal in pedagogy, the subject of chapter 6: in the process of getting personal, or coming out, one creates the secret one would reveal, the position one would (re)claim. Writing on Rousseau's *Confessions*, the classic literary example of coming out from which I take the epigraph for my prefacing remarks, moral philosopher Sissela Bok describes the Enlightenment philosopher's self-disclosure as "an extraordinary blend of laying bare, disguise, concealment, and invention, of flaunting the self in public while yet nourishing a sense of mystery" (74). Self-disclosure necessarily entails passing.

Coming out is only the latest in a series of metaphors for the disclosure of the self. Getting personal, breaking silence, speaking up, coming out— these are the moral imperatives of our postmodern age. "Recently, in the academy," writes Diana Fuss, "some would say it is 'in' to be 'out'" (*Inside/ Out* 4). The desire to come out is particularly acute, and especially valued, at a time when the emphasis on crossing borders and breaking down barriers between cultures, classes, social groups, and disciplines is creating anxiety about who we are and what we do. Yet, as Bok says of metaphors of personal space, the metaphor of the closet, with its language of private space and identity boundaries, personalizes interpersonal, discursive practices, and thus that language should not go unchallenged (13). If coming out, after Sedgwick et al., is no longer an unqualified good, then passing (whether in its literal or figurative sense) need no longer have a negative presumption against it from the beginning. Writing on secrecy and concealment, Bok insists, "We cannot even begin with a moral presumption in either direction" (27)—that is, that secrecy is bad or good—for "one cannot always know what is and is not intentionally kept hidden" (9). Bok's moral imperative undercuts the opposition between coming out conceived as disclosure or self-discovery and passing conceived as intentional deception or appropriation. Does this blurring of distinctions render moral choice impossible? It can, Bok concedes, but it also makes ethical inquiry all the more imperative. Moral responsibility, she argues, requires being "mindful" of the processes of (self-)deception, appropriation, avoidance, and ignorance. We need "to watch how they are imputed: to whom, on what grounds, and with what power to bring about changes" (71–72). If for Ellen coming out is a way of both gaining and feigning control over some aspect of her identity, then Rosie's response as interlocutor reminds us that our control over our own identifications is no less circumscribed: *You* could be Lebanese.

Passing cannot be an impasse. The very premise that our subject positions can be neither safely inhabited nor safeguarded is itself a call to act, to run the risk of passing. Insofar as passing, as I have conceptualized it throughout this book, has to do with subjectivity understood as a practice and a responsibility, not as a position, we must be able to come out of the apparent impasse created by that risk and assume responsibility for our forms of passing. This kind of responsibility has commonly been figured as "coming out." But once coming out, as Sedgwick reconceives it, is no longer the antidote to passing, then taking responsibility for our forms of passing does not mean freeing ourselves from the dynamics of passing. While Bok points out that we cannot be responsible for what we do not know (e.g., the drowning of a child while we are asleep on the beach), we are responsible for our *forms* of ignorance and, Bok says, for those things that we should know because they are an aspect of our job or duty (we are responsible for the drowning if we are the lifeguard on duty or the child's parent) (68). For literature and writing professors, the practice that best figures this responsibility, with all its risks, is pedagogy.

The happy etymology that brings together "passing" in its social sense of identifying or accepting identification as a certain type of person and "passing" in its academic sense of conferring approval on another who can then move on to a new course of study makes pedagogy all the more salient as a site for exploring the dynamics of responsibility that *is* passing. Although years of writing on this project have resulted in my work finding a place in a newly emerging and ever-proliferating academic discourse on passing, my initial choice of the metaphor had to do with a desire to make the work I do—specifically, reading, writing, and teaching theory—relevant in the public sphere. Those of us in the humanities hear much these days about the need to make clear to the public what it is we do, and I hope this book has contributed to this end. However, my motivation was less the desire to make my work accessible to the general public than to make the work of pedagogy public, visible, so it might come to mean more than classroom practices, and what we do might come to intervene in the kinds of debates that now preoccupy us: for example, Who owns museum exhibits? What are the limits of sexual harassment? Who can speak as and for what? As examples throughout this book show, pedagogy in literary and composition studies, reconceived as forms of cultural studies, provides a site and a model for learning how to deal with the experience of subjectivity as passing and with the resulting awareness of oneself—one's self—in relation to others, to history, and to writing. In pedagogy—understood as the actual interactions among subjects within a public space and not as a set of procedures—we learn how to assume (to seize and to simulate) the dynamics of responsibility in postmodernity with its deprivatization of personal space.[3]

In this book I have attempted to show the necessity of taking the complexities we engage in our writing into public sites and practices. In this sense, the book serves a certain pedagogical function; it is an effort to make teaching more like writing, not to provide a road map for teaching. As Peggy Kamuf says in the introduction to the Derrida reader she edited, "By meeting this expectation, or submitting to this virtual demand for a reassuring map of unfamiliar territory, written material may be only too eager to find and take up its place on the map of known coordinates, so that it can be easily recognized by the largest number" (Derrida, *Reader* xix). This desire for recognition that motivates writing on pedagogy and writing on identity comes into conflict with the ethical imperative I call "passing." Passing is not the masking of some identity that would otherwise be fully present; rather, passing is the exposure of identity conceived of as ever fully present. To continue with Kamuf's metaphor, passing means "blotting out the cardinal reference points, thus making it more difficult to read off the coordinates" (xix). Likewise, the kind of pedagogy I have been advocating here, one obviously informed by Derrida's writing, is not simply *about* passing but is an effort to produce the effect of passing in writing and teaching. "'I never write *on* anything,'" Derrida writes. "'I seek above all to produce effects (on you)'" (qtd. in Kamuf xix).

Passing cannot be an impasse nor a resting point, and so I have called this last chapter in my book "Coming Out," not "Conclusion" (as I call the initial chapter "Prefacing Remarks," not "Preface"). "Coming out" emphasizes the transformative possibilities of passing, especially when we are called on to account for it. When some of my students complain that theorists read too much into things, when some critics complain that theory denies agency and others complain that theory leads to an infinite regress of qualification upon qualification, I take that criticism as a call to act and not as a justification for abandoning the responsibility that is pedagogy. The double bind of passing is, as Gayatri Chakravorty Spivak says of deconstruction, its "peculiar responsibility," and its strength is "its acknowledgment of radical contamination" ("Responsibility" 28). The logic that would conceive deconstruction as the exposure of error ("Responsibility" 39) or the exposure of a fraud (Crowley 9) creates the impasse that is then attributed to deconstruction as a practice of reading and writing. The fear of being exposed as a fraud is not only a fear of being read (B. Johnson, *Wake* 73), it is a fear of reading. And reading along with writing is our responsibility as literature and composi-tion teachers. If we are to assume responsibility for passing, we need to show how our forms of reading and writing have, in Susan Suleiman's words, "pub-lic relevance" (234). The academic's one obligation, says Spivak, is not to write on something carelessly read ("Responsibility" 35)—and, I would add, not to write something that can be carelessly read because it can "take up its place on the map of known coordinates."

By way of coming out, then, I would like to turn from performances of passing in fiction, drama, film, and popular culture to personal writings, where the relation between writing and identity seems to be transparent and open. Although some of the personal narratives discussed here are about passing as a social practice and others treat passing in its figurative sense, each refigures passing in the process of narrating a life. Too often passing is as-sumed from the beginning to be the purview of the privileged few—those whose body type, skin tone, class or professional status make passing possi-ble and desirable. In beginning with this presumption, we overlook the way resistance to passing can be a form of self-protection, as each of these mem-oirs suggests. If we do not begin with a negative presumption against pass-ing, we might find in that performance a structure of response that gets us out of the choice between an enervating cynicism that denies moral choice and a moralizing certitude that insists on it. Both responses, according to Bok, seek to protect the self from the knowledge of being beside itself (103). Of confessional writing she says that personal narratives place a particularly heavy obligation on the reader, who is taken into the writer's confidence and must learn to deal with the responsibility this knowledge entails (81). We must analyze, then, not only how the writer figures her or his identity in the text but also, as Lester Faigley has pointed out, "who the text calls on [us] to be" (72). When the text presents the experience of subjectivity as passing, that is indeed a "peculiar responsibility."

Shirlee Taylor Haizlip's 1995 memoir *The Sweeter the Juice* is the fruit of the author's lifelong dream and eventual quest to find her mother's family members who, around 1920, passed over and lived as whites. "Ten thousand people each year cross the visible and invisible color line and become 'white,'" writes Haizlip, "and the footprints of those who have crossed the color line become infinite and untrackable" (15, 34). She attempts to trace the "infinite" lines of her racial descent and in the process raises questions asked repeat-edly by authors of narratives of passing: Why do people who are capable of passing as white do so (like the author's maternal grandfather)? Why do oth-ers who are capable choose not to (like the author's mother)? And, the ques-tion that so disturbs Nella Larsen's Irene Redfield, why do still others who choose not to pass protect those who do (like the author's Aunt Mamie)? Behind all these questions readers can hear: What is race? What is color? Who are "we," we Americans who, as a people, are neither black nor white?

In Haizlip's memoir, passing is more than simply the topic or theme of the narrative. What begins as a form of racial betrayal becomes, in the course of the narrative, an apt figure for the peculiarly American crisis of identity she confronts. Passing, like coming out, names "the most crucial site" for the interrogation and contestation of identity categories in contemporary culture (Sedgwick, *Epistemology* 72). "In America," writes Anna Deavere Smith, "identity is always being negotiated" (xxxiii).[4] Haizlip undertakes the responsibility of that impossibility: to track the untrackable. In doing so, she responds to the ethical imperative to see in that impossible task not an impasse but the possibility of living and acting despite the instability and insecurity of our (self-)identifications. The history of the places, people, and politics that have touched, however tenuously, the lives of Haizlip's family over several generations becomes our story, the story of a racially mixed, racially divided, racially ambivalent America.

By coming to understand the extent to which racial categories are noncontinuous over time and are bound up with other cultural differences, Haizlip reveals that in tracing one's racial identity there is no "thing" to know (as Sedgwick argues there is no subject to come out "as"). "I began the search for my mother's family believing that I was looking for black people 'passing for white.' . . . What I ultimately found, I realized, were black people who had become white" (266). Here, "becoming white" is the result of assimilation and denial, just as earlier in the narrative "becoming black" is the result of politically charged racial classifications and segregation. For example, in the 1880 census, the author's maternal great-grandfather and his children were listed as "mulatto"; in the 1900 census they were listed as "black." Why the change in designation when, as the author quips, they were surely no darker? But becoming is also a matter of context and audience. When her classmates at Wellesley asked her nationality, Haizlip says, "It baffled me that people could not immediately 'see' what I was. Then it dawned on me that I had left my brown community behind and had become part of a totally different context. I could be a different race, if I chose. For the first time I began to understand how my mother's family had become white" (188).

After narrating many different experiences of how people "become" black or white, after tracing as best she can her mother's and father's families back to colonial times, and after finally tracking down her passing relatives, Haizlip asks, "In the end, or is it a beginning, what have I found?" (265). In a sense, the author finds herself (by locating her passing relatives) only to lose her-self: "All in all, I have grown a great deal less certain about the vagaries of race and know that I am ambivalent about its implications. . . . If asked, I would probably now describe myself as a person of mixed race rather than as black, although I know I will never lose my black feelings. My journey has made me more cautious in labeling or pigeonholing others" (267). More than a simple plea for tolerance, Haizlip's statement in the context of her life-writing reinforces Elaine Marks's point in *Maranno as Metaphor:* "If there is an ethical dimension beyond the simple plea for understanding and toler-ance that underlies this book, it is the plea that we view identity historically, psychologically, and linguistically in a more complex manner" (xvii). If Haiz-lip now calls herself "racially mixed" rather than "black," if in the end she comes to question her initial contempt for her passing relatives, it is not sim-ply because she has become more ambivalent about race or more tolerant of differences. It is, rather, that she has become more open to "dis-closure," in both senses of open-endedness and exposure. In this narrative, dis-clo-sure changes its meaning from exposure of the "true" self behind the pass-ing persona to exposure of more of the self in the process of coming to un-derstand the many ways in which one passes (or can be said to pass), consciously and unconsciously.

The process of writing this narrative of her search for those who crossed over leads Haizlip to question the concept of racial *essence* that informed her initial contempt for passing. It is this concept of a given identity that the passer at once denies (by passing) and affirms (to safeguard her or his pass-ing identity). As this memoir movingly reveals, the impoverishment that the passer suffers does not lie in giving up a prior identity; instead, and paradox-ically, it is precisely that fiction of a fixed, given identity that the passer must embrace all the more fiercely. That desire for or belief in a fixed, unproblem-atic, essential identity gives rise to potentially debilitating fears that some-one else might try to deprive us of it.

What Haizlip comes to accept is the conception of subjectivity as an open and endless question, an ongoing process of learning, and the possibilities implied in that conception. Finding an identity to inhabit means, as she testifies, learning how to live with ambivalence and open-endedness, what John Caputo terms the "dissemination of *ethos*" (262). If the passer is irre-sponsible, it is not in trying to live under a "false" identity; rather, it is in relinquishing the struggle with her or his own historically constituted iden-tity by denying one part of her or his racial past. It is this struggle that Haiz-lip has engaged in by writing this memoir, and in doing so she has come to have sympathy for her passing relatives' loss of that defining experience. It is this struggle that makes her writing responsible and ethical, not simply tolerant or confessional.

The infinite and untrackable footprints left by our ancestors' forays across visible and invisible boundaries of identity make it possible to say there are very few, if any, "real" white Americans, Haizlip declares. "In other words," she says, "many Americans are not who they think they are" (15). The irrecoverability of those untrackable footprints of racial inheritance, and thus the never fully realized project of recovering a grounding identity, keeps alive the process of struggling with our self-identifications and our racially prescribed positions. If we do not put too much faith in ultimately finding a stable identity that could ground our actions and beliefs, if we do not long for the comfort of closure but yield to the open-endedness of dis-closure, then we could have faith that what is real, which includes our racial history, can never completely govern what is possible, as Drucilla Cornell argues in reference to the utopian moment of deconstruction (*Beyond Accommodation,* chap. 2).

In a 1990 lecture at the University of Chicago entitled "No Passing," Barbara Johnson argued that passing is acting as if one could determine one's subject position, as if one were an autonomous subject without heritage, family, or history. This is how Haizlip's passing relatives had to act, choosing to cut themselves off from their heritage and their history and denying that heritage to their offspring as well. To reject passing in this sense, as Haizlip does, is not to claim a racial identity as one's own but to reclaim a heritage and a history, as she also does. At the end of her search, and at the beginning of her memoir, Haizlip writes: "I have been called Egyptian, Italian, Jewish, French, Iranian, Armenian, Syrian, Spanish, Portuguese and Greek. I have also been called black and Peola and nigger and high yellow and bright. I am an American anomaly. I am an American ideal. I am the American nightmare. I am the Martin Luther King dream. I am the new America" (15). When one chooses to pass, or to let oneself pass, as so many identities, then it could be said that one has performed a political act.

Similarly, the struggle with his own historically constituted identity is what Alain Finkielkraut undertakes in his autobiographical narrative *The Imaginary Jew,* a work of intellectual history. Finkielkraut offers a scathing critique of his own earlier political identification as a leftist, for his politics led him to exploit his Jewish identity without the cultural memory that would root that identity in social history, a spiritual tradition, and the concrete, daily lives of Jews. He writes that "Jew" served him as an identity, one that he hoped to suggest to others, a point Gregory Jay also made at Jane Gallop's confer-

ence on pedagogy. To be a Jew was, for Finkielkraut, to be a symbol of oppression. He was in essence passing, not in the usual sense of disguising his
Jewishness, but in the sense of using it, "unveiling" himself to others (171),
"making a spectacle of [his] difference" (172). Behind his liberal appearance
lay, as he calls it, an "insidious constraint"—that is, "the obligation to conceive of Judaism in terms of self and identity" (178). History had become for
him a matter of "ideological self-legitimation" (viii). Finkielkraut's term for
this kind of fictive identity, for this peculiar form of passing as a Jew despite
the fact that one has a birthright to that name, is "imaginary Jew." Like my
use of "passing," "imaginary Jew" is an effort to name what has never been
considered as a category of identity (15).

In reclaiming a cultural memory and a historical past in his confrontation with Judaism, Finkielkraut insists that he has not become more authentically Jewish. His is not the story of "the victory of [his] authentic self" over
the image of authenticity he previously wore as a Jew. "The word 'Jew' is no
longer a mirror in which I seek my self-portrait, but where I look for everything I'm not, everything I'll never be able to glimpse by taking myself as a
point of reference" (179). Like Haizlip's, Finkielkraut's moral journey has
been a process not of finding himself but of losing himself in accepting the
ethical obligation to struggle with his identity. He is still passing, in the sense
that to present an image of oneself to others is always to strike a pose, "for
there is finally no getting away from the stage" (172); however, now his passing is an ongoing process of producing, as he sees it, an authenticity that is
never simply in opposition to the inauthentic.

Finkielkraut's point of departure, as David Suchoff says in his introduction to *The Imaginary Jew,* is Sartre's existentialism with its "firm distinction
between inauthentic culture and the [authentic] self" (xi). Yet Finkielkraut's
writing discloses the very difficulty of that distinction, not only because
postmodernity, with its "proliferation of images, identities without substance,
and textuality-centered culture" (xv) undercuts the distinction, but because
the distinction itself can "short-circuit understanding," as Bok says of metaphors such as Sartre's "bad faith." Such concepts help us to see "the para-
doxes of human failure to perceive and react," Bok writes, yet as explanations
"they short-circuit understanding of the complexity that underlies our experience of paradox" (64). "As a result," Bok continues, "they permit some
people to impute clear-cut intention, directness, and simplicity to the intri-
cate processes of coping with information, while at the same time allowing
others to dismiss the questions of responsibility and intention altogether"
(64).[5] Bok commends Sartre for not writing a book of moral theory, for that
would have required him to offer criteria for deciding when someone was

acting in bad faith and would have sacrificed the "subtle understanding of human motives" presented in his writing (62). Similarly, if Finkielkraut had remained committed to the Sartrean distinction with which he began, he would have had to give up on the ethical obligation to risk passing.

In coming to terms with the ways in which he passes as a Jew, in coming to understand that his Jewishness is not simply a matter of personal or political identity, Finkielkraut engages in an "undoing of the self" (176) that I call "passing." Passing as I have reconceived it is the process of trying to divest ourselves of certain privileged positions in our engagements with others and in response to the demands made on us by our collective history and by cultural memory. But "privileged positions," as Haizlip and Finkielkraut show, need not refer only to those social positions or identity categories privileged in the general culture. It can refer as well to the notion of the self as a position unto itself. Writing about the slogan "We are all German Jews," chanted by non-Jews in support and solidarity with Jews, Finkielkraut voices his resentment as a young man at their appropriation of his identity when they had not paid their dues (17–18).[6] Yet he has come to see that his resentment could have been directed at himself as well. While the protestors temporarily passed as Jews, he was always passing as a Jew (18).

"I am a Jew, yet the figure designated by this statement can be located nowhere," writes Finkielkraut; "no sooner have I written [I am a Jew] than I sense a mistake, that an error in grammatical attribution of person must have occurred" (32–33). An error in grammatical attribution takes the pronoun as referential rather than as performative.[7] "As an imaginary Jew," Finkielkraut says, "I have long lived my faithfulness to my Jewish background in a kind of appropriation" (34). In opposing that pose, he does not offer another identity but instead undertakes the difficult process of assuming responsibility for his own forms of passing. As I argue in chapter 1, putting one's self-identifications at risk in this way, as Finkielkraut and Haizlip do, is the first step in an ethics of passing.

Alice Kaplan's 1993 memoir *French Lessons* provides a third example of personal writing that engages passing as an ethical practice. In this memoir, passing ostensibly has less to do with Kaplan's Jewishness than with her efforts to pass herself off as French—or, more accurately, her efforts to *become* French. Writing on her mastery of the difficult French "r", she says: "With this 'r' I could speak French, I wouldn't be screaming my Americanness every time I spoke. 'R' was my passport" (55). Mastery of languages becomes crucial to Kaplan's developing sense of identity as a college student. In her Swiss boarding school, she lies in bed at night listening to her roommates speaking German to each other, a language she does not know. But just by listening intently, as she says, discriminating consonants from vowels, verbs from nouns, she begins to break through their "secret" conversation. One night she hears the word "Jude" and knows her roommates are talking about her. "I *could* understand," she writes. "Just by lying there with my ear and listening, I could understand languages. And because I could understand languages, she [her roommate] couldn't get me" (47). Mastery of the language is crucial to passing as French, but paradoxically it also means facing her identity as a Jew.

In "André," the first chapter of part 3, "Getting It Right," Kaplan is studying abroad during her junior year in college. She is intent on getting it right, mastering not only the French language but what it means to *be* French, which she refers to elsewhere as "passing in French" (182). She meets André, sleeps with him, becomes obsessed with him, and eventually loses him to Maïté, the "real thing"—a woman, as she puts it, with accents in her name (89). "What I really wanted from André," she says, "was language" (86). "I wanted to crawl into his skin, live in his body, be him. The words he used to talk to me, I wanted to use back. I wanted them to be my words. . . . I was burning with race envy" (88–89). "Race" signifies that world of difference between André's use of French and hers (87). Language is both the passport to another culture and the sign of the authenticity of that culture that inhibits passing.

I teach Kaplan's narrative to illustrate the relation between language and identity. Yet my students have often missed this point, dismissing her youthful persona in "André" as silly, finding her foolish for trying to pass as French. More admirable, or at least likeable, in their view is the "freckled jock who could hardly speak French" and who delights in "playing the American mascot" (92). At least he's genuine, they argue; he doesn't try to pass as someone else. But Kaplan's invocation of the Marlboro Man to represent this man's pose suggests he is also passing. The jock can inhabit his American identity so naturally only because cultural images have created that identity for him to occupy. He has the sex and the body type to pass as the American. "A girl can't be a Marlboro Man," Kaplan concludes (92). One might compare Kaplan's situation as a junior abroad with the ex-colored man's situation in James Weldon Johnson's novel. When he finds out that he is colored, not white, he sets out to *become* a Negro by learning what it means to be that identity. He reads literature and history, studies music and dialect, and observes and imitates other blacks. Like Finkielkraut's intellectual autobiography, Johnson's fictional autobiography shows that being something is no guarantee that one will or will not pass as that identity. If the ex-colored man can acquire an identity in these ways, I ask students, then why can't Kaplan?

Yet my students' resistance to Kaplan's passing teaches us another lesson, one that Kaplan learns early in her schooling in French: namely, mastery of the self is as illusory as mastery of language. As a student in France, Kaplan meets Micheline, a doctor who specializes in *maladies du langage* (illnesses of language). Micheline tells Kaplan: "'Language is not a machine you can break and fix with the right technique, it is a function of the whole person, an expression of culture, desire, need. . . . Inside our language is our history, personal and political'" (98). This understanding of language complements the understanding of literature Kaplan had earlier gotten from her French poetry professor who taught her that literature is an experience of language and not an objet d'art. Kaplan writes, "Literature is essential to survival and impossible to understand. Literature lies and tells the truth about lying. Writing is the opposite of making something present, I learned from her. Writing is effacement" (75). Reading literature as language (not just for content or meaning) means coming to understand identity as historically, psychologically, and *linguistically* complex.

In her afterword, Kaplan concedes that passing can be a form of self-deception, but not to pass can be a failure of imagination: "Learning French did me some harm by giving me a place to hide. It's not as if there's a straightforward American self lurking under a devious French one, waiting to come out and be authentic. That's nostalgia—or fiction. French isn't just a metaphor, either—it's a skill. . . . I'm grateful to French . . . for teaching me that there is more than one way to speak, for giving me a role, for being the home I've made from my own will and my own imagination" (216).

If learning French gave Kaplan a home, learning theory through her graduate studies in French exposed the precariousness of that safe space. She writes of her resistance to Paul de Man and deconstructive theory, which was all the rage at Yale in the 1970s when Kaplan was a student there. She wrote her dissertation (before the de Man scandal) on French fascist intellectuals, not simply reiterating the leftist critique of fascism but doing a close reading of its texts. "Maybe I could have it both ways," she writes of her thoughts then. "I could deconstruct fascism, and I could show that intellectuals were just as subject as anyone else to fascist longings" (159). When the de Man scandal broke, Kaplan felt vindicated for her work and for her resistance to deconstructive theory; yet, she notes the irony: in writing an article about the scandal, she wrote in de Man's style, undercutting the emotional excitement and moral outrage she felt with analytical distance and "the confusing flourish at the end" (170).

Even before the scandal, however, Kaplan had learned the lesson of deconstruction. In spring 1982, during her first research trip to France, she interviewed Maurice Bardèche, the "last living fascist intellectual," as she calls him, who founded the genre of Revisionism that essentially denied the Holocaust. He wrote a charming letter in response to her request for an interview, welcoming her warmly. "A Jew being welcomed by a fascist," she thought at the time. "Maybe the labels didn't mean anything anymore?" (188) On her way to visit him, she stopped at the home of a friend of one of her former teachers. It turned out that this man's father-in-law had been killed because of the fascist propaganda of Bardèche. He asked her: "Have you thought about what it means to even agree to talk with this man? There has to be an ethics for your interview—you have to formulate an ethics for the situation you're going into" (189). His reaction to her proposed visit took her by surprise. "Ethics? Does ethics mean my behavior? Does it mean I have to decide how I'm going to react to Bardèche before I've even met him? Am I not allowed to smile? Should I shake his hand? None of these thoughts had occurred to me before. . . . Maybe that was for the better, I thought. Shouldn't I be open to surprises? Isn't that the point that I don't have to have a prepared response, that I should be ready for the accidents of a real conversation?" (189)

Here Kaplan voices the ethics of a deconstructive practice, one that is open to the accidents and surprises ("the surprise of otherness," as Barbara Johnson calls it [*World* 16]) rather than having a clear-cut position, a grounded morality. When Kaplan writes about the interview, she chooses to follow the advice of her former teacher, Linda Orr, though one could also think of Paul de Man. Orr had urged her "to put into writing the contradictions and challenges of the situation—not to make it too 'clean' or resolved" (194). Kaplan refers to this practice as "the freedom of writing v. the constraints of ethics" (199). I would rather call it the ethics of writing in the wake of deconstruction (to borrow Johnson's title).

Kaplan's memoir raises questions about the ethics of the kind of work we do, about the responsibility of intellectuals, and about the ethics of teaching. "How do I tell [my students] who I am, why I read the way I do?" she asks (174). The answer to that question for Kaplan is her memoir (and for me, this book), where teaching becomes a form of writing and where responsibility for who one is can be assumed through the very form her writing takes, as one final example from the memoir will show. As a student, Kaplan fell under the spell of Céline's musical prose. Desiring to know more about him, she visited the Museum of Resistance in Paris. The librarian greeted her request for information on Céline with suspicion: Why work on a racist anti-Semite, a fascist, a collaborationist? Kaplan told the librarian that she was certainly no fascist sympathizer, that her father prosecuted Nazis at Nuremburg. The effect was immediate; the librarian softened toward her. "The line about my father worked," Kaplan writes. "Except I was lying" (107). It's not that her father wasn't a judge at the Nuremburg trials; it's that she was passing as a Jew in the sense Finkielkraut elaborates. She was wearing her Jewishness as a sign of her moral rectitude, to ward off any suspicion aroused by her attraction to the racist Céline. What the spectacle of her Jewishness evades is the power Céline's writing had to move her. By accepting the name "Jew" she escapes, as Finkielkraut says of himself, "the vertiginous feeling of a dissolving self" (8). Kaplan's response to Céline brings to mind the response of Toni Morrison's narrator in *Jazz* to the racist Golden Gray. After projecting herself into the mind of this character and depicting his negrophobia, the narrator stops herself:

> What was I thinking of? How could I have imagined him so poorly? Not noticed the hurt that was not linked to the color of his skin, or the blood that beat beneath it. But to some other thing that longed for authenticity, for a right to be in this place, effortlessly without needing to acquire a false face, a laughless grin, a talking posture. . . .
>
> Now I have to think this through, carefully, even though I may be doomed to another misunderstanding. I have to do it and not break down. Not hating him is not enough; liking, loving him is not useful. I have to alter things. (160–61)

Kaplan's writing on Céline clearly reveals the fault lines in her identity as a Jew, a woman, a French professor, and an intellectual, as Morrison's novel exposes the "fissures" in the identity of the New Negro as well as the white southerner. In her writing, Kaplan wanted to avoid both the expected liberal critique of and the suspect apology for Céline's racist propaganda. More than that, she wanted to avoid being exposed as the American, the prudish, boring, inept critic who could never understand the writer's difficult French. On the contrary, she writes, she had studied Céline precisely to be "disturbed by a foreign language" rather than simply master the official French (117). Yet that disturbance reveals more than she had bargained for. In trying so hard not to be read *like* other American critics, Kaplan ends up reproducing in her work Céline's xenophobia (121). Passing as French may have given her a home, but that home is no protection against her own self-difference. Her writing exposes her to the truth that she wanted to expose in others by writing on fascist intellectuals: that intellectuals aren't really so high-minded (159). And *that* is the "peculiar responsibility" of Kaplan's writing.

In "The Wild Woman and All that Jazz," Drucilla Cornell asks, "Can a woman writer even tell the story 'true' if she narrates her story so as to pass as the 'good girl' whose image demands that she 'whiten' herself to the point of erasure?" (313) In Kaplan's memoir, as in Morrison's *Jazz,* which is the subject of Cornell's essay, "we are forced to confront the toll of passing on creativity" (Cornell, "Wild Woman" 313). In Cornell's sense, "passing" means pretending that the psychical fanstasy of Woman (or Jew, or intellectual, or racist) is "out there," something we can write on rather than something we write in relation to (314). It means writing as if one could separate "the 'messy' world of private fantasy and desire from the realm of public debate and sensible politics" (315). The ethics of Kaplan's memoir and Morrison's novel lies in these writers' refusal both to pass and to resist passing, which opens them up to the risk of being "beside themselves" in their writing, to the risk of "passing" in the sense I have been rehearsing in this book. Both acknowledge through the writing itself "the danger of the secret inherent in writing, that what is written remains to be known" (Cornell, "Wild Woman" 321). The willingness to claim "I have passed," then, becomes neither a shameful confession of inauthenticity nor a celebration of a boundary crossed but an imperative to act.

Like Virginia Woolf's Neville, I too ask, What then?

Notes

1. The passage is in the voice of Neville, a poet, a homosexual, and a product of the British public school system.

2. This exchange is my condensation of their dialogue, not a transcription.

3. Caller ID, pornography online, sexual harassment, cloning, the criminalization of reproduction—these are only a few of the many examples of such deprivatization. On reproduction as criminal offense, see Roberts (chap. 4).

4. Haizlip traces the emergence of the "old idea" Anna Deavere Smith speaks of in her introduction to *Fires in the Mirror,* an idea that roots American identity in clearly drawn lines—lines so clearly drawn, as Smith writes of Crown Heights, that they were ready to snap with the tension of keeping the boundary between black and white intact.

5. Yet intentions, Finkielkraut writes, are not the only thing that matter. Whether or not he set out to profit politically and morally from the suffering of the dead, the effect was the same: others saw in him "something other than" himself, namely, the dead Jews, and that gave him a moral advantage (11–12).

6. The occasion was the announcement, in May 1968, that Daniel Cohn-Bendit had been denied a visa to return to France. Finkielkraut writes of the march: "Jewish identity was no longer for Jews alone. The event taking place put an end to such exclusivity. Every child of the postwar era could change places with the outsider and

wear the yellow star. The role of the Just now belonged to whoever wished to assume it; the crowd felt justified in proclaiming its own exceptional status, which largely explains the exuberant cheer of its members" (17).

7. Finkielkraut here anticipates Judith Butler's point about the grammar of the personal pronoun. In reference to a statement she makes elsewhere in *Bodies That Matter*, Butler writes, "I use the grammar of an 'I' or a 'we' as if these subjects precede and activate their various identifications, but this is a grammatical fiction" (99).

WORKS CITED

Abel, Elizabeth. "Black Writing, White Reading: Race and the Politics of Feminist Interpretation." *Critical Inquiry* 19 (Spring 1993): 470–98.

Abrams, M. H. *Glossary of Literary Terms.* 5th ed. New York: Holt, Rinehart, and Winston, 1988.

Alcoff, Linda. "Cultural Feminism versus Post-structuralism: The Identity Crisis in Feminist Theory." *Signs* 13 (Spring 1988): 405–36.

———. "The Problem of Speaking for Others." *Cultural Critique* 20 (1991–92): 5–32.

Angels in America. Tony Kushner. Dir. Michael Mayer. Royal George Theater, Chicago. Fall 1994–Spring 1995.

Appiah, Kwame Anthony. "Is the Post- in Postmodernism the Same as the Post- in Postcolonialism?" *Critical Inquiry* 17 (Winter 1991): 336–57.

Aronowitz, Stanley, and Henry A. Giroux. *Postmodern Education: Politics, Culture, and Social Criticism.* Minneapolis: University of Minnesota Press, 1991.

Auerbach, Erich. *Mimesis: The Representation of Reality in Western Literature.* Trans. Willard R. Trask. Princeton, N.J.: Princeton University Press, 1953.

Austin, J. L. *How to Do Things with Words.* 1962. Ed. J. O. Urmson and Marina Sbisà. Cambridge, Mass.: Harvard University Press, 1975.

Awkward, Michael. "Negotiations of Power: White Critics, Black Texts, and the Self-Referential Impulse." *American Literary History* 2 (1990): 581–606.

Baker, Houston. "Everybody Knows the Real Thing, but Magic Brings Us Home: Notes for a Multicultural Age." Paper read at the conference "Thinking through Difference: Teaching Practices and Student Diversity." University of Chicago, Center for Continuing Studies. November 1993.

———. "Local Pedagogy; or, How I Redeemed My Spring Semester." *PMLA* 108.3 (May 1993): 400–409.

Baker, Peter. *Deconstruction and the Ethical Turn.* Gainesville: University Press of Florida, 1995.

Balsamo, Anne, and Michael Greer. "Cultural Studies, Literary Studies, and Pedagogy: The Undergraduate Literature Course." In *Changing Classroom Practices: Resources for Literary and Cultural Studies*. Ed. David B. Dowing. Urbana, Ill.: National Council of Teachers of English, 1994. 275–307.

Barthes, Roland. *Image/Music/Text*. Trans. Stephen Heath. New York: Hill and Wang, 1977.

———. *Mythologies*. Trans. Annette Lavers. New York: Farrar, Straus & Giroux, 1972.

———. *S/Z: An Essay*. Trans. Richard Miller. New York: Hill and Wang, 1974.

Bathrick, David. "Cultural Studies." In *Introduction to Scholarship in Modern Languages and Literatures*. Ed. Joseph Gibaldi. New York: Modern Language Association, 1992. 320–40.

Bauer, Dale. "Personal Criticism and the Academic Personality." In Roof and Wiegman 56–69.

Bauer, Dale, and Susan C. Jarratt. "Feminist Sophisists: Teaching with an Attitude." In *Changing Classroom Practices: Resources for Literary and Cultural Studies*. Ed. David B. Downing. Urbana, Ill.: National Council of Teachers of English, 1994. 149–65.

Bauman, Zygmunt. *Postmodern Ethics*. Oxford: Blackwell, 1993.

Belsey, Catherine. *Critical Practice*. London: Methuen, 1980.

Benjamin, Walter. "The Author as Producer." In *Art after Modernism: Rethinking Representation*. Ed. Brian Wallis. New York: Museum of Contemporary Art; Boston: David R. Godine, 1984. 297–309.

Berger, Gloria, and Ted Gest, with Jeannye Thornton. "Hill vs. Thomas: The Untold Story." *U.S. News & World Report*, 12 October 1992: 28–37.

Berger, John. *Ways of Seeing*. London: British Broadcasting Company and Penguin Books, 1972.

Berlant, Lauren. "National Brands/National Bodies: Imitation of Life." In *Comparative American Identities: Race, Sex, and Nationality in the Modern Text*. Ed. Hortense Spillers. New York: Routledge, 1991. 110–40.

Berlin, James A., and Michael J. Vivion, eds. *Cultural Studies in the English Classroom*. Portsmouth: Boynton/Cook Heinemann, 1992.

Bernstein, Richard. "Guilty If Charged." *New York Review of Books*, 13 January 1994: 11–14.

Bernstein, Susan David. "Confessing Feminist Theory: What's 'I' Got to Do with It?" *Hypatia* 7 (Spring 1992): 120–47.

Bérubé, Michael. "Against Subjectivity." *PMLA* 111 (October 1996): 1063–68.

Bhabha, Homi. "A Good Judge of Character: Men, Metaphors, and the Common Culture." In Morrison, *Race-ing Justice* 232–50.

Bly, Robert. *Iron John: A Book about Men*. Reading, Mass.: Addison-Wesley, 1990.

Bok, Sissela. *Secrets: On the Ethics of Concealment and Revelation*. New York: Pantheon Books, 1982.

Braidotti, Rosi. *Nomadic Subjects: Embodiment and Sexual Difference in Contemporary Feminist Theory*. New York: Columbia University Press, 1994.

Brantlinger, Patrick. *Crusoe's Footprints: Cultural Studies in Britain and America*. New York: Routledge, 1990.

Brodkey, Linda. "On the Subjects of Class and Gender in 'The Literacy Letters.'" *College English* 51 (February 1989): 125–41.

————. "Postmodern Pedagogy for Progressive Educators." *Journal of Education* 169 (1987): 138–43.

Brooks, Cleanth, Jr. *The Well Wrought Urn: Studies in the Structure of Poetry.* New York: Harcourt, Brace, and World, 1947.

Brooks, Cleanth, Jr., and Robert Penn Warren. 1938. *Understanding Poetry: An Anthology for College Students.* New York: Holt, 1953.

Brown, Sterling A. "Imitation of Life: Once a Pancake." *Opportunity: A Journal of Negro Life* 35 (March 1935): 87–88.

Butler, Judith. *Bodies That Matter: On the Discursive Limits of "Sex."* New York: Routledge, 1993.

————. "Contingent Foundations." Butler and Scott 3–21.

————. "For a Careful Reading." In *Feminist Contentions: A Philosophical Exchange.* Ed. Seyla Benhabib, Judith Butler, Drucilla Cornell, and Nancy Fraser. New York: Routledge, 1995. 127–43.

————. *Gender Trouble: Feminism and the Subversion of Identity.* New York: Routledge, 1990.

————. "Imitation and Gender Insubordination." In Fuss, *Inside/Out* 13–31.

————. "Lana's 'Imitation': Melodramatic Repetition and the Gender Performative." *Genders* 9 (Fall 1990): 1–18.

Butler, Judith, and Joan Scott, eds. *Feminists Theorize the Political.* New York: Routledge, 1992.

Callahan, Anne, "Critical Personae: The Face Value of the Paglia Phenomenon." Paper read at the President's Forum, Midwest Modern Language Association conference. November 1992.

————. "The Voice of Pleasure: The Troubadour Effect in Fictions of Heterosexual Desire." Ms. Copy in author's possession.

Caputo, John. *Radical Hermeneutics: Repetition, Deconstruction, and the Hermeneutic Project.* Bloomington: Indiana University Press, 1987.

Carby, Hazel V. "Body and Soul: Paul Robeson and the Modernist Aesthetic." Paper read at the Center for Gender Studies, University of Chicago. October 1997.

————. *Reconstructing Womanhood: The Emergence of the Afro-American Woman Novelist.* New York: Oxford University Press, 1987.

Caughie, Pamela L., and Reed Way Dasenbrock. "An Exchange on 'Truth and Methods.'" *College English* 58 (September 1996): 541–54.

Caughie, Pamela L., with Anne Callahan. "Virginia Woolf and Postmodern Feminism." *Virginia Woolf Miscellanies: Proceedings of the First Annual Conference on Virginia Woolf.* Ed. Mark Hussey and Vara Neverow-Turk. New York: Pace University Press, 1992.

Certeau, Michel de. *The Practice of Everyday Life.* Trans. Steven F. Rendall. Berkeley: University of California Press, 1984.

Chafe, William. *The American Woman: Her Changing Social, Economic, and Political Roles, 1920–1970.* New York: Oxford University Press, 1972.

"Chasing a Rainbow." Dir. Christopher Ralling. Public Broadcast System. February 1992.

Christian, Barbara. "But What Do We Think We're Doing Anyway?: The State of Black Feminist Criticism(s) or My Version of a Little Bit of History." In Wall, *Changing Our Own Words* 58–74.

Cohan, Steven, and Linda M. Shires. *Telling Stories: A Theoretical Analysis of Narrative Fiction.* New York: Routledge, 1988.

Cole, Catherine M. "Reading Blackface in West Africa." *Critical Inquiry* 23 (Autumn 1996): 183–215.

Collins, Patricia Hill. "The Social Construction of Black Feminist Thought." *Signs* 14 (Summer 1989): 745–73.

The Commitments. Dir. Alan Parker. TCF/Beacon/First Film/Dirty Hands, 1991.

Corliss, Richard. "Don't Read This Story!" *Time,* 1 March 1993: 57.

Cornell, Drucilla. *Beyond Accommodation: Ethical Feminism, Deconstruction, and the Law.* New York: Routledge, 1991.

———. *The Imaginary Domain: Abortion, Pornography, and Sexual Harassment.* New York: Routledge, 1995.

———. *The Philosophy of the Limit.* New York: Routledge, 1992.

———. "The Wild Woman and All That Jazz." In Elam and Wiegman 313–21.

Crenshaw, Kimberlé. "Whose Story Is It, Anyway? Feminist and Antiracist Appropriations of Anita Hill." In Morrison, *Race-ing Justice* 402–40.

Crowley, Sharon. *A Teacher's Guide to Deconstruction.* Urbana, Ill.: National Council of Teachers of English, 1989.

The Crying Game. Dir. Neil Jordan. Palace/Channel 4/Eurotrustees/NDF/British Screen, 1992.

Culler, Jonathan. *Ferdinand de Saussure.* Rev. ed. Ithaca, N.Y.: Cornell University Press, 1986.

Cutter, Martha J. "Sliding Significations: Passing as a Narrative and Textual Strategy in Nella Larsen's Fiction." In *Passing and the Fictions of Identity.* Ed. Elaine K. Ginsberg. Durham, N.C.: Duke University Press, 1996. 75–100.

Dasenbrock, Reed Way. "Truth and Methods." *College English* 57 (September 1995): 546–61.

Davis, Robert Con, and Ronald Schleifer. *Criticism and Culture: The Role of Critique in Modern Literary Theory.* London: Longman, 1991.

Deacon, Desley. *Elsie Clews Parsons: Inventing Modern Life.* Chicago: University of Chicago Press, 1997.

Dead Poets Society. Dir. Peter Weir. Warner/Touchstone/Silver Screen Partners IV/Witt-Thomas Productions, 1989.

"Degenerate Art": The Fate of the Avant-Garde in Nazi Germany. Museum Associates. Los Angeles: Los Angeles County Museum of Art, 1991.

De Lauretis, Teresa. *Alice Doesn't: Feminism, Semiotics, Cinema.* Bloomington: Indiana University Press, 1984.

Deleuze, Gilles. "Literature and Life." Trans. Daniel W. Smith and Michael A. Greco. *Critical Inquiry* 23 (Winter 1997): 225–30.

Deleuze, Gilles, and Félix Guattari. *A Thousand Plateaus: Capitalism and Schizophrenia.* Trans. Brian Massumi. Minneapolis: University of Minnesota Press, 1987.

Denby, David. *Great Books: My Adventures with Homer, Rousseau, Woolf, and Other Indestructible Writers of the Western World.* New York: Simon and Schuster, 1996.

Derrida, Jacques. *Acts of Literature.* Ed. Derek Attridge. New York: Routledge, 1992.

———. *A Derrida Reader: Between the Blinds.* Ed. Peggy Kamuf. New York: Columbia University Press, 1991.

———. "Différance." *Margins of Philosophy.* Trans. Alan Bass. Chicago: University of Chicago Press, 1982. 1–27.

―――. *Limited Inc.* Evanston: Northwestern University Press, 1988.

―――. *Of Grammatology.* Trans. Gayatri Chakravorty Spivak. Baltimore: Johns Hopkins University Press, 1976.

―――. "The Principle of Reason: The University in the Eyes of Its Pupils." Trans. Catherine Porter and Edward P. Morris. *diacritics* 13 (Fall 1983): 3–20.

Devi, Mahasweta. "Breast-Giver." Trans. Gayatri Chakravorty Spivak. In Spivak, *In Other Worlds* 222–40.

Eckstein, Barbara. "The Body, the Word, and the State: J. M. Coetzee's *Waiting for the Barbarians.*" *Novel* 22 (Winter 1989): 175–98.

Edmundson, Mark. "The Ethics of Deconstruction." *Michigan Quarterly Review* 27 (Fall 1988): 622–43.

Elam, Diane. *Feminism and Deconstruction.* London: Routledge, 1994.

Elam, Diane, and Robyn Wiegman, eds. *Feminism Beside Itself.* New York: Routledge, 1995.

Eliot, T. S. "Tradition and the Individual Talent." *Selected Prose of T. S. Eliot.* Ed. Frank Kermode. New York: Farrar, Straus & Giroux, 1975.

Ellison, Ralph. "Change the Joke and Slip the Yoke." In Gates and McKay 1541–49.

Emery, Mary Lou. "'Robbed of Meaning': Displacing the Other in 20th-Century Feminist Narrative." Paper read at the International Conference on Narrative. University of Wisconsin at Madison. April 1989.

"Ethnic Notions: Black People in White Minds." Dir. Marlon Riggs. California Newsreel and KQED-TV (San Francisco). 1986.

Europa Europa. Dir. Agnieszka Holland. Les Films de Losange/CCC Filmkunst/Perspektywa, 1991.

Evans, Greg. "Plays Striking Gold." *Variety* 353 (10 January 1994): 63+.

"Ex-Colleagues of Nominee Step Forward to Rebut Allegations." *New York Times,* 8 October 1991: A21.

Faigley, Lester. *Fragments of Rationality: Postmodernity and the Subject of Composition.* Pittsburgh: University of Pittsburgh Press, 1992.

Feingold, Mark. "Prisoners of Unisex." *Village Voice,* 6 November 1992: 109+.

Felman, Shoshana. *The Literary Speech Act: Don Juan with J. L. Austin, or Seduction in Two Languages.* Trans. Catharine Porter. Ithaca, N.Y.: Cornell University Press, 1983.

―――. "Psychoanalysis and Education: Teaching Terminable and Interminable." In B. Johnson, *Pedagogical Imperative* 21–44.

Felman, Shoshana, and Dori Laub, M.D. *Testimony: Crises of Witnessing in Literature, Psychoanalysis, and History.* New York: Routledge, 1992.

Fetterley, Judith. *The Resisting Reader: A Feminist Approach to American Fiction.* Bloomington: Indiana University Press, 1978.

Finkielkraut, Alain. *The Imaginary Jew.* Trans. Kevin O'Neill and David Suchoff. Lincoln: University of Nebraska Press, 1994.

Finley, Karen. "The Art of Offending." *New York Times,* 14 November 1996: A17.

Fish, Stanley. "When Principles Get in the Way." *New York Times,* 26 December 1996: A15.

Flax, Jane. *Thinking Fragments: Psychoanalysis, Feminism, and Postmodernism in the Contemporary West.* Berkeley: University of California Press, 1990.

Fleishman, Avrom. "The Condition of English: Taking Stock in a Time of Culture Wars." *College English* 57 (November 1995): 807–21.

Foucault, Michel. *History of Sexuality,* vol. 2. New York: Pantheon Books, 1978.
———. *The Order of Things: An Archaeology of the Human Sciences.* New York: Pantheon, 1970.
———. *Power/Knowledge: Selected Interviews and Other Writings, 1972–77.* Ed. Colin Gordon. Trans. Colin Gordon, Leo Marshall, John Mepham, and Kate Soper. New York: Pantheon, 1980.
———. "The Subject and Power." In *Michel Foucault: Beyond Structuralism and Hermeneutics.* Hubert L. Dreyfus and Paul Rabinow. Chicago: University of Chicago Press. 208–26.
———. "What Is an Author?" In *Textual Strategies: Perspectives in Post-Structuralist Criticism.* Ed. Josué Harari. Ithaca, N.Y.: Cornell University Press, 1979. 141–60.
Fox-Genovese, Elizabeth. "The Claims of a Common Culture: Gender, Race, Class and the Canon." *Salmagundi* 72 (Fall 1986): 131–43.
Friedman, Susan Stanford. "Beyond White and Other: Relationality and Narratives of Race in Feminist Discourse." *Signs* 21 (Autumn 1995): 1–49.
Frye, Northrop. *Anatomy of Criticism: Four Essays.* Princeton, N.J.: Princeton University Press, 1957.
Fuss, Diana. "Accounting for Theory in the Undergraduate Classroom." In *Teaching Contemporary Theory to Undergraduates.* Ed. Dianne F. Sadoff and William E. Cain. New York: Modern Language Association, 1994. 103–13.
———. *Essentially Speaking: Feminism, Nature, and Difference.* New York: Routledge, 1989.
———. *Identification Papers.* New York: Routledge, 1995.
———. "Reading like a Feminist." In *The Essential Difference.* Ed. Naomi Schor and Elizabeth Weed. Bloomington: Indiana University Press, 1994. 98–115.
Fuss, Diana, ed. *Inside/Out: Lesbian Theories and Gay Theories.* New York: Routledge, 1991.
Gallop, Jane. *Around 1981: Academic Feminist Literary Theory.* New York: Routledge, 1992.
———. "Feminism and Harassment Policy." *Academe* (September–October 1994): 16–23.
———. *Feminist Accused of Sexual Harassment.* Durham, N.C.: Duke University Press, 1997.
———. "Knot a Love Story." *Yale Journal of Criticism* 5 (Fall 1992): 209–18.
———. *Reading Lacan.* Ithaca, N.Y.: Cornell University Press, 1985.
———. *Thinking through the Body.* New York: Columbia University Press, 1988.
Gallop, Jane, ed. *Pedagogy: The Question of Impersonation.* Bloomington: Indiana University Press, 1995.
Gallop, Jane, Nancy K. Miller, and Marianne Hirsch. "Criticizing Feminist Criticism." In *Conflicts in Feminism.* Ed. Marianne Hirsch and Evelyn Fox Keller. New York: Routledge, 1990. 349–69.
Garber, Marjorie. "'Greatness': Philology and the Politics of Mimesis." *boundary 2* 19 (Summer 1992): 233–59.
———. *Vested Interests: Cross-Dressing and Cultural Anxiety.* New York: Routledge, 1992.
Gates, Henry Louis, Jr. *The Signifying Monkey: A Theory of African-American Literary Criticism.* New York: Oxford University Press, 1988.

———. "Transforming the American Mind." Paper read at Northwestern University, Evanston, Illinois. February 1990.

———. "White like Me." *New Yorker,* 17 June 1996: 66–72+.

———. "Whose Canon Is It, Anyway?" *New York Times Book Review,* 26 February 1989: 1+.

Gates, Henry Louis, Jr., ed. *"Race," Writing, and Difference.* Chicago: University of Chicago Press, 1986. (First published as special issues of *Critical Inquiry* in 1985 and 1986.)

Gates, Henry Louis, Jr., and Nellie Y. McKay, eds. *The Norton Anthology of African American Literature.* New York: W. W. Norton, 1997.

Gennette, Gérard. *Narrative Discourse: An Essay in Method.* 1972. Trans. Jane E. Lewin. Ithaca, N.Y.: Cornell University Press, 1980.

George, Diana, and Diana Shoos. "Issues of Subjectivity and Resistance: Cultural Studies in the Composition Classroom." In Berlin and Vivion, 200–210.

Gilroy, Paul. *The Black Atlantic: Modernity and Double-Consciousness.* Cambridge, Mass.: Harvard University Press, 1993.

Girard, René. *Deceit, Desire, and the Novel: Self and Other in Literary Structure.* Trans. Yvonne Freccero. Baltimore: Johns Hopkins University Press, 1965.

Giroux, Henry A. "Resisting Difference: Cultural Studies and the Discourse of Critical Pedagogy." In Grossberg et al. 199–212.

Gould, Timothy. "The Unhappy Performative." In Parker and Sedgwick 19–44.

Graff, Gerald. *Professing Literature: An Institutional History.* Chicago: University of Chicago Press, 1987.

Graff, Gerald, and Bruce Robbins. "Cultural Criticism." In *Redrawing the Boundaries: The Transformation of English and American Literary Studies.* Ed. Stephen Greenblatt and Giles Gunn. New York: Modern Language Association, 1992. 419–36.

Greene, Gayle, and Coppélia Kahn, eds. *Changing Subjects: The Making of Feminist Literary Criticism.* London: Routledge, 1993.

Grossberg, Lawrence, Cary Nelson, and Paula A. Treichler, eds. *Cultural Studies.* New York: Routledge, 1992.

Grosz, Elizabeth. "Ontology and Equivocation: Derrida's Politics of Sexual Difference." *diacritics* 25 (Summer 1995): 115–24.

Grumet, Madeleine. "*Scholae Personae:* Masks for Meaning." In Gallop, *Pedagogy* 36–45.

Guillory, John. *Cultural Capital: The Problem of Literary Canon Formation.* Chicago: University of Chicago Press, 1993.

———. "Preprofessionalism: What Graduate Students Want." In *Profession 1996.* New York: Modern Language Association, 1996. 91–99.

Haizlip, Shirlee Taylor. *The Sweeter the Juice: A Family Memoir in Black and White.* New York: Simon and Schuster, 1994.

Haraway, Donna. "Ecce Homo." In Butler and Scott 86–100.

———. *Primate Visions: Gender, Race, and Nature in the World of Modern Science.* New York: Routledge, 1989.

———. "Situated Knowledges: The Science Question in Feminism and the Privilege of Partial Perspective." *Feminist Studies* 14 (Fall 1988): 575–99.

Harding, Sandra. "Who Knows? Identities and Feminist Epistemology." In *(En)Gendering Knowledge: Feminist in Academe.* Ed. Joan E. Hartman and Ellen Messer-Davidow. Knoxville: University of Tennessee Press, 1991. 100–120.

———. *Whose Science? Whose Knowledge?: Thinking from Women's Lives.* Ithaca, N.Y.: Cornell University Press, 1991.

Harper, Phillip Brian. *Framing the Margins: The Social Logic of Postmodern Culture.* New York: Oxford University Press, 1994.

———. "'The Subversive Edge': *Paris Is Burning,* Social Critique, and the Limits of Subjective Agency." *diacritics* 24 (Summer–Fall 1994): 90–103.

Hartman, Geoffrey H. "Higher Education in the 1990s." *New Literary History* 24 (Autumn 1993): 729–43.

Harvey, David. *The Condition of Postmodernity: An Enquiry into the Origins of Cultural Change.* Oxford: Blackwell, 1989.

Hassan, Ihab. *The Postmodern Turn: Essays in Postmodern Theory and Culture.* Columbus: Ohio State University Press, 1987.

Heilbrun, Carolyn, and Judith Resnick. "Convergences: Law, Literature, and Feminism." In *Beyond Portia: Women, Law, and Literature in the United States.* Ed. Jacqueline St. Joan and Annette Bennington McElhiney. Boston: Northeastern University Press, 1997. 11–52.

Hekman, Susan. "Truth and Method: Standpoint Theory Revisited." *Signs* 22 (Winter 1997): 341–65.

Henriques, Julian, et al. *Changing the Subject: Psychology, Social Regulation, and Subjectivity.* London: Methuen, 1984.

Hertz, Neil. "Two Extravagant Teachings." In B. Johnson, *Pedagogical Imperative* 59–71.

Himmelfarb, Gertrude. "The New Advocacy and the Old." In *Advocacy in the Classroom: Problems and Possibilities.* Ed. Patricia Meyer Spacks. New York: St. Martin's Press, 1996. 96–101.

Homans, Margaret. "'Women of Color' Writers and Feminist Theory." *New Literary History* 25 (Winter 1994): 73–94.

hooks, bell. *Black Looks: Race and Representation.* Boston: South End Press, 1992.

———. *Outlaw Culture: Resisting Representations.* New York: Routledge, 1994.

———. *Talking Back: Thinking Feminist, Thinking Black.* Boston: South End Press, 1989.

———. *Teaching to Transgress: Education as the Practice of Freedom.* New York: Routledge, 1994.

———. *Yearning: Race, Gender, and Cultural Politics.* Boston: South End, 1990.

Hooper-Greenhill, Eilean. "Counting Visitors or Visitors Who Count?" In *The Museum Time Machine: Putting Cultures on Display.* Ed. Robert Lumley. London: Routledge, 1988.

Hostert, Anna Camaiti. *Passing: Dissolvere le identità, superare le differenze.* Rome: Castelvecchi, 1996.

Hull, E. M. *The Sheik.* London: Evelyn Nash, 1919.

Hurst, Fannie. *Imitation of Life.* New York: Collier, 1933.

———. Letter. *Opportunity: A Journal of Negro Life* 13 (April 1935): 121.

———. "The Sure Way to Equality." *Negro Digest* June 1946: 27–28.

Hutcheon, Linda. "The Post Always Rings Twice: The Postmodern and the Postcolonial." *Textual Practice* 8 (Summer 1994): 205–38.

Ignatiev, Noel. *How the Irish Became White.* New York: Routledge, 1995.

Imitation of Life. Dir. John M. Stahl. Universal, 1934.

Irigaray, Luce. *An Ethics of Sexual Difference.* Trans. Carolyn Burke and Gillian C. Gill. Ithaca, N.Y.: Cornell University Press, 1993.

Jardine, Alice, and Paul Smith, eds. *Men in Feminism.* New York: Methuen, 1987.

Jarratt, Susan C. *Rereading the Sophists: Classical Rhetoric Refigured.* Carbondale: Southern Illinois University Press, 1991.

Jay, Gregory. *American the Scrivener: Deconstruction and the Subject of Literary History.* Ithaca, N.Y.: Cornell University Press, 1990.

———. "Taking Multiculturalism Personally: Ethnos and Ethos in the Classroom." In Gallop, *Pedagogy* 117–28.

———. "Values and Deconstruction: Derrida, Saussure, Marx." *Cultural Critique* 8 (Winter 1987–88): 153–96.

Jefferson, Margo. "Arguing Culture and Identity: A Matter of How, Not Who." *New York Times,* 4 February 1997: B1–2.

Johnson, Barbara. *The Critical Difference: Essays in the Contemporary Rhetoric of Reading.* Baltimore: Johns Hopkins University Press, 1980.

———. "No Passing: Sula, Passing and the Lesbian Continuum." Frederic Ives Carpenter Lectures. University of Chicago. 1 May 1990.

———. *The Wake of Deconstruction.* Cambridge, Mass.: Blackwell, 1994.

———. *A World of Difference.* Baltimore: Johns Hopkins University Press, 1987.

———. "Writing." In Lentricchia and McLaughlin 39–49.

Johnson, Barbara, ed. *Pedagogical Imperative: Teaching as a Literary Genre.* Special issue of *Yale French Studies* 63 (1982).

Johnson, Cheryl. "Participatory Rhetoric and the Teacher as Racial/Gendered Subject." *College English* 56 (April 1994): 409–19.

Johnson, James Weldon. *The Autobiography of an Ex-Coloured Man.* 1912. New York: Hill and Wang, 1960.

———. Preface to *The Book of American Negro Poetry.* In Gates and McKay 861–84.

Kahane, Claire. *Passions of the Voice: Hysteria, Narrative, and the Figure of the Speaking Woman, 1850–1915.* Baltimore: Johns Hopkins University Press, 1995.

Kakutani, Michiko. "Fiction and Reality: Blurring the Edges." *New York Times,* 25 September 1992: C1.

Kaplan, Alice. *French Lessons: A Memoir.* Chicago: University of Chicago Press, 1993.

Kaplan, Caren. *Questions of Travel: Postmodern Discourses of Displacement.* Durham, N.C.: Duke University Press, 1996.

Kaplan, E. Ann. *Motherhood and Representation: The Mother in Popular Culture and Melodrama.* New York: Routledge, 1992.

Kauffman, Linda. "The Long Goodbye: Against the Personal Testimony; or, An Infant Grifter Grows Up." In Greene and Kahn 129–46.

Kearney, Richard. *The Wake of the Imagination: Toward a Postmodern Culture.* Minneapolis: University of Minnesota Press, 1988.

Keating, AnnLouise. "Interrogating 'Whiteness,' (De)Constructing 'Race.'" *College English* 57 (December 1995): 901–18.

Krupat, Arnold. *Ethnocriticism: Ethnography, History, Literature.* Berkeley: University of California Press, 1992.

Lacan, Jacques. "The Insistence of the Letter in the Unconscious." In *The Structuralists: From Marx to Lévi-Strauss.* Ed. Richard De George and Fernande M. De George. Garden City, N.Y.: Anchor, 1972. 287–323.

————. "Seminar of 21 January 1975." Trans. Jacqueline Rose. In *Feminine Sexuality: Jacques Lacan and the Ecole Freudienne.* Ed. Juliet Mitchell and Jacqueline Rose. New York: W. W. Norton, 1982. 162–71.

Lahr, John. "Dogma Days." *New Yorker,* 16 November 1992: 121–25.

Lakritz, Andrew. "Identification and Difference: Structures of Privilege in Cultural Criticism." In Roof and Wiegman 3–29.

Lane, Harlan. *The Mask of Benevolence: Disabling the Deaf Community.* New York: Knopf, 1992.

Larsen, Nella. *Passing.* In *"Quicksand" and "Passing."* 1928, 1929. New Brunswick, N.J.: Rutgers University Press, 1986.

Lauter, Paul. "Introduction: The Politics of Curriculum Transformation." *Radical Teacher* 37 (1989): 2.

Lawrence, D. H. "Gloire de Dijon." *The Complete Poems of D. H. Lawrence.* Ed. Vivian de Sola Pinto and Warren Roberts. London: Heinemann, 1972. 217.

————. "Matriarchy." In *The Gender of Modernism: A Critical Anthology.* Ed. Bonnie Kime Scott. Bloomington: Indiana University Press, 1990. 224–27.

————. *Phoenix: The Posthumous Papers of D. H. Lawrence.* Ed. Edward D. McDonald. New York: Penguin, 1978.

————. "The Woman Who Rode Away." In *The Woman Who Rode Away and Other Stories.* Ed. Dieter Mehl and Christa Jansohn. Cambridge: Cambridge University Press, 1995. 39–71.

Lentricchia, Frank. "Last Will and Testament of an Ex-Literary Critic." *Lingua Franca* (September–October 1996): 59–67.

Lentricchia, Frank, and Thomas McLaughlin, eds. *Critical Terms for Literary Study.* Chicago: University of Chicago Press, 1990.

Lott, Eric. *Love and Theft: Blackface Minstrelsy and the American Working Class.* New York: Oxford University Press, 1993.

Lubiano, Wahneema. "Black Ladies, Welfare Queens, and State Minstrels: Ideological War by Narrative Means." In Morrison, *Race-ing Justice* 323–61.

Lydon, Mary. *Skirting the Issue: Essays in Literary Theory.* Madison: University of Wisconsin Press, 1995.

Lyotard, Jean-François. *The Differend.* Trans. Georges Van Den Abbeele. Minneapolis: University of Minnesota Press, 1987.

————. *Pacific Wall.* Trans. Bruce Boone. Venice, Calif.: Lapis Press, 1990.

MacDonald, Christie. "Personal Criticism: Dialogue of Differences." In Elam and Wiegman 237–59.

MacIntyre, Alasdair C. *After Virtue.* South Bend, Ind.: Notre Dame University Press, 1981.

————. *Whose Justice? Which Rationality?* South Bend, Ind.: Notre Dame University Press, 1988.

Malraux, André. *Museum without Walls.* Trans. Stuart Gilbert and Francis Price. Garden City, N.Y.: Doubleday and Co., 1967.

Mamet, David. *Oleanna.* New York: Vintage Books, 1993.

Marcus, Sharon. "Fighting Bodies, Fighting Words: A Theory and Politics of Rape Prevention." In Butler and Scott 385–403.

Marks, Elaine. *Marrano as Metaphor: The Jewish Presence in French Writing.* New York: Columbia University Press, 1996.

Martin, Biddy. "Introduction: Teaching Literature, Changing Cultures." *PMLA* 112 (January 1997): 7–25.

Mazza, Cris. "Is It Sexual Harassment Yet?" *Is It Sexual Harassment Yet? Short Fiction.* Boulder, Colo.: Fiction Collective Two, 1991. 193–223.

McClary, Susan. *Feminine Endings: Music, Gender, and Sexuality.* Minneapolis: University of Minnesota Press, 1991.

McDowell, Deborah. "Introduction." In *"Quicksand" and "Passing."* Nella Larsen. New Brunswick, N.J.: Rutgers University Press, 1986. ix–xxxv.

McGann, Patrick. "Two Comments on 'Teaching and Learning as a Man.'" *College English* 58 (December 1996): 964–66.

McGee, Patrick. "The Politics of Modernist Form; or, Who Rules *The Waves?*" *Modern Fiction Studies* 38 (1992): 631–50.

McLaughlin, Thomas. "Introduction." In Lentricchia and McLaughlin 1–8.

Melman, Billie. *Woman and the Popular Imagination in the Twenties: Flappers and Nymphs.* London: Macmillan, 1988.

Miller, J. Hillis. *The Ethics of Reading: Kant, de Man, Eliot, Trollope, James, and Benjamin.* New York: Columbia University Press, 1987.

Miller, Nancy K. *Getting Personal: Feminist Occasions and Other Autobiographical Acts.* New York: Routledge, 1991.

———. *Subject to Change: Reading Feminist Writing.* New York: Columbia University Press, 1988.

Miller, Susan. "*In Loco Parentis:* Addressing (the) Class." In Gallop, *Pedagogy* 155–64.

Modleski, Tania. *Feminism without Women: Culture and Criticism in a "Post-feminist" Age.* New York: Routledge, 1991.

Morgan, Thaïs. *Men Writing the Feminine: Literature, Theory, and the Question of Genders.* Albany: State University of New York Press, 1994.

Morley, Sheridan. "A Table for Two." *Spectator,* 10 July 1993: 38.

Morrison, Toni. *Jazz.* New York: Knopf, 1992.

———. *Playing in the Dark: Whiteness and the Literary Imagination.* Cambridge, Mass.: Harvard University Press, 1992.

Morrison, Toni, ed. *Race-ing Justice, En-gender-ing Power: Essays on Anita Hill, Clarence Thomas, and the Construction of Social Reality.* New York: Pantheon, 1992.

Mullen, Harryette. "Optic White: Blackness and the Production of Whiteness." *diacritics* 24 (Summer–Fall 1994): 71–89.

Muscatine, Charles. "Reading Literature: From Graduate School to Elementary School." In *Profession 1996.* New York: Modern Language Association, 1996. 115–20.

Nelson, Cary. "Always Already Cultural Studies: Two Conferences and a Manifesto." *Journal of the Midwest Modern Language Association* 24 (Spring 1991): 24–38.

Nelson, Cary, Paula A. Treichler, and Lawrence Grossberg. "Cultural Studies: An Introduction." In Grossberg et al. 1–16.

Nicholson, Linda, ed. *Feminism/Postmodernism.* New York: Routledge, 1990.

Paglia, Camille. "Academic Feminists Must Begin to Fulfill Their Noble, Animating Ideal." *Chronicle of Higher Education,* 25 July 1997: B4–5.

———. "The Strange Case of Clarence Thomas and Anita Hill." *Sex, Art, and American Culture: Essays.* New York: Vintage Books, 1991. 46–48.

Paris Is Burning. Dir. Jennie Livingston. ICA/Off White Productions, Inc., 1990.

Parker, Andrew, and Eve Kosofsky Sedgwick, eds. *Performativity and Performance.* New York: Routledge, 1995.

Patai, Daphne. "What's Wrong with Women's Studies?" *Academe* 181 (July–August 1995): 30–35.

Patterson, Orlando. "Race, Gender, and Liberal Fallacies." *New York Times,* 20 October 1991: D15.

Pease, Donald. "Author." In Lentricchia and McLaughlin 105–17.

Piper, Adrian. "Cornered." Permanent Collection. Museum of Contemporary Art, Chicago.

———. "Passing for White, Passing for Black." *Transition* 58 (1992): 4–32.

Poovey, Mary. "The Abortion Question and the Death of Man." In Butler and Scott 239–56.

———. "Cultural Criticism: Past and Present." *College English* 52 (October 1990): 615–25.

———. "Feminism and Postmodernism: Another View." *boundary 2* 19 (Summer 1992): 34–52.

Porter, Carolyn, "History and Literature: 'After the New Historicism.'" *New Literary History* 21 (Winter 1990): 253–81.

Probyn, Elspeth. "Perverts by Choice: Towards an Ethics of Choosing." In Elam and Wiegman 261–81.

Rabinowitz, Peter. "Against Close Reading." In *Pedagogy Is Politics: Literary Theory and Critical Teachng.* Ed. Maria-Regina Kecht. Urbana: University of Illinois Press, 1991. 230–44.

———. "'Betraying the Sender': The Rhetoric and Ethics of Fragile Texts." *Narrative* 2.3 (October 1994): 201–13.

Rajchman, John. *Truth and Eros: Foucault, Lacan, and the Question of Ethics.* New York: Routledge, 1991.

Reed, Christopher. "Through Formalism: Feminism and Virginia Woolf's Relation to Bloomsbury Aesthetics." In *The Multiple Muses of Virginia Woolf.* Ed. Diane F. Gillespie. Columbia: University of Missouri Press, 1993. 11–35.

Rich, Adrienne. "Compulsory Heterosexuality and Lesbian Existence." *Blood, Bread, and Poetry: Selected Prose, 1979–85.* New York: W. W. Norton, 1986. 23–75.

Richards, I. A. *Practical Criticism: A Study of Literary Judgement.* New York: Harcourt and Brace, 1929.

Riggs, Marlon. "Cultural Healing: An Interview with Marlon Riggs." *Afterimage,* March 1991: 8–11.

Roberts, Dorothy. *Killing the Black Body: Race, Reproduction, and the Meaning of Liberty.* New York: Pantheon Books, 1997.

Robinson, Amy. "It Takes One to Know One: Passing and Communities of Common Interest." *Critical Inquiry* 20 (Summer 1994): 715–36.

———. "To Pass/In Drag: Strategies of Entrance into the Visible." Ph.D. diss., University of Pennsylvania, 1993.

Rollins, Judith. *Between Women: Domestics and Their Employers.* Philadelphia: Temple University Press, 1985.

Roof, Judith, and Robyn Wiegman, eds. *Who Can Speak? Authority and Critical Identity.* Urbana: University of Illinois Press, 1995.

Rorty, Richard. *Contingency, Irony, and Solidarity.* Cambridge: Cambridge University Press, 1989.

Ross, Andrew. "Wet, Dark, and Low, Eco-Man Evolves from Eco-Woman." *boundary 2* 19 (Summer 1992): 205–32.

Rousseau, Jean-Jacques. *Confessions.* New York: Knopf, 1992.

Ruddick, Lisa. "Ritual Killing and the Work of Gender." Paper read at the session "Anthropologies of Modernity II: Gender and Culture." Modern Language Association conference. New York. December 1992.

Ruddick, Sara. *Maternal Thinking: Toward a Politics of Peace.* New York: Ballantine, 1990.

Ryan, Michael. "Deconstruction and Radical Teaching." In B. Johnson, *Pedagogical Imperative* 45–58.

Said, Edward. *After the Last Sky: Palestinian Lives.* New York: Pantheon Books, 1986.

———. "Identity, Authority, and Freedom," *boundary 2* 21 (Fall 1994): 1–18.

———. "Representing the Colonized: Anthropology's Interlocutor." *Critical Inquiry* 15 (Winter 1989): 205–25.

Sauerländer, Willibald. "Un-German Activities." *New York Review of Books,* 7 April 1994: 9–13.

Sawhney, Sabina. "Authenticity Is Such a Drag." In Elam and Wiegman 197–215.

Schilb, John. "Cultural Studies, Postmodernism, and Composition." In *Contending with Words: Composition and Rhetoric in a Postmodern Age.* Ed. Patricia Harkin and John Schilb. New York: Modern Language Association, 1991. 173–88.

Searle, John. "Reiterating the Differences: A Reply to Derrida." *Glyph* 2 (1977): 193–208.

Sedgwick, Eve Kosofsky. *Epistemology of the Closet.* Berkeley: University of California Press, 1990.

———. *Tendencies.* Durham, N.C.: Duke University Press, 1993.

———. "White Glasses." *Yale Journal of Criticism* 5 (Fall 1992): 193–208.

Shenon, Philip. "For Fiction, and Fibbing, She Takes the Prize." *New York Times,* 26 September 1995: A4.

Sheridan, Alan. *Michel Foucault: The Will to Truth.* London: Tavistock Publications, 1980.

Shocked, Michelle. *Arkansas Traveler.* Liner notes. Polygram Records, Inc. 1992.

Siegel, Carol. *Lawrence among the Women: Wavering Boundaries in Women's Literary Traditions.* Charlottesville: University Press of Virginia, 1991.

Silver, Brenda. "Retro-Anger and Baby Boomer Nostalgia." Paper read at the Seventh Annual Virginia Woolf Conference. Plymouth, N.H. June 1997.

Silverthorne, Jeanne. "Exits and Entrances." *Artforum* 31 (March 1993): 10–11.

Smith, Anna Deavere. *Fires in the Mirror: Crown Heights, Brooklyn and Other Identities.* New York: Anchor Books/Doubleday, 1993.

Smith, Barbara Herrnstein. *Contingencies of Value: Alternative Perspectives for Critical Theory.* Cambridge, Mass.: Harvard University Press, 1988.

Smith, Paul. "A Course in 'Cultural Studies.'" *Journal of the Midwest Modern Language Association* 24 (Spring 1991): 39–49.

———. *Discerning the Subject.* Minneapolis: University of Minnesota Press, 1988.

Smith, Valerie. "Reading the Intersection of Race and Gender in Narratives of Passing." *diacritics* 24 (Summer–Fall 1994): 43–57.

Smithson, Isaiah. "Introduction: Institutionalizing Culture Studies." In Smithson and Ruff 1–22.

Smithson, Isaiah, and Nancy Ruff, eds. *English Studies/Culture Studies: Institutionalizing Dissent.* Urbana: University of Illinois Press, 1994.

Sontag, Susan. *A Susan Sontag Reader.* Ed. Elizabeth Hardwick. New York: Farrar, Straus & Giroux, 1982.

Spack, Ruth. "The (In)Visibility of the Person(al) in Academe." *College English* 59 (January 1997): 9–31.

Spacks, Patricia Meyer, ed. *Advocacy in the Classroom: Problems and Possibilities.* New York: St. Martin's Press, 1996.

Spivak, Gayatri Chakravorty. "Displacement and the Discourse of Woman." In *Displacement: Derrida and After.* Ed. Mark Krupnik. Bloomington: Indiana University Press, 1983. 169–95.

———. *In Other Worlds: Essays in Culture Politics.* New York: Routledge, 1988.

———. "Responsibility." *boundary 2* 21 (Fall 1994): 19–64.

———. "Revolutions That as Yet Have No Model: Derrida's *Limited Inc.*" *diacritics* 10 (Winter 1980): 29–49.

———. *Outside in the Teaching Machine.* New York: Routledge, 1993.

Story, Richard David. "Theater." *New York* 25 (14 September 1992): 58–61.

Suleiman, Susan Rubin. *Risking Who One Is: Encounters with Contemporary Art and Literature.* Cambridge, Mass.: Harvard University Press, 1994.

Talbot, Margaret. "A Most Dangerous Method: The Pedagogical Problem of Jane Gallop." *Lingua Franca,* Winter 1994: 24–40.

Talk to Me: Americans in Conversation. Dir. Andrea Simon. Arcadia Pictures with Nebraska Educational Television/New York Cinema Guild, 1996.

Tarzan and His Mate. Dir. Cedric Gibbons. MGM, 1934.

Tate, Claudia. "Nella Larsen's *Passing:* A Problem of Interpretation." *Black American Literature Forum* 14 (Winter 1980): 142–46.

Tate, Claudia, ed., *Black Women Writers at Work.* New York: Contiuum, 1983.

Tompkins, Jane. "Pedagogy of the Distressed." *College English* 52 (October 1990): 653–60.

Tongues Untied. Dir. Marlon Riggs. Signifying Works, 1989.

Torgovnick, Marianna. *Gone Primitive: Savage Intellects, Modern Lives.* Chicago: University of Chicago Press, 1990.

Trebilcot, Joyce, ed. *Mothering: Essays in Feminist Theory.* Totawa, N.J.: Rowman and Allenheld, 1984.

Trotter, David. "A Horse Is Being Beaten: Modernism and Popular Fiction." In *Rereading the New: A Backward Glance at Modernism.* Ed. Kevin J. H. Dettman. Ann Arbor: University of Michigan Press, 1992. 191–219.

Tyler, Carole-Anne. "Passing: Narcissism, Identity, and Difference." *differences* 6 (Summer–Fall 1994): 212–48.

Wall, Cheryl A. "Passing for What? Aspects of Identity in Nella Larsen's Novels." *Black American Literature Forum* 20 (Spring–Summer 1986): 97–111.

Wall, Cheryl A., ed. *Changing Our Own Words: Essays on Criticism, Theory, and Writing by Black Women.* New Brunswick, N.J.: Rutgers University Press, 1989.

Wallace, Martin. *Recent Theories of Narrative.* Ithaca, N.Y.: Cornell University Press, 1986.

Walton, Jean. "Sandra Bernhard: Lesbian Postmodern or Modern Postlesbian?" In *The Lesbian Postmodern.* Ed. Laura Doan. New York: Columbia University Press, 1994. 244–62.

Weeks, Jeffrey. *Invented Moralities: Sexual Values in an Age of Uncertainty.* New York: Columbia University Press, 1995.

West, Cornel. "Theory, Pragmatism, and Politics." In *Consequences of Theory.* Ed. Barbara Johnson and Jonathan Arac. Baltimore: Johns Hopkins University Press, 1991. 22–38.

West, Robin. "Jurisprudence and Gender." *University of Chicago Law Review* 55 (Winter 1988): 1–72.

White, Hayden. "The Value of Narrativity in the Representation of Reality." *Critical Inquiry* 7 (Autumn 1980): 5–27.

Wicke, Jennifer. "Postmodern Identities and the Politics of the (Legal) Subject." *boundary 2* 19 (Summer 1992): 10–33.

Wiegman, Robyn. *American Anatomies: Theorizing Race and Gender.* Durham, N.C.: Duke University Press, 1995.

———. "Black Bodies/American Commodities: Gender, Race, and the Bourgeois Ideal in Contemporary Film." In *Unspeakable Images: Ethnicity and the American Cinema.* Ed. Lester D. Friedman. Urbana: University of Illinois Press, 1991. 308–28.

Williams, Patricia J. *The Alchemy of Race and Rights: Diary of a Law Professor.* Cambridge, Mass.: Harvard University Press, 1991.

Willis, Susan. "I Shop Therefore I Am: Is There a Place for Afro-American Culture in Commodity Culture?" In Wall, *Changing Our Own Words* 173–95.

Wimsatt, W. K. *The Verbal Icon: Studies in the Meaning of Poetry.* 1954. Lexington: University Press of Kentucky, 1970.

Without You I'm Nothing. Dirs. John Boscovich and Sandra Bernhard. Electric/M.C.E.G. Productions, 1990.

Wittgenstein, Ludwig. *Philosophical Investigations.* Trans. G. E. M. Anscombe. New York: MacMillan, 1953.

Woolf, Virginia. *Orlando: A Biography.* 1928. New York: Harcout Brace Jovanovich, 1956.

———. *A Room of One's Own.* 1929. New York: Harcourt Brace Jovanovich, 1981.

———. *To the Lighthouse.* 1927. San Diego: Harcourt Brace Jovanovich, 1981.

———. *The Waves.* 1931. San Diego: Harcourt Brace & Co., 1959.

Worsham, Lynn. "Emotion and Pedagogic Violence." *Discourse* 15 (1993): 119–48.

Zavarzadeh, Mas'ud, and Donald Morton. "Theory Pedagogy Politics: The Crisis of 'the Subject' in the Humanities." In *Theory/Pedagogy/Politics: Texts for Change.* Ed. Donald Morton and Mas'ud Zavarzadeh. Urbana: University of Illinois Press, 1991. 1–32.

INDEX

"'Women of Color'" (Homans), 182–89
Women's studies, 13, 69, 147–48, 154, 156–57,
 172–73, 177–78, 189, 191, 193
Woolf, Virginia, 53n33, 85, 97n6, 98n13,
 99n23, 100n33, 152–53, 157–58, 161, 162,
 167, 168, 171, 173, 174n5, 175nn8–9, 245, 259
World of Difference, A (B. Johnson), 47,
 49n4, 63, 85, 100nn32–33, 131, 136, 145n8,
 200n5, 257
Worsham, Lynn, 86, 188, 200n2, 202

"Writers, Intellectuals, Teachers" (Barthes),
 80, 81
"Writing" (B. Johnson), 3, 5, 56n53

Yearning (hooks), 50n8, 52n28, 61, 81, 85,
 100n28, 178, 192, 200n3
Yeats, W. B., 112

Zavarzadeh, Mas'ud, 177, 178, 180
Zollo, Frederick, 244n24

Pamela L. Caughie is an associate professor of English and director of women's studies at Loyola University Chicago, where she teaches feminist and critical theories, modern and postmodern literatures, and African American literature and criticism. The author of *Virginia Woolf and Postmodernism: Literature in Quest and Question of Itself* (University of Illinois Press, 1991) and numerous articles on Virginia Woolf, feminist criticism, and literary theory, she is editing a forthcoming collection of essays entitled *Virginia Woolf in the Age of Mechanical Reproduction* (Garland Publishing).

Typeset in 10.5/13 Minion
with Minion display
Designed by Paula Newcomb
Composed by Celia Shapland
for the University of Illinois Press
Manufactured by Cushing-Malloy, Inc.